'The author draws the "key players" in the rebirth of modern Manchester .... a vividness that might have eluded a conventional historian.'

Financial Times

'A flamboyant hybrid, conveying the nitty-gritty of municipal politics and private-public property deals with the zest and wit of the best journalism ... it is likely to become a touchstone for all chroniclers of modern Manchester.'

Times Literary Supplement

'Bursting with humorous, jaw-dropping, and intricately detailed tales.'

Manchester Evening News

'A fascinating and lively read ... Spinoza's book captures the secret of Manchester's revival.'

Literary Review

'Spinoza constructs a skyline of words to match the new Manchester.'

Louder than War

'Every great city needs a great chronicler. We are lucky to have Andy.'

Lemn Sissay

'This is a fabulous, compelling book with a cast of larger-than-life characters. First as observer, then as participant, Andy Spinoza has enjoyed a ring-side seat in the renaissance and development of Britain's most exciting city.'

Michael Crick

'Andy Spinoza knows the real story.'

Jon Savage

Manchester unspun

Manchester University Press

Manchester unspun

How a city got high on music

Andy Spinoza

Manchester University Press

Published by Manchester University Press
Oxford Road, Manchester M13 9PL
www.manchesteruniversitypress.co.uk

British Library Cataloguing-in-Publication Data
A catalogue record for this book is available from the British Library

ISBN 978 1 5261 6845 0 hardback
ISBN 978 1 5261 7406 2 paperback

First published in hardback by Manchester University Press 2023
This edition first published 2023

The publisher has no responsibility for the persistence or accuracy of URLs for any external or third-party internet websites referred to in this book, and does not guarantee that any content on such websites is, or will remain, accurate or appropriate.

Typeset
by Cheshire Typesetting Ltd, Cuddington, Cheshire
Printed and bound in Great Britain
by Bell & Bain Ltd, Glasgow

Is not the pastness of the past the profounder, the completer, the more legendary, the more immediately before the present it falls? More than that, our story has, of its own nature, something of the legend about it now and again.

Thomas Mann, *The Magic Mountain*, 1924

Contents

Contents

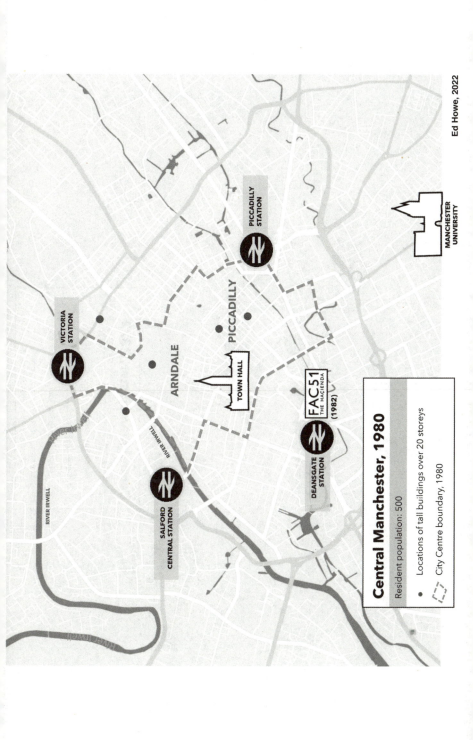

Central Manchester, 1980

Resident population: 500

• Locations of tall buildings over 20 storeys

City Centre boundary, 1980

VICTORIA STATION

SALFORD CENTRAL STATION

PICCADILLY STATION

DEANSGATE STATION

FAC51 THE HACIENDA (1982)

ARNDALE

PICCADILLY

TOWN HALL

RIVER IRWELL

RIVER IRWELL

MANCHESTER UNIVERSITY

Ed Howe, 2022

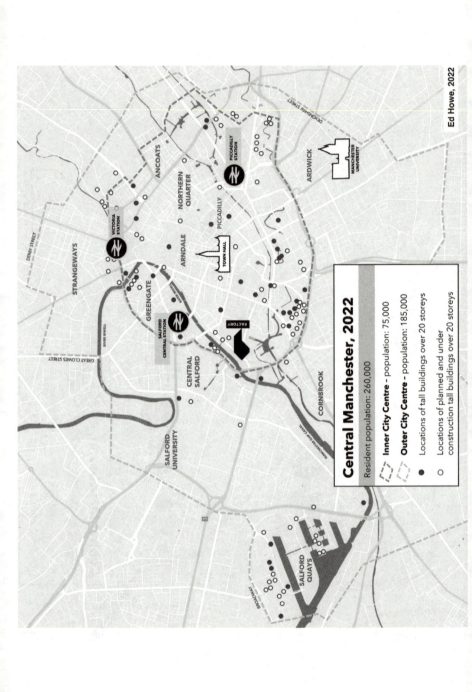

Central Manchester, 2022

Resident population: 260,000

- `⌐ ¬` **Inner City Centre** - population: 75,000

- `⌐ ¬` **Outer City Centre** - population: 185,000

- ● Locations of tall buildings over 20 storeys

- ○ Locations of planned and under construction tall buildings over 20 storeys

Ed Howe, 2022

STRANGEWAYS

ANCOATS

NORTHERN QUARTER

PICCADILLY STATION

ARDWICK

MANCHESTER UNIVERSITY

VICTORIA STATION

ARNDALE

PICCADILLY

TOWN HALL

GREENGATE

SALFORD CENTRAL STATION

FACTORY

CENTRAL SALFORD

CORNBROOK

SALFORD UNIVERSITY

SALFORD QUAYS

BROADWAY

RIVER IRWELL

DERBY STREET

GREAT CLOWES STREET

DEVONSHIRE STREET

MANCHESTER SHIP CANAL

Introduction: How a city got high on music

When I arrived in Manchester, it was sliding into the dustbin of history. It was 1979, and the shattered cityscape all around led to the unavoidable conclusion that the people of Manchester, and much of the North, were second-class citizens. Decline from Victorian greatness had begun in the 1920s, but now the city was reeling from steely-eyed, cold-hearted government policy to put old industries, and their political power bases, to the sword. Manchester looked like it was locked in a fatal post-industrial tailspin.

Life in the failed Hulme estate was an in-your-face existence straight from the pages of a J.G. Ballard dystopia. As a student, I would walk with my friends to the Haçienda nightclub from our flats, in which the council had given up housing 'normal' people. The journey was a mind-mashing meander through concrete underpasses and walkways, past the decommissioned Gaythorn gas works and the derelict Macintosh mills complex, the home of the rubberised raincoat still soot-blackened fifteen years after the Clean Air Act. Apart from us clubbers, the city centre seemed vacant – smashed-up, worthless, unloved and unused. As we revelled in the thrilling immersive aesthetics, it felt for all the world like we owned the place. Of course, we didn't own 'town'. We were at the fag-end of an epic economic bust and were just partying in the debris.

More than forty years later, I am reflecting on my time in the city from punk rock to the pandemic. From Peel Tower, a Victorian folly on the highest hill outside Manchester, at 1,100 feet above sea level, you can look down on the world's original modern city. With the Cheshire plain to the south and the waterways towards Liverpool in the west, the view from this or the other hill tops around the city offers up the entire metropolis in miniature: Manchester and its conjoined twin Salford, the only two major cities in the nation to share a land border, lie in a shallow bowl with uneven, undulating sides, like the work of a drunken potter. In the past two decades on my walks and cycle rides, from

1

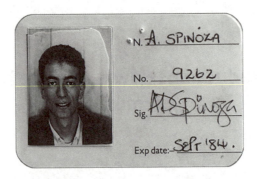

Andy Spinoza Haçienda card back and front

these vantage points I have seen the new towers rising like crystalline fingers from the base of the wonky, murky bowl that is Manchester.

What changes I have seen. Forgive me if I sound like the dying replicant in *Blade Runner*. It may not quite be 'attack ships on fire off the shoulder of Orion', but the centre has undergone an astonishing transformation, growing outwards and surging skywards. In 1982, the year the Haçienda venue opened, only five hundred people lived in the centre. Today that number is sixty thousand but the area that officialdom calls the city region's 'central core' (including Salford Quays and the Old Trafford sports stadiums) has today over-topped the 250,000 mark thanks to the building boom.

Those new Mancunians will be living in residential towers, a pipeline which is today set to make Manchester one of the tallest cities in Europe, with construction growth rates eclipsing Barcelona and Madrid. Buildings over twenty storeys high are set to more than double in number. Since 2018, 37 have been announced. In 2019 ONS data showed neighbouring

Manchester and Salford had the UK's fastest-growing and youngest-population city centres.

During the pandemic lockdowns, I returned to doing what I did as a new student – just wandering and watching. In those days of Sunday closing, the sabbath was the best day for idle meandering. With no one on the streets, and my gaze up to roof level, I could find visual delight in the architecture of the centuries past, seeing the same sights as the people who built the nineteenth-century city. As the Madchester T-shirt had it, 'And On The Sixth Day, God Created Manchester.'

If the city was on its knees by the early 1980s, the new millennium has seen a remarkable revival, with an astonishing jump in Manchester's success, confidence, investment and importance. Some also see brazen greed, disastrous planning and gross bad taste, and others feel that they just don't recognise the old place any more. At street level, people stretch to see upwards to the glazed Godzillas oversailing the streets with no pretence to blend in with the redbrick below. The jarring disparity with the historic buildings in size, massing and materials is what makes homecoming Mancunians point up, open-mouthed. Folk singer and broadcaster Mike Harding, a city-centre resident, objected to a nearby residential block, raging that 'the big money moved in and the dream was hijacked. Now Manchester looks like a city designed by a schizophrenic drunk with attention deficiency disorder.'

The city's leaders, looking back on what they have achieved, believe they have nothing to apologise for. They have laid down a drumbeat of growth, a policy of 'build, build, build' since the early 1980s, all against a soundtrack of world-beating Manchester music. The city's urban revival has made it the envy of its peers and rivals, and its music has swept the world, too. 'No Haçienda, no new Manchester' sounds outlandish, but my own forty-year span in the city's media reveals the links, the people and the processes behind the cause and effect of cultural forces on economic and planning changes. To understand how the North's skyscraper city has come to be, and how the changes have been definitively shaped by the music, I have picked out the key players, pivotal projects and critical events across a forty-year timeframe.

It all could never, of course, begin with just one eccentric and experimental building. And yet it did. The skyrocketing city of today began with a bunch of squabbling hedonists, anarchists, musicians and intellectuals opening a ridiculously outsize New York-style nightclub, for an audience that did not yet exist.

Forty years on, looking down the other end of history's telescope, we can examine the strange chemical reaction of pop culture, property and politics since it opened its doors in May 1982. Indeed, it is tempting to see the opening of the Haçienda as an act of political resistance. The force it gave the city is a story arc as much about political control, autonomy and identity as DJs, record sleeve design and debauchery. Today, with the city having prised some levers of power from London as part of seismic constitutional change, there are now over four decades of perspective, and a paper trail, revealing how the Haçienda/ Factory axis fired the starting gun for the new Manchester.

A typical pop-intellectual pirouette of Factory Records and Haçienda founder Tony Wilson was that, if the land between the Tigris and the Euphrates was the birthplace of civilisation, then nineteenth-century Manchester was Civilisation 2.0, when people left the fields to work with machines. For the people who opened the Haçienda, Manchester was the greatest city on earth: the first inter-city passenger railway, the first free public library, the birth of the co-operative movement, the first civic university, the birth of women's suffrage, the splitting of the atom, the first programmable computer, the isolation of 'wonder stuff' 2D material Graphene, the contraceptive pill, the test-tube baby, the place where Bob Dylan's audience infamously denounced him as a 'Judas' for going electric and, thanks to the pioneering Granada, the TV debuts of The Beatles and The Sex Pistols. And if Mr and Mrs Berners-Lee had not met working on the University of Manchester-Ferranti Mark 1 computer spun off from the maths department's original 'Baby' programmable machine, then their own baby, son Tim, would never have been around to create the World Wide Web. Compute this: the child of the Baby is the father of the World Wide Web.

The new 2021 red £50 note bears the face of Alan Turing, not only the daddy of modern computing at the university but also one of the very first humans to understand the profound implications of where his work was leading, to what we call today Artificial Intelligence. In Professor Stuart Russell's 2022 Reith Lectures, Turing is credited with the first prediction of machine learning, in a 1951 presentation he gave to Manchester's '51 Society and broadcast on the BBC Home Service. Turing prophesied: 'Once the machine thinking had started it would not take long to outstrip our feeble powers. At some stage therefore, we should have to expect the machines to take control.'

Russell made sure to credit the neglected Manchester location. Turing's work at the university's computing department sat on the same street where nuclear physics was born when Ernest Rutherford split the atom in 1917. This concentration of world firsts was not lost on Tony Wilson. For his mini-festival in 1998 to mark the fiftieth anniversary of the 'Baby', he highlighted a postwar British reticence which he believed had held the city back, telling me: 'Can you imagine if all these achievements in one street was in America? They would have built a great big theme park there!'

Northern taciturnity about the city's place in world history began to evaporate in the city-competition age. I was inspired to be a booster helping the original modern city to get a 'share of voice', as PR people say, on the platforms and channels which shape perceptions and change minds. There was a lot to be proud about, and to fight smug London media for attention for, but also a queasy chasm between the potential and the drizzly reality. The city today sits on the cusp of a new era – in 2D materials like Graphene, in life sciences, in metaverse software, as well as in art and culture. During the pandemic, we learned that tech can't improve everything. Forced to sample the metaverse, we found it to be more like *Meh*-chester; we need to see the look in other people's eyes, and not on a screen but under the same sky, no matter how dismally low.

The Haçienda was a unique enterprise, one designed for Manchester to celebrate itself. If that sounds like provincial backwater stuff, it set out, as we shall see, to be more cosmopolitan and provocative than London. Though its design was inspired by Manchester's heritage, it felt an international, even futuristic experience, just as Factory's fine art aesthetics seemed to place it far away from a dying industrial centre. The Haçienda was so sophisticated that it baffled the uncurious 'man in the street', a demographic Wilson despised. No permission was sought or needed from Westminster or Whitehall or even (or especially) of Manchester. No public money was spent, no government grants were applied for.

It was not just a place to get drunk, find lovers, take drugs, dance and see bands. Its very existence, we can see now, asked questions about what a city was, who it was for and in what new ways it could change. The 1953 prose-poem essay by Situationist Ivan Chtchcglov which inspired the club's name is about how the buildings and spaces around us shape our lives and imaginations. 'Architecture is the simplest means of articulating time and space, of modulating reality, of making people dream,' he wrote. Today's virtual and remote technology that lets us create new wraparound worlds may have weakened that claim. But with a historic devolution deal birthing a new power relationship with Westminster and locals now calling their city 'Manc-hattan', or more ironically, 'Manctopia', today's Manchester is the way the founders' dreams have turned out.

The pandemic is a punctuation mark, but history reminds us that there will be no full stop. Like a virus, Manchester mutates. Even in the tightest lockdowns

Factory Records and Haçienda founders Peter Saville, Tony Wilson and Alan Erasmus
(photo: Kevin Cummins)

of 2020 and 2021, with near-empty streets hosting shuttered bars and cafés, the building-site cranes continued to dance across the skyline to an accompaniment of power saws, kling-klanging steel and crooning hardhat Sinatras.

Today's high towers are for some grossly out of proportion to the Victorian city they sit in − a case of the new Manchester getting above itself.

Factory Records and Haçienda founder Rob Gretton (photo: Kevin Cummins)

Yet Manchester first led the world in Babel-like structures. The nineteenth century saw hundreds of factory chimneys fly up to heights of 300 feet. In William Wyld's 1852 painting *Manchester from Kersal* the pastoral foreground is dominated by a forest of belching smoke funnels, and a German visitor observed that this was the first city anywhere where the chimneys lorded it over churches.

Building big and brutal is a Manchester tradition. When the council tore down eight city blocks of narrow medieval-patterned streets and ginnels and replaced them in stages with the Arndale Centre, Mancunians called it the biggest toilet block in the world. Notorious gangster Jimmy Donnelly recalled in his memoir, 'The social scene, in which you could walk from den to den and drink from dawn to dusk, was lost.' A year before L.S. Lowry's death in 1976, writer Phil Griffin bumped into the artist gawping at the windowless monolith, clad in its reviled bile-yellow tiles. 'Oh no,' sighed the old man. 'Who let them do that?' Novelist Howard Jacobson said Mancunians claimed a warped sense of civic pride: 'Ugly we may be, but our ugly's bigger than yours'. In June 1996 the local wags declared that it took the IRA to do what many had wanted to for twenty years. No victimless crime, the 3,300 lb bomb injured over two hundred people and ended many small businesses, Swiss Re at the time describing its

£400 million of claims as the world's biggest non-natural disaster in insurance terms. Clearing the site, though, helped redesign an entire side of the city, and there is hardly a voice that says that it was not done well.

The city is unrecognisable from that of my arrival in the late 1970s, brimming with new buildings, and old buildings put to new uses: music venues, entertainment arenas, hotels of varied styles and stars, leisure and sports facilities, modern offices and workplaces, celebrity-fronted restaurants and bars, and residential apartment blocks. It has gone from a post-industrial disaster zone to a wild success in attracting a worldwide wall of money. Even during the pandemic, analysts continued to hymn Manchester's financial promise beyond the capital's maxed-out yields. City of London investment vehicles, sovereign wealth funds, UK and foreign pension funds, Far East safe-haven money, fleeing Hong Kongers, even 'mom and pop' investors, all are sinking their money into Manchester.

Politically, too, there is a beefed-up confidence. When city-region mayor Andy Burnham, who has not been slow to supply his Manc music credentials to the electorate, faced down Prime Minister Boris Johnson in a row about Covid funding in summer 2020, it was not a spat about a piffling £5 million. This was about the power dynamic between Manchester and London. The fresh-faced mayor with the Oasis eyebrows seemed to be channelling the same force which has been pushing the city's success, pride and now its buildings, outwards and upwards for two hundred years.

I have spent my entire adult life in the few square miles of the city centre and neighbourhoods around it. Drawn first here from London by punk rock and its influencers, I was another young dude just happy to carry the news, scribbling reports from the music-scene frontline. Then, inspired by those on a mission to revive the city's glories, I joined in the regeneration game, throwing in my lot with the Manchester movers and shakers of the new millennium.

Factory Records and the Haçienda, I submit, gave the kiss of life to a dying city, and sparked a chain reaction of hubris, scandal, money and power politics still playing out today. It is impossible to say that Manchester would have been a better or worse city if the Haçienda had never been built. It is only possible to say that it would have been a very different city.

Place names: A stranger's guide

Manchester is just forty-five square miles, but this thin strip of land carries a multitude of meanings, memories and myths, stories and stereotypes. 'Manchester' will trigger as many associations as there are readers, so some geographical (and psycho-geographical) housekeeping is required. It's complicated, but you need to know the difference between the City of Manchester and 'The City', and between the Northwest and Lancashire. And what was 'Granadaland', and 'Englandsnorthwest'. Manchester and Salford are essentially two parts of the same city, even though 'Manchester' came to be the label for the whole noble mission of the late twentieth-century regeneration (alongside a deep simmering rivalry between them). Complicated, yes, but then ideas of regional identity and loyalty have, due to Brexit, become rather more consequential than they used to be: Manchester's geopolitics is pointing the way to the future – in 2022 government levelling-up policy, following the pioneering Greater Manchester 2017 model, is set on installing regional executive mayors nationwide.

Manchester has for centuries been more than a place, a shorthand for ideas and ideals. In the eighteenth century, German traders coined the name Manchesterthum, meaning something like 'Manchesterism', which came to have a derogatory meaning among socialists, due to the nineteenth-century shock city's rampaging commercial mentality. It rose as a centre specialising in the manufacture of textile products, as being a bucket into which clouds from the Irish Sea dumped rainfall produced the damp conditions that keep textiles well. When a Promethean blast of capitalism threw up the nineteenth-century city, Disraeli declared it 'as great a human exploit as Athens'. The degradation of lives amid the mushrooming chimneys described by Friedrich Engels in his 1845 *Condition of the Working Class in England* provided the ammunition for Karl Marx's *Communist Manifesto*. Engels noted how dependent the towns around the city, today the town centres across Greater Manchester, were 'purely industrial

9

Manchester from Charlesworth, Derbyshire, September 2022 (photo: Andy Spinoza)

and conduct all their business through Manchester upon which they are in every respect dependent'.

An awestruck Alexis de Tocqueville wrote in 1835, 'From this filthy sewer, pure gold flows.' Manchester's lifeforce ushered in what A.J.P. Taylor called the last Hanseatic city, 'a civilisation built on trade', giving rise to orchestras, libraries and learning as well as the escapism of another first, the proletariat. Even today, it's a city which parties hard, and it markets itself on the New York subway with posters proclaiming 'Manchester. A city which thinks a table is for dancing on'. Below is a quick guide to this exceptional patch of land and the various place names which it inhabits and adjoins. We start wide-screen, taking in the northern panorama, before zooming in on Manchester (and Salford).

The North of England

The North comprises the Northwest, Yorkshire and the Humber and the Northeast, a territory of around 15 million people which has spawned countless stereotypes born of how historic counties helped splutter the industrial revolution into life, giving rise to extremes of poor and rich among crowded urban and wild natural landscapes. 'The North' is generally defined by poverty and disadvantage, leading to the notorious cliché of the divide between it and 'the South', as well as the revealing marked difference in English accent – 'This is not a Barth, this is a bath. This is the North' as the popular poster has it. It's a telltale sign of class and geography, yet the 2011 arrival in Salford of

This is Not a Barth (image: Statement Artworks)

BBC Radio 5 instantly created a new class of broadcaster fudging the issue, using flat northern vowels in words like 'Newcastle' and 'class' in their otherwise Received Pronunciation. Put aside for now the 2019 election-deciding 'red wall' and its consequences, for our purposes all we need know is that Manchester fancies itself rotten and thinks of itself as the capital of the North.

Northwest England

'I am from the mad north-north-west,' declares Hamlet, Shakespeare drawing on ancient beliefs that insanity and melancholy blew down South from 'up there'. Despite this, no one ever said at the holiday disco, 'Hi, I'm from Northwest England.' Useful maybe for weather forecasters, the Northwest of England has no administrative role, merely overlaying the boundaries of its constituent counties with the government's purpose to collect statistics. One of the nine official regions of England, it is made up of Cheshire, Cumbria, Greater Manchester, Lancashire and Merseyside counties, with a combined population in 2011 of just over seven million. As the region's largest city, Manchester is perceived as the capital of the Northwest, but perhaps unlike other regions such as Yorkshire and the Northeast, any claim to a cohesive Northwest identity crumbles in the face of its diverse landscapes, economies, lifestyles and cultures.

The Northern Powerhouse

Not an actual place, more a promotional brand name for global investment and a handle for electoral gain, coined by Chancellor George Osborne in a June 2014 speech in which he anointed Manchester as its foremost metropolis, part of a seismic shift in the political landscape leading to devolutionary trends and constitutional changes. It's a badge which has fallen out of favour, as under the Boris Johnson government the 'NP' was eclipsed by the even vaguer mantra of 'levelling up'.

'englandsnorthwest' and the Northwest Development Agency

In 1998 the Labour government installed the Northwest Development Agency (NWDA) to drive economic growth in 'englandsnorthwest' – the grammatically challenged brand it tried to affix to the region. In lavish tourism and lifestyle campaigns, media luminaries Stuart Maconie, Peter Hook and Faisal Islam were lured into fronting PR activity, in Manchester Grammar School old boy Islam's case, to give two fingers to the capital with a campaign titled It's Grim Down South. The NWDA was no mean effort, with a budget of £176 million and a staff of 180. It had powers over planning policy that overrode councils, and channelled £1 billion a year of central, European and other funds into the region. The coalition government killed off RDAs in

2012 but the NWDA was always a leashed pet of central government. When Factory founder Tony Wilson referred to the agency's Warrington HQ as 'the perineum of the Northwest' (which he usually took pleasure in doing while compèring events sponsored by it), he was referring not just to his antipathy to its location but to its very conception. However, he saw new regional powers encouraged by the Labour government in this period as a real prize to shoot for, and I have included an account of his eccentric 2004 campaign for a Northwest representative assembly.

'Granadaland'

Compare the NWDA's failed attempt to create a regional unity with the warm and cuddly regional identity cultivated by the extraordinary broadcaster Granada TV. Named after the sun-drenched Spanish city for the region with some of England's wettest places, it boasted a bolshie, quasi-republican attitude seen in its preference not to play the national anthem at closedown. It had beamed high-quality popular programmes to both the Northwest and Yorkshire from 1956 until 1968, when its franchise to broadcast across the Pennines was removed. The furious founder, southerner Lord Bernstein (no relation to the future council CEO), had drunk deep at the well of Manchester self-importance and declared he would raise the matter with the United Nations. From the early 1960s, 'Granadaland' became the channel's descriptor for its new footprint − Cumbria in the north down to Cheshire, and from the Isle of Man eastwards to the High Peak. It was less a logo or a branding campaign, and more a simple turn of phrase uttered by its Northern-accented presenters, which included Michael Parkinson, Bob Greaves and the leading man of this book, Tony Wilson. The folksy charm of this now half-remembered fairytale name for 5,500 sq mi of TV signal reach became an intangible territory of the imagination, encouraging an identity-by-stealth in a region with little else to unify it.

Lancashire

Anyone for Mancashire? Manchester used to be in Lancashire. As a newcomer in the late 1970s, I was struck by 'Lancs not Mancs' graffiti, dissent from the Local Government Act which in 1974 abolished Lancashire's traditional boundaries and cast many of its inhabitants into the new counties of Greater Manchester, Merseyside and others.

The whole bundle of identity confusion can be seen in the global brand of Lancashire County Cricket Club. The team plays home matches at Old Trafford in front of its 2013 'dock container' grandstands, architect Gavin Elliott citing nearby Salford Quays and the Haçienda as post-industrial influences. The stands are painted the vivid vermilion of the red-rose county but are situated in a part of the borough of Trafford which many simply see as central Manchester. Confused? The old Lancashire also included Liverpool. I did say it was complicated.

The redrawing of the map of Lancashire in 1974 was a messy business. The traditional county area lost territory to both Greater Manchester and Merseyside, and parts of the Lake District to another new construct, Cumbria. There are numerous people today for who Lancashire remains intact, because they hold as an article of faith that the Local Government Act did not abolish the 1889 historic county border. The feeling is not confined to scrawl on pub toilet walls. At many a Manchester business dinner there was the familiar form of The Loyal Toast – 'The Queen, Duke of Lancaster!' – made because Lancashire is a county palatine (one whose ruler was granted powers exercised elsewhere by the monarch) and Lancaster is its county town.

The deep roots of Lancashire identity survived the new council agglomerations. The timbre and tone of popular entertainers George Formby, Eric Morecambe and Gracie Fields display Lancastrians' apparently innate ability to entertain, which still floats through our airwaves daily. The Lanky burr is almost the official accent of BBC pop music – Sara Cox, Guy Garvey, Mary Anne Hobbs, Vernon Kay, Liz Kershaw, Stuart Maconie, Mark Radcliffe and Marc Riley, some from Greater Manchester, but most have the enduringly appealing Lancastrian character (along with their ex-colleague Shaun Keaveny), a loquacious likeability that lives on in the space between our ears. It's a territory which also gave us Chris Evans, Steve Coogan, John Thomson and many entertainers too numerous to mention. Note: such natural radio entertainers John Peel, Craig Charles, Janice Long, Kenny Everett and Liza Tarbuck come from within the old Lancashire borders, but they are Merseysiders, another Whitehall fabrication and a very different republic of the mind. If Liverpool has a part to play in the revival of modern Manchester, it was to show that confrontational class war – waged by its Militant council regime against central government in the 1980s – was a calamitous course which demonstrated to Manchester's leaders that there were better ways to emerge from the post-industrial age.

Greater Manchester aka the Manchester City Region aka 'the city region'

'Greater Manchester' is a metropolitan county of ten local authorities gathered around and including the City of Manchester. It may be home to 493 sq mi and 2.8 million citizens, but apart from officialdom, no one calls it by its name; no one has ever identified as a 'Greater Mancunian'. From 1969 to 1974, the government label for the conurbation was the Orwellian acronym SELNEC – South East Lancashire Northeast Cheshire – so things have arguably improved. As a geographic county, 'GM' is used by the Office for National Statistics for key data and census material. In 1974 the ten Greater Manchester boroughs – Bolton, Bury, Manchester, Oldham, Rochdale, Salford, Stockport, Tameside, Trafford and Wigan – grouped together informally as the Association of Greater Manchester Authorities (AGMA). After the abolition of the Greater Manchester Council in 1986, an evolving mix of collaborative governing arrangements led to, from 2011, the ten councils' ever-closer partnership in the Greater Manchester Combined Authority (GMCA). In 2017, under the historic devolution deal with government, an executive mayor election was won by former Labour MP Andy Burnham, and for a second time in 2021. In 'DevoManc' the ten councils took greater powers from central government, banding together to run economic development, health, housing, police, social care, skills and transport. The first deal of its kind, this new political context is fundamental to the future of the Greater Manchester City Region (aka the 'Manchester City Region' or simply 'the city region'), which since the late 1990s has been supported by GM-wide public sector agencies – Marketing Manchester (tourism), MIDAS (investment) and Manchester Enterprises, now Growth Hub (business support, training and skills), comprising what is widely termed the 'Manchester family'.

Salford

Pevsner remarked that the fact that Salford is 'not administratively one with Manchester is one of the most curious anomalies of England'. Manchester and Salford are cities which, very rarely in the UK, are joined back-to-back on dry land. A Norman baron is said to have rent the two places asunder with a stroke of the pen. Salford became a borough in 1844 and a city in 1926, despite Home Office civil servants dismissing it as 'merely a scratch collection of 240,000 people cut off from Manchester by the river'. Salford, while sharing a land border with Manchester, is indeed sited in a meander of the River Irwell and its name means 'ford by the willow trees'. During the English Civil War, Salford's Royalist forces mounted a brief siege across the Irwell of Manchester's Parliament supporters which history recalls 'did little to improve relations between the two towns'. Even today, little fellow feeling exists, with these Labour heartlands often bedevilled by behind-the-scenes civic rivalry.

Salford never had a grand centre like Manchester. Its historic commercial heart was the docks. Two classic accounts of Salford defined the working-class North – Walter Greenwood's 1933 novel *Love on the Dole* and Robert Roberts's 1971 autobiography *The Classic Slum*. When generations of TV soap addicts tuned into the world's longest-running drama *Coronation Street*, most believed they were watching life in Manchester, and not Salford. The Manchester brand was always stronger. When Sir Rocco Forte opened his Lowry Hotel on the Salford bank of the River Irwell in 2001, Salford councillors choked on the swanky lunch they put on to honour the hotelier prince; he told them he had used Manchester as the hotel address. The BBC, in contrast, ensured that its 2013 relocation from London to MediaCityUK is accurately described as Salford, finally helping its star to emerge from Manchester's shadow. The 2021 opening of the lovely 156-acre RHS Bridgewater garden at Worsley is also attracting many previously unlikely to visit Salford. None more unlikely, perhaps, than Chinese premier Xi Jingping, who slept over at the Lowry on 22 October 2015 on a UK state visit.

The City of Manchester

The City of Manchester on the map is a mere 44.6 sq mi of land in the shape of a fat finger, dropping down from Heaton Park in the north to a narrow tip in the south, and taking in Manchester Airport. Official statistics in mid-2019, the last pre-pandemic point of meaningful measurement, revealed that the city, governed by Manchester City Council, was the fastest-growing in the UK, its population of over 555,000 enjoying one of the youngest age profiles in the nation, with neighbouring Salford enjoying the second fastest growth. Its emblem is well known as the worker bee, but its upstart character is better revealed by a coat of arms featuring a trading ship, for a city 35 miles from the sea.

'The City'

Nothing to do with the City of London. It was used between the mid-1990s and 2021 by Manchester insiders to describe the strategic consciousness of the city's leadership, when the phrase 'The City thinks' meant 'what Howard and Richard think', and the strategies and tactics preferred by CEO Sir Howard Bernstein and political leader Sir Richard Leese. The term has fallen out of use since Bernstein's and Leese's retirement from their top-ranking roles (though both are heavily involved in city regeneration) and the 2017 election of Andy Burnham to Greater Manchester mayor. In 2017 Joanne Roney replaced Bernstein and in 2021 Bev Craig replaced Leese in their respective roles, two women chiefs (the political leader an out gay woman) for a city traditionally known for its high-profile male champions in the national arena.

Manchester city centre

The city centre today is the bullseye of the Greater Manchester dartboard, radiating energy out of a dense, agglomerated business and lifestyle centre which is circled by the radial M60 outer motorway and inner ring roads. The Victorian centre at its core was built from the local red Triassic sandstone by the whiskery, top-hatted merchants, factory owners, traders and inventors whose statues dot the centre and decorate the town hall. Today their mills and monuments are overshot by sleek new towers which bookend the city centre at the western and northern ends of Deansgate, the city's backbone since Roman times. At the northern end is the CIS Tower, the Co-operative movement's 1962 tower.

CIS Tower (photo: Peter J. Walsh)

For three decades Manchester's highest, it was seen by proud citizens as a beacon lighting the way to the future. A youngster like Clint Boon, the Inspiral Carpets' keyboardist, told me on his return from a tour of Japan how he measured his ambition against it: 'Until the band went abroad, I had never seen a building taller than the Co-op tower.' Today, there are many buildings around the same height or higher. Property data specialist Urbinfo reports that, as of August 2022, there are 55 buildings in 'Central Manchester' over 20 storeys, 41 of which have been built since 2000, with 30 completed since 2010. The wave is growing: another 23 buildings over 20 storeys are under construction, and another five are at pre-construction phases. A further 35 have planning approved. If they are all built, there will be 118 tall buildings, double the number today.

Today the CIS Tower looks a stunted lightweight compared to brash new boys at the other end of town – the Beetham Tower and the new four-tower Deansgate Square complex poised above the city's world-renowned

Beetham Tower in clouds (photo: David Blake)

heritage below. These glazed monsters loom over the cobblestoned Castlefield district where the Romans built a fort on Mamucium, 'the breast-shaped hill', and where the city's original go-getters joined up road, rail and canal to put a rocket under the industrial revolution. The historic city centre of Castlefield, Deansgate, Albert Square and Ancoats is just two square miles, but the centre cannot hold, pushing out as clusters of high buildings sprout up in former urban edge-lands. This effect was first seen in the 1990s with the urban heritage park Castlefield, then west into Trafford and Salford with residential schemes, and later with the tower block explosion in Greengate, a lacuna of land technically in Salford. The hipster neighbourhood of the Northern Quarter emerged in the 1990s and has rippled out into the 'doughnut ring' of rough fringe districts like Ancoats, New Islington and Angel Meadow, which now have a city-centre character. Unlike older cities where nobles gifted land, the city centre has almost no historic parkland. In 2019, by contrast, there were still 59 surface car parks across thirty undeveloped acres on former industrial sites in the centre, which is now fast growing upwards as well as outwards, with a pipeline of tall towers greater than that of most major European capital cities. Pedants carp that the towers are not skyscrapers compared to American or Middle East versions, but they have not seen the upper levels of Deansgate Square or Beetham Tower disappearing into the dank blur of grey. Manchester is on so much closer terms with its lead-coffin-lid sky than sunnier cities.

'Central Manchester' – the expanding city centre

There are borders on an official map, and then there is the way people live in their city and the way they feel about it. Manchester's momentum is creating a new, larger outer centre, spilling out and taking in Ancoats, Castlefield, Greengate and central Salford and Salford Quays, and parts of Trafford around the Old Trafford football and cricket grounds. ONS figures for 2020 revealed over 220,000 living in the combined inner and outer city centres, 30,000 more than in 2015. Take a taxi, tram or bus from Piccadilly or Victoria Stations, and in fifteen minutes you can be in MediaCityUK or the Lowry Centre at Salford Quays, or at the Old Trafford sports stadiums. You have gone beyond the Manchester boundary, but people call it 'Manchester'. Urban planners forced to deal with this pulsating zone of boundaries messed up by new buildings, money and movement call it 'the regional centre', or 'the central core', and have described it as 'the primary economic driver for the Northwest'. Research in summer 2022 for this book by data specialist Urbinfo estimates that the new *de facto* central Manchester is now home to over 260,000 people. While we wait for new ONS data to confirm these extraordinary numbers, they also align with official 2022 findings that Salford has one of the UK's fastest-growing populations.

'Town'

No one calls it the 'regional centre' or 'Manchester city centre'. It's called 'town'. As in 'I work in town' or, 'We're going out into town'. This is to the displeasure of city boosters for who the word feels a bit twentieth-century, sounding limited and provincial, not international and glossy. It's redolent, too, of the 'dirty old town' of Ewan MacColl's evergreen Salford ballad. No matter how much the brochures portray the vibrant, modern, cosmopolitan world-class European city, no matter how many shiny glass towers rise above it, 'town' is what people call their Manchester city centre.

1

The city calls

To the centre of the city where all roads meet, looking for you.
'Shadowplay', Joy Division, lyrics by Ian Curtis (original version,
when band named Warsaw)

In the month I arrived in Manchester, photographer Kevin Cummins stopped to record a street scene in the city centre. The black-and-white photo 'Corner of High Street and Cannon Street, October 1979' evokes an ambience of urban shabbiness – squared. It's one of *those* Manchester days. Along a vacant corner of rough ground, a leaden sky presses down above the heads of sodden pedestrians waiting at bus stops. Two banjaxed traffic poles at crazy angles emerge from the puddle-strewn pavement, adorned with hazard tape. A destroyed advertising poster, one of those faux-abstract art photos used in the late 1970s to sell cigarettes, lies in pieces below a sheared-off hoarding frame. The building elevation, and the scene it overlooks, is crushingly depressing.

Why did the supreme visual interpreter of Manchester music culture put the camera lens to his eye? Maybe he was simply taken with the composition, the aftermath of an accident. It's clear, though, that it spoke of a greater plight, a sad and pathetic sight in the heart of a city which had once the led the world and was now reeling powerless from brutal economic and social forces.

The photo, which sits alongside his portraits of musicians in his collection *Looking for the Light through the Pouring Rain*, evokes a humiliating loss of civic pride. Approach the same site today, and you won't find Cannon Street. As if a mercy killing has taken place, it has been expunged from the map, master-planned out of existence in a new street layout following the 1996 IRA bomb.

The image crystallises my experience of Manchester in my first year of student life. I lived in Chandos Hall, a tower-block university residence. I had received a letter saying that, as I had not applied for a room, I could have the

Cannon Street, October 1979 (photo: Kevin Cummins)

last one available among the three thousand new students. This random factor had a central influence on my life, which has been interwoven with the fortunes of the city centre. My room was the nearest on the entire campus to the city centre, a stone's throw from the main station. Trains to Liverpool chugged mere yards past the building. When I arrived at Manchester Piccadilly, the taxi drivers refused to take me to my new home. 'You can see it from here!' one shouted, pointing to the building. 'You can walk it.' Dragging my hi-fi and records in a suitcase the size of a small wardrobe was an exhausting welcome. My little room was soon reverberating to Buzzcocks, Television, The Slits and Talking Heads: jerky, nervy music for angsty youths like me, all elbows and cheekbones.

As an eighteen-year-old arrival in the autumn of 1979, I got a daily close-up view of a city beaten up by recession. Manchester was dazed and bruised and in A&E. I wandered without any intended destination around the second-hand bookshops and greasy-spoon caffs and investigated tatty living-room-sized pubs like the Jolly Angler and the Grey Horse. I turned my ankle on century-old cobblestones, and my Dunlop Green Flash tennis pumps fell apart trudging through the rain. I noted the ranks of elderly people keeping warm on Arndale Centre benches, and my eye was taken by the sight of walking wounded, men with limps and other disabilities who I assumed were victims of industrial injuries.

I was not unused to sights of dereliction. I was familiar with the insalubrious sights of London's East End when my parents would drive my two younger brothers and me back around where they grew up, where parts of Shoreditch and Spitalfields still looked bomb-damaged from the war. At Petticoat Lane market, tramps and pedlars would lay out pathetic trinkets and domestic junk for sale. 'These are the true existentialists,' my dad said to me. 'They have to make their life again every day.'

School was Minchenden, a big comprehensive with a multicultural catchment; the redbrick lower school was a dead ringer for the rowdy comp in the TV series *Grange Hill*. My fellow pupils and friends were English, Cypriots, Indian, Pakistani, West Indian, African, Italian, Irish and, like me, Jewish. While doing A-levels, in the holidays I washed dishes in bankers' canteens in the City of London. The 29 bus home took me back to my family's 1930s Metroland semi in Southgate. An upstairs seat on the Green Lanes route through Turkish and Greek Cypriot street life allowed glimpses of card games in rooms above grocery stores. My part-time kitchen porter jobs meant I knew my way around the reggae record stalls in the markets of inner-city Dalston, and I started exploring the pubs and venues where the angry new punk rock music was being played.

Even though family life was loving and lively, I was angry, too. My sixth form was made special by a group of teachers led by Mike McHale who introduced us to films, plays, opera and holidays in the UK and abroad. But my adolescence took place against a background of twisted and confusing emotions. At twelve, I accidentally overheard a family conversation and discovered that I was adopted.

When I took the fact of my origins in, I was on the floor of our living room reading the *London Evening Standard* and watching the teatime TV news. The knowledge provoked no tearful explanations and anguished conversations with my adoptive parents, David and Loretta. I simply shrugged it off and relegated my existential revelation to somewhere in importance below the next school trip or football match; something to deal with later. It would take nearly twenty years to discover I was born in an East End nursing home to a Jewish mother, with no record of my father's identity.

I have read truly awful tales of adoption trauma, especially of adults who blame their emotional issues on being separated from their birth parents. Some go to their graves bitterly cursing their fate. I didn't feel like that. Instead, in retrospect, I instinctively grasped that I could use the blank slate of my past. I could create my own story, not weighed down by the intense relationships that come with DNA. My natural-born younger brothers Marc and Robert rowed with Dad, teenage testosterone leading to heated confrontations. I was different. Dad knew I was bookish and thoughtful. In Mum's description, I was 'deep'.

My parents were second-generation Jewish diaspora, from family lines which had come to London from the Netherlands, Latvia, Lithuania and Poland around the turn of the twentieth century. Now their adopted son was the first on either side to go to university. One grandad was an on-course dog-track bookmaker before the war, in which he was a military policeman, the other was a backstreet bookie and air-raid warden. I grew up in a colourful tribe of tough, hard-grafting Jews. Most relatives earned their living in the *schmatte* business as cutters or wholesalers of cloth, or tailors or market traders. They were also cab drivers, roofers, hairdressers. No one had a boss, they all ran their own thing.

Hairstyling was my parents' way out of the smoky, crowded East End. Mum ran her own salon at the age of sixteen. My dad's uncle Louis, a flyweight boxing champ in the Desert Rats, tutored Vidal Sassoon at TV celebrity Raymond 'Teazy Weazy' Bessone's in Bond Street, and Dad was an ambidextrous stylist and trichologist, making wigs for stars like Barbara Windsor and providing expert opinion in civil-court cases against crimpers who burned instead of permed their clients.

If I felt I did not fit, it was in that most obvious way; I did not look like anyone around me. As awkward teens do, I was forever measuring myself; against my cousins, so dishy they modelled for covers of teen girl mags, and against my brother. Marc was in the year below me but was well-built and grew a beard at thirteen. In his first week at secondary school, he took on the biggest boy in my year for a public scrap on the playing field, egged on by a huge crowd. The whole school could tell we weren't naturally brothers. At sixteen, I was a gawky 6 ft 2 in beanpole, but the origins of my life went unmentioned. My unspoken turmoil was something I had to negotiate alone.

To find myself, I needed to go elsewhere. My mission to liberate myself began with talk of university. It seems improbable today, but government practice was to pay those with A-levels a more than reasonable grant from public funds, and their rent too. In return, I was required to read books, poems and plays, and write about them. I was one of the 5 per cent of eighteen-year-olds (today it is nearer 50 per cent) for whom studying for a degree was the next step on the educational assembly line.

Despite the enveloping warmth of the clan who had accepted me as one of them, I could not help but feel like an outsider, and Manchester was calling.

The place seemed football-mad, as I was, and all the gripping television, from *World in Action* to *Crown Court*, had a Granada logo. As a teenager my week hinged around Thursday lunchtime, when I picked up my order of music 'inkies' *Sounds*, *Melody Maker* and *New Musical Express* and spent hours in my bedroom wolfing down the scribblings of Manchester-based writers Paul Morley, Jon Savage and Mick Middles. Along with Malcolm Garrett's graphics for manager Richard Boon's Buzzcocks, like an alternative tourist board, their work gave the city's death throes a perverse glamour for alienated youth. And through history lessons I learned that the metropolis had an epic history as a crucible of radicalism from which poured forth protest, progress and provocation.

The city boasted a tumultuous historical energy which seemed to live on in the modern day. From the massacre at Peterloo, the eye-witness accounts of Engels and the formulations of Marx, through to the early trade unions and the Suffragettes, the Chartists and the Free Trade movement ... all this merged with modern pop culture into a swirling continuum in my mind. 'Manchester' was a movie on perpetual loop in my head, a revolving cast list of George Best, the Pankhursts, L.S. Lowry, the Moors Murderers and the cast of *Coronation Street* all set to a playlist of Joy Division, Jilted John and the mournful brass of the hit TV soap's opening credits. The seventeen-year-old me could no more have escaped Manchester's gravitational pull than Stan Ogden could have walked past the Rovers Return without nipping in for a pint.

I did not know it yet, but these influences were to combine with the power of place to create a new me. I was destined to become part of what Factory and Haçienda founder Tony Wilson called, in the early 1980s, 'the interesting community', the city's outsiders, rebels, artists and misfits. Somehow, over decades, and impossible to conceive at the time, they set the style for a new Manchester, as the city got high on music, ditching municipal socialism for global high-finance, elite culture and *grands projets*.

Maybe it was the inland port which brought the sailors and their vinyl records, or the US army base at Burtonwood, near Warrington, but Wilson always claimed that Manchester kids had the best record collections. Elton John's *Life* reserves special mention for its clubs, where he played piano with groups like The Ink Spots: 'People talk about Swinging London in the mid-sixties, but those kids in the Twisted Wheel were so clued-up, so switched-on, so much hipper than anyone else in the country.' A decade later, many of the back-to-backs where those kids had grown up had been cleared for modernist housing projects. The two eras sat uneasily side by side, the 1970s generation caught between a crumbling redbrick past and a jerry-built concrete future.

The built environment was expressed in the culture, and the city's music from the late 1970s to the end of the twentieth century expresses an overriding sense of place. The buildings and streets which the musicians grew up around are a crucial influence. Mick Middles writes in *Factory* how the ghosts of Little Peter Street, where Joy Division practised in the top floor of Tony Davidson's rehearsal rooms, had left their impression in the music. The former mill 'was a place where tortuous hard work had taken place. You could simply smell it.' The dismal interior 'became an integral part of the Joy Division image; it darkened the visuals and, some might say, darkened the music also'.

The emotional desolation of the music and the ruined cityscapes torn down and remade by merciless forces are captured in Jon Savage's interviews with the band. In both the *Joy Division* documentary and the book *This Searing Light, the Sun and Everything Else – Joy Division: The Oral History*, singer Bernard Sumner looks back, saying: 'you were always looking for beauty because it was such an ugly place … I was surrounded by factories and nothing that was pretty, nothing. So it gave you an amazing yearning for things that were beautiful …'

From the start, Joy Division's music evoked architectural epiphanies, from reviewers' 'cathedrals of sound' to Kevin Cummins's *NME* images of the band in a snowbound Hulme, in his words 'a landscape in which the four figures become part of the composition'. For their first TV appearance, the Granada TV director intercut their performance of 'Shadowplay' with reversed-out film footage of US freeways and suburbs, supplied by Wilson, a visual interpretation of the music's conjuring up of alienating human-made landscapes.

Andy Warhol's muse, the German chanteuse Nico, told Professor Richard Witts that she moved to Manchester in the early 1980s because it reminded her of Berlin after the war. (His biography *Nico: Life and Lies of an Icon* reveals it was more about a reliable supply of heroin). The grimly evocative ruins of Mancunia are an overstated myth for Witts, who believes Manchester should be noted instead for its muscular modernist rebuilding exercise in the 1960s and 1970s, a grand bid for a flagship city that the civic leaders modelled on Chicago. The city's 1945 and 1961 plans were designed to sweep away the grime and chaos of unplanned Victorian sprawl worsened by wartime bomb damage, an understandable postwar reaction which aspired to an idealistic new urbanism.

In 1967 Harold Wilson opened the city's Mancunian Way, the nation's first urban motorway outside London. Bestriding the centre, it was a potent symbol of the prime minister's 'white heat of technology' economic vision. The city's postwar rebuilding was defined by 25 major modernist concrete, glass and steel buildings for commercial and institutional use, from the CIS Tower to the Royal Exchange theatre's 'space pod' and the gigantic Arndale Centre. 'Contrary to the view promoted in the Factory story,' Witts commented, 'the image that Manchester presented to the world was not of a derelict city but a comprehensively modern one – one that had got it wrong.'

Owen Hatherley's 2010 book A *Guide to the New Ruins of Great Britain* pinpoints the missed opportunity for a socially progressive utopia, a blueprint for a future city of multilevel elevated walkways and bridges. Both the Hulme estate and the Arndale Centre were the work of Manchester practice Wilson and Wormersley, which through its links to Sheffield's 985-unit Park Hill (the most brutal single building of the nation's experiment in concrete brutalism) was influenced by New Babylon, a 'dynamic labyrinth' variant of modernism. Manchester's version of this was a disaster. In the university precinct, the 'streets in the sky' walkways were at different heights and couldn't be connected up. Huge inner-city concrete estates at Ardwick, Beswick and Hulme were completed by 1972, but poor design and construction meant that much of the new housing was quickly uninhabitable.

Modernism was the architectural expression of a postwar belief in progress. So, not only can the Haçienda can be viewed as the first project of today's Manchester, it can also be seen today as the final piece in the city's postwar campaign of modernism, in Witts's words 'a commercial contribution to a public post-modern design project'. It is only with the passing of time that we can turn the telescope around and look back through the other end, investigating the detail of a daisy chain which reveals the Haçienda not only as a cultural fire starter but as the point at which the modernist period concluded, and pivoted to the new city fast rising up today.

Narratives of mental anguish are commonplace in the marketing of young music artists today. Such openness was not the case in Ian Curtis's era. That such personal despair expressed through his lyrics, disturbingly cathartic performances and Joy Division's music could be the source of a city's staggering revival is worthy of detailed examination. On this reading, Manchester's reinvention was made possible by the global sales of Joy Division's music, an austere sound of space and mystery, with high bass guitar, unexpected drum patterns and doomy, open-ended lyrics interpreted with deep retrospective meaning after Curtis's death. The majestic mystery of the music powered the group's myth, which became a classic emblem of the city in the collective imagination. Curtis's suicide is today referred to by Professor Jon Savage and Peter Saville with cold truth as the 'equity' behind Factory (the company's capital ran to Wilson's £4,000 inheritance), and the tormented Curtis's death is viewed by

Saville as a 'sacrifice … he felt so authentically and passionately about what he was saying that ultimately he gave his life for it.' Says Savage, 'The first album said, "I'm fucked." The second album said, "we're all fucked."'

The band did not have to describe the grime and the rubble of the city, and how those surroundings shaped people's lives; rather, what emerges is a post-industrial Manchester state of mind. There is not a single mention of Manchester lyrically in Joy Division's *Unknown Pleasures*, but could this phenomenal work of art have sprung from anywhere else at that time?

Intriguingly, while growing up in Manchester was just as emotionally traumatic for Morrissey as it was for Curtis and Sumner, he flatly rejected Joy Division's cultural entitlement when he told Nick Kent in *The Face*, 'To me, it's all just … legend.' In The Smiths' lyrics, the city is the heart worn on the record sleeves, in the neighbourhood and street-name poetry of Strangeways, Rusholme and the roof of the Holy Name Church, not to mention the suffering little children – which, as Morrissey was forced to explain to outraged tabloids for using it as subject matter, could have been his fate too at the hands of 1960s Moors Murderers Ian Brady and Myra Hindley, who sprang from the back-to-back terraced streets of north Manchester.

The Fall's frontman and lyricist, Mark E. Smith, had a keen sense of cultural geography. He rejected Factory Records because he said he hated students and the label's office was based in Didsbury, the student central of south Manchester bedsit-land. The Fall's early songs are disturbing, often hilarious hallucinations, alighting on the local specifics in tracks like 'Lucifer over Lancashire', the Northern sprite myth in 'Fiery Jack', or 'Rowche Rumble', which was Smith's expression for the sound of crates of tranquilliser pills being unloaded at Salford's docks. John Cooper Clarke blended the grimy onomatopoeia of Salford township names – Ordsall, Seedley and Weaste – into 'Beasley Street', a dark caricature of Northern grime: 'Keith Joseph smiles and a baby dies / In a box on Beasley Street', referring to a key architect of Thatcherism while pandering with exquisite sick humour to the prejudices of southerners. Steve Diggle of Buzzcocks was inspired by 'the percolation of people on Market Street' to write their hit 'Harmony in my Head', after the mid-1970s disruption of the city centre. He says, 'The beauty of that old industrial environment definitely affected you, it makes you. Then the Arndale arrived, this big box. The little Victorian shops were disappearing. I was on Market Street and the song is about the sound of the people on the city streets.'

In the guitar band debut albums of The Stone Roses and Oasis you hear swaggering young Mancunians taking on all comers. Set on conquering the world beyond their horizons, they include only minor hometown markers – Noel Gallagher's tribute to Burnage record shop Sifter's on *Definitely Maybe*, and 'Mersey Paradise' in the Roses' chiming-guitar Arcadia; the river associated with Liverpool actually bubbles up in Stockport and snakes its way to the west coast.

Barry Adamson's 1989 *Moss Side Story* used his inner-city neighbourhood for a film noir soundtrack. Madchester era rapper MC Tunes' 1990 cover for *The North at Its Heights* reimagines Piccadilly as a graphic-novelised naked city. Stadium guitar group Doves touched on changing urban landscapes in 2005's 'Some Cities' ('Too much history coming down / Another building brought to ground'), but the song is about the personal rather than real estate. Elbow's 'Station Approach' sees Guy Garvey returning home out of sorts but so in tune with Manchester that he feels like he has designed the buildings he walks by.

The machine-made dance music of New Order, 808 State and Manchester university graduates The Chemical Brothers emerged in districts close to the Brunswick Street lab which pushed the buttons switching on the digital age in 1948. The university's Professor Fred Williams recalled how the display tube lights on the world's first programmable computer 'entered a mad dance … Nothing was ever the same again.'

What does Manchester's music heritage mean to the new Mancunians, those who arrive from distant lands, or those for whom The Smiths and Joy Division are 'dad music'? Everyone has their own personal city. For those mesmerised by the bleak images of Ian Curtis standing over the Princess Parkway in Hulme, or who purred at The Smiths posing in sepia outside the Salford Lads Club, the back-to-back conjoined twin cities were not just a backdrop: Manchester/ Salford is a sense of humour, a tone of voice, a way of looking at the world. But for many, the 'classic' Manchester and Salford in our heads, with its images, memories and meaning, has been fatally breached by the scale, style and signals sent by the high tide of shiny new obelisks. Will new music from the new Manchester have as distinctive a character as it did in the late twentieth-century city? If artists are shaped by the built environment, how will the transformation of Manchester's centre affect the culture it produces?

In Paul Morley's words, Manchester is not just a collection of streets, buildings and institutions, it is 'also a poem, a hallucination, a series of philosophies emerging in the shadows, centuries of colossal history colliding in one street …' My own story was destined to be an eye-witness to how the 'dirty old town' has become a mini-Manhattan. How did we get from the scuzzy Factory punk club in Hulme to the £210 million Factory arts centre announced by a Conservative chancellor in Parliament, rising up on the very site where Tony Wilson televised the insurrectionary Sex Pistols in 1976?

Winston Churchill said, 'We shape our buildings, and afterwards they shape us.' Wilson took this a step further when talking about Joy Division: 'They were on that stage because they had no fucking choice.' The look in his eyes left you in no doubt that the quartet – raised in Salford and Macclesfield, brought together by Manchester – were artists in the grip of their demons. Much more than that: their searing art was a pure expression of the places which had made them.

2

A meeting in Moon Grove

Tony Wilson and I were in a stranger's living room. He was in an armchair, and I was sat on the floor, a twenty-year-old student nervously pushing buttons on a mono cassette recorder. 'Right, then,' asked the high priest of the Manchester music scene, 'what do you want to know?'

Today, when the magic comes from the computer in our pockets, it's easy to forget that magic then came from a box in the corner, courtesy of a cathode ray tube and a signal broadcast to it. The people in the box spoke directly to you, and they were the gods of the age. And while it was clear, especially to youngsters, that many talking heads behind their studio desks were false gods with fake smiles and feet of clay, Tony Wilson was a veritable man-god, at the highest altitude, and on the sharpest edge of Manchester and its music.

As far back as I can remember, in thrall to the mediated Manchester I lapped up through music and the media, I had always wanted to be a journalist. Which is how I found myself face-to-face with Tony Wilson. As a final-year undergraduate, instead of time in the library, I hung out in the student union on Oxford Road where I was a connoisseur of the noticeboard, a long wall of leaflets and messages. One day in autumn 1981, scanning the wall peppered with bits of paper about events and small ads, I spotted a neatly written leaflet advertising a Fabian Society meeting, 'The role and responsibilities of the media in today's society'. The speakers' names hit me between the eyes – 'in conversation with Gerald Kaufman, MP for Ardwick, and Tony Wilson of Granada Television'.

Whoah. *The* Tony Wilson? The compelling ball of cultural confusion who pulled off a straight media career as a TV reporter, while simultaneously fronting a Northern art rock movement? Wilson was the guy in a suit and tie who read the teatime news on Granada TV but who had hustled his bosses into letting him champion new music. He was the impresario behind Factory Records, which released the records of the earth-spinning band Joy Division, whose charismatic lead singer, the epilepsy-tormented Ian Curtis, had killed himself by hanging earlier that same year, setting in train a creative explosion of iconic music, graphics and pop philosophy which forty years on still retains a cultural power that is honoured and celebrated worldwide.

Okay, Wilson may often have been photographed sporting – to us spiky youth – a wanky hippy scarf resembling a cravat. But for twenty-somethings, his presence loomed over the city. The live scene was jumping and in my first term in 1979 I had arrived in post-punk heaven, seeing The Fall at the Poly, The Cure at the University and the Boomtown Rats at the Apollo. I was badly pummelled by skinheads at the UMIST student union during a melee at a show by local punk group Armed Force. I shrugged it off. Such was the city, such were the times. Manchester was, as it is today, the biggest student campus in the UK, with up to ten thousand newcomers every autumn swelling the demand for live music. Students made the scene viable, and it was a cultural counterpoint to London, where the bastions of the corporate music business were based. In 1980, the city was the Ground Zero of a new music revolution and Wilson was right at the heart of it, having put on the first Factory live music nights at the Russell Club in Hulme with partner Alan Erasmus.

Following two seminal appearances by The Sex Pistols in 1976, bands like Buzzcocks and their New Hormones label under Richard Boon had shown how the corporates could be taken on, DIY-style, to record, produce and distribute music. Legions of independent labels like Wilson's own Factory Records followed; with typical Mancunian arrogance, the label had clothed the records in elegant graphic art by Manchester Polytechnic design graduate Peter Saville.

The chance of meeting Wilson was irresistible. He was a regular subject of music press interviews, and seemingly never shy of a quote or a photo. In fact, as presenter of *So It Goes*, the music show which graduated from Granada to national late-night ITV, his cringeworthy quips and strange, distant presenting style with the quality of bad acting had provoked vicious national press reviews. All this weirdly made him even more intriguing. If I could get to meet him, I thought it could give my own media career a kickstart. I was hopeful he could give a few minutes to a couple of bright-eyed and curious young student journalists – petrified at the thought of asking a famous person some questions, I needed a partner.

I found Ian Ransom in the union café. He was on the same American Studies course as me, a pale and interesting-looking Gary Numan lookalike from Kent, who was, improbably, even skinnier than me, and blessed with a gung-ho enthusiasm for anything outside of studying. Like me, he exclaimed 'mental!' a lot, in a positive context, and was not shy of using the word in the way that some today might say 'cool'. 'Mental!' was a response to reassure your peers that you were on their wavelength, that yes, like them, you were punky in your outlook and that, as life was dead boring in the early 1980s, with rampant unemployment, Fascist marches and bitter strikes in the world waiting for us outside university, that 'mental' was not only a fair description of society but a positive affirmation that you were, yeah, a fair bit mental yourself and up for doing new stuff. Even though he did not have media ambitions, I convinced Ian that this was an opportunity to launch our careers with an interview with the city's local legend and offer it up to the student union paper, the punningly named *Mancunion*, for a big feature garlanded with our bylines. I would bring the tape recorder and drive us there in my ancient Triumph Herald.

'Moon Grove? Where the hell is that?' We were pondering an *A to Z* in deepest Rusholme, the first district going south down Oxford Road from the university campus. We parked the ancient jalopy on Moon Grove, got out, and gasped. The Fabian Society event was being held not, as we assumed, in some community hall, but in a private house in an exquisitely preserved Victorian street. The evening roar of Wilmslow Road traffic vanished behind us, and the architectural setting encouraged the light to take on an antique glare, through the original glass streetlamps, of a bygone era. Like two chimney sweeps in the pages of a Dickens novel, we paced wide-eyed along the smoothed cobbles, past the original iron lamp posts and the beautifully maintained doorways and windows of Moon Grove. 'Mental,' we whispered.

With some trepidation at meeting the Wilson phenomenon in such unexpected circumstances, we made our way across the time-polished flagstones to the given address. The friendly middle-aged hosts opened the door and the pair of us were ushered into a tasteful living room. We took a seat on the floor as twenty or so people sat facing the two billed speakers. The object of our fascination was sitting cross-legged on a sofa, exuding his TV personality charisma in shoulder-length hair. Sat in his own armchair, and with his own media-enhanced aura, was the stiffly formal Gerald Kaufman, Member of Parliament for Ardwick, in suit, tie and pullover (and, I later learned, another Moon Grove resident).

The discussion was well under way. 'The way the media uses language is politically contextual,' Wilson opined. 'There's a hegemonic determination which is imposed by the language of those who run the culture. In the Granada newsroom, I have always tried to report the news from Northern Ireland employing the phrase "IRA soldiers" and the editor always spots it and replaces it with the word "terrorists ..." Hey, what more can I say?' He shrugged and waved his cigarette.

The veteran MP for Ardwick bristled. 'I don't think that last remark can go without the strongest response,' stated Kaufman, an ex-journalist who had written scripts for satirical TV show *That Was the Week That Was*. His punctilious enunciation was familiar from radio and TV. 'No responsible news organisation should even think about using the description you have suggested. Your editor is acting precisely as required by the fundamental principles of impartial and accurate news reporting. The British government is facing this terrorist threat, and I am disappointed that you, in your position of great responsibility, should even contemplate the manner of description you have just suggested. Terrorism is a criminal enterprise, Mr Wilson, and a danger to the stability of the public and the state.'

When the discussion was over, people were slapping Wilson on the arm. 'See you, Tone,' 'Cheers, mate,' and so on. I saw my chance and approached the pop culture deity. 'Tony, we're from the university student paper, please can you answer a few questions ...?' 'Of course, boys,' he replied, and asked his companions, who were gathering up their things, to hold on a few minutes.

'Sorry, just a moment while we get this recorder working.' I fumbled with an old Philips cassette recorder I had been given for my thirteenth birthday. It had been a reliable companion of my teenage years, its mono sound no matter in the days when lo-fi was a suitably crude standard for the era's DIY sensibility, perfect to record the three-chord punk thrashes heard on John Peel's Radio 1 show.

I set up the little cigar-shaped mic attachment and placed it on top of the recorder. I took a deep breath. 'What do you think about the way Ian Curtis's death has been mythologised?' Wilson paused. Had I overstepped the mark? 'Sorry Mr Wilson, if you don't want to answer that ...'

'No, no, I have no problem with it at all,' came the reply. 'I know I've been attacked. Let them say I'm a cunt, I'm a wanker, I'm a pretentious fucker, I had it all. With *So It Goes* I had every national paper slagging me, every single one of them. And you know what, when everyone says, "you're a cunt", "this man is fucking useless", you take it and take it and then you get used to it, and then it gets to the place where you just don't care.

'With Ian, it's a tragedy, such a waste, and it's affected all of his friends and all of the fans so badly. But the less imaginative members of our profession, the fourth estate, the sad fuckers in some of the media, well, thanks to their coverage, well that is all part of the myth now too."

I wondered how my intended publisher of the interview, *Mancunion*, might deal with the swearing, but I pressed on. 'Tony, can you tell us about the tombstone picture on the cover of the *Closer* album?' A voice butted in. 'Tony, the cab's here, it's time to go.'

'Sorry lads, I do have to go now.' As he was getting up to go, he added: 'I can live with the cover image. Because Ian was a friend of mine, and I was just someone who was happy to know him and be around him and witness his creativity, close up. That's all that matters, in the end.'

Walking on air about the quotes we had captured, we were ushered out of the house. I drove us home and pulled up in the car park of the council flats of the failed Hulme estate where I and many students lived. It was dark and the streetlamps illuminated the inside of the car. I couldn't wait, so, still in the driver seat, I put the cassette in the in-car player and rewound to the start. And I pressed play.

We heard my question, just about. And then a voice, or rather, only a ghostly shade of Wilson's voice, practically inaudible, under a loud whirring of the tape mechanism. All I could hear was the sound of a cassette tape whirring. And whirring. I strained to make out any of Wilson's precious utterances, the quotes that were going to get me my first published feature. It wasn't even semi-audible. It was all utterly, terminally unlistenable.

Instead of holding it near Wilson's face as a professional would, I had simply placed the microphone accessory on top of the cassette player. I had recorded the sound of a cassette machine in operation. The only content from the interview was a sound sculpture of the medium itself doing its thing. There was the ghostly voice-like sound of my interviewee in there somewhere, but as hard as I tried to focus my hearing, not a word could be clearly heard. I had interviewed the pop culture controversialist of the age, the provisional wing of the mainstream media. But the exact words of the Factory boss's pronouncement on the tragic end of the music shaman Curtis – these were never to be transcribed by me or read by the student readership of the *Mancunion*.

I had hoped this to be the calling card for my journalistic career, and I apologised to my partner for being such a prat. At least, we agreed, the experience had been appropriately mental. But without the words, I could not deliver my story or see it in print. Perhaps I could have tried paraphrasing as I have done here – but my lack of experience and confidence, on such a raw and sensitive subject, meant that the evening became merely a memory. My first journalistic act had fallen victim to technical ineptitude, my ambition snarked on the cassette spool of life. But I had tracked down the hip priest of the Manchester music scene and we had traded high-grade pop culture Q and A.

3

Dirty old town

It is like Berlin when they bombed it. I like the dead houses.
Nico to Richard Witts, *City Life* magazine, 17 February 1993

When John Bright, the MP and great orator of the age of Free Trade, addressed the city's grandees at the opening banquet of Manchester Town Hall in 1877, he asked the business and civic leaders, in their grandiose temple to power that their riches had built, to ponder what must have seemed unthinkable: the city's future decline. 'Great cities have fallen before Manchester,' he warned. 'Let us not for a moment imagine that we stand upon a foundation absolutely sure ...' His fearful prognostication did come to pass, but by the time the city was on its knees his audience were all long dead.

My student's bedroom was no more than fifty yards from the Done Brothers' bookmaker which took up too much of my student grant, and the Imperial Hotel, a grand old Victorian pub. The boozer served men who came in for a 'pie and pint for a pound', greeting each other across the bar with the refrain, 'Are you working?' as they removed their flat caps. Many were not. There were no backpackers with guidebooks in this city centre, no pet dogs being walked, or prams being pushed. Buzzcocks' manager Richard Boon recalled: 'Manchester seemed a vacant set.'

Like me, urbanist David Rudlin arrived to study in 1979 and would walk, as I did, from the town hall in the city centre, through the derelict Central Station, past the ruined warehouses of Castlefield, through the empty quays of Pomona and the dying docks of Salford Quays, to Barton Bridge in Salford. 'From the heart of the city to its edge, a distance of some six miles, we walked through uninterrupted dereliction,' Rudlin writes in his blog. 'We could have done the same along the Irk Valley to the north or the River Medlock to the east. Even in the city centre there were large areas of dereliction.' His first job after

Central Station, 1981 (photo: Ian Capper)

graduation, with the Derelict Land Grant team at Manchester City Council, was to demolish factories and cover the sites with grass.

The Conservative Party led by Margaret Thatcher won the May 1979 election after the strike-torn 'winter of discontent' with a manifesto to end rampant inflation, curb union power and launch an era of free-market capitalism. The official recession, during a worldwide slump after a spike in oil prices, occurred during 1980 when inflation peaked at 22 per cent, but its impact on Manchester lasted for much of the following decade. The old heavy industries were concentrated mainly in the city's engine room of east Manchester today known as 'Sport City' for Manchester City FC's stadium and an impressive array of other sports and leisure facilities. For decades before, it was home to the Bradford Colliery, a gas works, a steelworks and a chemical factory, a district which in the late 1950s was one of the most polluted places on earth, pumping out 12 tonnes of soot a day into the Manchester air.

In the city centre the 1967 Clean Air Act had hastened the gradual clean-up of the soot-blackened buildings, but a different type of cleansing got under way as the Thatcher government's monetarist policies delivered a Darwinian death sentence to industry which had been limping along for years. By the late 1970s and the Conservatives' victory, the industrial plants were wheezing behemoths, faltering under government policy and global economic forces. Manchester Steel in Bradford fell victim, amid reports that it was cheaper for British firms to import steel from Sweden than to buy it from Manchester. 'Like lumbering dinosaurs who suddenly met their meteorite, the big heavy industries of east Manchester toppled into extinction,' wrote Paul Taylor in the *Manchester*

Evening News. 'Wire works, engineering firms, factories of all kinds went out of business, throwing hundreds of men at a time – and they were mainly men – onto the dole.'

It was conscious economic policy for the Conservatives to let heavy industry go, seeing the job losses as creative destruction with political benefits. The decline decimated the unions representing workers in the large-scale workplaces, wiping away the labour movement challenge which helped topple previous Conservative prime minister Edward Heath. Other factors combined to hit all the Northern cities which relied on heavy industry for jobs: a high pound choked off demand, and government cuts in public expenditure reduced options for cities to create alternative work.

By 1983, inflation had fallen to 4 per cent from its 1980 high, but mass unemployment and the destruction of manufacturing industry was the cost. By 1982, national unemployment had risen to 12.5 per cent, making a mockery of the Tory posters which helped their 1979 election win, showing a long dole queue above the slogan 'Labour Isn't Working'. Between 1972 and 1984 the city lost 207,000 manufacturing jobs and its unemployment rate rose to 20 per cent. The number of jobs in the city of Manchester, only part of the wider conurbation, was over 700,000 after the war but had fallen to 430,000 by the end of the 1980s, due in part to population decline in the deindustrialising city.

In fact, the Thatcher revolution accelerated long-term downward economic trends. No chimneys had been built in the city after the 1930s and Manchester had been in steep industrial decline since the 1950s. Industries were inefficient after decades of under-investment from managements which let foreign innovators steal a march. The city had been suffering the flight of capital for decades, and manufacturing now moved decisively to places with cheaper labour.

Such macro-economic analysis did not ease the pain in the communities hit by mass unemployment. Disaffection and anger showed themselves in disturbances across Britain in 1981. In Moss Side, where the unemployment rate among young black men was 60 per cent, and controversial stop and search ('sus') powers were used, inner-city riots flared, as well as in so-called 'ghettoes' in Liverpool and London. Manchester reggae group Harlem Spirit's 1980 'Dem a Sus' expressed the moment for the black community. The riots in 1981's summer of social unrest in cities across the land had brought systemic racism into focus.

The disturbances lit a fire for protest music popularly expressed in the multi-racial Two-Tone movement of bands updating the Jamaican ska sound. Social comment springing from Midlands groups The Specials, The Beat and

The Selecter was squarely in line with punk's in-yer-face depiction of society's ills. The Jam's three-chord wonder breakthrough was 'In The City' ('there's a thousand things I wanna say to you') and the irresistible radical chic of The Clash's 'Hate and War' promised, 'I'm gonna stay in the city / Even if my house falls down.' As thrilling as they were, these London suburban and art-school perspectives which sustained punk into the early 1980s were voyeuristic snapshots of inner-city life. Media images of pitched battles between massed police and crowds of youths, against a backdrop of overturned police cars and burned-out shops, were straight out of the punk rock picture book. Urban unrest produced powerful imagery for the music press, record sleeves, concert posters and T-shirts, selling social comment music to politically conscious young music fans.

Whether politics was the mainspring of Manchester's late 1970s new music revolution is up for debate. Buzzcocks played the 1978 Anti-Nazi concert in Alexandra Park, Moss Side, headlined by reggae-pop crossover group Steel Pulse, but their music was free of slogans, or political ones at least; their buzzsaw-meets-Beach Boys chart hit 'What Do I Get' was a call for a redistribution of love and affection, not economic wealth. Perhaps the city's struggles were indeed more about personal liberation than placard-waving politics. Punk poet John Cooper Clarke's memory of his Manchester days is that 'punk rock was no exercise in socialism'. When it became the subject of 'sloganeering of activists, all the fun and imagination was kicked out of it'.

This tendency towards the individualistic might be surprising in a city so steeped in the collective traditions of organisation and protest. Yet time and again Manchester music rejected ideological sloganeering and took off for trips into the emotional and psychological interior – 'the soundtrack of the mind', as culture academic Bob Dickinson has called it. He identifies the influence of The Fall as the source of the emotional desolation in Joy Division's personal cathedrals. Dictatorial frontman Mark E. Smith explored the wrecked parts of the city, he writes, 'the parts with a past … empty synagogues in the snow'. Dickinson concludes, 'I don't think Joy Division would have happened without The Fall, because The Fall made it possible for musicians in Manchester to think of themselves as artists, as doing an act of art.' In Bernard Sumner's autobiography *Chapter and Verse*, the self-described 'introverted extrovert' repeatedly says that Joy Division's music came 'from within' even if it was, in his case, a response to 'the death of a community', when his Lower Broughton terraced streets were torn down and his family were swept up into new housing blocks.

The internalised desolation was matched by the modern ruins all around, so evocative to the likes of Nico. London had left cities like Manchester to crumble and rot, a lack of empathy by a government in the mid-1980s more excited by added-value services like tourism, design and finance rather than the fading practice of making things. This was the decade of the 'big bang' deregulation of financial services in the City of London. The legacy of bitterness that others had been selected for affluence while the North had been earmarked for decline remained heavy in the Manchester air in the 1980s. Morrissey's song 'Margaret on the Guillotine' on 1988 solo album *Viva Hate* captured the North's very real hatred of Thatcher and her methods – a song which, he revealed in his auto-biography, caused him to be interviewed by the Special Branch (though in a somewhat amiable manner, accompanied by a request for autographs).

When the Iron Lady visited Manchester on 11 December 1986, it was per-haps predictable that city council leader Graham Stringer, who had to come to power in 1984 in a left-wing takeover of the council's Labour Group of coun-cillors, would join a street demo against her deregulation of the conurbation's buses. On the day of her visit, Stringer (council leader for twelve years before becoming MP for Blackley and Broughton) attacked Thatcher in an open letter for stripping Manchester of £500 million of grants, leaving 50 per cent of its children on free school meals and 110,000 on housing benefit. The city was suffering 22 per cent average unemployment, compared to 12 per cent nation-ally. His letter ended, 'Remember, Mrs Thatcher, Manchester is the industrial city on which the wealth of the nation was built. Perhaps you are well named. Perhaps you want this city to revert to thatch, wattle and daub. But we won't let you.'

The prime minister was used to touring the nation's big cities and engaging with ceremonial mayors for whom the visiting premier was a highlight. But in Manchester 'The Lady' was snubbed by the lord mayor, councillor Kath Robinson, another of the left-wing group, who sent her apologies to organisers the Chamber of Commerce, at short notice on the night of the event. Chambers of Commerce were bastions of free enterprise and Manchester's captains of industry had paid £50 a head to don black tie for a reception and dinner in the Peacock Room of the Piccadilly Hotel, a 1960s modernist monument whose floor-to-ceiling windows overlooked the city's main square. Visitors from authoritarian regimes in socialist Manchester's sibling cities of Chemnitz, East Germany, or Wuhan, China, might have thought that the enormous portraits surveying the populace from the building were political leaders, and not in fact the presenters of commercial radio station Piccadilly 261.

Piccadilly Gardens may have been bedecked with Christmas lights, but Thatcher was about to be blasted from an unexpected quarter which took no account of the festive cheer. At regional business gatherings, she was used to an obsequious reaction. Her introductory welcome, though, from the Manchester Chamber president, John Morris, was far from friendly. The retired insurance broker attacked her employment secretary Norman Tebbit for claiming the North's wounds were self-inflicted. Reflecting the Chamber executive's position, Morris called for 'an end to central government and a move towards national government', part of a politely put but stinging rebuke about the North–South divide – something Thatcher refused to believe existed. As she sat stern-faced beside him, Morris criticised her government's southeast bias, declaring, 'We search in vain for some indication that Government is adopting its policies to take account of the problem.'

Clearly taken aback at the lack of warning from someone she had assumed would be 'one of us', Thatcher departed from her prepared text half a dozen times to respond. 'Mr. President ... Yes! You are telling me what I have got to do and I am telling you what you have got to do.' She ended by putting a brave face on such dissent from an unexpected quarter: 'Now, your predecessors made their own opportunities as you do ... You here tonight are their worthy successors and I honour you for it.'

That same year, Manchester celebrated a ten-year anniversary. It was a decade since The Sex Pistols had taken the stage at the Lesser Free Trade Hall. The two shows, the first in June 1976 to an audience of fifty, and then one in July to a larger crowd with Buzzcocks as support, have been the subject of volumes of memorialising. Audience members at the events which lit the blue touch paper of post-punk Manchester included, as well as the Buzzcocks, future music makers Ian Curtis, Peter Hook, Bernard Sumner, Stephen Morrissey, Mark E. Smith, Mick Hucknall, Martin Hannett, Billy Duffy and Marc Riley, and impresarios, image-makers and interpreters Richard Boon, Kevin Cummins, Rob Gretton, Paul Morley, Linder Sterling and Tony Wilson.

The Sex Pistols was a seditious art project comprising music, art and attitude which challenged everything. I turned sixteen in the summer of 1977 and, for many teenagers like me, their stance, sound and style somehow felt like they could change everything, too. They were a Situationist spectacle, punching a hole in reality. Critic Greil Marcus described their 'frightening seriousness'. Ian Curtis's wife Deborah, who attended the second show, wrote, 'After the performance everyone seemed to move towards the door as if we had all been issued with instructions and now we were to embark on a mission.'

The explosion of music following the 1976 gigs chimed with the depressing economic downturn of the mid-to-late 1970s. Mancunians who once counted on factory work, it seemed, suddenly had no jobs to follow their parents and grandparents into, a progression on which had been built communities whose identities were formed around the workplace and local football team, the pub and the church. The nihilism of punk rock hit a nerve, with the Sex Pistols' 'No Future' slogan holding a highly personal meaning to teenagers on benefits.

When in 1977 BBC1's *Brass Tacks* filmed at short-lived Manchester punk venue the Electric Circus, the studio presenter introduced the live discussion with vicars, councillors and DJ John Peel, starting with: 'Over the last twelve months punk rock has become almost a battle cry in British society. For many people, it's a bigger threat to our way of life than Russian communism or hyper-inflation.' The filmed report is of a gaggle of kids whose DIY dole-queue clothes are worlds away from London's art school on parade, King's Road. One lad with artlessly spiked hair, an earring and wraparound plastic shades pleads: 'I wanted to do something for *me*', 'cos look at me now, I'm nothing!'

This was the counter-culture spirit that the pop theorist in Wilson wanted to commemorate with the 1986 Festival of the Tenth Summer, a decade after the Sex Pistols shows. This was his opportunity to pay homage to a music form and culture which, outside of the music press, enjoyed no scholarly respect or main-stream acceptance. The city festival not only looked back but promoted coming developments in fashion, art and design, as well as music, across ten events from art shows to exhibitions, seminars and performances, the showpiece being the hiring of the G-Mex exhibition centre for its debut as a live music venue.

G-Mex was well known to original members of the Haçienda. When it opened in 1982, as they entered the club, across Albion Street sat the hulk-ing ruin of Central Station, whose defunct tracks stretched west to Liverpool, with faded 'ghost adverts' overlooking a glass-shard-strewn concourse, a loca-tion grimly notorious for its rail station bar where, in 1965, Moors Murderer Ian Brady had picked up his final victim, seventeen-year-old Edward Evans. Manchester Central rail station had despatched and received London trains from 1880 under its wrought-iron single-span arched roof, a feat of engineering 220 ft high and 90 ft wide. There are few iconic structures with which people can identify the city with one glance, but in the Manchester of the 1980s this was the most likely. The station had closed in 1969 and its rebirth in 1986 as a mammoth 10,000 sq m exhibition and meeting hall was almost the last act of the Greater Manchester Council before being abolished by the Conservatives in their bonfire of the metropolitan county councils. Renamed G-Mex (now

Manchester Central), it was opened by the Queen in March 1986 and, a few months later, ten thousand inheritors of the flame sparked by notorious anti-monarchists The Sex Pistols piled into the restored old station, and the high-riding Smiths closed their set with the galloping riffs of *The Queen Is Dead*, the title track of their new album.

There was a spat about who would close the show, and the honour went to New Order, after The Smiths had played, following A Certain Ratio, The Fall, Pete Shelley, The Worst and − as Wilson dubiously wanted to link back further − local 1960s raucous beat group Wayne Fontana and the Mindbenders. Compèring duties were split between Paul Morley, then in his ZTT/Frankie impresario pomp, and, with a nod to tabloid 'punk filth fury' headlines, Bill Grundy, the bibulous TV host who provoked The Sex Pistols into swearing live on the London teatime news.

There was another wrangle between the organisers and Morrissey over the filming of the event, of which no recorded footage has been seen. Factory direc-tor Alan Erasmus stalked around G-Mex with a camera crew, and I asked him if he could film the audience, remembering a recent viewing of *Monterey Pop*, in which an extensive tracking camera shot along lengthy queues of fans beauti-fully captures the 1967 California hippy moment in hundreds of faces. Erasmus acknowledged the point, but it was clear he had better things to do. It's a shame that we don't have that document of the post-punk, pre-Madchester music community, but at least the images by the Blackpool photographer Ian Tilton, of Morrissey's shirt being torn to shreds by his disciples, remain as an indelible record of that day.

With the festival finale at G-Mex, the city's music had come home. The late summer sun set slowly through the mammoth windows as the city's bands, who had won influence for and fascination with Manchester worldwide, played their sets. There was a tangible sense of an official acceptance that, within this remarkable piece of the city's history, the hometown had acknowledged the achievements of the artists who a decade before were vilified as a threat to soci-ety. As fine a day and night as the celebration was, the ironies were not lost on locals that what was originally revolutionary was becoming closer to the estab-lishment. Peter Saville exhibited his festival sculptures at the venerable City Art Gallery. 'The adolescent petulance of punk has passed over into lasting impact in a convergence of culture and commercialism,' Jim Aulich coolly observed in *City Life*.

Culture, then, even pop culture, was becoming noticed by the city's powers-that-be. The G-Mex event was the first major occasion when Wilson and officialdom met half-way in a partnership. Discussions began about where creativity and culture might lead the city. Culture was becoming understood as serious commerce. Though an economic sector whose output was hard to quantify compared to the old manufacturing industries, its intangible soft power was now being taken seriously. That Manchester music of all kinds commanded international respect, media profile and increasingly visitors was not lost on the city's decision-makers, who were also much exercised by the need for a new home for Manchester's three classical orchestras.

For all its history under the Hallé's great conductor Sir John Barbirolli, the Free Trade Hall, hastily rebuilt after the war, was deteriorating and almost obsolete as a classical music venue. In 1986, surveys, options and conversations were starting about how to replace it. Establishment Manchester chuntered that 'something must be done' about a new concert hall at black-tie dinners over crispy duck in Chinatown. Meanwhile, bohemian Manchester was setting the pace. The Haçienda on Whitworth Street West was soon joined in the mid-1980s by two alternative venues on the same thoroughfare, the Green Room and the Cornerhouse arts centre.

In fact, it would be ten more years before the Bridgewater Hall opened, the first civic building to go up in Manchester for more than sixty years. Its stage and gigantic organ are perched on 270 giant foundation springs usually used in earthquake zones, to prevent vibration from nearby traffic and trains. £42 million of government and EU funding was key to its completion in 1996, but the balance of its future financing was from the overall Barbirolli Square scheme's 350,000 sq ft of prestige office space which attracted professional firms as tenants.

The formula displayed the skill and dexterity of the city's leadership, showing that being smart with property could bring cultural reward. City council chief executive Sir Howard Bernstein later described the Bridgewater Hall scheme as a major demonstration of civic leadership. Here was a city that could do deals for everyone's benefit, a win-win for the public and the property market. 'The effectiveness of the partnership between the city council and the private sector was demonstrated conclusively,' he said, adding that for the city it was 'the most radical development ever seen because it, in effect, moved the commercial centre of the city 500 yards down the road and that was a pretty sensational move at the time'.

The hall was the springboard for its first chief executive Howard Raynor's mission to improve the quality of service in the city's hospitality venues. Sadly, his Manchester Standard crusade was rocked in 2011 with the well-liked former

RAF man's death from cancer at just forty-nine. While the prow-shaped exterior of the 2,400-capacity, acoustically enhanced hall was not world-class architecture, and the office scheme which enabled it was undistinguished, the whole development has settled comfortably into the changing city around it, creating a future stage on which the city's many cultures could enjoy music of all kinds. When Elbow played the Bridgewater Hall in 2009 backed by classical musicians, Guy Garvey quipped to universal appreciation in the hall, and to the large crowd watching on an open-air big screen nearby, that the Hallé Orchestra was 'the first Manchester band'.

4

All the news not fit to print

I had wanted to be an investigative journalist, digging the dirt on the establishment in my own magazine. Now I was in a courtroom of the Royal Courts of
Justice in The Strand, being sued for defamation. It was November 1987, and
the man going legal on me was constant national news.

Bury businessman Kevin Taylor was at the centre of police allegations that
he had criminal ties, as well as a friendship with Manchester assistant chief
constable John Stalker, which led to the senior cop being dropped from his own
inquiry into so-called police 'shoot-to-kill' methods against IRA suspects. It
was a tangled web which fascinated the media and the public, stretching from
the back streets of Manchester, where Taylor made his money by squatting on
bombsites before selling the land, to the Med where he holidayed on his yacht
with Stalker, to the RUC killings in fields and hay sheds of Northern Ireland,
the entire tale leading to speculation that the establishment was covering up
summary state executions by yanking Stalker off his investigation.

I was in London for a hearing to represent myself and other editors at our
alternative Manchester mag *City Life*, a cross between what's-on guide *Time Out*
and scurrilous *Private Eye* for the city. We had no funds for legal representation,
so it fell to me to attend the session. It was only a pre-trial hearing, but it felt
like I was already in the dock, answering questions put by Master Grant in his
wood-panelled chambers, with a plummy-voiced barrister representing the liti-
gant clearly an old hand at the process.

City Life, the alternative magazine I co-founded in 1983, had dared to get
involved in these matters of great national import. In fact, for their work on
the Stalker affair, our offices were frequented by investigative reporters Paul
Lashmar and David Leigh of *The Observer*, a duo regarded by many as the UK
equivalent of Woodward and Bernstein, America's Watergate investigators.
Leigh was quiet and self-contained and Lashmar was convivial, a regular at

London's Ronnie Scott's jazz club. The duo spent time in Manchester chasing up leads and contacts, and, through our own hard news reporter Ed Glinert, we built a supportive relationship in which they worked from our office in down-at-heel Stevenson Square, home of rag-trade wholesalers and Asian cafés.

The media revelations led all the way to the top of the British state. And now the man whom many of the media regarded as the fall guy for it all, Kevin Taylor, was taking us to court – and if he had his way, to the cleaners. He had a clear-cut case against us. *City Life* had reported details provided to the Greater Manchester Police committee, the publicly elected councillors who oversaw the force. We had flagrantly failed to use the hints and generalities other media had employed and had quoted unsubstantiated gossip and innuendo. The fact this came from the report which formed GMP's case against Taylor, and was included in the government dossier used to axe Stalker from his role investigating the Northern Ireland security services, was no defence: the information was privileged, a legal status meaning it should remain confidential. It was a schoolboy error to publish it, but our man Glinert put a brave face on it. His line was that by publishing we were confronting the police and calling their bluff – that they should bring charges against Taylor if they had so much on him (something GMP eventually did in late 1987 when it charged the Bury property developer and three others with conspiracy to defraud the Co-operative Bank).

Our appalling naivety had serious real-world consequences. We rushed the story into print with no deliberation, and by distributing the police's baseless allegations we were effectively promoting the defamation of Taylor. He had no criminal record. No one could have blamed him for suing us. Although we had no money for legal fees, a sympathetic lawyer, Basil Herwald, explained that the hearing was simply to confirm the pre-trial arrangements. It fell to me to take the London Euston train to the iconic centre of British justice, an intimidating experience for a twenty-five-year-old with no supporting lawyer present.

I was called forward and Taylor's barrister asked for the trial to be heard in Manchester. I readily agreed, thinking only how much a trial anywhere else would interrupt the production of our fortnightly magazine, which took up my every waking hour. When I enthusiastically nodded, Taylor's lawyer looked like the cat that got the cream. The presiding judge even asked me if I was sure. I agreed again. When I got back to Manchester, legally minded people explained the other side's delight – there was, understandably, a pro-Taylor sentiment in the city, with people wearing T-shirts on the streets in his support. A local jury was likely to be favourable to his cause, based on a growing popular belief from detailed media coverage that he was a victim of a stitch-up.

These were the consequences of publishing investigative journalism without a solid background in such specialist, high-risk journalism. We had set ourselves up as an 'alternative' magazine, to provide a different view of our city for people who felt, as we did, that the established Manchester media was biased, shallow and reactionary. This was the era of so-called alternative comedians and growing interest in alternative lifestyles. 'Alternative' is a term that today has died out, as by the early 2000s the internet was fast making everyone on social media or websites a publisher, undermining the power of media companies large and small by creating millions of individual points of view. Today, there is no dominant mainstream left to be an alternative to.

Back then, however, we were still operating in an age of powerful media gatekeepers. While our particular gate was small and unimposing, we were under legal assault, ironically, by a man whom we sympathised with. To us, Taylor was the victim of an establishment conspiracy, a patsy because he had light social links both to criminals – more petty than mastermind – and to John Stalker. The deputy chief constable had been photographed with Taylor and their wives on the businessman's yacht on a Mediterranean holiday, and this was seemingly enough (along with never-proven insinuations they were up to dodgy business) for Stalker to be kicked off his inquiry. Along with *City Life*, many established media commentators felt that Taylor was targeted as the authorities' way to discredit Stalker's unwelcome findings.

Taylor's criminal contacts were members of the Quality Street Gang, who had legendary status in the city's clubs, pubs and housing estates. QSG boss James Donnelly's jaw-dropping memoir *Jimmy the Weed* recounts how these hardmen got their name, when a Cabaret Club doorman shouted, 'here they come, the Quality Street mob' – referring to a jokey TV chocolates advert featuring gangsters in 1920s Chicago-style double-breasted suits and fedoras. Footballer Stan Bowles recalled that 'they were greater celebrities than the rock stars and footballers they partied with', and they were immortalised by Thin Lizzy's Phil Lynott in their hit 'The Boys Are Back in Town' – the rocker regularly partied with them at his mother Phyllis's legendary Whalley Range speakeasy which doubled as a B&B. John Cooper Clarke wrote in his memoir: 'They were just star fuckers pretending to be gangsters ... they were bad but they weren't evil.'

Taylor eventually dropped his case against us, perhaps when he realised that we had little else other than the shirts on our backs. In any case, Taylor had bigger problems than a local magazine. When the police finally charged him with conspiracy to defraud the Co-operative Bank with three others, the case collapsed when it came to court in January 1990. The evidence against him was so weak that the judge declared that the defence did not even need to make its case. The attempt to 'Get Taylor' failed, but he was a broken man. Financial problems caused by the whole farrago led to him and his family being evicted from their home in 1988. In desperate ill-health, he sued Greater Manchester Police and settled in 1995 for a reported £1 million, although the police did not admit liability. After undergoing heart surgery, Taylor died in 2001, aged sixty-eight.

The Stalker affair can be examined in mind-boggling detail in the ruined businessman's story *The Poisoned Tree* by Keith Mumby. It makes a forensically clear-cut case that the state's security services were out to rubbish Stalker's far-reaching inquiry which, it appears, would have imperilled an emerging but fragile peace agreement in Northern Ireland. *The Sunday Times* said of the book: 'Buy it you must if you care about the society in which we live.'

The deep dark nastiness of the Taylor business was a sure sign, if we really needed it, that we were not much more than inexperienced student radicals playing with the big boys. Ed Glinert was our Stalker affair correspondent and revelled in the notoriety, meeting informers, taking anonymous calls and receiving confidential documents in the post.

Glinert was a dangerous legend on the Manchester student political and media scene. He had the Mick Farren / Charles Shaar Murray rock journo look down − perma-stubble, Jewish Afro, small tinted glasses and a Lewis Leather motorbiker jacket seemingly welded to his slight frame. His reputation went before him not just because of his left-wing ideals but because he lived out his politics, fighting the power in print, and happy to take on authority in any form. He was a graduate of the 'kill your betters' school of 1960s radicalism. His first mouthpiece was the university's militantly left-wing, student-union-funded paper *Mancunion*, in which, under successive Labour-affiliated student editors, he scalded the university's awards system, reported approvingly on lecturer protests and built links with local trade unionists.

Glinert wielded a spiky staccato wit and was jumpy fun to hang out with. Sometimes there had to be very little in his reports to make it a story, but refraction through the mind of Glinert made it a *City Life* story. He would lambast career civil servants receiving honours as 'notorious bureaucrats'. To him, Cub Scouts and Girl Guides were 'para-military organisations'. Deploying his oceans of knowledge on football and music, he was forever compiling lists. Ed had a 'list for life', an attention to detail useful in his later work for *Private Eye*, where his hardcore political tipstering was rewarded with a staff job, and his entertaining, exhaustively researched city guidebooks for Penguin.

Back in the summer of 1983, however, we were simply two jobless ex-students wondering what to do next. We had effectively been driven out of the student union by a Liberal Democrat landslide for the student executive roles. As we had been Labour fellow travellers, we could no longer hang out in the *Mancunion* office, blagging records, gig tickets and freebies. We were however, encouraged by the 1983 NUS/Guardian media awards, which had made our *Mancunion* the Student Paper of the Year, and named me in the citation. Renowned campaigning *Mirror* reporter Paul Foot was a judge, we noted proudly. The award was nice, but neither of us had reporter's shorthand, media law or any experience of 'proper' journalism. And we were too arrogant, impatient and anti-authoritarian to do it the hard way, like doing a skills course.

'Why don't we set up an alternative what's-on magazine?' asked Ed, over naan breads at the Tandoori Kitchen, in Rusholme. 'Something like the *New Manchester Review*?' This was a city magazine in the classic radical news-and-what's-on format of London's *Time Out*, featuring early writing by aspiring critics Waldemar Januszczak and Paul Morley, but which folded in 1980 after five years.

It felt doable, something to shoot for. We roped in Chris Paul, another ex-student who, when he wasn't out road running, had skills in layout and design. We had to turn our talk into action, and for that we needed money. After long discussions about the emerging wave of government enterprise loans with a Royal Bank of Scotland manager, he granted us a mere £2,000 overdraft. We had asked for £10,000. The problem, we learned, is that our pitch had been queered by the flop of a Manchester title only the year before, after using up a £250,000 government-backed loan. *Flash* was an aptly named fiasco which came and went after only 13 issues.

To be fair to our bank manager, on the evidence of *Flash*, the market for something like *City Life* was something he and his over-managers couldn't see a future for. But as the overdraft was guaranteed by the government, with the two-grand offer, and £700 of our own, we were off. Renting out an office in a tumbledown building at the bottom end of Portland Street, we set up Medlock Publishing, a workers' co-operative. This model was pushed by me. Neither of the other two had strong feelings about it. I felt we should live our ideals through the business structure, and over the next few years our original trio was swelled by journalists and commercial and production staff, making running it as a co-op ever more challenging.

The structure was egalitarianism in action. However, without a hierarchy it set up a blank slate on which personality battles were fought, over both editorial

Andy Spinoza, Ed Glinert and Chris Paul, 1983 (photo: David Lubich)

content and commercial practice. The aspiring film critic Mark Kermode spent some time as a co-op member, and in his memoir *It's Only a Movie* describes in teeth-grinding detail the fortnightly co-op meetings, mainly a forum for dog-eat-dog personal attacks in which you were either steamrollered or fought back. Who ever said putting equality into action was easy?

Before the first issue in December 1983, we had put our feelers out to writers and photographers and held a meeting to explain our plan. They included pop writers Cath Carroll and Liz Naylor of short-lived fanzine *City Fun* and Bob

Dickinson, the latter bringing with him a rock and roll outlaw respect as he had travelled with The Clash in their tour van. Also throwing in their lot with us were Richard Witts, a classically trained musician and member of The Passage experimental rock group, Jim Aulich for the visual arts, and other specialist columnists on everything from dance to wine. As nightclub correspondents, I roped in Coventry soul boys Mick Anderson and Dean Johnson, university mates with extra-curricular studies in black music and amphetamines. We were going to be an A4 format black-and-white publication with a colour cover, we explained to our freelances, and we would be paying them the pathetic sum of £7.50 per contribution.

Our first issue of *City Life* in December 1983 was a fiasco, with a hideously dull front cover bearing a black-and-white photo of small boys watching a computer screen and the legend 'Best Christmas Micros'. We had decided, against our better judgement, to try a 'commercial' approach to appeal to parents, instead of photos of Lenny Henry on the cover. What made it worse was that I had been interviewed by reporter Rob McLoughlin for *Granada Reports'* TV news, which gave it a pre-Christmas promotional push. We printed ten thousand and had distribution to cover Greater Manchester's newsagents. Even with a cover price of 30p, we were to find out some time later, the launch issue sold just a thousand copies.

'Like the Loch Ness Monster, the Great Manchester Alternative Paper has surfaced once again. Is the beast here to stay this time?' The question was asked in *The Artful Reporter*, the widely distributed Northwest Arts Council paper. Writer Mike Harris deftly captured us, with Glinert described as a 'Micky Dolenz lookalike with the fast-talking, hectoringly insistent manner of a student activist', and Chris Paul as the 'softly spoken conscience of the group'. He wrote of me: 'Andy Spinoza is the frontman. He has the carefully shabby style of a Dexy's midnight runner and the inexplicably cautious manner of a Birmingham bomber being interviewed by the Special Branch.' Indeed, during our interview, I could smell his scepticism. Harris's piece wondered if we were the right people to stir things up in the city and questioned our radical commitment by wanting to broaden the appeal with entertainment coverage. 'In my day we were all International Socialists and proud of it,' he sniffed.

It was hard to get rid of the stink of the first issue. They say you only get to launch once, and we blew it. *City Life* should have died right then. But redemption was at hand. We got a grudging kind of 'not bad, keep it up' vibe from our contacts in the clubs, venues, theatres, wholefood shops and futon suppliers of Manchester. The general feeling was that something like *City Life* was badly needed. I chatted at the Haçienda bar on New Year's Eve to New Order manager Rob Gretton. He pushed his glasses back on his nose and asked, 'Can't you make it a bit more colourful?'

The Haçienda was busy burning money and we were happy to be a destination for some of it. The venue always supported *City Life* with big ads for its events. I was able to reply to Gretton with some good news. I had met with the city's star photographer Kevin Cummins and our covers were going to be very much more colourful from now on. In fact, he was giving us some unused New Order images from their recent US tour and Mick Middles was providing the words. It was the first that the band's manager had heard of it, but he didn't seem to mind.

'KC' was one of my heroes, the great image-maker of Manchester music. His images were branded into my teenage imagination, and he was doing strong work five years on. I had called on him at his studio and darkroom, a cheap ground-floor former warehouse in Baring Street, next to Piccadilly rail station in the neighbourhood promoted today as the groovy new Mayfield. He had seen the disastrous first issue, we seemed to get on and he said, 'I can help you. I will do the front cover photos for free.' I agreed to this no-brainer and went away with the New Order slides in my hand.

They showed Bernard Sumner's side-on profile, but Cummins had captured the singer's pretty-boy face at a 90-degree angle, his hair along the bottom of the cover. Sumner's clean-cut profile took up half the page, leaving the rest of the glossy cover for bright blue LA sky — perfect space for our logo and the cover text. The contrast with the first issue could not have been more striking and gave all the co-op members and freelance writers a morale boost.

Cummins had the pick of any celebrity jobs that came our way. In the next few years, I worked with him on one-to-one profiles, and he provided cover shots of Bernard Hill, Julie Walters, Alexei Sayle and Morrissey. We went to north London to visit the lovely Michael Palin at his London home and interviewed thespian wild man Richard Harris in his pyjamas at the Savoy. And I stood behind Cummins while he photographed Tony Wilson peering out from behind a striped Haçienda steel column, for our May 1985 cover on the club's third birthday, an image exhibited at the National Portrait Gallery in 2007.

Cummins always had a story from his dealings with his famous subjects. He asked Manchester United manager Ron Atkinson for some studio time to go with our interview. 'I'd need twenty minutes,' he told Big Ron, who shot back, 'You could make *Ben Hur* in twenty minutes, you can have thirty seconds.'

City Life No. 1, December 1983

He had to shoot on the fly, resulting in a most unflattering potato-like image of the football boss on the cover, and the exchange made *The Guardian*'s quotes of 1984. Having him as our in-house photographer gave *City Life* a more professional look, and, by the time he moved to London in the mid-1980s,

City Life No. 2, January 1984 – complete with wrong date on the cover

we had a pool of freelances who had been attracted by the quality of his work. As the finances stabilised, we were able to pay him a small fee for each cover he had provided; unless there is really no alternative no one should work for free.

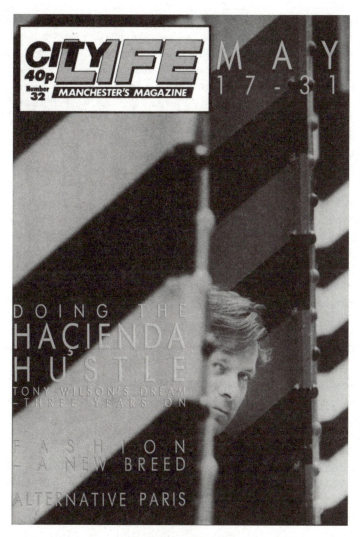

City Life No. 32, May 1985

Getting the finances on an even keel was a bruising rollercoaster ride. Advertising was at an okay level, and salaries were not going to capsize the business. Our wages were a pitiful weekly £75 for the three editors and new co-op members, administrator Caroline Auty, listings chief Mike Barnett and advertising salesman Mark Brookfield. Cash flow was our biggest headache. Our advertising income trickled in, payments months overdue. We liked our printers, a Lancashire outfit, but they refused to produce the next issue unless we paid them with money that we didn't have. We knew if we missed an issue we were dead, and with survival in mind we took our printing job to the Trafford Press, a subsidiary of the Co-operative Press, on Stretford Road.

There, in a beautiful old Victorian building, we laid out *City Life* No. 8 with a cover on the 1984 coal pits strike (a Cummins photo of miner with helmet). It felt like the end of a vanishing era of a collective, unionised culture. None more so than when, to speed up the mag's layout, I picked up a scalpel to help out. A cry went up: 'Down tools!' The whole room, about thirty men, walked away from their work. Chastened, I sat back down. The writing was on the wall for those workers and their restrictive practices. We had already decided to purchase new technology in the form of a typesetting machine, which would take written content from our cheap Amstrad 9512 word processors and give us freedom to design not only *City Life* but other publications too. I went past Trafford Press not long after. The grand old building was closed and shuttered, and I heard that the workers who had produced our publication had been made redundant.

Now we needed a loan to buy a typesetter on tick and applied for one from the city council's unit supporting co-operatives. A four-strong panel arrived in our first office on Portland Street to hear our business plan. Ten minutes in, there was a rap on the grotty old offices' beaded windows. A man wearing an anorak entered and bellowed: 'I am the High Sheriff of Salford and I claim all your goods and chattels!' Our previous printers had gone to law to get their money. The debt collector looked around the offices and realised there was nothing of any value. He didn't even take our word processors, worth £100 each, which would have ended *City Life* there and then. He left empty-handed, and what had just gone down, remarkably, did not stop us getting the city council loan.

In his book *My Trade*, Andrew Marr takes the reader on a pre-internet journey through every type of journalism in the UK but missed out the nation's alternative magazines like *City Life*. From his *Independent* editor's London office, it would have been easy to overlook the street-level titles like *City Life*, *The List* in Edinburgh and *Venue* in Bristol. His paper's regional reporters knew the value of mags like ours, though, which provided a different lens through which to view their cities. In 2006, *The Independent*'s Northern correspondent Ian Herbert wrote that *City Life* had 'tapped into the bohemian, scruffy, concrete place that

Manchester then was … Many still fondly remember the magazine's risky "Citizen" diary – though amid the revelations there were some spectacular mistakes.'

Herbert's fond memory of the news pages and the Citizen page – a silhouette with 1940s gumshoe hat and cigarette – conveyed the movie-influenced image of a private-eye-style newshound on a mission to reveal the city's secrets. Indeed, many of the stories were simply gossip or speculation and relied entirely on the trust that Glinert or another editor had in the source. We became the go-to for anonymous tip-offs from disgruntled employees, revealing everything from the Piccadilly Hotel disco's secret policy of turning away black people to the exotic range of weapons in the GMP armoury.

We attracted all manner of slightly odd, dirt-digging investigators into our offices. One provided a story asking questions about the property dealings of former Manchester lord mayor Harold Tucker. We were about to run the story when we received a last-minute injunction from Tucker's lawyer and had to print the magazine with a white space across two pages. Others which did appear resulted in stiff letters and occasionally we printed grovelling apologies.

Being beastly was just a way of life in the Citizen column. A not-untypical example of its extreme tanginess is this item about Cecil Franks, the Manchester-based MP for Barrow from 1983 to 1992. He was a favourite in our pages after the south Manchester rented flats he owned were reported for failing inspections. 'Where is mystery MP Cecil Franks?' asked the Citizen. 'That's the question all Manchester is asking, not least of all tenants of his sub-standard houses and the media who have come up against a brick wall in their efforts to track down the wayward Tory … Meanwhile the Citizen has been informed that Franks is safely trussed up in a private "clinic" following his latest nervous breakdown. He did however manage to slip past the guards to send a letter to the City's Environmental Health Director urging him not to put a closure order on the Franks-owned 105 Egerton Road.' This was classic Glinert. No legal action was forthcoming.

Getting entangled with the stories 'not fit to print', as the saying went, could be a murky business. Glinert was engrossing his meagre salary by passing stories to *Private Eye*. One about George Galloway, the War on Want CEO and Labour candidate for Glasgow Hillhead, rebounded when *Private Eye* promptly passed it to Galloway, who was a more long-standing informant to them than Glinert. The only revenge he could exact was to report in *City Life* how he was double-crossed.

Our funniest stories were always about Greater Manchester Police. We revealed that, when they needed identity parade participants, they took off to Moss Side where they paid £12 to eleven Rastafarians happy to provide this regular service, and that they gathered up red-haired chaps from the streets by offering them a fiver for the same task when the suspect was a 'ginger'. James Anderton, the city's top cop, was an oft-satirised Citizen regular, often about his love of the police band. His top-brass colleagues wanted to abolish it because instruments had gone missing so the 'top cop's top pop group' could do moonlighting gigs. We also mocked 'God's Cop' for his statement, widely discussed among the troops at GMP's Chester House HQ, that he was 'answerable to God, not man'. The Citizen pointed out that technically he was answerable to Norman Briggs, chairman of the Greater Manchester police committee.

With the super-arrogance of extreme left-wing youth, we railed against redundancies of any kind and cuts in public services, defended student militancy and took the mickey out of anyone we deemed to be hypocritical or posturing – such as left-wing councillors doing something that seemed not left-wing enough. We also lambasted our union comrades. The NUJ branch was 'the land of the rising beer-gut', and we attacked the hypocrisy of *Daily Mail* journalists for agitating for strike action when their reporting was rabidly anti-union. We tweaked the noses of the *Manchester Evening News* for missing the stories we covered. Their relentless attacks on the left-wing council meant that our exclusives, we boasted, had 'escaped the attentions of the local press hacks due to their obsession with the tiresome details of municipal socialism'.

The hard news, the what's-on guide, the bigger interviews and features … the overall mix gained a foothold. Working punishing hours that you would only do for yourself and a cause you believed in, we hung on and published fortnightly, not missing an edition for five years. We had been helped along by advertisers like the big entertainment venues, the city council, the theatres, the Haçienda, Factory Records and Paul Morley's ZTT Records. As these were the very organisations we were often slating, the whole thing was very Mancunian. You could slag your mates off, and they would still be your mates.

Gradually, it was the music that got the upper hand. Mark E. Smith wrote us a (surprisingly restrained) letter slagging off former band mate Marc Riley. Morrissey sent a postcard to Kevin Cummins about *City Life* No. 6, which he said 'moved me dramatically', asking if he could have a print of the photo on it. John Peel wrote to us asking for copies, we presumed more for the local band reports than the police band malarkey. London record labels had annual sub-scriptions. Cartoonist Ray Lowry, a hero of mine for his spiky, scratchy ink pen panels in the *New Musical Express* and his *London Calling* album art for The Clash, would drop off a sheaf of sketch-and-gag works about Elvis, Hitler and his other satirical pet obsessions.

It seemed natural to move into promoting gigs, mainly by offering free ad space and promotion for a cut of the door, and sometimes we even fronted the performer fees, including the 1984 gig at the Tropicana on Oxford Street which landed Simply Red a record contract. In this way, we started to build a bigger readership for the music than for the hard news. In 1987 I started managing a highly eccentric one-man act called Edward Barton, who had once been on *The Tube* TV show live, wringing hell out of an acoustic guitar and howling scar-ily. I liked Edward, a public schoolboy who claimed to have been educated at Sandhurst. We played football together and drank in the same Hulme pubs. So, when he asked me to direct his career, I fancied playing the Svengali. I pro-moted his next 'song', an unhinged, wailing affair, called 'I've Got No Chicken But I've Got Five Wooden Chairs', and sent a copy to the king of indie music, John Peel. Alone late one night in the *City Life* office, I called a BBC number during his 10pm-to-midnight show. I thought an assistant or answerphone might pick up, but the man himself gave a friendly greeting. 'Ah yes, Edward Barton, I was just looking at this one,' said the legendary taste maker. 'Hold on a minute, I've just got to put another record on,' he said in his languorous way. This all sounded very promising.

I was listening live to his radio show and the track that was playing ended – followed by thirty seconds of dead air. Then the music world's most influential DJ spoke to the nation. 'I've just taken a call,' he announced. I held my breath. Was he going to play Edward Barton? 'And on my way back, I've just tripped over the coffee table, and there's blood everywhere.' I held on to the phone for ten minutes, shouting, 'John? John?!' but eventually gave up. Peel had probably called for the BBC medical corps. On my first foray into artist man-agement, I had severely wounded our national music treasure. Despite Peel's play-anything policy which Joe Strummer uncharitably described in the music press as 'like a dog being sick on your face', my charge's record was never aired on the show. I later discovered that local PR Alison Bell knew Peel well. Going through her would have spared the bloodshed.

The city's music scene in the mid-1980s was on a roll, with The Smiths, New Order and Simply Red in the charts. Their divergent styles showed the variety of the cultural influences bubbling up in Manchester, from the kitchen-sink drama icons on The Smiths' sleeves to digital machine-made music and the city's deep love for soul music. Alongside the headline acts, city-based artists were releasing records and playing live shows on a range all the way from Peel darlings The Fall and Factory groups ACR and James to the jazz-soul of Swing Out Sister, Carmel and Yargo, the indie rock of The Chameleons, and a clutch of black hair-dyed Hulme bands, led by The Inca Babies and Big Flame.

A multitude of small, exotically named outfits were written up in our music pages, from The Man From Delmonte, Tools You Can Trust and Big Ed and his Rockin' Rattlesnakes. The indie scene attracted many mis-shapes and odd-bods to the city. We were happy to give a home to journalism from characters including Jon Ronson, the socially awkward future best-selling writer and broadcaster, and Mike West, the out-there Australian-born son of best-selling author Morris West, who wore his hair long down one side and shaved on the other.

On the live scene in the mid-1980s, gigs at the Haçienda were poorly attended, due to its dysfunctional acoustics and so, as well as the Boardwalk and the Band on the Wall, bands started using a new seven-hundred-capacity venue, the International in Victoria Park. (The club owner Gareth Evans came to know the fledgling Stone Roses there and became their manager.) With its conventional theatre-style layout and with the legendary Roger Eagle back in town as its booker, its success rankled with Tony Wilson, who told me: 'I wouldn't be seen dead in there, if you have to go there for work, I feel sorry for you and I hope you get well paid for it.' Sadly, I was not. The wages of the *City Life* co-operative had not advanced since our 1983 launch. The meagre earnings were eating away at our spirit and stamina, what with sixty-hour weeks, including two nights a fortnight spent without sleep while we laid out the edition in a manic 48-hour session.

We had managed to obtain National Union of Journalists membership after a heated discussion at the Manchester branch at the Press Club in 1984. Tony Wilson was in the room as the Granada TV union representative. We waited outside while the debate took place before we were called in to hear the decision: while our salaries were derisory, as we were responsible for our own exploitation and our publication was already on the streets, we were given union cards. We were doing the job of journalists, whether the union approved of our salary levels or not. The NUJ cards we carried were a proud symbol for us that we had the backing of our comradely peers in the city's citadels of press, TV and radio, even though in reality many saw us as untrained upstarts whose membership could only speed up the increasing erosion of earnings and working conditions, a quaint debate today when so many voluntarily write online for no payment.

There was more than money on hand, though. We lived the life of entitled media brats, getting free into gigs, films and plays, and sitting shoulder to shoulder with 'real' journalists at press conferences. We joked that we lived off the thin of the land — at art-show openings and movie review screenings, the sarnies, mini-sausage rolls and drinks came out. Positioning myself by the door through which the canapés entered the guest area ensured I could hoover up free scran. As a business, there was financial improvement thanks to the typesetting machine, as we inputted text and designed other publications. *City Life* had always had a Gay section, and we got good community reaction to the idea of its much-needed publication being run from our offices under Andrew Lowrey and Christopher Stocks. We took on the full publisher role for *Mancunian Gay* magazine, later *Gay Life*, and, as we grew, took on two full-time staff to produce it. Ebullient graduate Mike Hill joined as a restaurant reviewer and soon was appointed an editor. Mick Peek, a talented Poly graphics graduate, came in as full-time designer and overhauled the logo and layout, bringing an attractive cohesion to the look of the pages.

The new people and energy gave us stability and confidence, and in the mid-to-late 1980s the co-op employed 15 staff full-time. All were on the same salaries and had an equal vote on decisions. Sparks flew at the fractious meetings. Perhaps the co-operative structure had outlived its usefulness. When there were three, then seven of us, in the early days, there was a tight bond. We put so many hours in we were practically living together. The common purpose

National Union of Journalists card, 1987

started to fray when new members worked a standard nine-to-five, while others were putting in all-nighters. There was no prospect of pay rises. Chris Paul left when he took a job at Manchester City Council producing its job adverts. Ed Glinert was selling intel to *Private Eye* and others. I was the arts and features editor of the city's magazine, and I was doing washing-up shifts in Levenshulme bistro That Café, a crappy job made bearable by lovely mine hosts Joe Quinn and Steve King.

In summer 1988, a delivery man from our wholesaler-distributor W.H. Smith climbed the stairs to our top-floor office in the dilapidated corner building at 1–3 Stevenson Square, where since 1985 we had rented a 1,000 sq ft unit for £1 per square foot. He said, 'We've got some returns for you.' There was a rickety old lift and he and his colleague made many journeys schlepping boxes of unsold copies of *City Life*, pristine copies crudely strung together. The pair worked for an hour getting the boxes upstairs into a tiny anteroom we used for private meetings. When they left, you couldn't get in for the piles of boxes and bales of the unsold results of our heroic sixty-hour weeks, now trussed up for us to dispose of in an environmentally friendly manner.

The last five years swam before my eyes. The note left with us was a grim breakdown of the exact numbers of each issue sold. After years of delivering ten thousand copies of each issue for the newsagents and corner shops of the conurbation, we had increased our sale from one thousand of issue one to around three thousand each issue. The Greater Manchester population, including the hinterlands of Cheshire and the Peak District, contained 3 million people. We had been exhausting ourselves on a fortnightly basis to produce an alternative magazine for 00.1 per cent of potential readers.

It was spring 1988 and editing nearly a hundred issues of *City Life* was enough for anybody. I was soon to depart for a freelance life in which the *Manchester Evening News* paid decent rates. Less than a year later, the co-operatively run magazine went into administration and was rescued from financial purgatory by the *Manchester Evening News*. The anti-authority wildcat of a title was now a tamed animal, although very much part of the nation's liberal consciousness under the ownership of Guardian Media Group's GMEN division (which was sold in 2010 to Trinity Mirror, now Reach plc).

City Life is still the online brand for the *MEN*'s entertainment content. In 2022 my collection of three hundred issues was acquired by the British Pop Archive at the John Rylands Research Institute and Library at the University of Manchester, a resource for research into late twentieth-century Manchester. *City Life* has many legacies. The first proper job of digital ninja Andrew

Melchior, from Bury – the go-to guy for Björk and Massive Attack on their augmented reality ventures – was developing the GMEN-owned *City Life* website, which landed him a key role at EMI advising David Bowie on his pioneering expeditions in cyberspace. And the journalist behind the 2011 *Newsnight* scoop on Jimmy Savile's crimes against children inside the BBC, which caused a national storm when pulled by her bosses, was the late Liz MacKean, who I recall as a serious, diligent reporter uncovering her first campaigning stories for *City Life* in the mid-1980s.

5

A fiend dropping in

On my first shift at the *Manchester Evening News*, I was told that the world-famous thespian Lord Olivier had died. I was passed a slip of a paper with a handwritten Cheshire phone number on it. 'Can you call David Plowright at home? Get a quote from him on how his sister is, she's Olivier's widow, the actress Joan Plowright.'

I had interviewed the TV legend that was David Plowright at Granada TV press junkets, a straight-talking, courteous Northerner whose stellar career had seen him leading Granada news to the reputational mountaintops. He was the fearless editor who would tell his troops working on *World in Action*, 'Your job is to make trouble'. By now the TV company's chairman, I called him at home and passed on my respects, and he, a professional newsman to his boots, replied to my question about his sister in a helpful manner, with a line or two which I was able to type up.

The instruction had come from the paper's Diary editor Guy Meyler, whom I had briefly met after I had submitted a couple of stories, typed up and handed in to the paper's featureless modern offices in Crown Square. He had published both the pieces I submitted on spec, one about the Chinese community leader Loret Lee in the queue at the Cornerhouse cinema to see *Chinatown*. After our hand-to-mouth existence at *City Life*, I was impressed at how promptly the payment came through. Yes, we had slated the paper remorselessly at *City Life*, but now I was freelance, I asked myself, should I deny myself an income from providing words for a title which had employed George Orwell, Brian Redhead and Sir Harold Evans? The MEN sold up to 325,000 copies daily. Now I was a young dude carrying the news to a readership of around one million.

Meyler had called me soon after and booked me in for some shifts, paid at a day rate. He could tell from my contributions that I knew that the stories for his page did not necessarily have to be 'news'. They were about people.

Whimsical humour was preferred, about misunderstandings, mistakes, insults, disagreements, anecdotes, all of an order never going to trouble the news pages: this was the stuff of a Diary story. They were bite-sized morsels of mirth designed to help the reader digest a mountain of dispiriting news in the rest of the paper. If the readers could have a chuckle at the high and mighty on the way, so much the better.

The Diary was the home of off-cuts and 'funnies'. One day a fax arrived from the city's Central Library with a page from a 1930s street directory, which included an address in Hulme and the occupant's name, 'Matt Busby', then a player with Manchester City with his epic Manchester United years ahead. The door knocker at his back-to-back terrace had asked his occupation, and published it in the directory — doubtless on account of Busby's Lanarkshire accent — as 'Fruit Broiler'.

Such a high value was put on the Diary page of the *Manchester Evening News* that it employed two full-time journalists and enjoyed a budget for a third, a freelance. They worked five days a week, producing between them around six stories a day. The *MEN* paid excellent freelance rates — £25 for making the lead story and £15 for 'down pagers'. There was even a 'PS', a brief quirky item at the foot of the page, worth £7.50 for a tip-off. Perhaps the golden days of journalism had already been and gone, but it's worth holding that thought: three people working full-time on one page in 1989, something which continued for a decade more. I sensed that the Diary was seen by the hard-nosed news hacks as a well-upholstered journalistic cul-de-sac. The Diary was just one among fifty-plus editorial pages of a 96-page edition, of which the news pages were considered the most important, even if the most eagerly read reporters were probably the football writers. The paper employed four staffers in London, one for politics, three on showbiz. It had a staff canteen, an art department and even a motoring correspondent. Every Friday, it carried a book review by Gerald Kaufman, the MP I had witnessed debating with Tony Wilson in a Rusholme living room. (After Kaufman told a stranger at a concert that he did not waste too much time writing his pieces, as the pay was appalling, he was sacked – the stranger was a reporter, who passed the comment on to the editor.)

Despite the staff resources, I was amused to see that I would be writing my copy on old-school typewriters. Even *City Life* had word processors. To be fair, it wasn't long before a new ATEX system was installed, enabling journalists to send copy to the subs, and for them to design pages. I was also struck that my overseer Meyler seemed a bit posh for a big Northern city paper. I had expected the staff to be more Les Dawson than the comedy actor Terry Thomas, so his Royal Air Force accent and demeanour came as a surprise. Like the moustachioed Thomas, when he wanted your attention, he really did exclaim 'I say, Andy!'

The Diary page for many years had been the haunt of Duncan Measor, a recently retired chap who had become known as Mr Manchester, and whose bow-tied phizzog in hand-drawn caricature sat at the top of the page. This personality-led approach had not been transferred to Meyler, who without much fuss edited the page about the big city while commuting by train from Hebden Bridge in West Yorkshire. Later I was to discover he had an interesting hinterland, with a childhood spent in civil-war Spain and libertarian views on hard drugs you wouldn't have found in the editorial of the family newspaper, whose slogan was for many years 'A Friend Dropping In'. Mates of mine would often greet me with an edited shout of the tagline, replacing the 'friend' with 'fiend'.

Previously called 'Mr Manchester's Diary', the Measor and Meyler page seemed to me not nearly fiendish enough. It was hardly the rough stuff of a big-city paper gossip page. It dealt in stories about foreign consuls, chefs of fine-dining restaurants in deepest Cheshire, with hurrahs for the arrival of the Beaujolais Nouveau at the Midland Hotel, and free plugs for charity fundraisers by a gaggle of B-list celebs gathered around Mancunian legend Frank 'Foo Foo' Lammar, nightclub owner and drag artist who escaped the harsh tone the paper directed at other gay subjects, perhaps because he was an ex-bricklayer and, as Manchester-to-New York music writer Frank Owen recalls, literally knocked troublemakers' heads together as he kicked them out. The son of an Ancoats rag and bone man was a female impersonator, a north Manchester folk legend and hard as nails under the make-up and frocks.

The Diary was the newspaper's page reporting on the social life of the city centre. As I got more shifts, the long-serving staffers, the amiable Meyler and the ever-courteous David Harrison, realised I could bring a bit of edge. Five years of *City Life* meant I knew people in the changing Manchester, one that they didn't know or much understand. They started to trust me to attend press calls and dinners and report on VIP parties, and take interviews with writers, actors and anyone semi-famous being pushed at the paper.

I interviewed (on the phone) Salman Rushdie, Vanessa Feltz and Lily Savage, met several times with celebrated author and occasional returnee Anthony Burgess, and began to befriend some Coronation Street actors and Manchester City players. I was also gaining a certain amount of influence, as my senior colleagues started to respect my view on the value of a story or a tip-off.

I owed my opening on the paper to the newish editor. Wirral-raised Mike Unger had come from the *Liverpool Echo* in 1983, an incendiary appointment at the time for a Manc-majority newsroom. When he was appointed, the *Echo* newsroom staff faxed their Manchester peers with one line on an A4 page, scrawling the legend: 'Our loss is your loss'. My relationship was Unger was deeper than the average freelance hacking out a day shift, as I had interviewed him for a *City Life* profile, and he had written back a friendly note. He had asked Meyler to try me out.

Unger brought some talented journalists from the *Liverpool Echo*, including features sub-editor Eric Jackson, who commissioned many pieces from me, from 'go to Chorlton and find some alternative lifestyle types' to 'go to six pizza restaurants and review them'. Happy days.

From my Diary desk I could take in the whole features floor. While journalists typed away, pairs of youngsters hung around waiting for instructions. They were messengers, school leavers working placements at their first paid job after school. Many acted like they weren't paid at all, and seemed utterly uninterested in the minor but essential part they played in the epic production of the daily paper of their city. They were a mixed bunch, lads and lasses facing up to life after leaving school. It can't have been interesting work as they weren't involved in editorial, but stuff – mainly marked-up photographs or urgent paperwork – did need to get from one place to another on a busy paper publishing four editions a day.

The messengers were the human equivalent of the Victorian-era Heath Robinson-style vacuum pipe systems, like one I had seen in the Refuge Building on Oxford Road, an astonishing configuration of tubes running to all parts of the HQ, a mammoth network stemming from what looked like the grand pipe organ of movie villain the abominable Dr Phibes. Such infernal machines could move small objects around a building, but they could not scoot out on errands like buying fags and snacks. There was an office tale that deputy editor Jimmy Ross once asked a messenger to go out and buy him forty Senior Service cigarettes, adding 'but if they haven't got them, get me anything', after which the lad had returned with a pork pie.

On one of my early freelance shifts, I noticed one of the old newsroom sweats walking around with a photo of The Smiths in his hand. Hello, I thought, what's he doing with that? It transpired that he was looking for a messenger, though none were to be found, no doubt all enjoying one of their extended breaks. He passed by my desk with the photo, and paused, as if thinking, should I ask this freelance feller? But he kept on walking.

Later, it transpired that on that day he had needed some advice. The internet had not yet been invented. Who could tell him about a group called The Smiths, a young people's popular beat combo? Young people, obviously. When a couple of messengers came back from playing hooky, he asked them his burning question. Deadline was onrushing, and that day's *Manchester Evening News* first edition was to carry a story about bass player Andy Rourke of The Smiths in a Wrexham court on a heroin charge. Half-way down the office, I could see the silver-haired veteran showing a gaggle of lads a publicity shot of the band line-up.

Later, it became clear that he had asked the messengers who was who in the band. When the paper came out, the photo caption identified drummer Mike Joyce as the man up before the court. The messengers, being sixteen-year-olds with no clue about The Smiths, had fingered the wrong guy.

Soon after, I was having my hair cut at Dave Gerrard's old-school barbershop in Affleck's Palace. 'Hee hee, what a cock up by the *Evening News*,' chuckled Joyce's mate 'Demon Dave' as he wielded his razor. 'The paper had to pay Mike out quite a few grand for that cock-up.' Joyce's solicitor's case was not hard to make, and there was a price to pay.

Money was very much front of mind for the paper. Crunch times were coming as new social habits eroded circulation. The downward spiral started to bite into annual results. The paper had been economically dominant in the city for decades thanks to its display and classified advertising income. Improbably, this success had been to the benefit of left-leaning Britons, as the Manchester cash machine enabled *The Guardian* to ride years of low sales while still producing the strongly liberal voice which it had been founded to express by C.P. Scott in 1907. Despite its 1821 Manchester origins, almost all *Guardian* staff were based in London, having relocated there in 1964. It seemed ironic to me that, while Mancunia hosted only small outposts of *Guardian* readers, the proliferation of small ads in the not especially liberal *Evening News* paid the salaries and pensions of the nation's leading left-wing commentariat.

Under the rules of the Scott Trust, income from all the group's media was in the service of *The Guardian*. This financial dependence on Manchester's classified ad pages led to some stonking benefits for *MEN* staffers. In 1993, upon Meyler's retirement, I was offered the job of Diary editor. My contract included six weeks' paid holiday and a month's sabbatical every four years. Powerful journalist unions had used their industrial muscle over decades to argue that, if *Guardian* writers enjoyed a paid sabbatical to write their books and academic theses, then those who propped it up economically should be similarly rewarded. It appeared to me that many of the long-term senior staff, along with their peers at Granada TV, were a privileged corps, living comfortable lives doing rewarding media jobs. Hours not too long, great holidays, well-appointed residences in the suburbs. Shifts for most reporters were 7am to 3pm or 8am to 4pm.

My working day started at 8am, often coming in with an overnight report of a party or event. I would have to write the piece up for 9am. The page came back to me as a tabloid A3-sized photocopy with photos and headlines on it, and I could proofread and make changes at that stage. The first edition of the paper rolled off the Trafford Park presses in late morning and was on the streets at 12 noon. Later editions with updated news would be turned out during the day. When I went for my daily lunch stroll around Deangsate hoping to run into contacts and score some gossip, I would see people buying a copy from the street sellers, kiosks or shops. This became a pleasurable daily activity − watching strangers reading about what I had got up to the night before.

Most of the paper's staff got straight home after their day had ended. But it was my job to go to parties and events and file copy for the next day, so I would often go home for a couple of hours and re-emerge mid-evening with different clothes and my invite to a theatre first night, a record company launch or a novelist Q and A. Like most normal people, I was shy about striking up conversations with strangers. But holding a reporter's notebook and pen in my hands gave me the super-power of confidence.

It was a brilliant job to be out on the town representing the city's paper. I was a human pinball, zigzagging around the city's hotspots, when I wasn't on the desk taking tips on the phone or calling up sources to 'stand up' some gossip. My name was top of the list for any bar or restaurant opening party, and for celebs promoting their latest work. Variety was the spice of my life. I met football legends like Denis Law and Francis Lee at charity dinners and spent a toe-curling hour trying to get George Best, then deep in his alcoholic depression, to chat to me. US celebrities with something to promote, like country-pop singer Shania Twain or The Osmonds, were wheeled out to meet me.

Without formal training, I had no shorthand, but relied on my own 'scribblehand' and by memorising chit-chat, where paraphrasing rather than facts and figures could suffice for published quotes. One technique was to agree quotes with celebs. I was at the packed first night of Cameron Mackintosh's *Les Misérables* at the Palace Theatre when the set machinery failed at the interval, halting the show. As the famous VIPs filed glumly out, I approached Manchester City manager Peter Reid with a suggestion, and my report next day quoted him saying, 'It was a game of one half.' Sometimes I got the chance to put away the notebook and just listen. I spent a poignant afternoon with Ray Davies in the Midland Hotel, as he opened up about the toll on his family life that stardom with The Kinks had taken.

My beat could be an absurd circus and I liked the mix of characters I had to tangle with. The opening of Cheerleaders sports bar on Albion Street brought to Manchester the unlikely duo of the then all-powerful, later disgraced PR man Max Clifford, and boxing legend Muhammad Ali. How the two were tied up was unclear, and Ali's Parkinson's condition disabled him from a proper conversation with reporters. The former king of the ring was seemingly happy to greet a crowd of gawping boxing fans while Clifford orchestrated VIP introductions in a private area for celebs like the former hard-left Liverpool politician Derek Hatton, footballer Lee Sharpe and Tony Wilson to shake hands and pose for photos. All the while the hundreds of expectant drinkers watched patiently for Ali to leave − as Ali was a strict Muslim, all had been told, no alcohol could be taken while he was there. When he finally climbed the staircase exit, there was an audible sigh of relief, after which he came down the stairs again, all smiles, doing the James Brown 'I'm not done yet!' routine. This he repeated several times. The parched crowd were good about it. Ali was having fun, and no one was prepared to show him the door. Did he mischievously know he was depriving hundreds of lager-starved Mancs their Saturday night pint? When he made his final depart up the stairs and someone shouted, 'He's gone!' there was a cheer so loud it could have been heard at the Haçienda around the corner.

Among the anodyne *Coronation Street* and charity stories which were an inevitable part of the Diary's daily churn, I was also able to slip in many stories about the music scene – Mike Joyce bumping into Morrissey while the drummer was suing him for £1 million (they chatted politely and avoided the subject) or me ambushing Noel Gallagher on Oxford Street for some quotes on a rare visit home, thanks to a tip-off from paparazzo Eamonn Clarke.

I wanted the Diary page to be tangy. It didn't always fit in with the news pages around it, and I suspect the reporters did not regard me as 'one of us'. Nevertheless, this Londoner wanted it to be Mancunian – dry, direct and a bit stroppy. I was bringing the scurrilous *City Life* attitude to the mainstream family newspaper, and I credit editor Unger and the features editors under him. There wasn't a single time they pulled a story of mine because it would upset a subject.

The literary lunches put on by Waterstone's bookshop were terrific fun. Four writers plugging their books would gather for drinks before doing a turn for the

Max Clifford, Derek Hatton and Muhammad Ali at Cheerleaders opening

paying guests, and I could chat to the pick of them, like maverick Tory Alan Clark about his diaries. When I sat down with him in the Deansgate store's basement, manager Robert Topping yelled: 'Be careful, Mr Clark, this man is a gossip columnist!' Clark, famed for his acidic political memoirs, seemed unfazed. I recall telling Sebastian Faulks that I was sure his novel was very good, but my popular newspaper required I should focus on Bob Monkhouse on the same bill. When I read *Birdsong*, I was ashamed of denying Faulks's visit a mention for that heart-breaking book.

Working for the mass market meant I had to trade credibility points in. Some relationships became casualties. I had interviewed Morrissey for *City Life* about his *The Queen Is Dead* album in 1985 at the Portland Hotel, hearing out his eccentric, witty disquisitions on music, fame and Manchester. He had since invited *City Life* into his parents' Stretford home for a photo session for the cover of the hundredth issue in May 1988. Emboldened by this, I got a letter to him requesting an interview for my new berth. His letter back featured his trademark spidery signature: 'I dont [sic] seriously fancy my chances with the Moanchester Evening News … Another "miserable moors murders pop star" effort and Im [sic] off to Aberdeen to sell cut flowers. Now there's a threat!'

Morrissey onside or not, my Diary role was a foothold for writing features and pop reviews. I was sent to Paris for The Rolling Stones and Rotterdam for Prince, writing reviews to promote their Manchester dates. The famous were increasingly coming to the city. The bar and restaurant scene was bubbling with new openings, and Bill Wyman's Sticky Fingers chain didn't want to miss out on Manchester. When we met to promote his venture, he made clear his distaste for the way we described him as 'the wrinkly rocker', but I was the portal through which publicity would reach the market for his new posh burgers joint. My attendance at the October 1996 launch was to provide him with more publicity than either of us could have dreamed. The invite list included the usual Manchester faces of ball-kickers and soap-erati, but the restaurant's PR Rob Brown knew the city had some new faces, and got invites separately to New Order's Peter Hook and his recently estranged wife Caroline Aherne, whose Mrs Merton TV character had made her a household name.

I first met Caroline in my own small house in Levenshulme in the late 1980s. I came home to find her and my lodger Mark Tindall at the top of the stairs exiting his bedroom. He introduced her as a secretary working at the BBC and explained they had been writing scripts to submit to *Brookside*. Aherne's ditzy demeanour hid her laser-like ambition, and the next time I saw her was onstage as the comedy act Sister Mary Immaculate, her first step towards fame and a marriage to 'Hooky' in Las Vegas in 1994, a stormy union which ended acrimoniously two years later.

At the Sticky Fingers launch both she and her ex-husband turned up with their new partners. When they all gathered in the big main room, where guests snacked on nibbles and necked free drinks, it was petrol on smouldering firewood. I saw Caroline's new beau, Granada TV staffer Matt Bowers, walk over to Hook and throw a punch at him − but not before I had gestured to Manchester's premier 'pap' snapper Eamonn Clarke, saying, 'Quick, it's

City Life No. 100, April–May 1988

going to kick off.' His quick reactions captured the mayhem that followed, as Hooky's pal, the Haçienda manager Leroy Richardson, piled in to pull the brawlers apart – though he couldn't prevent the New Order bass player's kick landing in the stomach of his ex-wife. It was all over in seconds. I got quotes

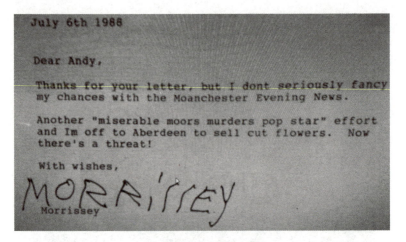

July 6th 1988

Dear Andy,

Thanks for your letter, but I dont seriously fancy
my chances with the Moanchester Evening News.

Another "miserable moors murders pop star" effort
and Im off to Aberdeen to sell cut flowers. Now
there's a threat!

With wishes,

MORRiSSEY

Morrissey

Morrissey letter, 6 July 1988

from everyone I could, though Aherne and Bowers left. In the morning, Clarke's photos were being loved by the news desk. There was some dismay that the picture editor had not paid freelancer Clarke for an evening job rate of £30, so he owned the copyright, a decision which cost the paper £20,000 in sell-on fees.

The *Manchester Evening News* splashed the photos and the story, my only front page byline. Meanwhile, Clarke tied up an exclusive deal with *The Sun* for the next day. This did not stop the four other tabloids – *Mirror, Mail, Express* and *Star* – brazenly scanning the *Manchester Evening News* photo and reproducing it, with varying and often dodgy results, on their own front pages. *The Sun* could not pay Clarke in those circumstances, but did provide the services of its lawyers Mishcon de Reya, who won him tens of thousands in damages from the four thieving papers.

I fancy that the photo Clarke took, of some of Manchester's most famous people bashing seven bells out of each other, has the composition of a Renaissance frieze, with the five participants neatly lined up, all playing their appointed role. The new Mrs Hook's shocked face looks straight at the camera, breaking the fourth wall. I fancied it might appear on *Have I Got News For You?* with smart-arse panellists suggesting witty captions: 'Intellectual Northerners discuss philosophy', or 'Mancunian relationship counsellors try new approach'.

The star bars were changing the face of Manchester. Sticky Fingers was in St Ann's Street, just round the corner from the strip of night-time businesses

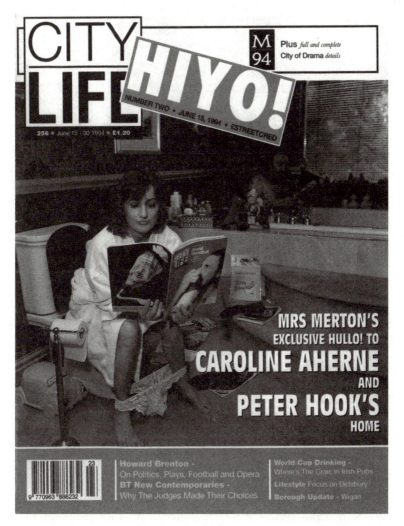

Peter Hook and Caroline Aherne, *City Life* No. 256, June 1994

including the influential J.W. Johnson's, set up by future leisure empire entrepreneur Tim Bacon. Other parts of town offered cheap property in run-down quarters. Jim Ramsbottom's Dukes 92 and Mick Hucknall's Barca kickstarted Castlefield as a destination, and the Factory–New Order axis put their money down on the Oldham Street bar they called Dry, giving rise to the Northern Quarter.

'A right hook', *Manchester Evening News* front page, 12 November 1996

Dry was the daytime haunt of the Madchester scenesters. Haçienda interior design guru Ben Kelly took its space, a whole city block deep, and created a huge socialising floor. Low seating broke up any solely vertical drinking vibe and at 24 ft the bar was the longest in the city, boasting tapas and 74 brands of whisky. A number of nightlife entrepreneurs followed along Oldham Street, including Dry copycat Isobar, live jazz venue P.J. Bells and, right at the north end of the street, the irrepressible cigar-chomping Dave Perkin, who opened the Frog and Bucket comedy club where Peter Kay and Johnny Vegas cut their stand-up teeth.

The Northern Quarter became the official designation of an area which had not needed a name before the early 1990s. It was simply a sprawling neighbourhood north of Piccadilly which had seen better pre-Arndale Centre days, when Oldham Street was a bustling retail thoroughfare. Now this stretch between Great Ancoats Street and Piccadilly corralled a higgledy-piggledy mix of rag-trade showrooms, lively old pubs, cheap curry houses and charity drop-in offices.

The area had created its own unique street-life, an osmosis begun in the 1980s by three major music-influenced enterprises – Dry bar, the growth of Affleck's Palace (the pop subcultural Aladdin's Cave where teen tribes came to buy DIY fashion) and, riding the city's buzzy wave of regen, Urban Splash's refurbishment of the former British Home Stores into the 84-apartment Smithfield Building.

Madchester came and went, with a Granada documentary for the ITV network featuring a young Stuart Maconie deconstructing the deep meaning of the designer urinals at Dry. 'Self esteem is a chic place to drink,' ran *The Independent* headline about how Dry was educating scallies in contemporary interior design. This improving purpose was lost on Shaun Ryder, who threw a bottle at a mirror behind the bar, and Liam Gallagher who smashed a vase. Managers Leroy Richardson and Mark Sullivan showed cool aplomb in ejecting the brattish celebrities, then calling me to get the tale in the paper.

Despite the area's roughhouse character, solicitors and business execs started to move in, as did Manchester United's PR chief Patrick Harverson, who left when he became Prince Charles's image manager. The council allowed the district to come up at its own speed, not forcing it, bestowing the Northern Quarter name only after it caught on in general conversation and culture. The council allowed the Northern Quarter Association of businesspeople and residents to take an active role in the area's regeneration, including selecting developers and ceramic street name signs by Wendy Jones and Liam Curtin.

Today's undisputed king of Britain's urban regeneration is Tom Bloxham, whose start in business selling Manchester music posters in the alternative lifestyle bazaar Affleck's Palace is well known. His first forays into property were in Liverpool; in Manchester people scoffed when he said buyers would fork out to live along Oldham Street, but he declared it could be the city's Covent Garden or Soho and he was proved right when his Smithfield Building flats were snapped up.

Many though felt the area's grubbiness was too far ingrained to ever be gentrified, London-style. 'Sometimes I think Oldham Street is an alternative care in the community scheme,' pub licensee and comedy promoter Dave Perkin joked, talking about the sad and the sozzled who stumbled and sang their way along the road that linked the city centre to the doughnut of deprivation bordering it. Perkin knew many of them as patrons in The King, his day-time karaoke pub over the road from Dry. For quite some years to come, there was just too much scuzzy poverty, too many addicts coming to Lifeline for methadone, too many thieves looking to roll a drinker separated from their pub-crawl mates, to change the offbeat chemistry of crummy Oldham Street.

These were the years when you could be at a bar in the Northern Quarter ordering a drink next to a world-famous singer or actor. For me running a gossip column, there was no need to be out every night, as it was easy to discover their regular haunts. From the office, I was sure to check in by phone or in person with the Haçienda, Dry bar, the Midland and Victoria and Albert hotels, the latter opened by Granada TV next to its studios.

The city's hotels were full the night in June 1992 when U2 played G-Mex, and I gate-crashed an exceptional rock and roll celebrity party. Leaving the band's concert in aid of Greenpeace, I bumped into music writer Stuart Maconie and photographer Peter Walsh, and the three of us walked into an empty back room. It soon started to fill up with very famous people hardly ever seen in dear dirty old Manchester. There were music stars Peter Gabriel and Chrissie Hynde with local guitar hero Johnny Marr, and, from the US, Lou Reed and film star Winona Ryder. There was no fancy food or flash cocktails, just some of the coolest, most talented people on the planet, all wearing black to signal how unflashy they were, and all in Manchester to signal their support for the work of Greenpeace's Stop Sellafield campaign.

What a buzz. These were proper rock stars, not the soap actor wannabes I often had to get quotes from. And there, I purred, was Kevin Godley, the leonine drummer of 10cc, my favourite pre-punk group. My heart beat fast as I told him, in my gushing enthusiasm, that I was with the local paper. He wasn't very chatty. Seconds later, a polite Irish voice asked me, 'Sir would you please come this way?' Floating on air, I was happy to oblige – was I being taken to meet Bono? – but a few seconds later the nice chap had vanished, and I was outside the room, elegantly ejected from the party of my life, alone in an empty G-Mex except for the roadies boxing up the tech.

These were the years when my phone at the paper rang not only from tipsters wanting some column inches for their club or bar, or from PRs plugging records or books, but also from national gossip pages. Piers Morgan was then *The Mirror*'s showbiz king who had started publishing photos of himself with celebrities in his reports. His proto-selfie schtick looked tacky to me. My snappers might snatch a jokey shot of me with a celeb as a personal keepsake, but Morgan's shameless approach made him a celebrity in his own right and took him all the way to the editor's job at *The Mirror* and beyond. Morgan was obsessed by Terry Christian and asked me for information about TV's pocket provocateur from Old Trafford. I didn't know much except that he had come to prominence on TV and radio shows seeking the voice of youth. Armed with a razor-sharp mouth and speaking in what, to many southerners, appeared to be a strong, almost caricature 'Manc' accent, he landed a presenter job on BBC Radio Derby, but came back to his hometown as a music specialist. The *Manchester Evening News* asked him to write a weekly

Andy Spinoza with Joe Strummer

music column, and the subs would ask me to check his copy, cackling when I said young Mr Christian 'sure put the punk into punctuation'. When a new Channel 4 show called *The Word* called and asked if I could recommend anyone 'up there', I suggested (as others did) Christian and also Jon Ronson, then a local freelance.

I was becoming known for my connections. In 1996 Chris Sievey approached me. He was better known as the cult comic character Frank Sidebottom, mostly known for wearing a head made of papier-maché and for exclaiming 'Oh blimey!' on children's TV. As younger men, he and Mark Radcliffe had

Andy Spinoza with Darcey Bussell and Tara Palmer-Tompkinson

Andy Spinoza with Coronation Street cast members

Andy Spinoza with Noel Gallagher (photo: Eamonn Clarke)

worked with Chris Evans in Sidebottom's Oh Blimey Big Band. After his death in 2010 there were many tributes but I knew him as an embittered guy with a manic urge to make money from selling stories about his old friends and associates. He kept on at me about a story that his old partner in tomfoolery Chris Evans, when he was up and coming, had broadcast a competition to win a car on late-night Piccadilly Radio. When he announced the winner live on air, Evans revealed that it was a toy car, to the winning listener's obvious anger at the jape. Sievey thought it was outrageous, and there are all sorts of

Andy Spinoza with Anthony Burgess (photo: Martin O'Neill)

broadcasting rules it would contravene today. But I couldn't see a national newspaper running that story without the aggrieved prize winner, now lost in time, as part of the package.

There was a bigger story, though. Sievey was adamant that his old partner Caroline Aherne had lifted her nationally famous comic character Mrs Merton from his Frank's World onstage revue and Piccadilly Radio shows. Sievey had devised and named Frank's female neighbour, and she had voiced the part of Mrs Merton for him. Aherne had gone on to enjoy huge fame by fronting her

Andy Spinoza with Alan Clark MP

own spoof TV chat show from 1993. By the time of Sievey's approach to me, audiences of nine million had made Aherne's 'Mrs Merton' and her Crimplene dresses, librarian glasses and surgical stockings a household name. (She went on to achieve what some regard as a tragicomic greatness worthy of Samuel Beckett with TV's sofa-bound sitcom *The Royle Family*, co-written with Craig Cash. Tragically, she was to die from cancer in 2016.)

Sievey asked me round to his house in Sale to pick up papers and notes – the proof, as he saw it, of the Mrs Merton intellectual property theft. In fact, there is no copyright on an idea, and he did not even have recordings. If he had consulted a lawyer, he would have known he had no case. It did have legs as a tabloid story, though. After the eccentric surrealist died, Radcliffe said he was 'one of the very few people I met whom I would call a genius'. A thwarted genius, it seems. There was a tangible bitterness from Sievey that his old associates had gone on to fame and fortune while his creativity had been largely unrewarded. His luck was in for the Aherne story. The *Mail on Sunday* reporter told me that his editors were obsessed with the Mrs Merton TV character. The aggrieved, cash-hungry Sievey had his say in print, his allegations making a double-page spread for the curiosity of middle England. My recollection is that this piece netted the man behind Frank Sidebottom around £4,000, after my own introducer's cut.

Gossip columns rely on tipsters, people who call with stories and tittle-tattle which may lead to one. Some want payment, others get a different kick from seeing their lead make a published piece. One of my unpaid sources was retired teacher Phil Hamer, a big man with a booming Welsh voice. He taught at Ordsall High School at the in-decline Salford docks and was always keen to see his former pupils doing great things as young actors and getting recognition in their home city. Hamer gave me the lowdown on rising local stars: like Ben Wong becoming a familiar face in Hollywood movies directed by Steven Spielberg, and Jason Done, a polite, taciturn young man who played a wounded soldier in the movie *The English Patient*, which required him to be kissed by Juliette Binoche – a take the director ordered to be repeated twenty times.

Another name which took my eye was that of the intense and compelling Christopher Eccleston. I had seen him in movies *Let Him Have It* and *Shallow Grave*, and TV's *Cracker* and *Our Friends in the North*, and thought him a remarkable talent. Hamer said I should speak to his old drama-school boss Keith Wilson, who ran the Salford Tech performing arts courses that Eccleston had come through. I wrote up a nice piece, describing him with tabloid brashness as 'a young British Robert De Niro'. I quoted the educator's reminiscences of the young Eccleston, including him taking to the stage in tights and make-up in his New Romantic teenage days. I thought it was a nice piece anyway. Not long after, I came to face to face with him on a Saturday night in July 1996 and learned that he was a very unhappy chappie indeed.

I was between nightspots and hungry. Pizza Express on South King Street was right next to South, my intended next stop and a great basement club night promoted by ex-Haçienda manager Paul Cons. The restaurant was a pivotal place for Manchester's media. It was always buzzy and reliable for a quick turnaround meal. As I walked in, Andrew Critchley, the finance boss of Nicola Shindler's Red Productions TV company, invited me to join his party. As I sat down, I recognised both Shindler and the chap on my left … ah yes, Mr Eccleston.

I introduced myself. 'I write the Diary in the *Evening News*,' I said. 'I wrote a story about you recently.' He snarled, 'That was *you* was it?' and threw a full glass of water in my face. The fiery glare he used to great effect on screen, it was clear, was no act now. I said to the gathering, 'I don't want to spoil anyone's evening, I'll leave,' and left the table, snaking my way through the chairs of the busy restaurant towards the exit. As I went outside into the street, I glimpsed a blur in my peripheral vision. I turned, but too late – the vein-bursting face familiar from TV had leapt out into my reality. 'If you write about me again, ya bastard!' he screamed in my face as he pushed me over a car bonnet, 'I'll fucking have ya!' Critchley pulled him away and ushered him back to their pizzas.

This will make a tasty story, I thought. The following Monday morning, I took a call from the top Granada TV press officer. Paul Tyrrell was a time-served reporter who had covered everything from death knocks to courtroom and had traded worn shoe leather for the chief PR job at Granada. 'Christopher has been to see me this morning and explained what happened on Saturday night.' Interesting, I thought … 'Yes, he told me how you approached his table and sat down next to him and his party.'

This was a clever reframing of the truth. I had done so only at the invitation of our mutual friend, I told Tyrell. I could see that, if I pushed the matter, I would be putting Critchley on the spot. Eccleston had been the best man at his wedding. I resolved to let the matter drop. Next time I saw 'Critch' we chuckled about the episode, which did land me with an unexpected dividend – a bottle of champagne. Matthew Norman of *The Guardian* diary column was hearing so many stories about the 'smug and irksome' Eccleston that he offered a bottle of bubbly for the best anecdote about him. The Guardian Media Group's internal logistics got me the fizz delivered to my desk by a messenger. Years later, when Eccleston strode out of the Tardis as the regenerated, leather-jacketed Doctor in Dr Who, I would tell my disbelieving kids about my real-life ruckus with the Time Lord. In recent years, his searingly honest disclosure of severe mental health issues has shed light on the personal pain behind his tortured tough-guy image.

One of the staple methods of getting a story was phoning the parent of a famous local person. In this way, you could often find about their next film or stage play, and who they would be starring with, before anyone had got round to putting out a press release. Stage and movie actress Jane Horrocks's mum Barbara was a delightful lady and always pleased to chat and tell you proudly what her daughter was doing when she wasn't supposed to. One day I found myself talking to teenage TV actor Anna Friel's father Des on the family phone. I was asking him if I could speak to Anna about whom she was dating – love matches were a staple of the page. I first met Friel in a queue going into a first-night musical. She was just gaining profile in the *Brookside* soap set on a Liverpool new-build suburban housing estate. Without the heritage of *Coronation Street*, 'Brookie' was more in tune with modern life, and Anna was from Rochdale and so, in our office parlance, was 'one of ours'. In interviews she told me that if she hadn't have gone into acting, she might have gone into journalism.

My desire for the story got the better of my qualms. I ran a piece speculating on who her latest beau was. It wasn't my proudest hour. As soon as the paper landed, I regretted falling into the national tabloid trap of intruding on celebrities' privacy just because you could, excused by the argument that the public had an insatiable appetite to know. For her part, Friel used a *Brookside* magazine interview to call out 'the Manchester press', and I knew that meant me.

If anyone these days wants any measure of the pre-internet power of the tabloids, exhibit one is Piers Morgan's diaries in which, as the *Daily Mirror* editor, he was scarcely off the phone to Prime Minister Tony Blair and chief spinner Alastair Campbell. The red tops' huge readerships, while down from their heyday peaks, were influential in shaping public sentiment, and the false entitlement this led to encouraged them to overstep the mark, as the later phone-hacking scandal showed.

It was around this time that actor Amelia Bulmore cut me off in conversation with 'you're such a tart, aren't you Andy?' and a friend of Steve Coogan's told me, 'Steve thinks you're charming but dangerous,' which must have been by repute as I don't think we have ever met. The Anna Friel episode, I knew, was a misstep, ethically and morally. No one was pushing me for the story. I pushed myself in the misguided belief that this was what celebrity reporters did. Yet I wasn't exposing dodgy councillors or corrupt coppers now. I started to question my treatment of celebs. Was I supposed to be following the national tabloids and chasing a younger audience? Or was I supposed to be toning it down for a family readership? Various editors gave me no steer, happy to get through the day while focusing on more important news pages. I thought hard about the choices I was making. I had gone from speaking truth to power to peddling celebrity tittle-tattle. From the Friel story on, I did not pursue tip-offs on the seamier side of celebrities' lives.

In June 1997, Unger left his post following a number of huge rows about editorial direction with commercial bosses who wanted a more advertising-led approach. He refused to take sport off the back page and replace it with TV, a sign of a creeping dumbing down of the paper facing an identity crisis in changing times. After an amicable negotiation about his exit, he was asked to clear his desk without saying goodbye to his staff. Deputy editor Paul Horrocks took over as *Manchester Evening News* editor and implemented the back page change. He too left me alone and seemed happy with my output. In 1997 he gave me a new title, Showbusiness Editor, my job now being to write one celebrity profile a day. Before, as Diary editor I had to find, write and check (with colleague Carl Palmer) six stories a day, for six pages, Monday to Saturday. I had become a human story machine turning out dozens a week. Now I was mainly twiddling my thumbs, I began to think of my next move.

I had actually applied for the top job which Horrocks had stepped up into, more to get noticed than in any expectation, and I did not get an interview. In this post-Unger era, the *Manchester Evening News* appeared to operate a behind-closed-doors method of selecting the top tier of the paper's editorial team. It was one that even today's employment laws around hiring and firing, with an ever-growing list of 'protected characteristics,' would fail to pick up. There was an unspoken belief that the senior editorial positions key to the paper's soul had to be people from north Manchester. Only people from the northern side of Greater Manchester — which for these purposes included Lancashire — could know in their bones the city's real character, the hot buttons and dog whistles any daily paper employs in everything from headlines, sports coverage, even the cartoons and reader competitions.

Under Horrocks, for the top jobs, the selections were almost always promotions from within. Already known to the decision-makers, their capability, attitudes, beliefs, sense of humour and football team would be known quantities. Applicants from south Manchester did apply for those posts, as I did, but it was futile. However experienced and capable, they could never get the role. The essence of Mancunianism, bosses believed, was in north Manchester. 'You're writing for Ancoats Annie and Beswick Bob' was the anti-intellectual advice uttered to me many times over. The implication of this mantra was clear: none of your pretentious fancy dan *City Life* nonsense here.

No southern jessie would ever get one of the top jobs — not a reference to London, but those from the more affluent southern districts of Chorlton and Didsbury, or Stockport, Trafford or the Cheshire towns. There was one brilliant journalist who had all the right attributes for higher office. Paul Taylor had a legal background but made journalism his trade and he excelled as much at murder assignments as editorials and pop music reviews. He was cheerful, a natural diplomat, and was courteous to all. He also ticked the unwritten big box, as he was Oldham-born and bred. When I mentioned to a colleague that he would make a great editor, he muttered: 'He'll never get the top job, he's far too intelligent. He might be from Oldham, but upstairs they think he's a south Manchester type.'

I was reminded of this Manc mindset many years later, in a meeting in which a property company and Manchester City Council staff were reviewing a new brand for a regeneration scheme just north of the centre. One of the council officers took in the gathering of marketing people and property developers, looked at the prepared hipster imagery and graphics and declared: 'This area you are branding is in north Manchester. You are all from south Manchester, and you have got to understand something: north Manchester is hairy-arsed Manchester.'

The title of the Greater Manchester borough with the most hirsute backside could be the focus of a fierce competition. My pick would be Salford, where *MEN* patch reporter Neal 'Killer' Keeling beat cancer to continue serving up compelling true crime and council stories for 35 years, and where the city's rabble-rousing agit-news *Salford Star* was first paid for, then defunded by the council after scathing takedowns sprinkled with industrial language. When it closed in 2022 after 15 years, its one-man protest movement of an editor Stephen Kingston told online news outlet *The Mill*, an altogether more thoughtful 'alt media' outlet: 'The old Salford doesn't exist any more. It's a different city.' Kingston has thrown his energies into creating a celebratory trail along Bury New Road, the Salford highway stretching from the city centre's HMP Manchester and the Arena, a route which influenced artists such as film-maker Mike Leigh, rapper Bugzy Malone and 10cc's Graham Gouldman, who wrote The Hollies' 1965 hit 'Bus Stop' on his way past the grotty Gothic mansions of Prestwich, where Nico and John Cooper Clarke lost years of their lives in an opium daze. This collection of names only hints at the curious atmosphere of the conjoined cities' hazy hinterland. Strangeways indeed.

The change in Salford was noticed even earlier by lovingly celebrated thespian Albert Finney, who brought Hollywood royalty Liza Minnelli to Salford for his 1968 movie *Charlie Bubbles*; local lore insists that he and his debut movie co-star 'romped', in tabloid-speak, among the Gothic headstones in Weaste cemetery, with the ghosts of Charles Hallé and Busby Babes for company: a grand Salford night out. In 1996, arguing that the coming Lowry Centre in would be a 'shining and terrific beacon for the world', the scion of a backstreet bookmaker dynasty declared that his hometown, whose docks were known as the Barbary Coast due to the exotic humanity which washed down the ship canal, had vanished: 'The identity of Salford has changed'.

No question, and the changes were not without friction. The cultural collision of regeneration and locals was crystallised in some tasty vignettes, from Ordsall youths targeting BBC staff who had ventured north in 2014, to brazen thievery at Sir Rocco Forte's Lowry Hotel which opened in 2001 on the Salford side of the River Irwell. The renowned hotelier installed a valuable bust of

Lowry by artist Harold Riley in reception, but it was snatched off its podium and walked straight out the hotel's doors. The master keys to every room also went walkies, costing £45,000 to replace. Welcome to Salford. Even so, the city's regeneration had an unstoppable momentum. The council held a competition in 2004 for the masterplan of its central districts. When the victor's name, an Italian starchitect, was conveyed to the press officer by his colleague, he told him: 'And the winner is … Fuksas! Good luck with that on BBC Radio Manchester.'

I had been up close and personal with hairy-arsed Manchester. Indeed, I had encountered the hot breath on my face of Bernard Manning, the racist comedian and the custodian, in many ways, of the old north Manchester belief system. I chose to interview the obese club owner and racist stand-up for *City Life*'s cover in October 1986 because he was 'a phenomenon to be analysed, not ignored'. Visiting his 'world-famous Embassy Club' on Rochdale Road, Harpurhey, was a reminder of how extensive were, and still are, the deprived communities north of the city centre: mile after grim mile of low-level housing and the remnants of once-thriving engineering supply chains, now reduced to scrap-metal yards and car-repair depots. And it was the same on the other arterial roads out of the centre, Oldham Road and Ashton Old Road. And west through Salford on the Regent Road. And northerly on the Cheetham Hill Road and past Strangeways jail on Bury New Road. It wasn't hard to see where Manning's fan base came from, and what the *Manchester Evening News* top brass saw as their readership base.

It would be wrong to paint the whole of north Manchester as illiberal, intolerant and reactionary. Indeed, radio talk shows on both Piccadilly and BBC aired authentic voices like Mike Sweeney, Allan Beswick and James H. Reeve, who told it straight but always reflected the warm-hearted, inclusive Manc character. The much-loved TV comedian Les Dawson was the essence of the old north Manchester – deadpan, lugubrious and making mill-workers' 'mee-mawing' (expressive miming over the noise of the looms) part of his routine. The much-loved Dawson, along with Roy Barraclough, was happy to cross-dress for their 'Cissie and Ada' sketches, something unthinkable in misogynist Manning's act.

Even so, being given an hour of Manning's time was a jarringly good experience for a liberal like me because – perhaps like debating with racially motivated 'red wall' Brexiters many years later – you could despise the malignancy of certain opinions, but you had to confront the authenticity of his experience. 'I've lived, y'see,' he told me. 'I've been poor. I've been rich. And rich is better.

We all had nowt when we was kids. I know what it's like … it's all money. It's all down to money.'

He lived in the relatively affluent pocket of Alkrington, part of nearby Middleton, where a close neighbour happened to be firebrand left-wing playwright and TV dramatist Jim Allen. But Manning's big house hadn't meant he had ditched the value system of Harpurhey, where he was still seen as one of the locals. He channelled the resentment and intolerance of many north Manchester residents living recession-battered lives. 'We've got the rich and the poor like any town,' he said. 'It could be better balanced. I don't know how they do it. I mean, I'm not a politician. We've got poor people where we shouldn't have poor people forty years after the bloody war. We've got Japan pricing us out of all the businesses – defeated nations!' He shook his head in disbelief, unable to comprehend how the folk of north Manchester could have gone to war (as he did) and won, then saw the losers enjoying greater prosperity.

Maybe we could have gone on to debate the consequences of the US role in the Second World War, the Marshall Plan and how the postwar flight of international capital took advantage of cheap labour elsewhere. But we had to move to the main course – the racism question. I witnessed his Embassy act, which, as Jewish writer Jonathan Margolis noted, could be incredibly funny when his comic content was not outright racism. Margolis wrote: 'I would maintain, as once did an article in *Marxism Today*, that Manning was a potential working-class hero, a master of the comedy of vulgarity and insult whom Chaucer would have admired, but who ruined it all by being racist.' Manning's act included vile insults that could never be dressed up as jokes, and from his Embassy he had quite simply become an ambassador for race hatred.

John Thomson was one up-and-coming comedian able to exploit the rancid Manning brand with subtle satire. The stand-up scene of the city was firing out comic performers and writers, many from Manchester Polytechnic, being given precious experience on regional TV by Granada, talents like Steve Coogan, Henry Normal, Caroline Aherne, Craig Cash, Dave Gorman and Chris Addison. Thomson was a gifted impressionist (as seen on TV's *The Fast Show*) who came to prominence in the early 1990s. I was leaving the Green Room on Whitworth Street one night when Johnny Dangerously (later John Bramwell, frontman of I Am Kloot) raced out and persuaded me back in to witness the debut of Thomson's character 'Bernard Right-on'. The physical frame did not need much work, and the voice was subtly, gruffly perfect: 'There was a Pakistani, an Irishman and a Jew – what a fine example of an integrated multicultural community.' In 2015 Thomson described how the act in today's stand-up circuit suffers with young audiences, who can be offended – they don't understand that it is a parody – and he has dropped it from his act. They have never even heard of Bernard Manning, the potty-mouthed personification of hairy-arsed north Manchester, the late twentieth-century heartland of the *Manchester Evening News*.

6

Left turn, U-turn

The final scene of the 1990 TV series *House of Cards* sees ruthless Prime Minister Francis Urquhart throwing his journalist lover from the roof of the House of Commons. In fact, you can clearly see the Manchester skyline all around, as the building standing in for the Palace of Westminster is Manchester Town Hall. While no one involved in the city of Manchester's politics during the preceding decade was dispatched in this way, the politics inside the grandiose seat of power during the 1980s was equally as brutal and compelling a spectacle.

Bar a brief, uncharacteristic Tory regime in 1970, the city had long been Labour in temperament as well as control, with a manufacturing trade-union base, and a radical protest tradition going back to Peterloo, the Chartists, the Free Trade movement and the Suffragettes. While the Conservatives had a sizeable minority presence for many years (opposition council wards migrated to the Liberal Democrats in the 1990s), Labour was in no danger of losing 1980s Manchester. However, no-holds-barred in-fighting began in the decade's early years between the old guard and the young pretenders – many recent graduates from university and inspired by the Militant 'fight back' in Liverpool. They fought bitterly within the Labour group over policies to combat the Thatcher government, which had set about with gusto on its manifesto promise of squeezing council budgets. In the wake of Thatcher's 1979 election win, the sitting Manchester Central MP Harold Lever was made a life peer, and leading councillors Graham Stringer and Pat Karney worked hard to support the selection of a former city councillor, the left-leaning Bob Litherland, who won the ensuing by-election in September that year, the first of the Thatcher era.

The policies of the 1974–79 Labour government had failed to win the general election and young councillors disillusioned by the party targeted the city party, grabbing key positions in charge of selecting candidates and writing manifestos. They accused the moderate leadership of managing decline, just like their national counterparts, and of cosying up to the private sector by offering council land for redevelopment. Karney was quoted in *Detonation*, Ray King and Andrew Nott's excellent detailed account of late twentieth century Manchester politics: 'We were a new phenomenon, and the old stagers didn't know really know where we were coming from or how to handle us.'

Karney was garrulous and breezy and a good foil for Stringer who, raised in inner-city Beswick and educated at the city's Central Grammar School and Sheffield University, had a dour demeanour which stood him in good stead as 'one of us' on the doorstep, in party meetings and with the unions. In 1982 Stringer challenged for the leadership but lost. The civil war that followed saw council leader Norman Morris complain about the left-wingers' tactics to Labour's National Executive Committee, which to Morris's dismay sent left-wing Liverpool MP Eric Heffer to the city to negotiate an uneasy, bad-tempered truce.

Two years later, the left's councillor candidate strategy paid off. Though the city party was still riven, thirty-three-year-old Stringer won the leadership battle on a platform to confront the government with all means at his disposal. The focus of the 1984 caucus he led was not always the traditional socialist objective of improving the lot of ordinary residents in a city plagued by housing and job shortages, crime and ill-health. The new regime was driven instead by ideological instincts. These were the years of idealistic young councillors and radical political gestures: measures like trying to abolish the Lord Mayor role and funding outside meeting rooms for gay and lesbian groups 'oppressed' by the town hall. A row over Manchester Fair stalls with homosexual content led to the departure of renowned horticulturist and parks boss Roy Bee, unenthusiastic about the ruling clique's insistence on gay and lesbian-themed flower beds in Piccadilly Gardens.

Such causes were alien to the mass of Labour voters. The portrait of the Queen was taken down from the Great Hall, the council voted to express solidarity with Irish Republicanism, and controversial Chief Constable James Anderton was challenged by the council's setting up of a police monitoring committee. These moves straight from the student-union playbook were gifts to the *Manchester Evening News*, which teed up a steady stream of 'Loony left' headlines for the disgust of its traditional working-class readership. 'I can't believe we were so out of touch with the Manchester public; it makes me cringe with embarrassment,' recalled Karney.

Council policy may well have become a series of gestures, but the *Manchester Evening News* was hardly the voice of moderation. In the wake of police chief

James Anderton's infamous 1986 speech about AIDS victims 'swirling around in a cesspit of their own making', the paper's editorial 'Speaking his mind' described him as 'a police officer and a deeply religious man' and 'a father and a lover of the human race'. The leader column declared that 'the Chief Constable has a right to his view … that AIDS is a question of morality, being no threat to those who live blameless lives'.

These were days of bitter enmity between the city's daily paper pandering to its readers' prejudices, and the new council hierarchy. Of course, there was a high-level dialogue, though better described as complaints, lobbying and rebuttals. The handwritten note that editor Mike Unger sent me after my *City Life* profile on him in 1987 hinted at the day-to-day attrition: 'I'm told that the city fathers were very pleased with my attitude towards them and that Pat Karney is thinking of framing the bit about them "being caring people about Manchester"'.

The identity politics meant the city was bracketed by national media with Liverpool, Sheffield and the Greater London Council under Ken Livingstone as hotbeds of extremism, another city captured by left-wing radicals. Yet, while all were solidly anti-Thatcher, the cities had nuanced differences in their stances. Liverpool's was outright revolutionary. Led by its controlling Militant faction, it decided on a head-on collision with the Thatcher government and refused to set a budget. The result was calamitous, resulting in personal surcharges and disqualification for 47 councillors.

Manchester's leaders were still intent on confrontation. Stringer's ruling left-wing faction debated tactics into the early hours in the only open post-pub-hours premises, gay hangouts like Manhattan, Napoleon's and New York. They faced down Thatcher with an attempt to refuse to set a budget in 1985, but the move was defeated by combined votes from moderate Labour and Conservative councillors. The next two years saw creative accounting tactics to tap council reserves, using clever ways to present finances to government to win more central grant, supervised by finance council chair Frances Done, a former KPMG accountant. This bought the leadership some time, but, when new rules capping the rates were introduced, it meant the 1988 deficit would be £100 million, even after a planned 20 per cent rate rise.

When the Conservatives won the 1987 election, the game was up for Manchester's young rebels. They had gambled on a Labour victory and lost. Despite their defiant 'no cuts' promise throughout the mid-1980s, the council was faced with either slashing budgets to balance the books or an open and illegal Liverpool-style revolt which would be crushed by brutal legal hardball.

Recalls Sir Richard Leese, then a rising councillor: 'The Labour group in 1987 put a bet on the Labour Party winning the 1987 general election. We lost. In 1987 we were rate capped. We were in the shit.'

Stringer and a key group of councillors changed tack dramatically. Leese authored a position paper outlining a face-the-facts ultimatum. He says: 'The debate was between the welfarist approach – people are poor, so give them more benefits – or the Labourist approach, get people into decent work. There was a clue in the name "Labour Party", we're about people working.' The energised discourse, says Leese, included wheeling business people into the town hall, one being Factory's Tony Wilson, to talk to Labour councillors 'about the world outside of our politics'.

'I wrote,' continues Leese, 'that the biggest issue we face is deprivation, and the biggest single cause was unemployment or low skill value employment, and we needed to tackle the causes of deprivation, not just deal with the symptoms. To do that we needed to create jobs. Given we were being cut to ribbons, it was pretty clear the public sector wasn't going to create jobs, we needed the private sector to do it. That was the thesis. And it won the argument. Jobs, jobs, jobs was our slogan.' A summer of persuasion followed: Stringer spent six weeks in the June and July of 1987 addressing every Labour ward group in the city, 24 trade-union meetings and a packed-out Free Trade Hall with 1,800 council employees. It was a calculated blast of cold hard realism for the city's rank and file. Stringer put his political career on the line, as his resignation was inevitable if his proposed U-turn had not carried the day. So compelling was the case he made that the new policy was carried by a large majority of the city Labour party.

Although the new strategy kept ideological priorities of anti-discrimination and the environment, it accepted that job cuts were inevitable. Manchester was now playing by rules set by the Thatcher government. It was, confirmed Stringer some years later, effectively a capitulation to their loathed political masters in London. A few far-left councillors accused the leadership of 'bottling out', but they were now marginalised voices, dismissed as hopeless romantics.

The upshot of the 1987 Stringer ultimatum was rapid. The leader wrote to environment secretary Nicholas Ridley with a message which was in essence, he said, 'You win, we want to work together with the government'. The new Manchester pragmatists were ready to do business. This process was less a dramatic *volte face* than a gradual transition, as a new realist generation gradually took up critical posts. An early act was to break with fifty years of policy to sell council land, for a new Siemens headquarters on the Princess Parkway which took shape in Didsbury, today still one of the city's most satisfying newer land-mark buildings. There was a councillor revolt against the new policy in the early 1990s, when a caucus in the Labour group put a candidate up against Stringer. 'I think Graham won by 14 votes,' says Leese. 'So it only needed 7 people to change their vote. And this was a fierce debate. But that was pretty much the end of it.'

Manchester's leadership entered a new entrepreneurial period, bringing together the talents of Stringer and Leese with the deputy chief executive Howard Bernstein, a team which was to power the city forwards into new opportunities and undreamed-of collaboration with private business. The main way Manchester could now finance a better future was to compete for cen-tral government funding competitions, European grants and private invest-ment. With the new ground rules clear, the government installed the Central Manchester Development Corporation (CMDC) in 1988 with a £100 million budget and fifty staff to stimulate property development. The urban devel-opment corporation was an intervention model for problem locations, often where the government did not trust the council to deliver. The new agency combined private sector know-how with seconded council staff to make devel-opment happen. Strange when looking back from today's Manchester, but the CMDC's remit was not to populate the city centre through new homes but to breathe life back through commercial property schemes.

With the CMDC chaired by James Grigor, a genial Scotsman with a long career in industry, the government tasked him and chief executive John Glester with levering private investment using government funds. The pair could have been Thatcherite boot boys determined to make life hard for the city council. Yet the CMDC executive were prepared to meet the council half-way – and the key to success was whether the council, unused to being lorded over in planning matters, was prepared to be a genuine partner. The scene was set for two poten-tial outcomes – either a stand-off in which non-cooperation would produce just an urban planning sclerosis or an unlikely partnership between traditionally daggers-drawn parties.

By the late 1980s, all the accompanying talk of regeneration seemed merely aspirational. The daily reality of Manchester city centre mocked the ideas of those who talked of loft living and café culture. Regeneration is hardly a quick process: buildings take days to demolish but years to plan and construct. With city-centre living still a dreamers' gleam in the eye, even the superficially easy part, the leisure sector, was mired in conflict and controversy. Thanks to out-dated licensing laws, the challenges to get outdoor seating and late drinking licences were constant bugbears of the pub and club sector. The ideal of the continental-style, so-called '24-hour city' was a concept which remained just that for many years. Regulations which had been applied in the mid-1960s to curb the centre's seething backstreet scene music, dance clubs, late-night drinking dens and gambling backrooms – much of it swept away by the Arndale Centre – were still rigorously enforced. Tough guy TV actor George Sewell told me of policing's deadening effect on Manchester social life. The 1960s city, he said, 'was great – casinos, nightclubs, the lot … One minute it was like Las Vegas. The next it was like Morecambe.'

In the 1980s this was the same draconian legal framework in which Manchester's pubs and clubs were regulated, though public entertainment licences were under a separate regime. It was a confusing web of legislation, and in the dance-mad Manchester of the early 1990s the interpretation of these laws by councils, police and magistrates was sorely resented.

Between them, the police and magistrates limited the number of venues, applying an unofficial ceiling of 220 licences in the city centre, and new licence applications were rejected on the grounds of need. The urban timetable remained as it had been since the 1960s crackdown – the centre emptied out of commuters at 6pm, pubs shut at 11pm and clubs at 2am, and club owners could be prosecuted if people danced after 2am. The police quota led to a market in existing licences. In the case of Paradise Factory in 1993, owners Carol Ainscow and Peter Dalton, desperate to open in the former Factory Records HQ, paid £10,000 to acquire a licence which would have cost them £12 if no quota had been applied.

The situation was stifling the economy of the city centre. Frustrations came to a head in the early 1990s when the city council called a round table at the Institute of Popular Culture (MIPC) at Manchester Polytechnic (now Manchester Metropolitan University). Phil Bell of Oldham Street jazz club P.J. Bells summed up the frustration: 'Magistrates who live in Wilmslow and Altrincham and who go to bed at 11pm don't understand that there are people who want to live a different lifestyle. They want to go out at 11pm and have a drink in a sociable environment.' Pat Karney, dubbed 'councillor for fun' over his responsibility for the city centre, addressed the room of music-venue owners and club managers: 'The council respects the creativity in this room, and we want to work with you for a better city centre.' Yet national government was still not on the same page. In 1992 Labour's spokesperson for cities, Keith Vaz, stated at a 24 Hour City conference in Sheffield that the UK did not have the weather for outdoor café culture. The MIPC was fond of countering that familiar objection with Norway's lead at the time for the greatest number of open-air café bars in Europe per head of population.

Council strategy was now very much focussed on jobs of any kind. The early 1990s economy was flat, and, with old factory jobs fading away, any jobs, even those in the more unstable leisure economy, were welcome. If the burgeoning night-time scene could provide them, the city's leaders were now ready to help create the right conditions for it. Longer-term strategies were being pursued. Manchester had got the sports event bidding bug as early as 1985, announcing its bid to be the British candidate for the 1992 Olympic Games, which it lost to Birmingham (the Games eventually went to Barcelona).

By 1992, however, Manchester was the official bidder for the 2000 Olympics, and while the national press made hay with the stadium venue's location of Dumplington and the *London Evening Standard* smirked at the idea of the Games among 'the rusting cranes of Mancunia', there was a very firm eye on the benefits of bidding and losing. There was not only the high profile of the bid process but also the gradual securing of grants to build a sporting infrastructure, a key part of the jigsaw which was to bring the right to host the 2002 Commonwealth Games. The perception of the city abroad weighed on the minds of civic leaders. How could a host city be taken seriously as a contender for a global event like sport's five-ring circus if it could not trust people to socialise with alcohol at times that international visitors would expect as normal?

The city council, it emerged as people talked, was as annoyed and tied up in knots as the bar operators. Not only did the police and magistrates interpret the lattice of licensing laws strictly, but jobsworths from the council's own planning, highways and environmental health sections were also guilty of blocking new enterprises. After the first clear-the-air session led by Karney, a 1993 conference brought together councillors, senior officers, police chiefs, magistrates, club owners and opinion-formers. The MIPC's Andy Lovatt recalled: 'The strange thing was that very few of these people had met before and interesting consensus emerged. People did want to make Manchester a more civilised place.' Karney described Manchester as being shackled by legislation in 1992, when outdoor tables were still not permitted. 'Did you know that an Act of 1692 bans dancing in the city on Sunday nights?' he told *City Life*. 'We are fighting the battle with music and dancing. The next stage will be liquor licensing.' He committed the council to reform of the licensing laws well before 2000.

The emerging spirit of co-operation demonstrated that the Puritanism of James Anderton's era was over. The new Chief Constable David Wilmot's thoughtful position was that while the police were bound by the law, 'there is an argument, with some merit, for liberalisation of the licensing laws', and he noted that recent loosening of drinking times in Scotland and England had 'not led to a significant increase in policing problems'.

The new dialogue between the politicians, publicans and club owners brought tangible change. The police agreed to stop objecting to new licences on grounds of need, which opened the floodgates for new bars and restaurants. Entertainment and alcohol licences were de-linked, which encouraged late-night clubbing. The number of licences leapt to 340, and in 1997 the police estimated that the city centre was hosting an average 75,000 visitors a weekend, more than double five years before. In the same year seven thousand people were now living in the city centre, mainly in refurbishments of former redbrick warehouses and mills. The century-old structures built for armies of low-paid Victorian workers doing back-breaking work were now becoming the habitat of residents for rest and recreation.

7

Village people and rock-star developers

Through the late 1980s the idea of urban regeneration was captured for the popular imagination by a television advert. In the 30-second commercial for Halifax Bank's cash card, an actor with boy-band looks wakes up in a handsomely proportioned loft. It boasts all the iconic signifiers: it's next to a railway line and there is a double bed, floor rug and exposed brick walls. Bicycles hang from the ceiling. Yawning, then dressing, he makes his way through empty city streets under the railway viaduct, waves hello at a cheerful newspaper vendor, and using his bank card at a cashpoint, extracts a wad of notes. The advert ends on a shot of the cute guy stroking his cat, reading a newspaper, on his picturesque balcony inside the appealingly dilapidated viaduct. All set to The Commodores' 'Easy (Like a Sunday Morning)'.

The advert's influence on the imaginations of the nation's twenty- and thirtysomethings went beyond the product being promoted. It crystallised the dream for those under the spell of European-style city living. The Halifax ad made the yearning for an urban lifestyle now part of the national consciousness. Even though everything about it screamed 'London' (where it was filmed), its look became embedded as the way urban regeneration should be, and ignited the idea that any town with empty railway arches could blossom. Indeed, who wouldn't want a dead cool yet homely loft, with all facilities nearby, and the cash spitting out of the walls? Easy like a Sunday morning, indeed.

The truth was that railway arches were more suitable for small business users. Empty old buildings littered the UK's towns and cities, and there was much media talk of loft living in the style of the Big Apple. Tony Wilson knew New York City, and for him Manchester's redundant redbrick monsters didn't offer the same dirt-cheap, massive living spaces. 'New York lofts are huge, freezing and cost next to nothing to rent,' Wilson told me. 'There's nothing like that in Manchester.' Years later, though, he tried it doing it the New York way in the 3,000 sq ft top floor of a former warehouse on Little Peter Street behind Deansgate Station, buying the shell for £80,000 and getting Haçienda designer Ben Kelly to fit it out at a cost of £230,000.

However ruined Manchester city centre was, the scuzzy, cheap property for a NYC-style loft culture wasn't available. As autobiographies of the city's artists from Patti Smith to Talking Heads' Chris Frantz describe, living for buttons in the Big Apple allowed space for musicians and artists of all kinds to create great work and form creative communities. As has been proved all over the world, low property values produce conditions in which artistic people survive and thrive, and in which creative ideas flourish.

The scruffy Gothic grandeur of the 1980s low-rent city centre, combined with the allure of the Factory aesthetic, made for a fertile, if often furtive, creative atmosphere, in Paul Morley's words, 'stunted streets … loaded with surface tension and hidden networks'.

In 1985 Factory produced *Feverhouse*, Howard Walmsley's monochrome movie short, an unsettling Mancunian sibling to David Lynch's *Eraserhead*. In 1988 The Fall and Michael Clark staged punk ballet I *Am Kurious Oranj*: 'cross cultural terrorism' said critic Dave Simpson. A regular visitor to Hulme's Aaben cinema was future movie director and Olympic Games opening ceremony producer Danny Boyle, down from Bury for his education in independent film. Dave Haslam published cerebral fanzine *Debris*, Paula Greenwood's Playtime record label talent-spotted indie bands and Carol Morley tore through town in a traumatised hedonism she laid bare in her film *The Alcohol Years*. In the drizzly whirlpool of easy camaraderie, draughty pubs and cheap drugs, writers Glenn Patterson, David Peace, Jeff Noon, Nick Blincoe and embryonic poet laureate Simon Armitage composed their early drafts, and Joanne Rowling used her Manchester 'year of misery' in 1990 to dream up her world of wizard children in the city's greasy-spoon caffs.

In contrast to all the cultural energy, barely anyone lived in the centre. In mid-1980s Manchester, however, in the hollowed-out textile merchant neighbourhood, there was one resourceful guy who had enough space, know-how and devotion to the bare-brick aesthetic. To live in the city centre officially would require all manner of paperwork and permissions, but if you were tradesman-handy, you could live informally, if not quite off-grid, under the noses of the town hall officials only a few hundred yards away.

Dave Wilson of Axiom Lighting lived above his premises in what was Manchester's only authentic loft. Using his professional expertise, the Londoner rigged up a power supply so he could furnish and operate his bedroom, kitchen and other domestic needs across the entire top floor of the five-floor Victorian warehouse at 59–91 Faulkner Street in Chinatown. With his neon company logo above the door, he ran his design and manufacturing business by day and partied by night. 'Do they know you actually live here?' I asked him at one of his late-night get-togethers. He grinned as he shook his head and then shot me a serious look as if to say, 'Don't tell anybody!'

This part of Manchester, with its unbroken sequences of fine Victorian warehouses taking in Chinatown and Princess Street, resembles Manhattan's garment district. Evocative terracotta features on the front elevations, a grittier look with fire escapes to the back, these film noir settings from Albert Square up to the emerging Gay Village were deserted after dark in the 1980s. Manchester's Gotham neighbourhood was just begging to be regenerated. The time for city centres was coming. There was a momentum as people began to imagine what a revitalised city centre could be.

Progress was painfully slow. Close to Piccadilly rail station, the first privately developed conversion in the mid-1980s was the 1908 Granby House, the first of the city's classic building stock to become apartments. The first building earmarked for government cash by the Central Manchester Development Corporation was 42–44 Sackville Street. Beatrix Campbell in *The Guardian* quoted a city insider recalling that the CMDC 'came riding into town with saddlebags bulging with money … we could access money for stuff we wanted to do'.

The CMDC bought 42–44 Sackville Street for £1 million in 1991. The solid, imposing Grade II listed building went up in 1870 hard by the Rochdale Canal, enabling its merchant occupiers to load textiles from barges right into the four-storey goods warehouse. The city in its pomp was a global draw for the ambitious and entrepreneurial. A list of the building's original occupiers reads like a Premier League football team: Berger, Greatorex, Nordlinger, Pinto-Leite, Meyerhof and Nathorff. Over a century later, with King Cotton dethroned, the 1980s tenants were tiny operations drawn to cheap rents in divided-up spaces for small creative businesses: photographers, designers and music promoters.

The graphic design trio Central Station Design's studio was inside. Matt and Pat Carroll (cousins to Happy Mondays' Shaun and Paul Ryder), and Pat's wife Karen Jackson, were free-thinking artistic talents. They went on to design the band's sleeves and make art exhibited in galleries worldwide. Their vivid colours and outlandish painterly graphics graced the Mondays' records and T-shirts, including the 'Stone Age alphabet' on the cover of *Wrote for Luck*, a new loose typeface for the young baggy generation. Their creative process could be described as 'very Happy Mondays'. They would arrive at the studio, have a drink, sometimes something stronger, turn the music up loud, and do their work. Usually at night. So, a visit to them in my *City Life* days to collect artwork was always an experience. While waiting for them to open the locked heavy front door, I could observe the solid black form of the old building loom up, the moon reflecting off the canal. It was always eerily quiet, and odd to consider that this dark and silent vista was in the very heart of the city.

42–44 Sackville Street was the first big public-money purchase by CMDC. Its impressive floor-to-ceiling heights, robust brick and sandstone structure and the waterside location were not the only features which made it right for the city's first loft development – across the water ran Canal Street, the main thoroughfare of the Gay Village, which was transitioning from its seedy 1970s manifestation. The use of 'Gay Village' had grown steadily and informally in the 1980s. Manchester's gay and lesbian community had grown significantly during the decade, thanks to the left-wing policies of the city council, which took its progressive policy cues from the Greater London Council. Manchester council promoting itself vigorously as an equal opportunity employer meant that many able civil servants were tempted to leave the employ of councils in towns where they felt uneasy about being 'out'.

There was a furtive, behind-closed-doors aspect to the old Canal Street, when the waterside was home to a string of bars including the city's short-lived Playboy club, where men were men and women were bunnies. All that was blown away when Manto opened in 1990 in Unity House. Owners Carol Ainscow and Peter Dalton raised the roof of the late nineteenth-century working people's reading room, added a large balcony and let the world see the party through the full-height glass frontage. 'I felt sick of having to knock on doors and hide,' said Ainscow. Other bars of all kinds followed, and Canal Street was soon being described as one of the world's top gay locations. The value of the pink pound was being acknowledged, if not actively embraced, by the new political leaders, seen when Manto was the first city venue permitted to put out street chairs and tables in a council-supported challenge to archaic licensing rules.

One evening at Manchester Town Hall a few years later brought home how gay culture was embedded at the heart of the city council. In my role as PR agent, I arranged for Haçienda DJ and musician Mike Pickering's group M People to perform at the city's annual Christmas lights switch-on in 2000. A staple of many civic squares across the land, in Manchester the event was an annual showpiece with a line-up of glossy acts. It pulled in huge crowds of families from the estates and suburbs for a free teatime party in Albert Square, after which the surrounding pubs and eateries would be heaving.

The stage was on the town hall steps and after M People had topped the bill and sent the crowd of happy kids home singing 'Search for the Hero', I accompanied the band to a reception in the lord mayor's parlour. My role was to introduce them to the city's top people. Pickering and the group's soul diva frontwoman Heather Small moved down the line-up shaking hands and making pleasantries. We started with the mayor and his consort in full civic chains and regalia, followed by the chief executive and the council leader. But the M People halted at the next VIP, an extravagant drag queen with a full Carmen Miranda-style headpiece. The most important dignitary after the city's top brass gushed adoringly over Heather Small. Taking it all in her stride, she rolled her eyes in hilarity and drawled. 'Only in Manchester, Mike!'

The council leadership had got wise to associating their aspirations for the city with its pop exports. In March 1996 I reported for the *Evening News* on a glitzy occasion as Manchester Town Hall's main hall reverberated to a late-night disco after a civic award for Take That (minus just-departed Robbie Williams). Surrounded by the twelve Ford Madox Brown murals depicting the city's history, leader Graham Stringer spoke in their honour and handed out framed certificates. Lord Mayor Joyce Keller said: 'The council does not under-estimate the work of pop artists. They do a great job for the city.'

The chart-topping boy band had exported a different side of Manchester to the world than that of the *avant-garde* Factory output, or the rowdy late 1980s Madchester scene. Here was a likeable, good-humoured, high-tempo pop package for girls of all ages to enjoy, not to mention their gay following. In many ways, the Take That phenomenon was an echo of the city's 1960s pop groups. There had been no civic recognition in their home city for Freddie and the Dreamers, Wayne Fontana and the Mindbenders or Herman's Hermits after their remarkable feat in spring 1965 when the trio of Manchester combos held the top three positions in the US Billboard 100. The groups were written out of the 'British Invasion' narrative, dominated by how the Mersey Sound's Scouse accents conquered America.

This city leadership were not going to miss the opportunity their political forebears had passed up. Besides, Take That was managed by Nigel Martin-Smith – a model agency boss and nightclub owner whose businesses were based in the expanding Gay Village. Property developers are well tuned in to the ripple of rising values visible around a genuine lifestyle scene, particularly one not manufactured by official or corporate forces.

The neighbourhood was heating up. Enter Harry Handelsman and the Manhattan Loft Corporation. The smooth German property developer was behind loft-living schemes in run-down parts of London which had captured the zeitgeist, their buyers striving for that Halifax TV ad aesthetic. The suits at the CMDC liked his style, and his business model, which was to strip the interiors back and sell the shells to occupiers up for the bespoke fit-out challenge. A puff piece in *The Independent* property pages ran: 'In Manchester … the idea of smart urban living is only just starting to gain hold … Moss Side could find itself twinned with Greenwich Village, rather than the Bronx.'

Tasteful brochures were handed out along with the canapés at the smart launch, and Handelsman proudly declared that these were to be the city's first New York-style apartments. But he got cold feet about the viability of its model in Manchester, something which did not help the local property market. The word went out that the city was not yet ready to embrace New York or London loft living, but locals complained that London prices were being asked by developers who didn't understand Manchester.

The time-limited CMDC shut up shop in 1996, having spent £90 million of public money which attracted £430 million investment. One of its final acts was to pay £75,000 towards glazed coloured bricks on the exterior of the Haçienda, a recognition that the government-installed corporation had drunk the Kool Aid – youth culture was now being officially seen as part of the real economy. 'We are planning for the millennium,' said manager Paul Mason, who had brought a professional business approach to the troubled madhouse. His job interview in 1986 let him know what he was in for, when he had to help Alan Erasmus separate his fellow club owners Gretton and Wilson from brawling on the floor. 'I thought the whole thing was so bizarre,' recalled the real-ale-loving manager from Nottingham. 'I just had to take the job.' Despite Mason's diligence and the stylish new facia, the Haçienda was stumbling towards closure. Its last manager Jon Drape (who went on to promote Festival No. 6 among other live music events), called me at the Diary to help promote the sale of replaced pieces of the dancefloor, a sad bid for cash and a precursor for its eventual dismantling and charity auction some years later.

Its frontman Tony Wilson and CMCD chief Grigor had become something of a double act at city centre receptions, the avuncular older man and a giggly Wilson chinwagging each other over complimentary drinks. At his organisation's closedown, Grigor asked in a newspaper column, 'Who will take up the baton of regeneration?' Not Handelsman, who walked away from the Sackville Street scheme. The gauntlet was picked up by the woman behind

Manto's success. Carol Ainscow had started out in property by buying, refurbishing and renting out big old houses in her hometown, Bolton. She was an out gay woman emerging as a player in the braying, boastful male world of property, and The City – the increasingly common term for the emerging Bernstein–Leese power axis – liked what they saw. Her Artisan Holdings took on the Sackville Street building that scared Handelsman off and started to sell the completed lofts in 1996. An avid hockey player who cited Glaswegian Alex Ferguson as a personal hero, she was renowned as a tenacious negotiator, in 1993 buying Factory's Princess Street offices for a bargain £340,000 from the receivers carving up the crashed record label. Ainscow and partner Peter Dalton turned it into the three-floor disco Paradise Factory, which extended the Gay Village towards Oxford Road.

Shockingly, Ainscow died in 2013 at the age of fifty-five, suffering a brutally rapid decline after a sudden brain tumour. Her remarkable career – in 2007 the *Sunday Times* Rich List named her the eightieth richest woman in the country – ensured her legacy in the Gay Village and in landmarks including the former Express newspapers printworks on Great Ancoats Street – the 1930 classic building in glass and black Vitrolite panelling which became her company HQ, part of a development of 70 homes, 140,000 sq ft of offices and the Crown and Kettle pub.

Friends gathered at her funeral and remarked that she felt it was important to be respected more than liked, and that people loved her for that anyway. Ainscow's company was Artisan Holdings, and the priest at her family's Catholic church paid tribute to the hard graft she had displayed 'in building up her property business, Urban Splash'. His slip says it all about the power of a memorable brand. Urban Splash, under Ainscow's friendly rivals Tom Bloxham and Jonathan Falkingham, had become the archetypal city-centre regeneration developer. Bloxham was and remains the rock-star urban developer of the last thirty years. There are wealthier and bigger development companies, and more brash or controversial ones, but Urban Splash set the style for the city-centre revival many others tried to copy.

Bloxham's business origins lie firmly in the Manchester music scene. Born in Hampshire, he came to study at Manchester University in 1983 and was soon selling posters in the student union's markets. Realising that most of the available posters were old hippy images, he started selling Manchester music album covers. The Smiths and New Order did better sales than the Athena tennis girl scratching her bum. As his business grew, he took a stand in the city centre's 'alternative emporium' Affleck's Palace on Oldham Street.

By renting out two floors, he learned about letting space to other businesses, and a property entrepreneur was born. He became entranced by the possibilities of Smithfield Buildings, an entire city block further up Oldham Street, and its potential for characterful apartments. Bloxham moved swiftly when the opportunity came, with the entrepreneur's killer feel for change in the air, despite all appearances: 'When we bought the Smithfield Building the main tenant was bust,' he said. 'The owners were bust and the mortgage bank in possession was bust – and that was the time for gut feeling and decisive action.'

In his 1999 landmark Urban Task Force report *Towards an Urban Renaissance*, Lord Richard Rogers praised Urban Splash for pioneering urban living in the Northwest, describing Smithfield Buildings as 'a catalyst for entrepreneurial and creative activity, attracting people to live in the area and locate new business'. Lord Rogers called for a more European city-centre style of living and generated a new wave of thinking. He advocated homes on brownfield land and for regeneration led by design excellence, which led to the setting up of the Commission for the Built Environment. A policy turnaround in the way government viewed cities was under way. Regeneration projects began to receive generous public funding, and private lenders got the message. Once-untouchable urban neighbourhoods began to be seen as the future of the nation, and the word 'urban' was not inevitably followed by 'blight', 'decay' or 'jungle'.

Emboldened by Lord Rogers's words, Bloxham invited him to chair an architecture competition for his new Timber Wharf development on the western edge of the city centre, planting the flag of regeneration where conventional developers feared to tread. Urban Splash became a byword for place making, encouraging public activity and new uses in written-off places, and carving out new identities for so-called failed neighbourhoods. Traditional developers carped that he was expert at exploiting public grants, but the jealously could not stymie Bloxham's rise.

Quite apart from the music-poster business which led to and bankrolled Bloxham's early property interests, there was another strong relationship between the rock star developer and the rise of city-centre living – Bloxham's own love of the club scene. He became Manchester property's carouser-in-residence. And, with his rackety entourage in tow, he was a generous setter up of tabs in the Haçienda cocktail bar and the other nightspots along Whitworth Street like the Venue and the Brickhouse.

One night on the town he stumbled across one of his earliest developments, a former paper factory tucked into a side street near Oxford Road, which he turned into open-plan apartments in 1994. 'We were rolling out of the Haçienda when we found Sally's Yard,' said Bloxham. 'In the beginning there was no plan; when we saw an opportunity we went for it.' He credited the music culture with priming his own motivation: 'I'd often walk around, perplexed at how quickly it became a ghost town each night. There were pockets of vibrant cultural scenes starting to emerge; my good friend Tony Wilson's infamous assault on the music scene and the renowned Haçienda nightclub started a cultural appreciation that permeated everyday life … when we first established Urban Splash in 1993 we hoped we could bring the physical architecture to match a new cultural scene.' The friendship was on display at an extraordinary fortieth birthday bash at Manchester Town Hall, where Wilson compèred a 'This Is Your Life' celebration, inviting guests to bask in the glory of Bloxham's life and works to date.

Urban Splash was to end up owning Sankey's Soap, an uber-cool nightclub which in 1994 stuck its neck out by setting up DJ decks in Beehive Mill, an Ancoats cotton mill dating back to 1820. These days the neighbourhood is the hipster epicentre of the city, but, in the 1990s, clubbers were taking their lives in their hands just walking the five minutes from Piccadilly. Now workspace, as a club it had a stop-start existence, but Sankey's opened the eyes of the property market to Ancoats benefiting from pioneering public realm work by council urbanist Lyn Fenton, artist Dan Dubowitz and others in the early 2000s.

As his company took flight, so did Bloxham's personal ambition, and he emerged as the predominant developer-influencer in the new Manchester, exploiting the interrelationship between the physical regeneration and daring, often elite culture. The energetic charisma that Bloxham and architect partner Falkingham displayed in creating over £1 billion worth of developments could not alone have carried Urban Splash through recessions and challenges that traditional house builders run shy of. Rather, they rejected conventional thinking and cookie-cutter design, educating themselves with every old building and tricky urban site, hiring the best available people and proudly declaring they were selling 'homes, not units'.

The media love Bloxham for his urban transformations and the jaw-dropping before-and-after photos. The *Financial Times* described Urban Splash as 'the housing market equivalent of a designer fashion label'. A journalist rarely leaves an interview without reporting the Bloxham oath, the same one sworn by the ancient Athenians: 'We shall leave this city not less, but greater, better and more beautiful than it was left to us.' The regeneration of my adopted city was, I believed, a noble and righteous cause. In 1999, having left journalism to set up a PR agency, I was chuffed to win a pitch to represent Urban Splash and promote their plans for the Cardroom estate. The failed housing scheme on the very edge of the city centre had been depopulated, and there were not even enough people to keep the local pub going. The government body English Partnerships awarded the Millennium Community site to Urban Splash solely on the basis of its previous work. Bloxham hired the colourful architect Will Alsop to develop the new vision, which evolved after long and deep consultation with the remaining locals, who were offered new homes in the street they had lived in. Alsop, a *bon vivant* with a hairy biker look, would knock on locals' doors with the introduction: 'Hello, I am the architect and I have come to knock down your house.'

These days named New Islington, twenty years on, the neighbourhood now has a small park, a marina with residential moorings, a health centre and a primary-age Free School sponsored by Urban Splash. Other developers have piled in on the back of the Urban Splash schemes. The area now features the work of numerous architects in a mix of styles, including quirky low-rise canal-side homes with oversized Dutch gables by the FAT practice. But it is some sliced fried potatoes, that Northern icon, which take the eye. From the fertile avant-garde mind of Alsop, who would draw his schemes with a thick black pen in one hand and glass of red wine in the other, the exuberant Chips building has 142 apartments, stacked in nine storeys but arranged in a layer of three wonky, 100 m long rectangles – the fat 'chips' of the building's name.

Echoing the ethos of the Factory and Haçienda conspirators, Alsop told Lynn Barber of *The Observer*, 'Architects are the only profession that actually deal in joy and delight – all the others deal in doom and gloom. Yet it's surprising how many architects dress as though they're accountants, and behave like accountants.' This unique building must be the closest realisation in post-Haçienda Manchester of the architectural wit and wonderment proclaimed in the radical Situationist manifesto which dazzled the club's founders. Chips even has that most arresting and rarely seen visual feature – writing on its walls, featuring outsize names of local waterways in a serif typeface.

By his own admission Alsop was not good with finances, and what clients or funders saw as the impracticality of his wavy-line visions meant very few of his Burgundy-enhanced sketches were made real. His book *Supercity* in 2004 was thought daft by mainstream commentators for its idea that the Northern cities could function better as one mega-conurbation – a concept which enjoyed greater success under George Osborne when he took its basic notion and branded it the Northern Powerhouse.

The lead for Urban Splash on the New Islington development was Bloxham's lieutenant Nick Johnson. *The Sunday Times* architecture correspondent Hugh

Pearman recalls Johnson's impact in 1990s design circles, with his professorial specs, Paul Weller-styled hair and immaculately tailored threads by his wife Jenny Thompson. The trained surveyor from Bolton had taught building design at Yale, and he hit UK regeneration circles like a blast of Northern cool, leading in 2007 to a key role with the quango the Commission for Architecture and the Built Environment. Johnson became a major influence in the city, not just for his trenchant views on good and bad building design but also for his Atlas bar at the western end of Deansgate. From 1994, the triangular redbrick drinkerie (co-owned with Thompson and architects Ian Simpson and Rachel Haugh) – a former car repair shop now all reclaimed floorboards and plywood-clad arches – was the hotbed of the hip design resistance, standing outside Deansgate rail station like a proud indie puffing its chest out against creeping big business. In the late 1990s its husband-and-wife managers led a charge against corporates muscling in on the city, forming the Manchester Independents group to champion young businesses and lobbying the council to resist the design blandness of big leisure plcs and listed companies.

National chain Whitbread had opened no fewer than four bars in the Gay Village after the success of Manto, and Johnson told *The Guardian* in 2000, 'The city took on the challenge to raise the quality of the built environment partly because we independents wouldn't stop banging on about it…. we want to allow independent operators to flourish and add a richness and dimension that we desperately need.' Thompson added, 'they [big chains] just want to make the money and get out. Unfortunately, they've frightened away a lot of the creative people that used to come to town. There is no heart and soul in Manchester any more.'

The city was starting to listen to the city's design-educated bright sparks as the new millennium turned. Martin Wainwright in *The Guardian* acutely caught the nuance that "the independents' movement is not gunning for the corporates, only against their dominance'. Johnson told him that the city centre was looking better 'not by belligerence but by clever negotiation' and that outside investment was essential to civic success. Manchester was increasingly a city that big business could do business with. That was brought home with emphasis when the outspoken Johnson and his co-owners sold Atlas, the city's spiritual indie flagship, to listed pubco Punch Taverns (though today it is back in independent hands). Without Johnson's contacts, drive and intellectual arrogance, and with Atlas no longer the base of the anti-corporate lobby, the Manchester Independents lost their moral force and soon faded away.

8

Haçienda hitman

On the night of 18 January 1989, TV presenter and pop culture impresario Tony Wilson approached the hulking redbrick Haçienda nightclub on the outskirts of town. At 9.30pm on a Wednesday just after new year, the scruffy end of Manchester city centre should have been quiet, but tonight Whitworth Street West was in uproar.

I was already there, notebook in hand, outside the venue jointly owned by his Factory record label and its globally successful band New Order. My job was to cover the event for the next day's *Manchester Evening News*. There was a big and noisy crowd milling around in the street instead of inside the club. I watched as Wilson, a man with 'Entrepreneur' in his passport, but far more suited to the intellectualising of pop culture and media soundbites than running a business, found his usual way blocked by the hundreds gathered outside the double-door entrance. Normally, security men would push open the doors for him and he would jauntily wave to the staff behind the ticket-office window who sat under a large-format photo of him in black tie, Wilson's outsize visage smirking at clubgoers as they stepped up to hand over their cash.

The portrait was an ironic parody of the cult of personality, but it fuelled the public perception of a local boy who got a Cambridge education, returned to his roots and now, through his TV celebrity status and his cultural and business interests, had become a kind of rock and roll lord mayor who proclaimed that his hometown was the most important city on the planet. A relentless booster of everything Manchester, Wilson was both egotist and joker, all the while happily accepting that the joke was on him.

Like all arrivals, Wilson would usually be greeted by a chilly draught down the neck and a semi-audible sound system pumping out low-frequency bass rhythms, the sound muffled due to a sound-baffler curtain of opaque vertical plastic strips. It was if you had stumbled into an unauthorised staff party at an

113

industrial cold storage unit. All this was a tease of design genius. As they pushed through the curtain, clubbers would face a 'wait for it' moment in what Wilson called interior architect Ben Kelly's 'narrative of space'. Only once they stepped through a grey, sharp-angled portal could they fully take in the post-industrial cathedral-like space, the Gothic silhouettes of strobe-lit dancers swimming among the chunky girders and lighting gantries high up in the rooflight.

To enter on one of the wild nights of the Haçienda was to be hit by an immersive shockwave of music, lights and the body heat of 1,200 clubbers – on the raised dancefloor, on podiums, on the stage and in the seating areas, and on the high balcony above, a pulsating, multi-head-bobbing, arm-waving life-form moving to the beats of the new electronic sounds coming out of Detroit, Chicago and New York.

In the daytime, the only sign of any presence was an exquisitely discreet nine-inch-long marble plaque engraved with 'Haçienda – FAC 51'. At weekend nights, this was the busiest corner in town and Wilson had made his entrance hundreds of times since the club opened in May 1982. Tonight, though, he couldn't get near the double doors. They were shut and his way was barred by the crowd. The security team in black bomber jackets waited for talkback on their earpieces. Wilson stood back from the throng and declaimed some words into the wind along the lines of 'If you let me in, then we can open the doors', but no one gave way.

Haçienda dancefloor (photo: Peter J. Walsh)

Tonight's chaos was because TV cameras had come to the Haçienda. ITV network show *The Hitman and Her* filmed in nightclubs and then broadcast the results at 1am and again at 4am, its viewers just home from a night out and wanting to carry on the party. Almost by accident, Granada TV had created a cult post-pub show attracting a national audience of youngsters gawping at their contemporaries out on the town. When the Haçienda date was announced, *The Hitman and Her* had raised eyebrows among the city's scenesters, the DJs and designers, musicians and journalists. The show was derided by the Haçienda faithful, the in-crowd who picked up on the new dance music emerging from the nightclubs of the US and Spanish party islands. Its schtick was to rock up to the sticky-carpet discos like The Ritzy in Leeds and Mr Smith's in Warrington, the kind of musically unadventurous nightspots attracting hick locals desperately seeking excitement.

It teamed the incongruous pair of bouncy, pig-tailed sidekick Michaela Strachan with besuited pop producer Pete Waterman, a man whose deep love for and knowledge of black dance music went back to 1960s Northern Soul clubs. He knew what made kids dance, and, as a songwriter and studio producer with the Stock Aitken and Waterman hit machine, his chart success with Kylie Minogue, Jason Donovan and Rick Astley had inevitably earned him the tabloid nickname of 'the Hitman'. Their arrival on Whitworth Street West captured the moment that the new music jumped the species barrier, as a generation of club-goers tuned in to witness a whole new scene changing the happening city of Manchester: new sounds, and new ways of dancing, dressing and behaving.

The TV show heralded a new youth attitude which has been alternately labelled as a movement of apolitical, braindead hedonism or identified as a radical anti-establishment protest against the social order, in which artists like Jeremy Deller believe that the fight for the 'right to party' – and the 'Rave' itself – was a radical political act against an authoritarian government. That debate was yet to come. The night the high-street crowd crashed the Haçienda was a sliding-doors moment for popular culture, the moment when the club's bosses, a colourful bunch of dreamers, druggies, misfits and intellectuals, were forced to realise that their lab experiment in pop culture had created something becoming impossible to control. Brought together that night by the magnetic attraction of television cameras and a new music trend were a range of audiences and interests: the influx of young people from across the Northwest hot for the new music; media TV and record business executives scenting new audiences and income; and, undercutting the party vibe, the growing presence of opportunistic gangsters also seeking new and lucrative markets. Many clamouring to get in just wanted to see themselves on television, but the cameras had also lured out brazen, hardened criminal elements into Wilson's pop culture playpen.

Pacing up and down and eyeing the crowd outside, the famous owner could see evidence of the club's changing clientele. At this time, the Haçienda was more an edgy bohemia for urban hipsters, but tonight's crowd were not in-the-know club-goers, clued up to the dress codes and slang of the emerging scene. Instead, the TV had attracted a racially mixed crowd of streetwise teens and twenty-somethings. Wilson, like everyone else on the city's music scene, could see the change happening during 1988 as the council-estate kids who shunned his venue, known as an indie rock hangout, were increasingly drawn there. Tonight, the TV filming was the talk of the town, and the crowd contained ticketless troublemakers known to door staff, who badly wanted in. With no physical way to stop them, the security team had shut the doors and called the police.

The night has never figured highly in the histories of the pop culture which swept all before it in the late 1980s. In the oceans of words written about the Haçienda, it's become an intentionally forgotten event. Music aficionados recall it with embarrassment, such as DJ Jon da Silva's tweeted reply when fellow DJ Dave Haslam posted some YouTube clips from the night, 'Oh gawd … this is hardly footage one wants to be reminded of …' Jacques Peretti in *The Guardian* did make the night one of the Top 50 key events in the history of dance music in 2001, pointing out that, between the programme being commissioned and filmed, the rave music phenomenon happened. The programme was such an anomaly, he noted, 'Because in the days before reality TV, it was one of the few places in the schedules where you could see real people doing real things – looking bored, getting drunk and trying to get off with each other'.

In early 1989 the kaleidoscope of pop culture was twisting and turning, creating a new soundscape and fresh collaborations. In 808 State, you can hear the sound of a city's borders melting as north Manchester duo The Spinmasters and Bolton's mouthy Martin Price teamed up with south Manchester experimentalist Graham Massey of fiercely avant-garde Biting Tongues. 808 State's spacy 'Pacific State' was a crossover pop chart smash, following the combo's founder Gerald Simpson's seminal 'Voodoo Ray' sounding like the spectre in the system-built housing block, and the absolute Detroit-meets-Moss Side moment in 1988 when the underground dance culture took off.

Not only was drum-machine-led music becoming cheaper and easier to make with little or no tuition or experience, but new sampling software which translated analogue sounds into digital information made it easy to lift rhythms, riffs, vocals and all manner of sonic content to create new music. This broad new dance music genre was given the interchangeable terms House music (after Chicago's Warehouse club), Acid House, Acid or Rave music. There was another critical element, and it was pharmaceutical. During 1988, a small scene had been bubbling underground, mainly in Manchester and London, propelled by the emerging music and ecstasy, the illegal new drug whose effects were perfectly suited to enhancing enjoyment of the new sounds.

When *The Hitman and Her* came to town, in early 1989, what most people think they know about the Haçienda had not happened yet. The club was not yet a global byword for the Madchester youthquake. Financially, it was getting back on an even keel after several years of heavy losses. These were regularly made up from 'benefit' gigs by New Order, the band which had become – through gritted teeth – a cash cow for the club and its parent music label Factory Records.

From 1989, after the TV show aired what was still an underground culture, an entire generation grew their hair out, necked new pills, and wanted to know where to get the stuff which made those kids on the TV dance, in that abandoned, mad-eyed way, for hours on end. *New Musical Express*'s Danny Kelly wrote, in a phrase journalists would think twice about now, that 'ecstasy made white men dance', a statement at the time no one found fault with. They could see what was happening in clubs, parties and illegal raves all over the land, and it was felt to be a straight-ahead description of an unmistakable phenomenon.

The Haçienda's promotional leaflet illustrated the subcultural gulf between the venue and the programme, knowingly titling the event '*The Hitman and Her* Experiences the Haçienda'. YouTube clips show Strachan interviewing a young man who blurts, 'This is what real club music is all about. No one at the Haçienda wears striped shirts from Top Man.' Waterman plays up the mismatch, putting on an exaggerated madcap demeanour, as if to say 'Wow, it's all mad here!' As they gawped at the new clothes and dancing, many viewers witnessed a youth culture in transition. While many of the girls still have frizzed-up hair and look closer to 1987 than what we think of as 1989, in the boys we can see the way clothes would be worn for years afterwards – a bright, baggy and loose fit all round, with sightings of dungarees, ponytails in buns, and, in the defining statement for the new look, the shirt untucked and worn outside the trousers. Shaggy the beatnik from the cartoon Scooby Doo was the new fashion template.

Haçienda leaflet for *The Hitman and Her*, 18 January 1989

The new dance was all about the arms. Feet were firmly planted on the floor and the movement was in the upper body. As academic Steve Redhead noted, the 'trance dance' upended the whole idea of the dance in previous pop music history. For a start, the dancing was everywhere; the dancefloor burst its boundaries and spilled over on to chairs, tables, in the dark corners under the balcony initially designed for intimate conversations, and on to a Haçienda stage originally built for professional performers. The moves, which needed no expertise whatsoever, were asexual and negated the male gaze, says Redhead: 'Instead of, as usual, the female body being subjected to the ever-present look, the dancers … turned in on themselves, imploding the meanings associated with exhibitionist dance.' Happy Mondays' frontman Shaun Ryder and his mad-eyed dancer partner Bez moved like manic flowerpot men on the Haçienda stage, teaching a new generation a new dance. The show's producers had for once dropped the usual professional dancers, realising this was the wrong place for its dance troupe with its 'proper' disco dancing.

Most on 'the scene' were giving tonight the swerve. The Haçienda faithful believed that, if the chain-store-clothed hicks were coming to town, the programme was bound to be a cringing embarrassment, and something not to be seen on when broadcast. How had the night come about? I had asked around, and it seemed that Waterman had called Wilson with his customary puppyish enthusiasm with the request and Wilson, employing one of his favourite adjectives, thought the idea was 'wonderful'. From the available footage, it seems that Wilson did not appear in the broadcast edit. Perhaps he had picked up on the cool crowd's disdain for the tragically low hip value of the show. Club DJ Mike Pickering, whose Nude Night every Friday played hard House US imports to local, racially mixed, non-student crowds, appears briefly; mildly embarrassed, his brief interview ends abruptly as he escapes to the DJ booth.

Pickering's tracks had evolved from the Electro genre of the mid-1980s, also championed by local DJ Greg Wilson, who had seen clubbers coming from what he called 'the Factory side of town' to his nights at Legend. These DJs' 12-inch records featured tough, militant beats and basslines embellished with a range of sonic toppings – electronic beeps, bloops and, later, playfully wobbly basslines. By 1989, these styles were merging with more summery and soulful 'Balearic' styles. Around 10pm on the TV show's night in Manchester, however, filming had not yet started, and the production was behind schedule. Hundreds of would-be revellers still crowded the entrance, on the wide pavement at the traffic-light junction on the edge of the city centre. Several police vans parked on one corner, with officers sat inside, though several were on the street scanning the crowd.

The pair of senior officers in command seemed relieved when they saw Wilson arrive. As he strode up and down outside the entrance area unable to penetrate the crowd, a Coventry accent cried out, 'What's going on then, Tony?' Not a frustrated clubber this time, but the floppy-haired Waterman bouncing up and down with the buzzy chaos of the situation. 'Hi Pete, hello, hello, don't worry, we'll sort it out, we'll sort it out,' declared Wilson loudly, so as many could hear as possible.

The police officers turned to the pair, both now joined by various TV and club colleagues, all looking to the local hero to resolve the matter. Among the vehicles on the street was a TV production van, cables running along the pavement and into a side door. Their screens monitored the interior and Wilson used the opportunity to view inside. He emerged soon after and conferred with the police officers, who indicated they were happy to let the situation play out, as long as he could deal with it without further incident. The crowd was becoming impatient, with occasional female screeches and shouts of 'Sort it out, Wilson!' carrying across the throng.

As he scanned the milling crowd and talked with the TV crew and police, he noticed me. 'This is your fault!'" he shouted across at me. Police officers, Waterman, TV assistants, Haçienda bouncers, all turned to see whom he had aimed this at.

I gestured quizzically, as if to say: 'Really?'

'You put it in the *Manchester Evening News*!'

I shouted back, 'You put leaflets out, so it's hardly a secret gig is it? I just reported it was happening.'

There was something a bit pantomime about our exchange. It benefited both of us. It put him in the role of responsible nightlife proprietor berating a member of the irresponsible print media. And I, playing the role of plucky newspaperman bringing the steaming hot news to the masses, could take pride that my professional duty had been done – a little proud, also, that the *Manchester Evening News*, whose declining circulation was put down to being an older reader's paper, could occasionally get the youth out.

My overnight report the next day ran at the top of the page, headlined: 'It's chaos as club revellers roll up.' The article was in Diary style, in the first person, an affectionate piss-take required for this page of gossipy entertainment news. 'Chaos reigned outside the Haçienda night club in Manchester last night when hundreds of revellers turned up in unexpected numbers for the late night TV disco show *The Hitman and Her*. So fearsome was the crush at the club's entrance that TV presenter Anthony Wilson could not get into the club he part-owns … Wilson eventually slipped in his club via a side door, but an unluckier would-be disco dancer left out in the cold was David Liddiment who as Granada TV's head of entertainment is Wilson's boss – and the executive producer of *The Hitman and Her*.'

It was all good knockabout stuff. I knew, from many interviews and conversations with Wilson, that my relationship with him was sound.

What I didn't include in my light show-bizzy report from that January night in 1989 when *The Hitman and Her* cameras rolled, was an episode of gangland viciousness which took place once the cameras stopped rolling. Most of the crowd had emptied out and the house lights were on. Bar staff with brooms were starting to brush up empty drink cans. Just as I was about to leave, from my spot on the balcony I could see that something was kicking off … it was clear that two people were annoying each other very badly indeed.

I watched from above with a small group of club staff and TV crew as a tattooed, bald man with Hell's Angels biker-style facial hair, in denim jeans and leather waistcoat, faced up to a taller and expressionless black man. The biker was conspicuous by his utterly inappropriate clothing for the club and the music, testament perhaps to the magnetic pull of TV. The two had already done squaring up, they were now running towards each other, head-to-head, like two jousters. Except every time the biker got near his adversary, out of the taller man's hand flew an extendable metal weapon which landed full on his opponent's head time after time. It was a bloody encounter, only ending when manager Leroy Richardson pulled the victim into an exit door and away from, I learned later, a feared gang boss.

I went down the stairs and out, appalled by what I had seen, and wondering how such a weapon could get into the club on such a high-profile event. Wilson and Waterman were not around to witness it. There were no police there at the time. It was clear, however, that the club's owners were fast having to wake up to the fact that what made their club nights go with a bang was an illegal market making fortunes for criminal gangs. The TV event foreshadowed a legion of nights to come which were almost operatic in their intensity, in which an existential battle for the survival of the club would test the reputations, practices and principles of its founders to breaking point.

Wilson and the club's owners and managers had been used to problems on the door, unsavoury characters who made life difficult for the staff and, once inside, demanded free drinks from the bar. They were impossible to ban and in fact, in the early days of the ecstasy boom, rival Manchester firms tolerated each other to keep the booming underworld economy ticking along.

The heavy mobs circled the Haçienda marketplace like sharks in a feeding frenzy of drug dealing as the pills poured in from the Netherlands and elsewhere.

Even these hard cases realised that clubbers needed a functioning club for them to have a marketplace. Reformed criminal Jason Coghlan told *Vice* in 2016: 'If [the clubbers] knew what was making this a safe environment to watch all these fucking celebrity DJs, they'd have probably got straight out back on the bus and fucked off,' he said. 'This is not fucking Disneyland, this is not a fucking ice cream van. People selling narcotics are fucking drug dealers, gangsters … every one of us were walking heavy, making sure that if anyone came out and started making noise, they'd be dealt with.'

James Brown asked in the *New Musical Express*, 'How does Wilson come to terms with presenting a clean club when he operates within a culture where artistic creativity is frequently inspired by going beyond the law?' Wilson replied: 'I've said for years that, as far as running the club goes, we have to exist within the law … I'm able to talk about a culture which in many ways is stronger than punk. That it's wonderful. It doesn't necessarily mean that I advocate drug use.'

There have been many similar revelations, notably those of club co-owner and New Order bassist Peter Hook in his brutally honest inside story of *The Haçienda: How Not to Run a Club*, with its handy guide to the city's different gangs, their leaders and the extreme methods with which they defended their markets. It may lead anyone to wonder how it was possible for an entire generation to cite the Haçienda as the defining positive experience of their youth, when all around was a whirlpool of cynical and extreme violence. Hook writes: 'Wilson was aware of the paradox … he was, after all, a casual drug user himself. So, to find his own moral cut-off point in the drug culture, he needed to look in the direction of organised crime.'

Manchester is a place where all the threads intertwine, where improbabilities disappear in a cosmic collision of history, horror and humour … on his first day at the Manchester Ship Canal Company, 'Hooky' was given the desk George Best used during his Manchester United apprenticeship; the Madchester-era Haçienda ticket desk was run by Fiona Allen, granddaughter of Britain's last Chief Executioner (when he didn't run his pub, hangman work not being regular); and, when 'White Tony' Johnson, a gangster who tormented the club's security team, was gunned down, it was revealed that he had been raised by Winnie Johnson, the mother of twelve-year-old Moors Murderers victim Keith Bennett, whose body was never found after he was abducted and killed in 1964.

To these perverse ley lines of Manc-coincidence, we can add more undeniable proof of absurdity in the alignment of Manchester's stars. Wilson's work for serious TV news dried up after a disastrous *World in Action* interview with Conservative minister Sir Keith Joseph, which folklore speculates was performed while on an acid trip, but which Wilson blamed on manic stress after his car broke down on the motorway to London.

And if he had been alive more than thirty years later to hear Factory being affectionately cited in the House of Commons by George Osborne, the ideological heir to Joseph's hard-right austerity? That, the serious broadcaster-cum-moonlighting impresario living a surreal double life might readily have acknowledged, was because he could only be utterly out of his skull on mind-bending substances.

9

Cash E-conomy

I feel close to the rebelliousness and vigour of the youth here ... nobody can deny that here, behind the windows of Manchester, there is an insane love of football, of celebration and of music.

Eric Cantona

The year before *The Hitman and Her* came to the Haçienda, it seemed to those on the Manchester club scene that they were a small community experiencing a parallel universe. In 1988, being in the social scenes around the city's music and media felt like you had been given a key to the door of an alternative reality.

If you had tasted its fruits, you were a member of a secret society. In your new head-spinning existence, normal people continued with their commonplace, everyday world. That world, the one with which you were tediously familiar, would turn as usual, humdrum life carrying on day by day. The sun rose in the morning and fell in the evening, that's if you could see the life-giving sun through the low cement-hued sky. Yet if you were in on a secret, at night-time a dazzlingly vivid Manchester would open up, and holding the two realities in your mind produced a bizarre cognitive dissonance on a city-wide scale.

Mancunian humour tends towards the laconic. In the place that brought forth the cathartic Gothic genius of Joy Division and the uplifting miserabilism of The Smiths, even Manchester's comedians were a parade of hangdog expressions and laughter in despair, from Les Dawson to Victoria Wood. Think Colin Crompton, the lugubrious social club compère on Granada TV's *Wheeltappers and Shunters Club*: downbeat humour for a hard-knock life.

No wonder that drugs both legal and not were, and still are, for many the mainstay of surviving Manchester. Legal intoxication drives the city's night-time economy, with pints, shorts and shots flying down the hatch in the city's pubs, hotels, nightclubs and the many 'style bars' of the city centre. Drinks companies have for years targeted the city's leisure society with new product taste tests and focus groups. Manchester is a blinder of a booze city, and it can be judged somewhere on the spectrum from harmless relaxation all the way through to personal addiction and social damage.

During the spring and summer of 1988, however, thousands of young people stopped drinking alcohol as black-and-white lives turned technicolour. What might have formerly been a night out getting plastered had become an intense, supercharged experience, thanks to a new mood-enhancing illegal Class A drug. Ecstasy was the street name for the psychoactive pharmaceutical MDMA, originally synthesised in 1912 for medical uses, and revived in the 1960s by American psychotherapists. Used recreationally in Boston among cliques of professionals, and on the West Coast in couples counselling, it was found to foster empathetic feelings and emotional openness. When psychotherapist Leo Zeff tried the drug in 1977, he nicknamed it 'Adam', believing that it not only stripped out inhibition but put users in a state of primordial innocence. In Manchester, youngsters couldn't 'Adam and Eve it' − MDMA was whooshing them into a state of euphoria. The drug's psychedelic amphetamine quality produced a mass 'one love' vibe as large nightclub crowds got high collectively, enjoying waves of sensation and emotion which lasted for hours. Club owners and promoters began to enhance ecstasy's sensory effects on their clientele by adapting their music, lighting and decor.

By 1988, ecstasy was being mass-manufactured in the Low Countries and distributed by well-organised criminal gangs who had long established connections in Amsterdam. Probably the very first consumers, in 1987, were some ne'er-do-wells from Salford's Little Hulton estate who, when they weren't thieving or poisoning pigeons for laughs, had started a raw and ragged band Happy Mondays which made a scuzz-funk racket unlike any other music: sound collages of rasped doggerel over sleazy bass and jagged guitar. The drug exploded in Manchester after Mondays' singer and lyricist Shaun Ryder and dancer Mark 'Bez' Berry returned from a club night in London with a boot full of tablets.

In Ryder's autobiography *Twisting My Melon* he recalls his first use of the drug in summer 1987. He was caught with a bag of ecstasy but let off by a police officer believing they were legal energy pills. Knowledge that it was a Class A drug seemed very much the preserve of the clannish family and friends around the Mondays. 'It wasn't until early 1988 that the E scene really started to kick off,' said Ryder, 'and by the summer of '88 we blew the roof off the Haçienda.' This state of consciousness was mostly experienced on a weekend, though committed practitioners (most studies conclude the drug is not addictive) could go on a three-day bender or more. Ryder recalls that hardened users like him and his mates often had a pill for breakfast without thinking of the health risks.

I first met Ryder at the Ladybarn flat of his cousins, graphic designers Pat and Matt Carroll. They introduced me to Shaun and a glassy-eyed girl companion. It was clear she was coming down. It was Sunday teatime, but it was still Saturday night in Shaun's head. He was totally wired and fizzing like a firework. On the television was the music-over-newsreel show *The Rock and Roll Years*. Ryder mainlined the TV show like a drug – exclamations, curses and shrieks poured out of him, as he machine-gunned out mad perspectives on the programme's pop history shrapnel. Just being Shaun Ryder, he was quite a show.

Living for the weekend was giving way to the '24 Hour Party People' lifestyle, journalist Mandi James observed: 'The Friday/Saturday night flirtation with club culture has become a full-time, total commitment. What was once a brief encounter, an occasional messy, one-night stand, has become a deep and meaningful relationship, a fact of life.' Ecstasy tablets for £15 a pill found their way into friendship groups supplied by small-time dealers, who were also hairdressers, shop workers or aspiring musicians, like Jeff 'the Chef' Cunningham, the chatty small-time dope dealer who fell into the role of chief supplier to the Haçienda queue.

In her book *And God Created Manchester*, the twenty-year-old Sarah Champion from Chorlton, a *wunderkind* who was penning features at the age of sixteen for *New Musical Express*, wrote: 'Morrissey went for a night out, had a bad time, then wrote a song to depress the rest of us. Old Manchester. Raincoats. Gloom. Misery. Except things changed somewhere down the line … the city partied, [sic] one nation under a groove.'

From the Cromford Court flats above the Arndale Centre, DJ Mike Pickering could see over to the tower blocks of Miles Platting. The Angel pub sign had all the letters ripped off except 'E' and, in the grim housing scheme behind it, one of his Haçienda regulars had rigged up a strobe light in his flat on the top floor. 'He rings me up really late,' said Pickering, pointing to the tower a mile away. 'I look out the window and there he is, the strobe's on, and he's dancing.'

A drummer in a band I knew who sold a few pills to mates had business cards printed, and underneath his name the single word 'Drums'. A mutual friend told how he had been a passenger as the 'Drums' supplier drove around the city one sunny day, high on ecstasy. In his state of *jouissance* he purposefully slow-bumped the car of a pretty girl driver, simply so he could bring about a meeting, a chat-up line and the offer of his card offering 'Drums'.

The goofy 'one love' vibe of 1988 couldn't last. The scene was souring as the year turned. The so-called '1988 Summer of Love' seems in retrospect more of a media construct, with a few journalists on titles like *i-D* and *The Face* as blissed-out as the scene they were writing about. In reality it was the preserve of a select in-crowd stumbling on a world of new pharmaceuticals and musical innovation in clubs in Ibiza, in Manchester and in London's Shoom, a prelude to the mass-participation mayhem of 1989.

It's hard to underestimate the impact on the city's music and social history of the Happy Mondays' car journey back from London. The first place it showed up was at Mike Pickering's Friday Nude Night at the Haçienda. This proved to be a key pivot from the Haçienda's early days, when moody rain mac-wearing Northern lads gripped their bottles of lager and plucked up the nerve to dance to Grace Jones's 'Nightclubbing'. Thursday was a student night of indie and dance crossover under Dave Haslam, and Saturday was a unique melée of hair products and leather trousers as hairdressers partied with their blow-waved Cheshire clientele. But Nude Night on Friday attracted black kids from inner-city neighbourhoods who appreciated Pickering's US-sourced tunes. The music was harder than the other sounds around town. The Haçienda management were wary at first. 'They'd say "it's too rough,"' Pickering told me in 1989. 'I said, "it's a rough city, it's our city."'

Once the supply of ecstasy floated around town, Pickering watched the change from the Haçienda DJ booth, perched like an eagle's nest above the dancefloor. 'As soon as they got hold of E the whole place went berserk,' he said. 'It was like a tidal wave … Ecstasy made the white kids dance. You could see the black kids who had been the main dancers getting moved over a bit because of all this rave dancing.' Asked to describe the atmosphere at the Haçienda and other rave clubs to a London journalist, a clubber declared: 'It's like a goal being scored at the football – for five hours.' Not everyone was ecstatic, soul purists like the late *Black Echoes* journalist and DJ Dean Johnson among them, 'House music was essentially fast music for cool black dancers. None of this arm-waving. Like all sub-cultures, once the media got involved, it was ruined.'

Pickering remembers how there were various scenes at the club, from 'black kids to working class kids from sink estates who rubbed shoulders with homosexuals and bohemians alike'. Andrew 'Saltz' Anderson of dance group the Jazz Defektors was an original Haçienda regular. His ensemble inspired the dance scene at the city's basement Berlin club which led to their appearance in the movie *Absolute Beginners* alongside David Bowie. 'Saltz' described the liberating new ways in which the daily social relations he encountered as a black man from Moss Side was very different in the Haçienda: 'People's musical tastes changed, their attitude towards black music … Now, there's a big percentage who feel they don't need the drug to reach that state. To be able to remove themselves from the drug. And feeling, "was it the drug, or was it us"? If they capture the same vibe without the drug, we've got a serious utopia.'

The loved-up atmosphere was, however, being cut with some harsh ingredients. Through 1988, frightening, violent incidents were becoming the norm. While they did not usually disturb the enjoyment of most of the clientele, who hugged and trance-danced obliviously, intimidation on the door, or fights between rival gangs, became a regular worry for Haçienda staff and owners. Financially, there was a hit for the club as well. Pilled-up clubbers, not needing alcohol, were drinking only water or soft drinks to slake their thirst, extinguishing income from selling booze. 'The club took money like blotting paper, and it cost a fortune just to keep it rolling,' said New Order's Bernard Sumner in 1992. 'I sometimes think that if I could turn the clock back I wouldn't do it again … the Haçienda is now known all over the world, but it has caused plenty of headaches over the years.'

By the summer of 1989, there couldn't be many people who felt underinformed about the new scene. On 24 June 1989, what the media called Acid or Rave was out of its box. Clubbers' party weekend became a full-on Monday morning hangover with *The Sun*'s front-page banner photo of tranced-out clubbers. Under the 72-point headline 'SPACED OUT' the nation's biggest-selling daily tabloid splashed on an illegal rave near the M25 motorway, and the Haçienda was fingered in accompanying reporting as the North's mothership for the new drug and music culture.

In July 1989, sixteen-year-old Claire Leighton, from Cannock in Staffordshire, became the first known ecstasy victim in Britain. After taking a tablet in the Haçienda, she suffered a horrendous rare reaction and died from organ failure. The inquest into her death heard that she had taken the drug before without ill-effects. As well as a tragedy for her family and friends, it was traumatic for the club owners and a collective slap in the face for users who had drunk the Kool-Aid, to borrow from a previous generation, and believed that ingesting chemicals illicitly produced by organised criminals was a risk-free pastime. The same month, happy-go-lucky Jeff the Chef was caught dealing outside the City Road Inn across the road from the club, and received a four-and-a-half year sentence, serving three years in Strangeways. He was the first person in the north to be caught in the new police crackdown. 'I took prison as an experience,' he says. 'New Order still send me guest list tickets.'

As well as that reality check about ecstasy's dangerous thrill, a debate raged in the music press about the creative validity of the scene. Tim Booth of the indie group James, whose first single had been released on Factory, wrote a letter to *New Musical Express* accusing it of 'trying to give house fans the status of valiant revolutionaries surrounded by the conservative forces of oppression. Well, I'm sorry but this state only exists in the heads of a few far-out minds ... I am not impressed by any movement that seems to be based squarely on a drug.' Manchester DJ Greg Wilson warned that that the hallucinogenic effects of ecstasy had started a new surge in LSD use, and cautioned: 'Clubs are the wrong environment to take acid ... Back in the 60s, they preached setting, being with people you trust, in your own environment, in a club you can't control that.'

By 1990, the Haçienda was in the throes of a prolonged bad trip. Claire Leighton's death had made it a national byword for the dark side of clubland. Another dance music club, the Gallery on Peter Street, had been shut by the police because of the criminality it attracted. This knocked on more drug dealing at the Haçienda, and in early 1990 Greater Manchester Police applied to revoke the licence. The police declined requests for paid officers to patrol the door as at football matches, and when called to deal with live incidents, such as men carrying illegal firearms into the premises, they simply told staff to deal with it, as an astonished Peter Hook recounts in his Haçienda book.

Crime was being committed on a widespread scale inside the cathedral of love and hugs, but Wilson openly talking up the drug culture in the music press was seen by senior officers as rubbing it in. The licence would be granted again, said the authorities, only when the club could prove it could curb the drug-taking and violence. The legal impasse led Wilson to hire one of the most famous barristers in the land, George Carman. The diminutive Lancastrian was no stranger to the Manchester circuit or indeed the city's wine bars, which he would take to after a hard day in court and commandeer a piano. He had successfully defended comedian Ken Dodd against tax fraud charges and Liberal Party leader Jeremy Thorpe against conspiracy to murder. When he took on the case, reportedly his first piece of advice for the Haçienda management was aimed squarely at Wilson: 'For God's sake, shut that man up!'

While 'Killer Carman', an appropriate nickname perhaps for the job he had accepted, drew up his case, Wilson lobbied behind the scenes to gain support from an unexpected quarter. The city council enjoyed an overwhelming

Labour majority, and it now took a once-unthinkable stance – lending official civic backing to one of the city's biggest crime hotspots. On the back of a growing profile and music economy, its councillors could see the benefits of the Haçienda to a post-industrial city, now bidding, in spite of London sniggers, for the 1996 Olympic Games. City leader Stringer pledged council backing, writing to magistrates that it was an economic asset making 'a significant contribution to the active use of the city centre core,' and got MP Bob Litherland to pen a similar defence.

In May 1990, The Stone Roses played Spike Island in Widnes, Cheshire to 30,000 sun-drenched fans, the movement's Woodstock-lite moment. *The Sunday Times* ran a cover feature on Manchester. The city seemed on the crest of a wave. Wilson was getting a Malcolm McLaren-style buzz from appearing to be the ringmaster of it all, teaming up with film-makers Keith Jobling and Pete Shotton aka The Bailey Brothers to pitch a city-set crime movie to US film studios. *The Mad Fuckers* failed to excite Hollywood, though it did coin the term 'Madchester'. A further unlikely boost was provided by the US magazine *Newsweek* which in July 1990 put 'Stark Raving Madchester' on its front cover and explained the new phenomenon for Main Street USA: 'Punk was menacing; the new music is buoyant, almost goofy. The fashion grafts British football gear onto American hippie glad rags – with a soupçon of the Jetsons' futurism. The philosophy is simplistic, the politics nil. And the whole package, still nameless and leaderless, was created in Manchester, England. The kids call it Madchester.'

The UK entered recession at the end of 1990. Jobs and incomes suffered and house prices, the great British metric of economic optimism, were going backwards. In a city losing traditional industries, the blossoming importance of the night-time economy meant the Haçienda was playing a role, however marginal, in bringing income and publicity for the city. While not blind to the crime it attracted, the council asked the police and licensing authorities to work together for the civic good. In true money-burning Haçienda style, the legal battle had cost the club £250,000, but it resulted in a six-month reprieve granted in January 1991. The police asked the owners to put their house in order, a decision hailed as a victory by clubbers and the city's leadership. The first night of reopening was titled 'The Thanksgiving', with hordes of Manchester's artists turning out for the British live debut of 'supergroup' Electronic, assembling Johnny Marr, Bernard Sumner and Neil Tennant. With the police reporting 'a positive change in direction', the night heralded a new co-operation between cops and club.

Unfortunately for the unlikely new crime-fighting alliance, warring gangs continued to vie for supremacy. Violent incidents involving guns around the club entrance had become commonplace. The Haçienda had become the focal point not just of the city's music scene but of feuding Manchester gangs. While few clubbers fell victim to the problems door staff faced, the club owners felt that bringing in London security to run the door would remove local faction fighting. This only raised the temperature, however. Staff were threatened with a gun, an incident which Wilson believed was beyond the pale. In his version, shots were fired in the air. He was adamant this was a watershed needing drastic action, and, while his co-owners were divided, his insistence that the club close won the day. The Haçienda voluntarily shut its doors.

Wilson called a press conference that made national news on Wednesday 30 January 1991. The *Manchester Evening News* covered it the same day, editor Mike Unger asking me at 10am to write a feature on a one-hour deadline, my brief to explain to its mass readership the Haçienda's importance to the city. As a Manchester stringer for the weekly *New Musical Express*, sending them tips and reports, I was in regular contact with news editor Steve Lamacq and deputy Iestyn George (though the office phone was answered by Mary Anne Hobbs with the same breathless enthusiasm familiar from her radio shows). The newswires were buzzing and George was straight on to me. Lamacq wanted a report. It ran under the headline 'Haçienda that! Official' in the next week's *NME*.

Ironically, of course, the voluntary closure followed the club's recent victory to retain its licence. After lying empty for twelve weeks, it had reopened after £100,000 of security measures, including an airport-style metal detector, body and bag searches, external video cameras on swivel mountings, and infra-red cameras covering the inside crannies where police alleged that cash and drugs changed hands. My *NME* report quoted Wilson: 'The Haçienda is closing its doors as of today. It is with the greatest reluctance that for the moment we are turning the lights out on what is, for us, a most important place … We are quite simply sick and tired of dealing with instances of personal violence.'

The club's gun incident and voluntary closure made it clear the new measures had not solved anything. After more discussions with the police, it reopened in May 1991 with a night dubbed 'The Healing', but all parties knew this was wishful thinking. The money, gangs and guns followed the city's illegal drugs market across the city, but the Haçienda's notoriety, profile and scale seemed to encapsulate all the issues in one media-friendly package. In the summer of 1991, I was commissioned by *The Face* magazine editor Sheryl Garratt to write about the Haçienda's troubles and the wider implications for clubland. My feature headlined 'Clubbed to Death?' in its August edition that year started with perhaps the most sobering example yet how the club was now trapped in a pincer between the authorities and hardened criminals. At 2am on Sunday 23 June 1991, 1,200 people emerged from the Haçienda after a night's hard partying and straight into a bad dream. Outside, dozens of Tactical Aid Group police officers, complete with riot shields and CS gas cannisters, had sealed off the entrance and rear exits. A police helicopter wheeled overhead in the eerily bright early morning light. As the dazed clubbers filed out through a gauntlet of police, their faces were recorded by a Greater Manchester Police video unit.

It was the strongest police reaction yet to a violent incident at the club. A gang of men, frustrated at the 'House Full' sign on the shuttered, security-heavy new front entrance, had gained entry after attacking security staff with knives at a side door. Six door staff were stabbed, and ten men were arrested in the crowd's police-controlled exit. Four, from Salford, were charged with offences of affray and assault. A doorman said of one of his colleagues, 'He's had enough. He was stabbed five times and his lung is still leaking. That's enough for anybody, isn't it?' In *The Face* I described how the euphoria of three summers had faded to reveal the ugly reality of a city in recession: 'The party is over and the Haçienda, once on the highest high of all, with its TV presenter frontman, pop star patrons and big-name DJs, is having the nastiest comedown of all.'

Madchester was draining away. A weekend festival in Heaton Park promoted by Alan Wise in August was a flop – Cities in the Park was well undersold and the booked acts' managers lined up outside Wise's trailer to demand their fees in cash before they went on. The staging, techies and security staff were 'knocked'. So much for the brotherly vibe. This period also saw a sharp and murderous escalation in gang feuds between the loose affiliations of Moss Side, Cheetham Hill and Salford firms. The point-blank gunshot execution outside a Cheetham Hill pub of 'White Tony' Johnson, a notorious nuisance on the Haçienda door, might have given the impression that the gangs were well organised, but many US-style drive-by shootings showed the reality of out-of-control young bucks. GMP intelligence had Moss Side down as the focal point of warring drug gangs in a trade worth £20 million a year. A police source put the criminal hard core at fifty people and revealed that they liked to stash their guns under the beds of their girlfriends' kids.

Senior officers began to realise that crime prevention might be better aided with the Haçienda open. The club's self-imposed three-month closure had cost another £175,000 on top of Carman's bills, so the hierarchy had no choice but to get on with working more closely with GMP and making drug-free, law-abiding clubbing an appealing prospect. Infra-red cameras and body searches weren't anyone's idea of a banging night out, but they were the price if the club wanted to make its tenth birthday party in May 1992. Half a dozen undercover police became club regulars. 'They're cool,' said the ticket office's Rebecca Goodwin. 'The right clothes, the right dancing. They look sorted. You just can't tell.'

The club's tenth birthday is one of my best Haçienda memories. Manager Paul Cons put a fairground wheel on the canal-side behind the club, and the weather was unseasonably summery. Before things got too wild, who should appear but 'the Hitman and Her' – not Waterman and Strachan, but the catty nickname for council leader Graham Stringer and gay city-centre councillor Pat Karney, bestowed by *City Life* columnist Stephen Stroud.

It was a night that seemed problem-free, but, that same summer, the seriousness of plainclothes police activity was graphically played out before my eyes. After a 2am turnout of the club, my girlfriend Lynne and I got into my car, parked on the pavement outside. As we were belting up, a modern-day Manchester vignette played out before us, the actors framed by our windscreen. In the car in front something furtive was going on. A guy in the back seat was leaning towards the driver. Any impression that the two were swapping football stickers evaporated when suddenly a white police van screeched to a halt, jolting forward as it braked hard. Seven or eight uniformed officers appeared from nowhere and the boy in the driver seat was yanked out and dumped in the back of the van. The doors clanged shut and it sped off. The backseat guy, sporting a fashionably floppy fringe and a T-shirt over baggy jeans, nimbly exited the car and disappeared. The uniformed officers ignored him. The car in front was now empty. Lynne and I looked at each other wide-eyed. It was over in seconds and looked like an undercover sting of a drug deal.

These were volatile days, with 'Gunchester' becoming an off-the-shelf media cliché. That the fun desired by large numbers of the young was illegal led to a jittery, wired ambience, and a night out was undermined by the anxiety about the undercurrent of violence. Despite the police activity, there was still big money to be made. A former pupil at Orsdall High School, 'Steve', was interviewed in *City Life:* 'All the publicity about Madchester helped make the drug culture. Thousands waiting for a buzz, no advertising, no production costs, hardly any labour costs and no taxes. It's a businessman's dream isn't it?'

The better days of this entrepreneur's dockside district had long gone, and it was one of the Salford wards with the lowest local election turnout in the whole of Greater Manchester; the neighbourhood crime gangs commanded a respect eclipsing that of their democratic representatives – in 1992 only 15 per cent voted in local elections.

Damien Noonan of the feared Ordsall gangland family was at times the head doorman of the Haçienda, the desperate owners even sending the giant hard-man along with dapper, diminutive licensing lawyer Anthony Lyons to meet with a senior police chief. One episode captures the mood of the time, as all kind of hustlers scented a way to make fast money, often using reckless methods. A famous TV actor I was friendly with invited me for a meal at the Basta Pasta restaurant off Piccadilly, saying he wanted to discuss an idea. Over freshly made pasta he outlined a plan. Sick of his treatment at the hands of tabloid reporters, he wanted to hoodwink the red-top press and provide himself a big pay day.

He was a regular target for the tabloids, and knew they were hungry for big stories about TV stars like him. This was the blag: he would be in the Haçienda on a Saturday night and, when the place was rocking to its rafters, his associate would fire gunshots into the ceiling. In the ensuing chaos, the celebrity would exit the club, making his way to a remote rural location. I would contact the papers on his behalf and offer them his story: 'How I fled from gangland figures who wanted me dead.' All for the right price.

I was aghast, and not only at the thought of having to conduct an auction with tabloid jackals on a false premise. The idea of firing a gun inside a packed club, and the whole range of things that could go wrong, from accidentally shooting someone to causing a mass panic, ran through my mind. And who were these gangsters he was supposedly running from? The Salford mob, maybe? I was hoping he would crack into one of his winning smiles, but I could tell he was serious. It was clear he felt he had the connections to get the gun inside despite the hi-tech door kit, and that he could ensure the shooter could also melt into the night.

I held back from questioning his sanity but outlined to him the possible unintended consequences. Whether it was this counsel or whether common sense overcame him, thankfully his crackpot idea never came to pass.

This was the period when Haçienda regulars the Happy Mondays and their mindset reflected an amoral approach to the cash economy that was an everyday reality. Textiles were the city's historic trade and a free-enterprise approach to music-scene fashion meant many of the Madchester groups sold more T-shirts than records. The group was even discovered by a market stall holder, Phil Saxe. He sold unfashionable flared denims at the Arndale Market to what he called 'The Boys' – 'they went to the Ritz back then, the Haçienda was for students,' said Saxe, the group's first manager.

Outside gigs, illegal merchandise flooded the streets, punters exiting the shows offered cheap unofficial products. The pirating centre for 'snide' clothing was, and remains, the Cheetham Hill area nearby Strangeways prison. With the prison's distinctive tower looking down, street lookouts keep watch for backstreet producers of raids by trading standards officers. The neighbourhood was also home to legal businesses like the media-friendly Joe Bloggs brand. Fashion boss Shami Ahmed rode the Madchester style wave with his label, hogging headlines with 20-inch flared jeans. Yet his Bentley and Park Lane apartment were more likely the product of his family's pound-shop retail chain Pennywise. 'JB' was derided by the cool crowd but that didn't stop Ryder and Co. grabbing all the freebies offered, and the brand sold in High Street chain stores was worn on TV soaps by youthful *Brookside* and *Coronation Street* cast members.

The Madchester T-shirt became default clobber for the younger generation. The band James and frontman Tim Booth had gone from indie darlings to a stadium rock act with the annoyingly catchy anthem 'Sit Down', and they rode a tsunami of T-shirt sales with their naive flower cartoon. Designing a cotton tee was not beneath cerebral Peter Saville's design agency, either. When a malapropism by Granada TV veteran David Plowright amused the Haçienda crew – the titan of hard news asked Wilson about 'the Hallucienda' – the club commissioned from Saville's agency in its honour a luridly beautiful graphic of a bio-organism, implying the altered state of a drug experience.

The ravers' uniform was seen everywhere – baggy flared jeans, primary colours all over, Kickers on the feet, hoodies and beanies up top. Affleck's Palace on Oldham Street was the mecca for the new fashion trends, what the music press called 'Scallydelia' – blending the working-class style trends of Liverpool 'scallies' and Manchester 'perry boys' with the new drug associations. In the alternative emporium's warren of stalls, Leo Stanley' Identity created a fashion craze with his Northern Pride T-shirts. Stanley was selling five hundred 'Manchester North of England' T-shirts a week. A committed Catholic who embraced the drug culture, he declared, 'Jesus was a raver. He preached love, peace and let's everybody get it together.' Another of his T-shirts 'And On The Sixth Day, God Created Manchester' became the scene's slogan, sold to the growing numbers of backpacking and sofa-surfing youngsters for the street life, gigs and the chance to meet the bands in the Northern Quarter clubs and bars.

The cash economy feeding frenzy took hold among the groups. Shaun Ryder and later Noel Gallagher were personal friends with some of the biggest ticket touts in town. If their fans had paid inflated prices for their shows, they know where to look. Ryder was brazen about it. I interviewed him before the Mondays' G-Mex show in 1990 and asked him if he felt under pressure from Factory to make sure their new album was a chart success. 'The only thing I'm worried about right now is how I'm going to sell my ticket allocation for G-Mex,' he replied.

The blag culture was in full swing. The second-hand record stores stocked vinyl picked up by the local freelance journo pack from plugger Tony 'the Greek' Michaelides, then sold on. Pop into his Princess Street offices and you could swap gossip with his assistant Marc Riley (post-The Fall, pre-BBC radio) and other local music champions like Key 103 nice guy DJ Pete Mitchell. The talk of the town was the Mondays' entourage of drug suppliers, ticket touts, merchandise sellers and petty thieves, all chasing fast times and easy money. Their live show promoters also took an unconventional approach. When wannabe promoters Jimmy 'Muffin' Sherlock and John Kenyon tried to hire G-Mex to put a Mondays' show on there, they were shown the door. The next week, the Mondays' mates went back in as Night-time Promotions with a suitcase of cash and counted it out for the gobsmacked jobsworths. £40,000 deposit paid, the gig was on for late March 1990, and, when it sold out, the pair added a second the following night. Who were these chancers out of nowhere, taking on local promoters like Danny Betesh of Kennedy Street, who had been operating since the 1960s and had put on The Beatles?

Kenyon and Sherlock pulled off the G-Mex sell-out shows. When I saw the brochure on the first night, it was full of pictures except for two pages titled 'Revenge of the Scallies' — a freelanced feature I had written for the *Manchester Evening News*. It was word-for-word, except for my missing byline. I now had to shake down the promoters for nicking my words. I harassed the pair whenever I saw them out, finding Sherlock a hard-to-dislike charmer. Finally, in the Haçienda cocktail bar he took out the thickest bundle of £50 notes I'd ever seen. 'There's your money, Andy,' he smiled as he peeled off two for me.

This was also the time when on leaving the Haçienda you'd be tipped off about an early-hours rave. In August 1989, after the club's shutters came down, I drove with my girlfriend Lynne and DJ Justin Robertson, who knew the location, to the Ashworth Valley outside Rochdale. Billed as Joy, it is reputed to be the acid house era's first free outdoor rave in the North, thrown by Anthony and Chris Donnelly, who later created street fashion house Gio Goi. The brothers were nephews of the notorious Jimmy 'The Weed' organised crime boss, who later described in detail how his firm was behind Joy, estimating that eighty thousand ravers attended over the weekend. Thanks to the outlaw chic of the Mondays and their circle, an association with wideboys and grifters was now in vogue. The Madchester photographer Peter Walsh captured the scene's characters amid the eerie light of a Northern England late summer sunrise. Among his subjects were Lynne and me. Our connection proved more long-lasting than many chemical romances. We married in 1991, and still are.

A big part of the music scene of this period, and of independent pop culture ventures, was played by one of the city's most interesting historic buildings. 23 New Mount Street was a Grade II listed Victorian monster in Collyhurst, just outside the city centre, and its new incarnation was the brainchild of John Lancaster. A warm and friendly Stockport man, he created serviced offices grouped around an atrium and café in the interior of the five-storey, 50,000 sq ft building. A forerunner of today's co-working spaces, it offered affordable, easy in and out rents for an exotic range of small creative businesses. Its 1869 origin was appropriate for independent thought and cultural action, as the first home of the Co-operative Printing Society, churning out Co-op newspapers and other labour-movement publications, horse-drawn out from the goods entrance on School Street.

Andy Spinoza with Lynne Cunningham at Joy, 1989 (photo: Peter J. Walsh)

Now pouring forth from the same portal was a flood of late twentieth-century leisure wear – boxes of cotton T-shirts bearing the image of a cartoon cow wearing sunglasses and the legend 'Cool as Fuck'. 23 New Mount Street was the base of Oldham indie chart success Inspiral Carpets and their savvy manager Anthony Boggiano, who ran an impressive fashion sales operation as well as his act. The Inspirals' first album sold two hundred thousand copies worldwide, but it was a common quip around town that they shifted more clobber than records. 'Bodge' would hand me my press tickets for the band's shows in his office and ask me if I could help their roadie, an impassive young man with a Monkees-style bowl-cut called Noel, schlep boxes of T-shirts into their merchandising van. I knew Noel Gallagher from the Haçienda, where he inhabited the same spot every Saturday night with Oasis' first radio plugger Liam Walsh. It was impossible not to notice that, while the entire place was throwing arms in the air, whooping and gurning ecstatically, the elder Gallagher seemed to be on a one-man mission to prove that, amid all the madness, he could remain as undemonstrative as a living statue. Such cold-bloodedness proved useful when Oasis sacked his pal Walsh's outfit in their first wave of success.

23 New Mount Street was a hive of networking. Gallagher met Wigan photographer Brian Cannon there, leading to cover photos for the band's Oasis albums. Also based there were promotions firm Red Alert, publishing house Wordsmith and influential electro DJ Greg Wilson and his Murdertone record label. It was home too of the short-lived black music station Sunset Radio, and it was from the top floor of what is possibly Manchester city centre's highest spot, as the land rises north along Rochdale Road, that The Spinmasters Darren Partington and Andy Barker pumped out dance shows to the city and what they called their 'roughneck' mates.

With their raucous cry of 'A big shout going out!' The Spinmasters had a big following at Thunderdome, where they served up Detroit techno to council-estate kids. For those close to that hardcore scene free of trendies and students, it was the proper sound of Manchester before baggy jeans and wah-wah pedal guitar took over. Sunset Radio had an official radio licence and during the day was run by soul aficionado Mike Shaft, a BBC Radio Manchester stalwart. But every Tuesday night for three years from 1990, 808 State and Spinmasters' driving beats gave it a pirate radio feel ('Tune coming at you, Slow Bongo Floyd, this is a mad tune this! Go out and buy it cos the lad needs some clothes!'). Driving on summer evenings hearing their gravel-voice namechecks of the city's cast of Runyonesque street-life, over an upbeat rush of club floor-fillers, was an exhilarating rush.

Sunset did not last, and many of the creative businesses faded away. Digital start-ups were taking over and looked to sleeker, more wired-up and networked spaces in which to talk tech over artisan coffee. 23 New Mount Street's destiny was, as with many of the city's grand old buildings, as expensive city living spaces. Today the building contains 66 restored apartments and townhouses. The conversion revealed characterful features including the Co-op building's original timber floors, cast-iron columns and exposed brickwork. In 2016, the developer marketed them as 'high growth buy-to-let locations with strong yields' with the offer to invest from £199,000. The minimum deposit required was £45,000, a price tag well beyond the wherewithal of the street-smart rough-necks who had previously made it their musical home.

In the summer of 1992, to mark the Haçienda's tenth anniversary, Tony Wilson commissioned writer and journalist Jon Savage, a former Granada TV researcher and a long-time Factory collaborator, to edit a celebratory book, *The Haçienda Must Be Built!* In a softback A4 publication of 100 pages of articles, photographs and graphics, Savage interviewed prime movers like the Factory directors and managers, New Order band members, DJs and band managers. It included a small number of original pieces commissioned from journalists, including me. It was not a detailed brief, more, 'You've been close to it all, write what you want'.

The request was an invitation to get a few things off my chest. I wrote about the way pop culture's sexual politics seemed to have changed, and the Haçienda's role as a space where some backwards attitudes had taken hold. I was hardly going out on a limb. The *New Musical Express* had created a storm in November 1991 when the late Steven Wells, always happy to interrogate the politics in music, had skewered Happy Mondays' Shaun Ryder and Bez with their own prejudices. In his interview he revealed their openly hostile attitude to gays at a time when it seemed that a hoodlum gang mentality had taken over the Haçienda brand.

The band's motivation behind giving that interview was to give Ryder a platform to dispel any notion, as recently reported in the *News of the World*, that he had once been a sex worker. 'Lads who come from where I come from don't like being called a fucking faggot,' he said, '… that's probably the worst thing you call someone.' And Bez weighed in, too. After countless nights in the Haçienda teaching a generation a new dance to music produced by gay men in the US for gay nightclubs, he declared: 'I hate them. Faggots are disgust-ing.' Savage himself highlighted the contradiction by using a quote by Mike

Pickering in a headline: 'A lot of the best DJs and the best clubs in America – the Scallies don't realise it but they're all gay.' Paul Cons had also recently started the monthly Flesh night, a wild carnival with male dancers in cages and massage tables, which also opened up the decks to the club's first female DJs, Paulette Constable and Kath McDermott. Publicity-savvy Cons added a line to the tickets stating that 'management reserves the right to refuse admission to known heterosexuals'. Even so, some of the heavy mob were curious and could gain entrance whether welcome or not. Writer Sarah Champion said at the time: 'I always thought it was really weird that the homophobic macho idiots co-existed in the Haçienda with the beautiful young boys.'

Happy Mondays' interviews were always car crash affairs packed with unfiltered tales of criminality, yielding up often hilarious escapades which made Shaun and Bez sound like Fagin and the Artful Dodger. As I was also employing an equally frank approach, it led me to think, perhaps naively, that Wilson would take a free-thinking approach to all things in the book. Surely, he might tolerate some thought-provoking dissent among the celebratory tone? The reality of Madchester's message to the world, I wrote, was that theirs was a city where gays don't count.

I tried to nail the reactionary trends and contrast it with some original club principles. In the early years of the Haçienda it leaned towards what Wilson called the 'interesting community', an offer derided as arty student crap by those who later became Madchester ravers. Indeed, when it came to matters of audience tastes, often asked why his club was struggling for numbers, Wilson was apt to quote the late Sex Pistol Sid Vicious, who when asked about 'the man in the street', replied: 'I have met the man in the street and he's a cunt.'

The C-word was as problematic in the 1980s as it is now. Wilson knew it was offensive for many, but he wanted to make a point. It does lead, though, to thoughts about how such an unlikely mish-mash of Situationist-inspired radicalism, fashionable left-wing gesture politics and old-school Northern prejudices were all mixed up in the libertarian attitudes of those behind hip Manchester's hothouse.

Since opening its doors, Wilson's 'gift to Manchester' had formulated some extraordinary, sometimes chaotic or absurd, often high-risk escapades in live performance and music culture. The launch was followed by film nights, fashion shows, jazz dance groups and literary readings by the likes of writer William Burroughs, when the audience sat cross-legged on the floor, hippy-style. Bands who went on to conquer the world, like Culture Club, Simple Minds and Orange Juice, played to crowds who endured the infamously murky acoustics in a Victorian warehouse which Wilson and his partners, in their typically muddled way, had designed to emulate their favourite New York nightclubs. Only later, when Madchester exploded, did the owners come to regard the cathedral-like space, now perfect for mass dancing, as a preordained gift from the pop culture gods.

In spring 1982, to create a noise with the opening, the controversialist in Wilson drove him to hire foul-mouthed comedian Bernard Manning. After his lead-balloon audience reaction, he waived his fee, he said out of pity for the owners. The 1,500-capacity, design and clientele were beyond the comprehension of the obese proprietor and MC of the city's tinsel-curtained Embassy Club, where pints were served by waiters in white butcher's aprons. Ben Kelly would visit from London to see who was using the spaces he had designed, and observed: 'I was shocked by how deeply uncool people looked. They hadn't figured out how to be cool in this cool space.' In 1985, on the club's three-year anniversary, The Smiths' Johnny Marr's waspish impression in *City Life* captured the milieu: 'Androgynous men, androgynous women, fur clothes, punk pensioners, watered-down Coca Cola – my favourite place.'

My submitted piece to Savage for the book contrasted the current consciousness with the Haçienda's early days, which began with a members-only approach. As a final-year degree student I had handed over my passport photos and £5.25 for a credit-card-sized membership card. The first ones were in Saville-designed stainless steel, but, as the run of these ended, the club moved to laminated plastic cards sporting pink and yellow stripes; I still have my one from September 1983, number 9262, with my photo. Hillegonda 'Gonnie' Rietveld, singer with Factory band Quando Quango, now music culture professor at London South Bank University, processed the cards. The volunteers for the pop-culture experiment, she said, were 'adventurous people. Anything went. People were still discovering the space. It was a blank slate.'

The unsettling, subversive writer William Burroughs and deeply unpleasant stand-up Bernard Manning were the widest of cultural parameters. For some, though, the Haçienda was rolling back the wrong barriers. Journalist Neil Riley saw red at Christmas 1983 when promoter Alan Wise hired female strippers for the onstage entertainment. Riley and some friends drenched Wise in beer and were thrown out. 'I accuse the Haçienda management of cooperating with perversion of entertainment,' wrote Riley in *City Life* in January 1984. 'They have toyed with bad taste too often … Let's dance anyway, but to our own song, not to a tune that's out of time.'' Riley knew how bad pre-Haçienda Manchester was for out gay men like him. For Riley and others, the space was precious, and he expected great things, not racist jokes and strippers. Two of the club's early-days managers were women, Penny Henry and Ellie Gray, and the latter told me: 'I think the owners and other managers constantly battled against their Northern chauvinism. They tried. But there was a boys' locker room mentality.' Musician and writer Richard Witts later observed, 'There are no happy women in the Factory story.'

An early performance at the Haçienda by Linder Sterling's Ludus could not have been more different from a racist stand-up. It confronted audiences with music and art exploring taboo areas – menstruation, sado-masochism, fetishism. The group's manager Cath Carroll celebrated one Ludus show by leaving red ink-stained tampons in the men's toilets, and Linder – more widely known as a 'sexperimental' visual artist through her Buzzcocks sleeve designs – ended her performance by opening her coat to reveal a huge dildo. 'I think the general consensus was "That's disgusting,"' says Carroll, who went on to become a Factory artist, playing with androgynous images in her own work. 'I feel very tired of heterosexuality,' she told *New Musical Express*. 'It's not something I feel entirely comfortable with.'

My article explored the notion that Factory had knowingly exploited the Mondays' cynicism and small-mindedness for notoriety and record sales. Savage called me to explain that it 'had pushed the wrong buttons' with the directors, and that he would like to work with me on an amended version. I had pushed their own boundaries too far. Wilson and the others were bruised from years of struggle with the gangs, the authorities and the media. Now with the homophobia controversy they didn't need someone close to them giving them grief in their own book. At first, we tried to edit certain sections, and I even received a photocopied page of the book proof with Savage's edits in black pen. But soon after, he told me that the piece could not run. Instead, he said, they wanted to use my gang wars article from *The Face*.

There was a taker for the unedited original version, which *City Life* editor Mike Hill published in July 1992 with the line on the cover: 'Exclusive! Censored. The article The Haçienda banned.' I didn't see it like that. The Haçienda book was for, about and by Wilson and Co. to celebrate the club and its achievements. It was a speculative punt by me to test the limits of his intellectual tolerance. It was entirely up to him, Gretton and the others what went in it. In the published version in *City Life*, though, I was able to express what many people felt strongly at the time: 'The Haçienda must take its share of the blame. The best club in pop culture's capital was often, at Madchester's dizzy heights, a deeply unpleasant place, crawling with bimbos and their pistol-packing sugar daddies. We danced on, oblivious – oblivion was where we wanted to be – to the undercurrents: it was hip to be thick, cool to be a criminal. Girls adopted the stoned-chick look. Clubbers dressed down and worse, they thought down.'

This paragraph was one which Savage's black pen had crossed out in the aborted 'compromise version'. By airing my views in *City Life*, I was reflecting the widespread feeling at the time that intelligent discourse had lost out to fashionable monosyllablism. Media influence and public take-up of the Mondays' tar-thick 'Manchestoh' accents – which older Mancunians pinpoint as the accent of the Salford docks – came to be used by anyone striving to sound like 'real' Mancs. Interestingly, it was noticeable that an earlier Salford generation containing Sumner, Hook and poet John Cooper Clarke owned softer tones. Mondays' slang expressions 'top', 'nice one' and 'double plus good' were being overused to the point of parody, encouraged by Wilson's claims that Shaun Ryder's lyrics were as incisive as Bob Dylan's and profound as those of W.B. Yeats.

Even if that were true, the Haçienda at its heights was not exactly full of sensitive poets. To an increasing number of people, the widely used term 'scally culture' to describe the new youth behaviours put the 'moron' into oxymoron. Madchester's bow-legged, flared-jeaned swagger was popularised by Ian Brown and Liam Gallagher. When the HMP Manchester riot took place in April 1990 the 25-day televised spectacle gave the nation some idea of the kind of people the Haçienda door staff were facing. The prisoners' protest on top of the roof prompted the wisecrack: 'What are the Happy Mondays doing on top of Strangeways?'

In 1992 Ryder came off heroin temporarily only to succumb to crack addiction as his band blew £150,000 of Factory's money in Barbados recording their final album *Yes Please!*, the overspend being the final straw for the company's finances, and it crashed later the same year. Despite everything, Wilson supported Ryder's epic commitment to William Blake's proverb that 'the road to excess leads to the palace of wisdom'. He told *The Guardian* in 2000, 'Everything had to go wrong. Happy Mondays had to discover crack cocaine in Barbados! New Order's album had to be two years late! Claire Leighton had to die, of a tablet bought in Stockport, but in the Haçienda! There had to be an international property collapse! Do you want me to go on?' Looking back in 2020, Ryder recalled: 'I'd out-smoked meself, out-e'd meself, out-charlied meself, out-whizzed meself, out-drunk meself.'

10

Simply regeneration

It is easy to forget how big a deal Mick Hucknall was in the global music business in the 1990s, and the story of how his worldwide success helped build Manchester city centre's regeneration after the Haçienda led the way is little known.

His group Simply Red were an established chart act by the end of the 1980s, and in 1991 the 'flame-haired singing star', or the 'carrot-topped singing sensation', to use the tabloid descriptors that annoyed him, released the album *Stars*. In 1991 it outsold all others, not just in the UK but in Europe too, and not just for that year but for all of 1992 as well.

Selling tens of millions of albums, plus busy touring worldwide, meant the former Manchester Polytechnic student raised by a Tameside single-parent father had become a *bona fide* star. Yet Hucknall was not typical of the superstar elite club he had joined. He had, let us not forget, seen the Sex Pistols at the Free Trade Hall in 1976 and he pursued his love of abstract painting into a fine art course at the Poly. His first recording saw him fronting mutant punk-R&B outfit The Frantic Elevators, with a cover photo of him frenziedly putting a gun to his mouth. When dredged up by the tabloids during his starry heyday, the image shocked his army of fans among the nation's suburban mums and young marrieds. He told me in a 1985 interview that his favourite music was early records by Buzzcocks and The Fall, music unlikely to feature in the collections of his mainly female fan club, whom he was obliged to meet after shows for photos, and whom he described affectionately as 'the dumplings'.

Hucknall was an unusual celebrity in many ways – he kept his Victorian semi in Old Trafford and was not shy of expressing strong left-leaning politics, leading to panel appearances on BBC shows like *Question Time*. 'Red' stood for his hair, his football team and his politics, the latter so often swerved by artists wanting mainstream commercial success. Simply Red exploited the 'hard times' chic seen in the early 1980s style magazines of the recession-hit UK. For the cover of the group's debut album *Picture Book*, Hucknall sported a Great Depression-era look, looking wistful in a working man's cap over his ginger curls.

After the first flush of success, Hucknall spent a year residing in Milan on tax advice, but then he returned to his home city. His management company was based in Princess Street, where with the aid of a fax machine and prodigious helpings of cannabis, his wily manager Elliot Rashman handled media approaches, kept his ears open for new talent by hiring radio and club DJ David Dunne, and became interested in the slowly reviving city centre.

A Mancunian graduate in American studies, Rashman was a charismatic huckster who first saw Hucknall perform in early versions of Simply Red while running Manchester Poly's live gigs. He offered to manage his career and helped form the band's line-up on the first album. Someone who took his life lessons from the music and drugs counter-culture, Rashman was prone to some eye-watering takes on life, the universe and his hometown, and became a favourite of Granada TV, which often booked him as an audience 'firelighter' on its raucous weekly debate *Upfront*.

I had known Mick Hucknall since the *City Life* days and had got to know Rashman when bringing in copies of the mag to sell in the student union shop. Our pop music reviewer Robert Graham and co-editor Chris Paul had seen the band perform, and soon cajoled the rest of us into witnessing an intimate gig at the swish basement Manhattan Sound club, off Spring Gardens. Here was a red-haired, Mancunian Al Green, who had been schooled by Northern Soul guru Roger Eagle in the best soul and blues. 'The carrot-topped crooner from Tameside', as my Diary page later liked to call him, boasted a rich and sexy falsetto. Backed by a classic brass section, it really kicked as a live soul sound. With the frontman's back story of abandonment as a baby by his mother, and a hard upbringing in Denton by Stockport barber father Reg, who relied on parenting support from his neighbours, no one could say his blue-eyed soul was emotionally inauthentic.

Everything about Mick was intense and passionate. He shot a highly competitive pool game in the pubs of Hulme, displayed his knowledge of great dance music at his Wednesday night Poly disco, and was not shy about his love for United and his avowed hatred of the Tories. He was a lover man too, juggling female relationships. Mick and I were reasonably friendly, because, as the band rose, I was able to get his interviews in the local press.

Rashman persuaded us that *City Life* should promote his still-unsigned band's biggest show yet. We would stage the show and take the door money. He would invite some London record business talent scouts. The hype would be good for all concerned and we might even make a profit. So, in November 1984, I sat on the door of cheesy Oxford Street disco the Tropicana taking the entrance money. Next to the cash box, I had a list Rashman had given me of the 'comps' – the names for free entry for record company scouts. What I hadn't expected was that all on the list, plus more, turned up – more than sixty in all.

The upshot was twofold: *City Life* became surely the only promoter to lose money putting on a Simply Red show, and the band got a record deal from performing among the Tropicana's plastic palm trees. The company signing them up was US label Elektra and their respectful, mature approach – in contrast to the million-pound advances being waved under Rashman's nose – was a smaller advance of £60,000 but allied to a sophisticated 'artist development' approach to build a long-term career.

Rashman had sought support from an experienced and imaginative partner, establishing a business pairing with Andy Dodd. A former promoter and arts administrator from the Wirral, he exuded a zen-like presence, referring to the need to have an 'interesting existence' as well as make money, and provided the thoughtful yin to his partner's yang, which had a tendency towards drama and confrontation. Generally, Rashman and Hucknall looked after the creative side and Dodd did the business, including transferring the contract to WEA when Elektra was closed by its parent company.

Dodd had started a town-planning degree before his passion for live music led him to programming the schedule at Chester Arts Centre. He joined Ian Croal at the Manchester office of the Jazz Centre Society and by the early 1980s they were promoting 75 per cent of the nation's live contemporary jazz and world music. JCS saved the Band on the Wall (BOTW) when its founder Steve Morris could not continue, thereby making the stage available for a serious contribution to the nascent punk scene in the late 1970s.

There is a lot more to Dodd than being one of the managers of Mick Hucknall's heyday. Since the mid-1990s, after first boot-strapping the finances of the struggling venue with his own funds, he subsidised the painfully slow process of expanding the BOTW into two adjoining buildings. Buying the three properties, putting them in trust, applying for public-capital grants and then handing ownership to the new BOTW means he has personally guaranteed

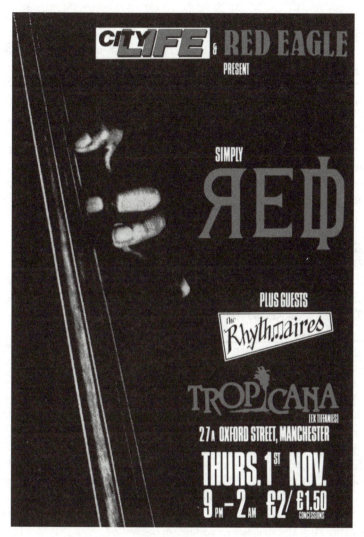

City Life advert for Simply Red at Tropicana, 1984

not only the venue's survival but overseen a threefold rise in its property value. 'The Band', which has at least the same cultural impact as London's Ronnie Scott's, reopened in early 2022 with two stages, larger capacity and pin-sharp sound systems.

One night when Dodd's duties doubled as the venue's sound mixer, he saw Hucknall's first band The Frantic Elevators and didn't like them. A decade later, things had moved on. Now Hucknall was a millionaire through the success of his 1986 ballad 'Holding Back the Years', including a number one in America, it would have been easy for him to cut his Manchester roots, in the time-honoured fashion of the Northern pop star made good, ever since The Beatles left Liverpool. His stateside fame meant he was given the respect by his American music heroes when they came to town, though, when invited by Curtis Mayfield to take the stage at the International 2, it was to the sound of audience laughter when the soul man announced him as 'Rick Hucknall'. A gig by Bobby Womack promoted by Roger Eagle at the International 1 descended into farce when the messed-up American legend asked Hucknall up to sing with him, but couldn't remember the words to his own hits.

After the *Picture Book* album was a hit, Hucknall was getting the bus into town from his Old Trafford semi, as if still living the life of an aspiring musician. Though a superstar, he would stride in and out of the clubs on Whitworth Street West, where he knew the managers and the door staff. Hucknall's sartorial style included a wide-brimmed hat and cane. It was a ballsy look to carry off. Clubbers would bitch behind his back about his showmanship, but, as I was always telling London journalists, fame hadn't changed him – he had an arrogant swagger about him when he was unknown, and he could handle the attention, both welcome and unwanted.

If Manchester was where he decided to base himself, it was also where much of his money ended up. Having secured an entire block in Chinatown for Hucknall's pension, Dodd and Hucknall looked to develop property and partnered with a small bar and restaurant outfit, Hale Leisure. The owners Eamonn Dwyer and Aidan Clancy were an Ant-and-Dec-style double act known as 'the Murphia', used because no one could remember which was which. I think it was Dwyer who visited me at the *Evening News* office with Dodd's property partner Simon Bate. I wrote the story in my page the next day. Never mind Planet Hollywood, move over Arnie and Bruce, the story said: our own world-famous celebrity Mick Hucknall is opening his own bar-restaurant.

Barca opened in two very large railway arches in Castlefield in June 1996. Its name matched the council's Catalan Square outside, inspired by the leadership's visits to Barcelona in pursuit of the city's two failed Olympic bids in the 1990s. Credit for the delightful transformation of historic Castlefield, however, was due more to Salford than Spain. Bookmaker Jim Ramsbottom had read up on the historic importance of the world's first industrial transport complex and fell in love with the crumbling factories and warehouses. Salfordian 'Rambo' had a city-wide chain of bookies, but his Deansgate office was on the edge of Castlefield, and his fascination with the area's history grew as he wandered, chain-smoking and lost in reflection, every time a punter took him for a big win.

Gazing with increasing interest at the ghostly remains of the city's origins, he saw opportunity. Buying the oldest standing warehouse in the city, Merchant's Warehouse, for just £25,000 for the scrap value of the bricks and timber, he secured £4 million of public funding and private money to convert it to offices. He performed similar miracles with other glorious old buildings which became offices, apartments and the Dukes 92 pub in the old stables on the 92nd lock of the Bridgewater Canal.

Underneath the elevated train line to Liverpool and with the Rochdale and Bridgewater canal junction outside, Hucknall's Barca was a two-level affair with a swanky first-floor restaurant offering lovely views of the historic, newly blossoming neighbourhood. The ancient cobbles all around were not ideal for high heels but the VIP launch party attracted the white stiletto brigade, Hucknall family and friends, and Mick's own hero-object and now close pal Alex Ferguson. Hucknall loved playing football at celebrity charity matches, but Ferguson told him: 'You haven't got the legs for football.' With the paparazzi prowling outside, due to Hucknall's distaste of being fronted up by snappers while strolling the streets – 'My music is for sale, I am not!' he snorted – I was happy to take the photo of the pop star and football boss clinking glasses which went to the papers.

The Barca party photo cemented the widespread perception of a bromance of two famous people living with the pressure of life in the public eye. 'We found we had a lot in common,' said Hucknall. 'We're both working-class boys with an interest in the labour movement, we'd bettered ourselves and come out of a certain amount of poverty.' Hucknall, who, media estimated, was worth £10 million after selling 26 million albums, could have added that both were proud of their tough regional cities.

No one who visits Castlefield fails to be impressed. Pop producer Pete Waterman moved his hit factory into the 1858 Venetian-style Congregational Church in the late 1980s, recording Rick Astley's 'Never Going to Give You Up' there, before selling it for offices in 2006. However, the fact that the area is the last word in how to blend historic with modern is thanks to a bookie-turned-local history buff. Rarely has self-made money been so well-versed in heritage, or better advised by well-chosen architects. Developer Ramsbottom

Barca launch. Ferguson and Hucknall (photo: Eamonn Clarke)

was a fast-talking, senior 'mod' with ciggie ash on his neat suits and a bracing, Salfordian turn of phrase. Developers coming to the area after him 'were dipping their bread in my gravy'. When he struggled with the council to get an artisan market under Castlefield's arches, Rambo explained to them it would differ from the city's other markets – 'our market won't be selling second-hand bog rolls'.

Castlefield was the place to take visitors with good taste. In 2001 I took the top brass of global luxury brand Hermès for dinner at Barca after the launch of its first Manchester store. The venerable nineteenth century company was run by a courteous old-school French family, and the entire party purred with delight at the sympathetic restoration of the surrounding buildings by Ramsbottom's architect Roger Stephenson. In heaven among the Victorian vista of redbrick, they trilled: 'This whole area has been done beautifully, so right for the history. In France, this area would be so "ticky tacky"!' I reassured them there were no plans for the aesthetic to be ruined by fancy neon lighting and plastic signage. (The summer 2022 opening of an elevated garden inspired by New York's High Line on the 330 m steel Castlefield Viaduct drew attention to its disgraceful fall into neglect under its landowners the city council and Peel.)

Indeed, there were influential voices which argued that the historic quarter should be designated a UNESCO World Heritage Site. Surely the UN's blessing would boost tourism and be a feather in the city's cap? Not so. Privately, some in authority were horrified when, in 1999, Castlefield was put on the UNESCO 'tentative' list, the process through which it could be inscribed as a World Heritage Site. They were aware of the restrictions the awarding body put on building anything new, not only on the site itself but also nearby or even within sight of it. Indeed, those issues were to bedevil Liverpool, which was only too happy to accept the garland in 2004 for its waterfront district and has ever since torn itself apart in disputes about new development.

In Manchester, the council and the music business were taking tentative steps towards each other. In January 1996 Rashman hosted the city's most powerful official in his VIP box at the new 21,000-capacity Manchester Arena. This was not the chief executive Arthur Sandford, but his deputy. The council's number two, Howard Bernstein, was the increasingly influential power behind the throne as the city's top official neared retirement, and he would have been justified at some personal pride over his role in creating the new facility, built over Victoria rail station, which Rashman praised for its 360-degree audience sightlines and its backstage, allowing easy access for the modern-day caravan of trucks, tech and roadies. (Hucknall was hired for the topping-out ceremony along with TV's chimney-demolisher Fred Dibnah, teaming up old and new Manchester.)

In Manchester's bids for the Olympic Games, many scoffed at what they saw as a laughable, quixotic tilt at windmills. Yet Bernstein was making sure Manchester was getting a modern venue which would never have come without the bids. The new Manchester Arena was to provide a critical pivot for the city, with the council clearly setting its sights on becoming the entertainment capital of the North. Needing complex property contracts around 'air rights' over

Victoria Station, it was built as an American-style sports arena, but has been far more successful hosting big music events.

Following his experience with Hulme and the Bridgewater Hall, Bernstein and his lieutenants knew their way round securing public cash. Of the Arena's £52 million cost, £35.5 million was from government grants and £2.5 million from European funds. This was the kind of trickle-down sought by the leadership – the taxis, the hotels, the restaurants all benefited, even if the jobs as concierges and waiters were part-time and low-paid.

In its first two decades it has been calculated that the venue brought £3 billion of spending into the city. At the 2016 private event marking its twenty years of operation, Bernstein told the invited guests, 'Not many places would have thought about building the biggest indoor arena in the world, as it was back in the early '90s, over a railway station.' The £35.5m million government cash was, he said, 'the single biggest public grant that was made for a facility of this kind ever and there has never been one since'. He continued: 'I've always believed that how we actually drive culture … will always be part of what makes Manchester different.'

When the rising city official and the music manager sat down together for the Simply Red show, one of a three-night run back in the band's home city, Hucknall was possibly the most well-known Mancunian after the city's footballers, celebrated in the red-top papers for his lusty lifestyle, including dating tennis champ Steffi Graf and taking movie actress Brigitte Nielsen to the Haçienda. Of more pragmatic interest to Bernstein, however, was that, mostly unknown at the time, the Simply Red office on Princess Street had a hotline to Labour Party leader Tony Blair, which only a year later became a very busy line between No. 10 Downing Street and manoeuvring Manchester.

Bizarre as it may seem, the Blair party regime destined for power in 1997 had no fellow feeling for Manchester. His government contained a large number of heavy-hitting Northeast MPs in a party bitter at the city's record of working with Tory governments on regeneration. In 1996 US writer Stryker McGuire coined 'Cool Britannia' for a *Newsweek* cover feature, which became a vacuous London media cliché. However, there was an actual cool, if not frosty, relationship between the party and the Labour city delivering the public–private partnerships that an out-of-power Labour could only talk about. Manchester was finding to its dismay that the command-and-control of regional cities by the centre was something that the Labour Party machine shared with Westminster and Whitehall.

Unlike other cities hoping and waiting for Labour to win and build a new Jerusalem, Manchester simply cracked on with building its own future infrastructure. The Arena was a prime example, its funding made possible because Manchester had been on good terms with successive Conservative governments. Strange to think that The City, a Labour machine run by Leese and economy led by Bernstein, might be concerned how it would be treated under a Blair leadership seeking to capitalise on John Major's wobbling government. An evening in Rashman's VIP box, then, was a way for Bernstein to tune into the political mood music.

After Labour's 1997 landslide victory, Hucknall's outspoken support for the party made Blair pay attention to Manchester, and it brought about a three-way love-in between Blair, 'Red Mick' and Manchester United's Labour-supporting manager Alex Ferguson, with Labour king of spin Alastair Campbell making it a quartet. This mutual appreciation society had created a Manchester back channel into the highest office in government. As a confidant of the Simply Red operation, I heard many a story of how the PM's powerful gatekeeper Anji Hunter – the woman known as Blair's office 'wife' – had been in touch to ask for concert tickets, celeb contacts and personal appearances from Mick, and not just for office staff – Blair attended at least one show by the group in the mid-1990s before he became prime minister.

Behind the all-conquering commercial sound of Simply Red, Rashman was a music biz mastermind, a radical thinker and in his own way as much of a disruptor as Tony Wilson. Rashman agitated for artists to leave record companies' exploitative clutches for the risky world of internet sales, and followed Dodd's push to form Blood and Fire, a label re-issuing classic Jamaican reggae.

Rashman opined about 'people magic', when creative people hit it off. But he could be caustic. I assumed that he and Bernstein, both Jewish Mancunians and close in age, would find some common ground. I was in the same box at the show where they met, but not privy to their conversation, so I enquired afterwards if the two had got on. The council chief's sartorial style – fashionably baggy suit and turned-up trousers – was the subject of a Rashman snipe: 'Yeah, we got on okay, but he must have Hitler as his tailor.' No people magic there then. However, the meeting predated and cued up a close working partnership between the other half of the Simply Red hit machine, Rashman's co-manager Andy Dodd. He bought out Rashman in the early 2000s and he was to make the millions from Hucknall's royalties have a major impact on Manchester city centre.

Behind the all-conquering commercial sound of Simply Red, Rashman and Dodd were music-biz radical thinkers, in their own way as much visionaries as Wilson, with whom they co-founded (with Wilson's partner Yvette Livesey) the music industry convention In The City. At the first event in 1992 they initiated The International Managers Forum, later renamed The Music Managers Forum and now a four-thousand-strong global representative body.

The council led by Leese and Bernstein, by now being commonly referred to by the shorthand 'The City', welcomed new property entrepreneurs like Hucknall and Dodd. The Simply Red camp had got the development bug, and the fruits of Manchester's music exports were being invested back in the city which made them. Hucknall ended up in Surrey rock-star country, while the Gallaghers have invested 'nish' in their hometown, and the feuding brothers whom many see as 'Proper Mancs' live in the celebrity-and-cocaine circuits of London's Primrose Hill and the shire counties.

While he was hardly a hands-on developer, leaving Dodd and his team to it, Hucknall's royalties transformed the prospects of one of the city's most shameful sights, one which hit visitors arriving by train. Exiting via the station approach on to London Road, they could not miss the plight of the derelict Joshua Hoyle building opposite. This fine 1906 six-storey warehouse in brick, terracotta and glazed ceramics boasted a lovely corner entrance crowned with an octagonal turret. It did not enjoy protected status and, ominously, owner NCP had earmarked it for demolition for a car park. The building looked like it was not long for the world, but public-spirited local architect and original Haçienda member Dominic Sagar ensured it was listed and protected.

Simply Red money, public grants and a Scottish entrepreneur rescued the Joshua Hoyle. Shareholder-investors Hucknall, Dodd and Rashman, using the consultancy talents of Simon Bate, attracted the Glaswegian star hotelier Ken McCulloch to open a two-hundred-bed Malmaison hotel. The scheme was not without controversy, as the next-door Imperial Hotel, the 1907 birthplace of the Professional Footballers Association, had to make way for a later extension. It was a sad lesson that, when regeneration momentum takes hold, you cannot save every building simply because it has some history to it.

The hotel launch in March 1998 was a watershed for me. I had become friendly with Dodd, and in late 1997 he suggested I start a PR firm, starting with me handling his leisure business interests. Plus, he said, Mick Hucknall could do with some positive stories in his Northwest audience heartland. I was well disposed to the idea of working for myself, based at the lockkeeper's cottage at the 91st lock on the Rochdale Canal, which Dodd had turned into his offices.

Having given notice at the *Evening News*, I started with me and my Filofax, stuffed with contacts from my twenty years of reporting, and a mobile phone clipped to my belt. All very late twentieth-century, as was the agency name, Spin Media. I had been nicknamed 'Spin' since primary school, and everyone used it, so it was a no-brainer as personal branding for a showbiz and leisure PR agency. The name was to prove problematic later, but at the time it was a trendy expression for smart and slick presentation, not yet associated with manipulation and deceit. A more immediate concern for my wife Lynne and I was, with two daughters under five and a third baby on the way, how we would pay the mortgage. But I could see the exciting changes in Manchester. I wanted to be in the room where it happened, not merely to be called in afterwards to interview the decision-makers.

The Malmaison opening was my first launch. It was a blast, as endless supplies of champagne disappeared down the necks of Mancs determined to show their Glaswegian partners a thing or two about epic boozing. It was an even bigger result for McCulloch, who on the same day sold his hotel empire for £35 million to US pension fund American Patriot and promptly relocated to Monaco. Simply Red's 1999 album *Love and the Russian Winter* flopped, but Hucknall's pain was cushioned by a seven-figure pay-out for his stake in the Manchester slice of the Malmaison sale.

The agency's first national account win was to launch the George Foreman Grill in the UK. My partner Daniel Kennedy and I spent two days in London with the 'king of the ring' whose portable indoor grill-on-a-slope – 'knock the fat out' – was a household name stateside. We toured the pugilist-turned-entrepreneur around the media studios and hit the jackpot when we landed him on the Jonathan Ross TV chat show. Sat in the Green Room during filming, we were amazed when Ross brought out the 'Lean Mean Fat-Reducing Grilling Machine' he had bought on holiday. Paul McCartney was on the sofa alongside Foreman, and 'Wossy' quipped to Macca: 'You might have sold millions of records, but you haven't got your own grill, have you?' While ITV shows were governed by strict Ofcom rules on product placement, with heavy fines, the BBC deemed the product editorially relevant, and our PR blitz drove sales of one million grills in the first three months.

Business opportunity was in the air. My silent partner had another client for me. As one of the many Manchester United fans of Irish descent, Dodd, with some others had approached Alex Ferguson, the club's manager, about arranging his testimonial during the 1998–99 season – not only a football match but also a golf tournament, a horse-race day, several dinners and eventually a concert by Simply Red, all to give the boss, at that time still an unknighted commoner, a financial thank you.

The purpose behind the testimonial was for United fans to express their gratitude in a way, they felt, his employers never did. Their view was that whatever Ferguson was being paid (a reported £1.5 million a year), it wasn't enough. An external committee formed, including chairman Dodd, the Birthday greetings cards millionaire Ron Wood and Kieran Toal, the former United reserve who was studying the law, and is now a prominent Manchester solicitor. They wanted to pay him tribute both financially and emotionally after 13 years in which, at that point, he had steered United to four premier league titles and three FA cups, among other honours. In football, the art of managing a winning side and then regenerating new teams at the same club was possibly the toughest job in world sport, and it was one at which Ferguson was the master. For once, the use of 'legend' was not hyperbole.

With a team stuffed with big name players like local boys the Neville brothers and pin-up Ryan Giggs, the 'Great Dane' goalie Peter Schmeichel, the emerging celebrity of David Beckham and the recently departed Eric Cantona, Fergie could easily be overlooked. Other managers, it was felt, had become hugely wealthy for failure, picking up eye-watering payments when sacked. Yet Fergie had not been rewarded by United's owners for his sustained success, as any leader of a worldwide brand would be.

Dodd and Toal suggested to Fergie that I handled the PR. I had met him and his wife Cathy at a reception at the Palace Theatre when they attended a musical, and found the off-duty footy boss pleasant company and nothing like his fearsome image. At the first committee meeting, I played the Cassandra role and prepared the organisers, and its hero, for bad news. I did genuinely think that Fergie, who had an unassailable reputation as one of the gods of the game, and a proud supporter of socialist causes, would get criticism for the tax-free testimonial income.

'I think we will get a rough ride over the tax issue, and I think we should prepare for some awkward questions,' I ventured. The committee members looked nervously at Fergie, who was quite sanguine, replying, 'No, I don't think we will get a rough ride at all.' He was firm about it, and I was not about to contradict him. As it transpired, I had underestimated the influence that Ferguson had over the football media. Such was the respect for his achievements (and the fear he might withdraw media access to players) that the testimonial year was reported entirely straight by the media. At his testimonial race day at Haydock Park, BBC sports reporter Clare Balding delivered an impressive live interview with Ferguson about his love and knowledge of horse racing. Earlier, though, she took me to one side and implored me to prevail upon him to grant the BBC more football interview time, referring to a spat between him and her bosses. I could only tell her that brokering any such rapprochement was well above my pay grade. In any case, the United manager clearly knew his own media value, and with it came a muscle he was not shy of flexing. Still, I couldn't work out what he liked and didn't. On my telling him he would be a shoo-in for a turn on Michael Parkinson's chat show, he replied: 'Him? He's a clinger-on!'

My business partner Dodd thought some bonding with the Ferguson clan was in order, so I accompanied him, along with Mr and Mrs Fergie, to the opening night of Hucknall's Paris nightclub Man Ray. The four of us were en route in a people carrier when heavy traffic immobilised us in the narrow roads around the Champs-Élysées. The driver said we could walk the rest. Fergie was out like a flash, leaving his spouse stranded, so I accompanied her while we found our way there. Inside, we were sat at a long dinner table in full view of fifteen hundred people, and our table started to fill up with diners: Sean Penn, Naomi Campbell, Johnny Depp, Johnny Halliday and Kate Moss took their seats. A couple sat down on my right, U2's Bono and wife Ali Hewson. I told her that I had come with Alex Ferguson. "Who's Fergus?" she asked me. Only a few months before, as a gossip columnist I'd have been writing up her amusing ignorance of the famous football figure. Now I was a trusted confidant.

In March 1999 with Fergie by my side at a press conference at Manchester Town Hall, we launched his testimonial season. The tabloids sent their snappers and the story made the *News at Ten* 'And Finally …' feature. Throughout the year only one dissenting press voice injected a shot of vinegar into the Scotsman's glass of sweet media sentiment. David Conn of *The Independent* ran a feature after the showpiece United versus the Rest of the World game in October 1999, which estimated the money Ferguson was to make from the year at £2 million and delved into its tax-free status.

What many Manchester City fans hated was the thought of an army of people only delighted to pay good money for events celebrating Fergie's success. There was further salt in their wounds. By amazing good fortune, between announcing the testimonial year and its extended finish, Ferguson had steered the team to an unprecedented treble of Premier League, FA Cup and Champions League, the latter achieved with two astonishing late, late goals which gave rise to the shell-shocked manager's phrase 'Football … bloody hell' often used in moments when otherwise intelligent people struggle to sum up the unpredictable, compelling nature of the game.

Ferguson, Hucknall and United players Giggs and Neville (photo: Eamonn Clarke)

No testimonial committee could have planned it better. The climax of the extended campaign on 1 April 2000 was a dinner at G-Mex for a thousand people, paying £100 each to dine on Arbroath smokies and medium-rare Scottish beef steak by chef Paul Heathcote, and to hear tributes from sports and TV personalities including Eamonn Holmes, artist Harold Riley and, on a recorded video message, Prime Minister Tony Blair. Until that point, the only possible friction had been the fashionably late arrival of the Beckhams, which some close to Ferguson felt was a bid to upstage him.

158

This had been a season of tension between Fergie and his now most famed celebrity player. I had been in the manager's office for an 8am testimonial meeting when one of his legendary spy network phoned in with intel about his player breaking the club curfew. 'He's been told', Fergie gravely muttered to his informant over and over. 'He's been told.' Their relationship started to deteriorate around that time, and Ferguson observed that celebrity and football are a difficult combination. 'He was never a problem until he got married,' he said of the Beckhams in one of his autobiographies.

With Posh and Becks safely seated with other team players and WAGS, the scene was set for the many giant screens dotted around the hall to play the words of the nation's leader. PM Blair's communications chief Alastair Campbell was in attendance at Fergie's VIP table. As the Blair video message played, there was some limited hissing and booing, but after a few seconds these gave way to respectful silence as his tribute played out. Considering there were a thousand people, mainly men, who had been knocking back the booze all night, I thought the collective courtesy was remarkable. When Hucknall came on to the stage, placed centrally to give all a good view, the crowd granted him total silence as he sang a spine-tingling acapella of Nat King Cole's 'Nature Boy' yards from the Glaswegian hardman, who looked mildly embarrassed at the naked affection of the performance.

On the Monday morning, the *Manchester Evening News* had a different take. My successor on the Diary, Rob Meakin, was, unknown to me, in the hall and saw an opportunity to have a pop at the Labour Party. His sympathies towards the minority Liberal Democrats on Manchester council were well known, and the article gleefully reported that the Blair video 'was met with a chorus of boos' and that 'eyebrows were raised' at Campbell being the winner of a raffled prize trip to Canada – 'the premier's media guru … isn't reported to have returned the tickets'.

The paper hit the streets at 12 noon in the city centre. Around 12.20pm, Ferguson's son Jason called me from his car while driving through Cheshire. The former Sky Sports TV football match director had switched career to become a football agent, and had brought his confrontational style into the testimonial committee. 'Alex is not happy,' he growled. 'Why didn't you shut that story down?' I explained that the journalist did not inform us he was going, that he was skewing the story for a political angle – and anyway, if there were a few boos, that was a fact, even if the story exaggerated it. And even if I knew that Meakin was in the room, how could I, in his phrase, 'shut it down'?

The report couldn't be denied factually. So, seemingly out of frustration that the gloss had been taken off a glittering night, the Ferguson clan kicked the dog, that mutt being me. 'Alex is very disappointed,' said Jason as he ended the conversation. 'You've embarrassed him in front of Alastair.' To my mind, the call had the king of spin's fingerprints on it. The Labour Party machine had a rapid rebuttal unit, and it seemed it was working efficiently. If Jason was in Cheshire, out in the sticks, it seemed impossible that he could have seen the first-edition paper so quickly, unless someone with access to it had alerted him.

It was only fish and chip paper, but the politicisation of a wonderful night left a sour taste. It ended my involvement in the testimonial year, except that the committee members told me a sorry tale that relationships had worsened after the arrival of Ferguson junior, who saw pound signs where they didn't exist. The gig, the race day, the dinners all washed their face but weren't money-spinners. 'Can't you tell Alex what Jason's doing?' one of them asked me, saddened at insinuations that they were profiting from their involvement. I thought better of getting between the former Govan shipyard-trainee-turned-sporting warrior, and the son he had brought into the ever-enriching business of football. The players earned enough to make the hair-dryer treatment worth it, but I considered my work done. Meanwhile, Jason's activities as a footballer middleman were to be the subject of much media reporting in future years.

Despite the way things ended, the experience of working with Fergie was hugely enjoyable. I noticed that, wherever he went, he had time for the cleaners, door staff and catering staff, going out of his way to spend a few seconds to say hello. I had suggested to Lis Phelan of Marketing Manchester, also a member of the testimonial committee, that he should receive the Freedom of the City, an idea that she steered towards the council, and the honour was bestowed with great publicity in February 2000, shortly after he received his knighthood.

Meanwhile, the property interests of Fergie's pal Mick Hucknall were moving ahead. After the Malmaison Hotel's success, Dodd teamed up with Simon Bate and Nick Payne, bringing them as shareholders into his Westport Developments, and Hucknall invested in its projects. Bate was a partner at accountant Levy Gee when he looked after Simply Red drummer Chris Joyce's purchase of an old Knott Mill building for a recording studio, music sparking regeneration again. The deal opened a portal into real estate projects suited to the singular talent of the softly spoken Bate, who stood out in the property crowd with his imposing height and charming manner.

Bate's fertile mind devised Westport's audacious £6 million scheme to remodel 50,000 sq ft of redundant railway arches on Whitworth Street West to create a new boardwalk of bars and restaurants. In June 1999, Westport hired my agency to launch the site, named Deansgate Locks. It was a derelict and invisible property asset until Bate's ingenious plan for public access to the arches by building footbridges across the Rochdale Canal. My task was to get everyone who might take an interest, and spread the word about it, to a big old party in the mammoth hollow space. The overall shell was to be partitioned up for eight separate units, but, for now empty, it looked as big as the inside of the cavernous G-Mex, its neighbour on the north side.

How to get the property world to engage with potential leisure operators? This called for a collision of worlds: brewery reps meet property agents, quantity surveyors meet bar runners. My agency partner Daniel Kennedy had launched Planet Hollywood in London; he printed up an invite with a hint of intrigue about 'Manchester's inner outer space' and hired Bobby Langley – a pal of Liam Gallagher and an in-crowd DJ – for music scene cred. As the *Northwest Business Insider* property awards were being held next door at the Midland Hotel the same night, we wrote to the big dogs of the property world: come for an early evening livener before the awards, and, yes, you are welcome in black tie.

The result was a Fellini-esque social mash-up as dinner-jacketed corporate grandees rubbed shoulders with kids in anoraks and trainers, all meandering through the scuffed moonscape beneath the high arches, a smoke machine enhancing the offbeat scenario. The evening was talked about long after, and the combination of corporate and street soon delivered – the leases on Deansgate Locks' cavernous arches were snapped up by bar groups, restaurants and the first outpost outside London of the Comedy Store. The clash of penguin suits and streetwear had worked its commercial spell.

The influence of the Manchester music scene on the changing face of the city was unmistakable: the music culture was pump-priming the growth of a new city centre. But there were voices asking how healthy it was for an entire city to be appearing to remake itself around alcohol consumption, a public health issue which has never put the brakes on growth. There were questions, too, about the missing pieces for the pioneers moving into the city-centre pads. Where were the GP and dental surgeries, schools and grocery shops?

Those of us close to the noble mission for 'urban regeneration' aspired to the civilised lifestyle of European cities, where three generations mixed happily in the streets and squares. Owen Hatherley inserts those quote marks in his scathing polemic *A Guide to the New Ruins of Britain*, noting the almost religious tone of New Labour's cities policy. Yet the ideal was proving elusive. Instead of a continental-style utopia in which parents could raise their offspring, and for seniors to retire to (though small plucky numbers of both groups tried), living in Manchester city centre felt more like a Club 18–30 holiday camp with rather less sunshine.

It has often seemed as if city-centre transformation was being floated on an ocean of booze, its prospect for success swaying precariously on the foundations of an endless bout of rowdy drinking. In 2016 photographer Joel Goodman's night-time image of police, drunks and gawping onlookers enjoyed worldwide viral status when it was plucked from the *Manchester Evening News* photo gallery and tweeted out to spiralling fascination; cyberpunk writer William Gibson was among tens of thousands retweeting it and Wikipedia founder Jimmy Wales bought a copy. It was hardly the airbrushed global profile any city wishes for, and the alcohol-led city centre revival is still a source of conflict between business and some fed-up residents, a divisive issue that those driving the new Manchester have often struggled with.

11

Planet Hulme, city conversations

They say normal people don't live in Hulme. Just skinny freaks with skinny dogs.
Just kids with crazy-paving eyes, junk up their nose, needles in their arms. Just
aspiring musicians, who seek superstardom yet never get past their local pub. Just
little rich kids living it rough, sleeping with the cockroaches under their pillow, so
they can pretend they're as tough as the rest.

Sarah Champion, *And God Created Manchester*, 1990

Focused on jobs and investment, Manchester had committed solidly to the
regeneration game by the early 1990s. Where there was an opportunity, there
was Manchester, with its civil servants and consultants primed for the number-
crunching, form-filling and lobbying to win funds on offer. The city had bid
for and won the Festival of Expressionism in 1992 and the City of Drama in
1994. Following Rio de Janeiro's inaugural hosting, the second Earth Summit
took place in Manchester in 1993. In the competition culture set up by central
government, Manchester was shouting 'Over here! look at us!', determined to
be always first up and best-dressed.

While many put the IRA bomb of 1996 as the defining moment in this process, the partnership between Manchester and successive governments, more
often Conservative ones, had begun earlier, with the winning of £37.5 million
City Challenge funding to redevelop the failed Hulme estate. The inner-city
district on the centre's southwestern edge was a bold and well-meaning but
cack-handed urban planning revolution. Designed as a complete 1960s modernist neighbourhood, it swept away the cramped, unsanitary ranks of back-
to-backs where 132,000 lived in 1945. Across 230 acres, thirty thousand homes
were demolished and in their place were built six Brutalist estates, with concrete
deck-access blocks of six to nine storeys modelled, seemingly without irony, on
architect John Nash's Georgian crescents in Bath, interspersed among 13 tower
blocks.

The new Hulme's five thousand homes were built and occupied by 1972, but the 'city in the sky' soon became a crime-ridden dystopia. Badly constructed buildings left gaps between walls and floors, bedevilled by damp, mice and cockroaches. In 1974 a five-year-old was killed in a fall from a high walkway and the council stopped housing families there. In 1975 a tenant survey revealed that 96 per cent wanted to leave. By 1984, 59 per cent of Hulme's adult male population and 68 per cent of its young people were unemployed, and the same year the council said that many of the flats were in such poor condition that they would be rent-free.

On his first day at Manchester Polytechnic in 1988, Richard Davis was told Hulme was a dangerous, lawless place, to be avoided. The Brummie photography student went there straight away, and found it, he said, 'so damn photogenic … a lot of it was derelict, whilst what was occupied tended to consist of a diverse mix of artists, musicians, drop-outs, ex-students and the unemployed, the kind of people mainstream society seemed to reject'.

The big flats designed for families provided space for studios and rehearsal rooms. Some were turned into recording studios, others into unlicensed clubs which knocked through walls, like the fondly remembered rave-era Kitchen. Davis photographed the young Lemn Sissay and Steve Coogan amid the

Steve Coogan in Hulme (photo: Richard Davis)

Travellers in Hulme (photo: Richard Davis)

crumbling concrete (though Coogan lived in art-deco apartments in nearby Fallowfield, amusing neighbours with his proto-Alan Partridge habit of sitting in his sports car for long periods, gently pressing the accelerator to appreciate the souped-up tenor of the engine).

Hulme was designed and built for over twenty thousand people, but by the mid-1980s only eight thousand lived there. Some saw Hulme as Manchester's version of Copenhagen's Christiania or Berlin's Kreuzberg, a creative hub left by officialdom to its own devices. New-age travellers overwintered their convoy in Hulme and held car-burning festivals for the residents. The street-art collective Dogs of Heaven burned effigies of Margaret Thatcher on Bonfire Night 1990. Hulme's attraction to young people for both cheap living and radical politics gave the area a unique schizophrenia. By the end of the 1980s, a third of its population had university degrees, on a par with the leafy suburbs. Another third had no qualifications at all. Urbanist David Rudlin says of his time there, 'It wasn't a divided area – qualified and unqualified, most people were unemployed, looked the same, drank in the same pubs and ran the gauntlet of the same muggers and drug dealers.'

There was a green produce home-delivery company Marlarkey, and even an arthouse cinema, the Aaben (Danish for 'open'): all muted lighting and 1970s soft furnishings, its groovy interior seemed styled by Bang and Olufsen hi-fi. While celebrated by writers and nicknamed the People's Republic of Hulme by the community of drop-outs, artists and 'alt' lifestylers, in urban planning terms it was a gigantic foul-up and was bleeding council resources.

Perhaps the biggest cultural contribution the new Hulme made to future Manchester was the chain of events caused by the sweeping away in the 1960s of Stretford Road, one of the busiest shopping streets in the city. In the urban war zone which Hulme had become, the Clopton Walk precinct only just about managed to retain a newsagent and an off-licence behind graffitied vandal-secure exteriors. A windowless brick box was the social club for the city's bus drivers, variously called the Russell Club, the Caribbean Club or the PSV (for Public Service Vehicles). This became the short-lived live music venue known as The Factory. With promoter-collaborators Alan Wise and Roger Eagle lending their booking experience, the charmless building was hired out for gigs by Tony Wilson, moonlighting from his TV job, and his actor friend Alan Erasmus. The Factory's place in the city's cultural journey was fleeting but critical, an experience which gave the fledgling entrepreneurs the confidence to set up first Factory Records and then the Haçienda.

It also introduced Joy Division and photographer Kevin Cummins to an area they had no reason to venture into before the Factory nights began. When I lived there for two years from 1982, the student residents nicknamed it 'Planet Hulme' for our immersive other-worldly experience of life in such a hard-edged widescreen environment. Cummins's imagery of the band on Epping Walk bridge in the snow for the *New Musical Express* – after which it was known as 'Joy Division bridge' – showed how such extreme urban voyeurism could create a resonant media-fuelled myth. 'Hulme-ans' like me were there for cheap rents and the closeness to our lectures, but as we criss-crossed the concrete pathways, bridges and walkways on giant stilts we carried Cummins's monochrome tableaux in our heads.

The government's response to the inner-city riots of 1981 and the social problems in the big urban areas was the City Challenge funding competition. Manchester was one of the twenty winners nationally, but, intriguingly, the city's success may well have been nudged along because of the ructions at the very top of the Conservative Party. Cabinet dissent and the challenges to Thatcher, from Poll Tax protests to Geoffrey Howe quitting over Europe, flushed out a long-speculated Conservative leadership bid from Michael Heseltine in autumn 1990. Thatcher stepped down but 'Hezza' did not have enough votes to win, and her preferred candidate John Major emerged as victor. He immediately asked Heseltine to take up his former role as environment secretary, and this reinstatement was to prove critical to Manchester's fortunes.

As environment secretary between 1979 and 1983, Heseltine's crucial role in the revival of Liverpool, where he is still feted to this day, is widely known. The social conscience of the Tory party wrote a famous memo to the cabinet called 'It Took a Riot'. In Manchester's case, however, his bond to the city was smoothed by chance personal relationships. Politics and policies may be laid down in tablets of stone, but things get done when people get on. As Ray King and Andrew Nott's *Detonation* revealed, the city was to benefit from a personal connection. The city council leader Graham Stringer had been at university with Heseltine's private secretary Phil Ward and, furthermore, he had been best man at Ward's wedding.

Heseltine lost no time in visiting the Northern cities. At a meeting at Manchester Airport, Stringer, with the city's theatres boss Sir Bob Scott whose idea it first was to tilt for the five-ring global sporting circus, summarised the second Olympic Bid for the 2000 Olympics that had been presented to the International Olympic Committee by his predecessor Chris Patten. Bernstein recalled Heseltine, at first cool on sports as a regeneration lever, shouting 'I love it, I love it!' £70 million of funding came through rapidly for the Manchester stadium site and a new velodrome, along with the full-blooded backing of Her Majesty's Government for the bid process.

More success was to come with money to rework Hulme for the second time in twenty years. Before the City Challenge was announced, Heseltine had received a presentation from the council and its development partner AMEC. Heseltine viewed the mixed-tenure model, a blend of social and private housing, with great interest and he took a helicopter tour with Stringer to get a bird's-eye view of the immense failed estate, marvelling at the scale of the botched design and human mess below. Leese later said, reported by Ray King and Andrew Nott, that the government-designed contest was an uncanny match for Hulme: 'It's one of those things you can never prove, but after that, City Challenge as a concept was announced … [it] was almost a response to Hulme; it fitted the circumstances of the area perfectly.'

A big requirement for winning funding was getting tenant support for the new Hulme. The residents were very different from those in the late 1960s when compliant families in the terraces were uprooted by a paternalistic council. The new residents included articulate operators like Charlie Baker of the remarkable Homes for Change housing co-op, an entire ex-council block of 75 flats around an enclosed open space. Many others, though, were simply party animals or drug-dependent waifs and strays. When *Area News*, a council-funded paper for Hulme and Moss Side, was closed after it asked tough questions about City Challenge, freelance journalist Andrew Orlowski was driven to publish *Bad Press*, an underground 'micro-zine'. The A3 concertina-format featured small type and minimal design, but squinting readers read him making life difficult for the council, going through minutes of meetings, and carrying spiky reports on public consultation. Orlowski challenged how much of a say the residents were really being given. He thrust *Bad Press* into the hands of people at pubs and in queues. He recalled: 'I always thought it was very strange how Hulme community had an identity and was always gonna go its own way … as soon as the City Challenge came along, that disintegrated very quickly … people who you'd meet would say, "How did that happen?"'

Bad Press caused a stir in limited circles, but the stakes were too high to pander to a tiny outpost of bohemia. There was high-level momentum behind remodelling the 1970s Hulme experiment and demolition began in 1992. Another Hulme gradually took shape, one which has come to be generally regarded as an exemplar of how to transform a district from an urban nightmare to a flourishing community, thanks to the Charlie Baker and David Rudlin-authored Hulme design guide which required developers, architects and planners to build mixed and varied communities in low-rise housing on connected streets, rather than estates like the gang-troubled Alexandra Park nearby, or on suburban-style cul-de-sacs. Property journalist David Thame says, 'It has been the UK regeneration default setting ever since … The idea of placemaking, now at the heart of urban regeneration, was born in Hulme.'

In a *Telegraph* feature in 1993, Michael Watts noted the 'ironic alliance between self-help Toryism and paternal Socialism'. Yet despite the close working relationship with the highest level of the Conservative government, there was still a traditional Punch and Judy game being played out for the public. Supporters of the main parties, and the media feeding both sides their diet of yah-boo-sucks commentary, may have found the reality of fraternising across party lines too discombobulating. Perhaps this explains why heritage minister Robert Key (also the 'Minister for Manchester' supporting the Olympic Games bid), when asked by *City Life* in March 1992 to comment on the city's future, said he believed it was bright, but added: 'I have one pre-condition to all this. That the biggest yawn of all, the boring, stultifying, ultra-conventional, crushingly establishment, Mogadon-induced failure of the unquestioning, uninspired party state that is the Labour party in Manchester, is removed.'

That the Tory minister for Manchester felt he could insult the leadership of the city he was charged to support says much about the public presentation of political relationships. Perhaps the portly Wiltshire Tory didn't get the memo from on high: the Conservatives were closer to The City than the average left-leaning *City Life* reader realised. When Marketing Manchester was established in 1997 to replace the city's visitor and convention bureau, its chairman, former Conservative MP Sir David Trippier, oversaw its £2.5 million budget, £1 million of it from local-authority-owned Manchester Airport.

I made the point in my newspaper column that it was curious that Labour councils' money was being governed by a Tory MP. It was strange that the convivial 'one nation' MP was regarded by Manchester's leaders as 'one of us'. Trippier was a former leader of Rochdale Council before he was Tory inner cities minister, so was used to working across party divides. Centrally involved with the CMDC (which had been disbanded in 1986), he had worked well with The City. He revealed in his memoir *Lend Me Your Ears* that he gelled with the council only after it rid itself of what he called its 'banana republic' period. The former Royal Marines Reserve officer wrote: 'The Lefties even got rid of the military silverware from the town hall … it went to Tameside and when Manchester eventually asked for it back they were told to fuck off.' Now they had done away with what he sneered at as 'ideological tripe', odd bedfellows Trippier and Stringer bonded through a shared love of Manchester, excited that they had many of the elements in place to bring investment and employment back to the city.

The relationships between civic and business leaders created in the ten years of the CMDC and Olympic bids were to be critical in the challenge to come, though not in any way that anyone could have imagined. The IRA bomb of 15 June 1996 was a cynical compliment to the resurgent Manchester. A European championship football match between Russia and Germany was scheduled for Old Trafford the next day (the game went ahead) and the city was packed with families and foreign tourists, plus legions of media workers. The 1,500 kg device was detonated on a busy Saturday morning outside the Arndale Centre. Thousands of shoppers were hastily evacuated after a telephoned coded warning, and no one was killed, but over two hundred people were injured. Swiss Re estimated that over £400 million insurance was paid for the world's most costly non-natural disaster at the time.

Wry jokes abounded about the terrorists' helping hand to remodel the loathed Arndale. Manc humour flourished, such as the tale of musicians Johnny

Bramwell and Bryan Glancy. The pair emerged from the Night and Day Café's basement dazed and bemused after a day of guitar riffing and spliffing up, wandering along empty Oldham Street in the evacuated city centre, until being ticked off and sent home by a police patrol. I wrote up a (drug-free) version of the story in my *Manchester Evening News* page.

It was no laughing matter for businesses in the twelve hundred buildings affected across 43 streets. As the impact sunk in, it was clear that national government was needed for finance and clout to help rebuild the northern side of the city centre. Cue the arrival of Deputy Prime Minister Heseltine. Ten days after the explosion, he was in the city, working again with The City — people he knew and trusted, from his close involvement in the transformations of G-Mex and Hulme and the funding of the Bridgewater Hall. In no time £21 million of aid was channelled Manchester's way from European and other funds. The image of Tarzan flying to the rescue was an irresistible one for the media. Heseltine wrote in his autobiography that he gave newly installed council leader Richard Leese his home phone number, adding, 'I believed this was a remarkable opportunity to create a great legacy from the outrage.'

The Manchester Millennium task force was formed almost overnight and offered to Howard Bernstein to lead. At that point, he was hot favourite for the top job at national regeneration agency English Partnerships but he said, 'I couldn't turn it down, this was my city.' Under his stewardship, he was to skilfully manage what he called 'the interdependence of public and private sectors' in a tight-knit group, notably the chairman Sir Alan Cockshaw of AMEC,

Howard Bernstein with model of reconstruction of city centre after the IRA bomb

Manchester-friendly Tory Sir David Trippier, the top government civil servant in the region Marianne Neville-Rolfe and leading councillors Pat Karney and Kath Robinson.

The IRA bomb had brought the 'Manchester mafia' back in the game, and it proved the right way to get things done. The subsequent international design competition used the opportunity to enhance the Manchester Cathedral quarter. The city centre took on a new shape, making use of the space left by the half of the Arndale Centre damaged by the bomb. Shops and restaurants opened up in the new Exchange and Millennium Squares. The new start was signalled by the striking glass profile of the Urbis museum.

In 1996 the two Olympic bids had attracted ridicule, but the city had made friends in high places, built media profile and gathered know-how. Eyes were fixed on tangible prizes and the new partnership machine led not only to the 2002 Commonwealth Games but to an array of facilities. As well as the main stadium, there were new swimming and tennis centres and a velodrome, plus further expansion in the Metrolink system (technically not the 'tram' as it is commonly called, but a light rail 'road running' network), which began stretching tentacles across Greater Manchester.

That the city was winning pots of money was given a cold hard look by urbanism and economics academics in 2001. In the book of essays *City of Revolution*, they looked beyond the boosterism and observed that Manchester had moved from an old economy, welfarist municipal city model to one which had fully embraced the realpolitik of neo-liberal economics. Faced with global forces it could never alter, they concluded that The City was now pitching for unstable, low-paid service jobs through centrally run beauty contests. In 2002 Professor Peter Dicken noted that Manchester, once a global player, dominant in textiles, chemicals and manufacturing, 'is in many ways now just another potential investment site in the global economic system'.

The City's invisible enemy was deindustrialisation. In 1961 the city centre was the main employment centre for the region, with 167,000 jobs in its small, dense business centre, but this had fallen to 98,000 by 1977. Between 1971 and 1997 more than one in four jobs in the city of Manchester were lost, two-thirds of all of the job losses throughout Greater Manchester. The leadership now saw their hope for economic regeneration in the service sector – precarious part-time work in bars, hotels, restaurants, the kind of leisure-economy work for young people which could not measure up to their parents' (usually their fathers') decently paid, unionised manual jobs in factories, mines, engineering and transport. The erosion of the urban core economy meant that there were few affluent residents in the city of Manchester itself. The high council tax bands were to be found outside the city boundaries. Little wonder that the council began to aggressively extract income from car-parking charges and fines from affluent residents of Trafford, Stockport and Cheshire who drove in for leisure and pleasure. A hot topic in the 2000s, it is a shadow 'tax' now accepted as a given.

Manchester had set out to be better at the regeneration game than anyone else. Having bonded in the early 1980s with comrades in the socialist cities of Liverpool, London and Sheffield, by the end of the decade Manchester was forging a different path, reinventing itself politically, a friend of national government and local business. The policy was underpinned by the belief that jobs would come from new city centre buildings and what was good for Canal Street was good for Rochdale Road. This philosophical change, as we have seen, was articulated by rising councillor and key Stringer ally Richard Leese, after the authority had been forced to accept government-imposed rate-capping and job cuts. When he succeeded Stringer as council leader in 1996, a *Manchester Evening News* profile, keen to inject some colour, painted the smart-suited Leese as a 'cross between a teacher and a country squire'. It quickly became clear that this relatively bland exterior concealed a brain as sharp as a bacon slicer, and a talent for gripping the detail and getting things done. 'Back then,' he said, referring to the journey from New Left to New Labour, 'we thought municipal socialism was the alternative to Thatcherism and we could take her on and win. We didn't … It triggered the debate within the party about setting a balanced budget and I was one of those who had to go out in 1987 and sell it.'

The pure maths graduate and former teacher from Mansfield, at this point a youth worker in Crumpsall, posed the hard questions in a Labour Party think piece: 'What were the causes of poverty? Unemployment, low skill, low wage employment … and in the late 1980s and early 1990s, it wasn't going to be us creating the jobs, it was the private sector.' This rationale has set the tone for the city's future economic policy ever since: Manchester was open for business, and the benefits of city-centre development would reach the deprived districts.

Academics such as Jamie Peck and Kevin Ward in *City of Revolution* have taken a more sceptical view of the policy as 'talking up, making over and trickling down'. This collection of studies gives credit, but perhaps not enough, to the activist energy which went into the Manchester model of regeneration, in which tight networks of business and council were proactively primed and capable to snap up whatever was on offer. The *Evening News*'s Ray King, the gregarious local government correspondent, spent many evenings socialising with politicians; he was with Graham Stringer when the council leader learned that a world chess tournament was up for grabs. A decision had to be made instantly and Stringer authorised the bid. The organiser's price was £1 million, Stringer was told. Yes, that would be no problem, came the leader's response. Though the opportunity came to nothing, a flabbergasted King had seen at first-hand how opportunistic The City had become. In 1997 when Britain won the Eurovision Song Contest, Lis Phelan suggested to The City that Manchester should bid to be host city for the next year's contest, producing national news. The jamboree went to Birmingham but Manchester had grabbed early head-lines and sent out its going-for-gold message.

The new mentality rejected passive victimhood. Deindustrialisation and central government control may have combined to beat Manchester down, but it began to operate a 'third way', a decade before such an approach was taken up by the Blair government in 1997. The council's left-wing slogan in the 1980s was 'Defending Jobs, Improving Services', but now it might well have been spin king's Alastair Campbell's New Labour principle, 'We deal with the world as it is, not as we would like it to be.'

If any in Manchester believed the common ground of the Labour movement would turn on the public-spending taps under Blair, they were wrong. The scything Tory cuts to local authority budgets were not reinstated under Labour, and the competition between cities remained the dominant way in which Whitehall doled out funds. In addition, roles performed by the old county councils were now delivered through other on-the-ground bodies which, despite their local footprints, still had to sing to London for their supper. Manchester, like its musicians, had the best tunes. The city had become a financial snake-charmer, adept at snaffling whatever public funding was available – private sector, regional, national or European – and peer cities today look at the track record with jealousy and admiration.

In the early days of the new millennium, the fellow-feeling first established between Tony Wilson and the council during the gang-plagued Gunchester days had evolved. From the first discussions with the music sector and licensing trade, there was more engagement, not as formal advertised public meetings but in behind-closed-doors dialogue. In back rooms in bars, or over dinners, as well as in organised daytime forums, all were buzzing with council people eager to hear what the new breed of mover and shaker had to say.

The accelerant in this process was the backfiring 1997 launch of a new logo and slogan for Manchester's tourism body, the Visitor and Convention Bureau; even the old-fashioned name hinted at a poverty of ambition. A protest group of emerging figures from music and property, including Wilson, Rashman, DJ Dave Haslam, graphic designer Trevor Johnson and Urban Splash's Tom Bloxham and Nick Johnson, lost no time in rubbishing the new approach. They formed the 'McEnroe Group' named after the stroppy tennis champ and his cry 'You cannot be serious!' Apollo Theatre manager Ian Coburn distributed the rebels' exasperated exclamation around town along with his venue's gig fly-posters. The group's base was Atlas on Deansgate, a minimalist design hang-out for the cool set. As a friend of the principals, I was notified of the meetings and turned up to network at the regular moanfests. Nick Johnson fumed: 'Manchester's Factory Records has given the world beautiful designs, and this logo looks like a cycling proficiency badge.' It was the strapline 'We're Up and Going' which attracted the greatest vitriol, in both the local and tourism trade media, as a pathetic new calling card to the world.

The episode raised several sharp questions among the people who were making things happen in the city centre, with their energy, creativity and money: How did such an abomination come to be approved? Did the people in charge not realise how Manchester was changing? And why weren't The City involving the people making the centre such an exciting place? The campaign had immediate impact. The well-meaning but ill-suited tourism boss Elizabeth Jeffreys departed to run tourism on the Isle of Wight, and the

The **McENROE** Group cordially invites you to an **EXHIBITION & PARTY** on Wednesday **16th JULY**, **7 - 9pm**, at **DUKE'S 92** annexe (Castlefield, Manchester).

McEnroe Group invitation

city leaders started to talk to the creatives. In a decade, the city council had gone from the kind of authority whose leading figures socialised with police chief James Anderton at charity dinners at Chinese restaurants Yang Sing and Kwok Man, to one whose newbie council leaders – none of them aficionados of acid house music – were forced to pay attention to voices normally frozen out of official decision-making. The 'We're Up and Going' fiasco propelled the music, clubland and property crowd right into the room where it happened.

Wilson recalled (in 2000): 'Suddenly in the early '80s, the word Manchester came not just to mean the centre of Manchester, it came to mean "the project", being the rebuilding of this whole Northern place. I always say that in the early '80s when we built the Haçienda we thought we were idiots, just individual crazies for some strange obscure reason in love with our city and putting some of our money back into the city. It was only by about '84, '85 that we realised there were a lot of other people doing exactly the same thing, also individually, on their own, separately thinking they were just the same idiots. Our city fathers, council leaders, were doing it, and we all thought it was in isolation, and suddenly by the mid-80s we realised we were all doing it.' In 1990 Wilson was getting excited about the idea of cities as village networks, writing in *The Face* about 'why my village feels so modern, and so alive. Look at the people you get to drink with. Look at the people you get to think with.'

In the early days, these engagements could be colourful mismatches. There had already been the Stringer–Karney double act turning up and leaving early, to the management's relief, before things got too wild at the Haçienda's tenth birthday party. During sessions to discuss this or that project or opportunity, Wilson would often hold forth about one of his hobby-horses. There were some issues Wilson opined on where he might rally some opinion, such as more support for the nascent digital sector. But he was on shakier ground when he complained about the way it had become increasingly hard to drive and park his car, a Jaguar JVC saloon with customised sloping slides that doubled as his mobile office. His friends cracked that his pimped wheels looked somewhat 'gangsta'. It was also one of the first cars in the country to have a built-in CD player. At one evening meeting Wilson piled in with 'We need to talk about cars, yeah? I've just got back from LA, and it was amazing, we were driving down Rodeo Drive and you can literally drive all day, with the roof down, you chat to people at traffic lights, everybody's cool, it's great.' The raised eyebrows must have expressed the mood of the room to Wilson, but he failed to apply the handbrake. 'And then you come back here, and you can't move because of the road narrowing that's going on, the new one-way streets, and parking wardens slapping tickets on you. If we want to be a modern world city, then we need people to be able to use their cars in this city centre.'

You couldn't see members of the creative community going to the barricades over this one. After some mumbling among the cast, the *coup de grâce* was delivered by Leese. He had become leader when Stringer became an MP in 1997 and was a skilled political debater, possessed of a sharp tongue. 'As much as we're interested to hear of your experiences on your trips abroad,' he said, 'there aren't many people who would claim that Los Angeles has much similarity to Manchester, not in the width of its streets, the layout of its city, or indeed in the number of sunshine days a year it enjoys.' He went on to outline a green vision for the city based on reducing car use, the growth of Metrolink and other low-polluting transport methods. This did not stop Wilson advocating for what many thought a lost cause, and he remained a noisy pro-car evangelist in the corridors of power.

These initial get-to-know-you events between the city leadership and maverick captains of the cultural industries grew into a default dialogue. When something important was coming up, The City increasingly turned to the music biz hucksters and lifestyle commentators for their views. One Wilson-led brainstorm in the upstairs room at Dukes 92 pub saw him ask, at the council's behest, for views on what could be done with Piccadilly Gardens, a constant problem location. He went round the table asking for ideas. Dave Haslam said: 'This is ridiculous, we aren't the people with the expertise for this.' Put on the spot, my idea was for a giant swimming pool, rather making Haslam's point. Alongside the chit-chat, one tangible result was the commissioning of a 'Manchester' typeface from design agency Hemisphere's Sue Vanden and Grant Windridge.

It was flattering for us youngish upstarts to feel as if The City regarded us as urban imagineers, and the 2003 Boho Index reassured The City it was on the right track. American academic Richard Florida published the hugely influential *The Rise of the Creative Class*. The old industrial economy had been replaced by the creative one, he asserted, and interesting places to live attracted openminded, tolerant innovators who produced new forms of economic wealth. Florida, professor of economic development at Carnegie Mellon University, said: 'When people with varied backgrounds and attitudes collide, economic growth is likely.'

Manchester topped Florida's first league table of cool in 2003. It joined San Francisco as leaders of urban bohemia in their respective nations. The Boho index combined census and demographic data with key criteria of gay-friendliness, ethnic diversity and the number of patent applications. The story generated much media noise in Britain and abroad, and, as the best PR is from an independent, well-respected source, gave all concerned in Manchester's regeneration a morale boost.

Today, the UN's Creative Economy unit puts the value of 'creative goods' – everything from music and fashion to media and digital – globally at almost $550 billion. The momentum Florida observed perhaps began in 1997 Bilbao, with its astonishing titanium-clad 'dream ship', the Frank Gehry-designed Guggenheim art centre. Spain had led the charge with the 1992 Barcelona Olympics, as much a festival of lifestyle and design as of sport. At the closing ceremony mayor Pasqual Maragall proclaimed, 'We have reinvented the city as a cultural phenomenon.' Ever since, buoyed by the media coverage and visitor figures for those Spanish cities, and encouraged by studies like Florida's, governments tried to revitalise failing industrial cities through art and culture. The Blair government particularly encouraged cities to turn their derelict industrial sites into cultural facilities with public-funded Millennium projects. Salford benefited from the £106 million Lowry Centre, which opened in 2000 and created a critical mass of development in the quayside location, leading to the BBC's MediaCityUK opening in 2011.

Manchester's talk-shops had brought the political leadership outside per-spectives from the hip new generation of business owners to take advantage of the national agenda. The University of Manchester urbanist Rosemary Mellor noted how this changed the way people were thinking about how life in the city was being presented, with the future framed by a philosophy of urbanity: 'Work and leisure, private and public life, day and night, were to be synthesized ... this pointed to a civilised lifestyle and the presentation of Manchester as "Glamchester" (*Vogue*, November 1997), and a model for urban regeneration in Europe.'

Could Manchester's economy really be revived through culture and leisure? In 1961, 167,000 people were employed in the 1.5 sq mi centre. In 1977 that had fallen to under 100,000 and by the mid-1990s the great reinvention had, for all the column inches and rocking city centre, failed the Leese test, that it was 'all about the jobs'. In March 1996, 50 per cent of Manchester and 40 per cent of Salford people were jobless, with only Trafford's employment rate of 76 per cent higher in Greater Manchester than the national average. The new leisure economy could never replace the mass employment of industrial yester-year, and one study found that, in the early to mid-1990s, for every 100 people leaving unemployment over a four-year period there were only 36 new jobs created, all part-time. The city may have appeared to be having a real good time, and the BBC moved its 'yoof' TV department under Janet Street-Porter up from London, but it did not last as the talent would not travel up North.

The leisure-society approach could not hide the real jobs gap. By the mid-1990s, city-centre living was still a slowly growing reality. 'Now the excitement's within easy reach', ran a developer advert showing a heterosexual yuppie couple carrying Habitat shopping bags, in *City Life*'s June 1997 'Livin' in the City' guide. How tender the green shoots of regeneration were can be gauged by the advert for 'Manchester's only 24 Hour Convenience Store, open for beer, wines and spirits during licensing hours' – a Spar on Oxford Street. Manchester was being hailed as the city of the new millennium, even if it had one only round-the-clock food and booze store. The style press and Lord Rogers's landmark 1999 Urban Task Force report did not seem to notice. They lauded the jumping night-time city centre as the model for UK city renaissance. In the national conversation, the London loft dweller in the Halifax TV advert had been usurped by Northern upstarts. Manchester had become the poster child for the way that cities outside the capital could find their new role in the world.

12

Suited, booted and branded

The world of rock and roll has little in common with that of the council jobsworth. The civil servants exercising authority on local councils are paid to organise and regulate our lives, and they have standards to abide by. We pay them through our taxes to be thorough, conscientious and dull. On the other hand, our creative geniuses in the field of popular music are the more fascinating, and often more commercially popular, the more dysfunctional they get. Sex, drugs and rock and roll in one world. Committee meetings and Key Performance Indicators in the other.

The interaction between the worlds of political governance and pop culture is usually an epic cultural cringe. Think of, as legend has it, a reputedly coked-up Noel Gallagher shaking hands with Tony Blair at No. 10 during the height of Cool Britannia, or David Cameron's confession of his love, while an Eton boarder, for The Smiths' tales of working-class Manchester — an excruciating revelation for Johnny Marr, whose public rejection made the unrequited advance all the more mortifying. A nation simply had to look away.

It was with high amusement, then, that I was able to witness the unlikely flowering of the bridge-building of leading lights from Manchester music and politics in the 1990s. It felt strange then, in a positive way, but feels even more peculiar today, the start of a process which has somehow spiralled over the decades into a Conservative chancellor of the exchequer gifting the city squillions for a new arts complex named after Tony Wilson's heroic but hapless record label.

In the late 1990s, as the increasingly joined-up conurbation began making winning government money a fine art, the business support services of the ten Greater Manchester councils (previously provided by Training and Education Councils) were combined in Manchester Enterprises (ME), an umbrella body for 15 organisations. Housed in Churchgate House on Oxford Street, it appeared that all had combinations in their names of the words 'Partnership', 'Regeneration', 'Training', 'Enterprise', 'Skills' and 'Business'. While this dulled the brain, this was not gratuitous. Each organisation had been set up to respond to a different pot of public money available and each had a separate CEO.

My knowledge of this Frankenstein's monster organisation became higher than the average citizen's when in 2003 my PR firm was invited in to raise public awareness of its work. The top dog at the apex of this pyramid was Richard Guy, and, when we went in, we were told he was in Majorca, from where he worked on alternate weeks. Running a major Manchester public sector institution from abroad was an impressive feat. Though there was no indication the work of the organisation suffered, Zoom was decades away and it was a rum arrangement for the time. Deprived of the chance to meet the man who was spoken of in respectful, awestruck tones by all, we duly took away the brief: to raise the profile of Manchester Enterprises.

We returned with our presentation, full of diagrams with arrows. 'Publicity for the 15 companies is good publicity for Manchester Enterprises,' we confidently proclaimed to the 15 company CEOs, the top man being in Majorca. 'And any good profile for Manchester Enterprises is good for the companies.' The bosses all nodded. We won the contract and congratulated ourselves on how smart we were.

When we were finally presented to Guy, he looked as dyspeptic as anyone heading up 15 organisations might be expected to. We had to explain who we were, and what his 15 CEOs had signed us up to. We repeated our pitch to him – that PR for Manchester Enterprises was good for all 15 companies, and vice versa. He fixed us with a stern look, and said, 'No, that's not right at all. That's totally wrong.' We were ushered out by an assistant, and I was grateful that the contract had been signed, presumably while the boss was in the Balearics.

In a sign that the city's music was making the local civil service pay attention, the organisation reached into the world of rock and roll in 2004 and yanked out a new marketing chief into its foggy world of management-speak and acronyms. That man was Colin Sinclair, and he had serious Manchester music scene credentials. Hailing from Worsley, the only remotely posh neighbourhood in Salford, he had spent a year as Salford University's student union president, elected on a Conservative ticket, which must have taken some nerve in the early 1980s. As a young graduate he had proper music business chops, having managed jangly indie-pop band The Railway Children, signed them to a major label and steered them to a Top 40 hit.

When taken on by ME, he had recently closed the legendary Boardwalk, the indie rock live music venue in the city. I had bumped into Colin and his father one day in the mid-1980s while they were sizing up the building on Little Peter Street close to Deansgate rail station. Sensing a market for live indie music from the undersold Haçienda gigs, from 1986 the former Sunday school's seven-hundred-capacity room became a staple fixture on the music circuit. The Boardwalk's bookings were organised by the super-capable Sue Langford, staging early shows by bands including Suede, Happy Mondays and The Charlatans. Ultimately it became even more famous for its rehearsal rooms where Oasis got their tight live act together before they became big, and for Dave Haslam's Yellow disco on Saturdays, which became renowned for its euphoric 'last night of your holidays' DJ sets. (The building had a hidden illustrious history; in 1943 after the Free Trade Hall was heavily damaged by German bombing, the top floor of the future indie venue became the rehearsal room for the Hallé under British-Italian conductor John Barbirolli, who, in an act of personal bravery and cultural solidarity, had returned to war-torn Britain from the safety of New York to helm the orchestra.)

As his success grew, Sinclair was called out for his increasingly corporate style around this time by music writer John Robb, the Blackpudlian punk who believed in the musical creed as more than a hairstyle and a record collection. True to the punk ethos, 'Robbo' pursued a non-acquisitive life, shunning the home-owning democracy. Sticking loyally with his band Gold Blade, who still tour extensively in the former Eastern Bloc, he rejects a materialistic, meat-eating lifestyle. He has happily lived for over thirty years in the same council flat in Hulme, where he maintains his Mohican and pumps iron on a strict vegan diet, as well as providing his growly tones as pop culture commentator for TV.

'What does Colin need a bloody big Jag in the centre of town for?' he sniffed. 'Manchester's a village.' Perhaps he might have had more sympathy if he had known the issues that the Boardwalk had during the Gunchester days – not as bad as the Haçienda, but just as paranoia-inducing if you worked there, which Sinclair did. He was no absentee owner and needed a big reliable car for his long drive home to Lancashire's west coast in the wee small hours. Transporting the night's takings in bulging bags of cash, he would have to floor the pedal to lose suspicious cars tailing him.

Now Sinclair was baggage-free. The golden boy of the city's night-time economy had gone into the straight world. Unlike the Haçienda crew, he had no record of unprofessional handling of drugs and crime issues. While at the Boardwalk, he had used his police contacts to become a reliable organiser of outdoor shows, including the city centre's Millennium Eve celebrations. He moved into staging skills festivals for youngsters at G-Mex, and then in 2004 he took over the role of Manchester Enterprises' marketing boss.

He ticked all the boxes. Hailing from the sexy and happening music scene which impressed city leaders, he was also a safe pair of hands for the Manchester establishment. A calm and unflappable demeanour from years of handling hustlers and needy musicians had given Sinclair the right stuff needed for public employ. The city's leaders found his attention to detail reassuring, and women civil servants found him an attractive addition to the ranks of stolid local bureaucrats.

Sinclair's unstoppable rise continued. Within a year, he had landed the role of chief executive of MIDAS, the inward investment agency. Landing this new role in 2005 was a serious personal coup, as the world was now his oyster. MIDAS was funded by all ten Greater Manchester councils to promote Manchester as a global business location. Now the former nightclub manager, used to accelerating away from late-night ambushers, was in the business of wooing firms from the US, India, China, Japan and Europe to set up shop in Manchester. He was part of the team which smoothed the path for the Bank of New York Mellon to open at Piccadilly, announcing that it was hiring eight hundred staff to process $15 billion of financial securities transactions a day. This was an inward investment coup; the New York connection was a new door opening, a chance to woo more investment. Handily, Factory and Haçienda cultural product was already an established export on the east coast. New York was as sexy an association for spiritual city kinship as it got in the early 2000s. Wilson and new girlfriend and business partner Yvette Livesey bounced their music business convention In The City between New York and Manchester.

With the BONY Mellon location deal signed, it was deemed that a series of trade missions to the Big Apple should take place. It was my PR agency's job to profile these, and the media responded with genuine fascination. Why would a New York bank set up in an archetypal grim and past-it Northern English city? Business journalists were genuinely interested that the city was reinventing itself as a financial centre. Not all were sold, though. *The Financial Times*, possibly the most influential organ for the kind of global CEO who spends their life on planes assessing new locations, opined: 'Despite its big ambitions, Manchester remains a shadow of its former self.' The reporter was William Hall, who had recently moved to the city to live and was left cold by the hype of boosters like me. Tasked with arranging these junkets was MIDAS's sibling body, Marketing Manchester, another of my clients. We prepped Big Apple reporters to meet the city's top brass at receptions, dinners and press conferences at which Lancastrian chef Paul Heathcote served up canapés of newspaper-wrapped mini-fish 'n' chips, followed by Manchester tart.

Manchester hit New York with a typically cooler-than-thou marketing masterstroke. Having learned from the humiliation of the 'Up and Going' launch, the city council ditched the idea of slogans and logos. Instead, they had hired a Creative Director, Peter Saville. The informal ear-bending from the city's hip new advisers had made its mark, prompting a review of the city's brand. A panel of advisers, including me, was assembled to hear some of the world's top place-branding experts make their pitch. Overseen by Susan Hunt, an Australian sports sponsor dealmaker who stayed after the 2002 Commonwealth Games and first introduced the notion of Manchester as a brand to The City, the selectors included Manchester graphic designers Trevor Johnson and Ben Casey, art-gallery owner Claire Turner and academic Justin O'Connor, as well as property developers Carol Ainscow of Artisan and Tom Bloxham and Nick Johnson of Urban Splash.

There was an impressive list of contenders. Designers with a Manchester connection like Assorted Images and Buzzcocks' image-maker Malcom Garrett were joined in battle with the veteran Michael Wolff of Wolff Olins, the man behind work for New York City which became a worldwide paragon of city branding. The small, bald branding veteran walked up and down the panel, looking us in the eye, and talking with gentle sincerity about Manchester, and how he thought he could fulfil the brief. Without actually coming up with any fresh suggestions – the inference was that his sky-high fees would start off that process – the genial seventy-year-old charmed us all. He had given a masterclass in soft selling without appearing to.

Even if Wilson had absented himself from the panel, there was only going to be one winner. Peter Saville was last up and he entered the room, sat down and perched his long black denim-clad legs on the table in front of him. 'Hello, I'm Peter Saville,' he said unnecessarily from beneath his beatnik fringe, 'and I haven't brought my portfolio, it is on show at Urbis and you can see it there.' He was referring to an exhibition of his work on at the nearby museum of the city. Urbis opened in 2002 as one of the bold new statements on the city centre site impacted by the 1996 IRA bomb. Funded by government Millennium Fund cash, it did not take long for all concerned to realise that its collection of exhibits was a canine repast of monumental proportions.

The City had delivered exactly what its hometown critics wanted. The academics, designers, journos and lifestyle entrepreneurs had been invited inside the civic tent, and informed of the opportunity to bid for a new cultural build-ing. Academic Justin O'Connor said: 'The two sides were looking for each other. The city wanted a landmark project and the people on the popular culture scene wanted to do something for the city.' Wilson had suggested a museum of pop, but O'Connor owned the big idea: 'But what we were really talking about was a museum of contemporary urban living.' This persuasive concept was welcomed by all involved. The Manchester architect Ian Simpson was appointed after a competition. Known to the council for his work on the city-wide version of the Hulme design code, his was the only shortlisted design to push the building to the edge of the site, leaving much of it open space, some-thing not in the brief but which struck a chord with The City.

The niggly questions about Urbis began. What was going to go in it? This was discussed endlessly in groups and committees, and the search went out for specialists to install the latest, grooviest future exhibits. Among the loose group of consultees who saw this as their chance to show the city how cool and design-literate they were, the issues surfaced. Didn't Manchester already have an excellent museum about the city's past, at the Museum of Science and Industry? Shouldn't Urbis be more of an interactive gallery where his-tory and the future of cities could combine? Doesn't screen technology, once installed, become obsolete very quickly? And was the planned 'travelator' to the building's prow really a thrilling sky-ride, or simply an escalator?

Thanks to the efficient project director Fran Toms, the government-funded Millennium project opened on time to national media coverage in 2002. My agency handled the launch, booking Tony Wilson to compère the media con-ference, who added personal notes about his German ancestors who came to Manchester, and talking up the regenerating promise of the place. But once people got inside, there were more questions than answers, the main one being 'Why is it so boring?' swiftly followed by 'Why can't you see out of the win-dows?' The reviews stank. Deyan Sudjic in *The Observer* described the building as hostile to the city around it, and complained that the only place you could see out to the city was right at Urbis's peak, a small window in what he called a 'Flash Harry' restaurant: 'It's a view that lets you understand far more of what a real city is about than any of the tat inside, all of which could happily have been consigned to a skip.'

Architect Simpson, whose star was rising in the city, had designed a build-ing clad entirely in glass which looked wholly transparent – until you were up close. Then you could see that, in fact, he had specified horizontal etched lines which travelled across the entire structure. Whether you were on the travelator, interacting with the weak exhibits or eating in the main restaurant, try as you might, but any clear view was obscured by the thick lines which allowed only tiny glimpses out, denying the instinct to want to look at your city from new vantage points. Simpson's belief that visitors would find favour with his irritating window design is one thing, but the failure to prevent it by his client, the city council, revealed the guru status that architects can hold among those in high office. A decade later, council CEO Bernstein wangled the relocation of the under-visited National Football Museum from Preston into Urbis, preventing it from becoming a white elephant. Perhaps the most lasting, popular use of the main Urbis site is Cathedral Gardens, tastefully landscaped public realm boasting costly paving that has been colonised by the skateboarder community.

Manchester's cool crowd edged away from the Urbis embarrassment. It was not the only design and financial blunder in the wave of Lottery-funded Millennium projects. The cost of the Millennium Dome in London overran to £1 billion and numerous attractions across the land – a pop music museum in Sheffield and something called The Public in West Bromwich – closed after failing to attract visitors. Perhaps the lesson about this type of project is not to design them by committee; the final word rested with the unsexy location of a defunct steel works in Rotherham which became Magna, an inspirational, per-fectly realised vision by Cheshire educationalist Stephen Feber. Based around the four elements of air, earth, fire and water, the 'science adventure centre' won the RIBA Stirling Prize in 2001 for Wilkinson Eyre architects, and Magna remained a staple and substantial day out for Yorkshire families for many years.

Feber was the also the force behind the award-festooned Eureka! Centre in Halifax, and – after my media launch of Magna – I introduced him to Saville over a coffee. They bonded over their mutual distaste for 'the dreaded football' and discussed the potential for the Museum of Science and Industry (MOSI, now Science and Industry Museum). It contained the extensive col-lection of buildings based around the railway warehouse serving the station from where the world's first intercity train left for Liverpool in 1830. MOSI was cheek-by-jowl with the Castlefield canal, road and rail interchange, where the Duke of Bridgewater's coal came from the 1761 canal, the bellows which were to fire up the modern world. MOSI was in Saville's sights. He had designs on the museum, believing its location, the crucible of the modern world, made it the intellectual motherlode for his emerging big idea for 'brand Manchester'. Despite his stellar record, though, Feber was resigned to his face not fitting in Manchester. Despite meetings with the senior ranks and his enthusiasm to work in the city, Feber was the best director MOSI never had and eventually went to Bristol as a consultant.

The man running MOSI in 2011 was marketing and museums specialist Tony Hill, who oversaw the opening of a new £9 million wing of interactive displays, and he had lined up Britain's best-known scientist, Professor Brian Cox, to launch its Revolution gallery. I was handling the PR but was distinctly nervous as the day approached and the famous physicist was in frozen far-northern Europe out of communication. Former pop musician Cox – a star around whom many personal assistants from academe, publishing and the BBC orbited – made good his promise and arrived back to publicise the new facility with his trademark enthusiasm, a personal brand which has helped Manchester's physics degree courses harder to get into than Oxbridge.

MOSI was a popular visitor attraction. Urbis was a flop. Saville had been nowhere near the Urbis project discussions, so in 2004, when delivering his pitch for Manchester's brand project, he was not tainted by its debacle. Factory's design genius could articulate with great clarity, and at great length, about the 'heritage', 'aura' and 'personality' of a brand. The selection panel voted three for Wolff and nine for Saville, and, after a three-month trial expertly shepherded by Susan Hunt, he was handed the brief, to 'bring to life the creative expression of Manchester's image and to help unify the way in which Manchester presents itself to the world'. Council leader Leese told the national press that Saville's job was not to come up with a strap line or logo. Instead, he said, 'We want an all-encompassing creativity that communicates to people who might live, learn, work and invest here that Manchester is on track to become a world-class city.'

I was curious about Saville's attitude at that time to his home city. Raised in Hill Top, a part of Hale, Trafford that he describes as 'the Bel-Air of Manchester', he was the one Factory founder who grew up in suburban afflu-ence, a security that gave him a voyeuristic sense of 'awe and wonder at a Gothic industrial drama'. He did not have to survive the city, as others did, but, where punk's anger was aimed at the monarchy or hypocrisy, he says: 'I was angry about the mediocrity of everyday existence – the art and design books I studied proposed a richer way of life.'

Saville graduated from Manchester Polytechnic in 1978 and almost immedi-ately became the superstar graphic designer of his generation. He became the touchstone for the way Factory presented itself and its output to the world. His beautiful Factory Records designs were followed by commissions from global entertainment, fashion and product corporates including Adidas, Givenchy,

EMI and the Pompidou Centre, and collaborations with exciting music artists and fashion designers. By the time of the Manchester brand project, his quest for an ever-sharper refinement of his aesthetic saw him working in international fine art circles. Says Saville: 'Manchester was the place that had made me and given me the unique opportunities of my career. Having spent my life working around the world I was ever more uncomfortably aware of how Manchester was perceived. But if someone is rude about your family you immediately want to defend it. I wanted the perception of Manchester to be more positive. I was aware that by the end of the twentieth century, the city did not know how to see itself and if there was no internal collective vision, how could there be an external one?'

True to his legendary rep as the designer who, in the interests of perfection, delivered Factory concert posters on the night of the show, he spent months getting under the skin of the new Manchester. The first report back of Saville was to a meeting of around three hundred people from the Manchester family of public agencies. Consultants and influencers like me were invited. The presentation was as lo-tech as could be imagined. A large screen hosted a slide show of photos, mainly black and white, which Saville talked through – examples of good and bad design, as he saw it, across the city. Many focused on street signage, as the blizzard of jarring official typefaces and styles was a source of irritation for him.

The images were followed by a massive list of words in a tiny, almost-unreadable size. For a man who had redefined modern text design, this non-design meant something, probably a signal of his disdain for the omnipresent PowerPoint. Whatever the conceptual purpose, what was presented was an eye-straining stream of tiny, unpunctuated text – factoids, observations, phrases and statements. This unconventional method eventually brought forth the main conclusion of his research. The torrent of wordage was the result of the preceding months in which he had walked the streets, taken photos and interviewed many VIPs, businesspeople and commentators. Now, only two words (still absurdly tiny) were on the screen. He had distilled all the information into a simple formulation: Original Modern. (Saville credits the lightbulb moment to typographer Paul Barnes, who first uttered the phrase in the pair's discussion over dinner.)

Manchester was the world's first modern city and therefore, ran the persuasive logic, these two words captured the essence of Manchester. And, true to the client brief, this was not to be used as a slogan. Rather, it was a 'brand positioning'. But it was also a stern invocation, a call to arms, a high bar to which the city should hold itself and its products. 'Original and modern should be the core brand values Manchester projects to the outside world and used to test whether everything from new buildings and transport infrastructure to future cultural events project the right message,' he said. Original Modern was not only a new kind of quality kitemark. It was a way of Manchester understanding itself before it could begin telling the world what it was, and could be. In the words of its glossy prospectus with commissioned pieces from Victorian art expert Tristram Hunt (on the Original) and social economist Will Hutton (on the Modern), it was 'a way of valuing what we do in Manchester and is a declaration for Manchester's future'.

In some ways, Saville had thrown his clients a hospital pass. The challenge was all but impossible for any city to live up to, as the confusion of type styles still visible in Manchester's signage today confirms. But the exercise focused minds. It also became an interesting test for how much criticism the city leadership was prepared to take in the media. Although in many ways it had made great strides since he left to make his international reputation, Saville wasn't one for flattering his client. His hire made news, and his clear-eyed views aired in public were not to The City's liking. As a star designer in demand in Germany, Japan and the US, his opinion had to be respected. 'Everybody says Manchester is a great city,' he said. 'It was a great city but now it is just all right – and that is not good enough.'

It wasn't that the hierarchy couldn't take such advice – after all, they had hired him to improve things. They just did not expect him to be saying it to the *Financial Times*, and this made for some tension. Whenever Saville's name was mentioned, Sir Howard Bernstein, newly knighted in the wake of the Commonwealth Games, was heard to loudly say to anyone, including me, 'Five minutes in that man's company is more than enough for me.' Another unforeseen turn the Original Modern project took was something the city initially said it did not want. No doubt as the result of voices asking what the practical benefit of the branding exercise was, and its cost, Saville was also asked to come up with a graphic. In his hands, this became the Manchester 'M' – not a logo but what he terms 'an imprimatur', a quite beautiful letter formed from parallel multi-coloured lines, alluding to both industrial heritage and digital culture.

In 2006, using the new approach, the suited-and-booted city elite jetted out to take another bite out of the Big Apple, focusing on new back-office finance jobs. Under a *Sunday Times* headline 'Manchester woos Wall Street' Bernstein explained: 'There's no open top bus for us ... You can go anywhere in Britain or

Europe and pick up the city's brochure. Everyone is the centre of the universe. We have never gone for that.' *The Observer* compared the ambition of Bernstein and Leese 'to the 19th-century captains of industry who first put Manchester on the map. After years of decline, the city's leaders believe Manchester is making its mark, this time in a world of changed technologies.' The big push was for financial and professional services firms to follow BONY Mellon from New York to Manchester. These white-collar jobs would sit nicely in the emerging Spinningfields district being developed by Allied London in the justice and civic quarter around Crown Square. Built in the 1960s and 1970s as homes for the courts, education offices and other public administrations, this concrete neighbourhood between the River Irwell and Deansgate was full of vacant featureless modern offices. It had been earmarked for redevelopment for some years.

Allied London was the council's preferred developer, led by Mike Ingall, who had risen from a surveyor managing office estates to developing the Brunswick scheme at Bloomsbury in London. After appointment to the board of Allied London, he had risen to run the business, and his interest in Manchester was sweetened by a growing bromance with Bernstein, who had taken the helm of the city council in 1998. It's undeniable that Spinningfields changed the face of Manchester, in one very obvious sense, that you have to look very hard to see any red brick, being all Modern and no Original. Peter Hook told *The Times* that he and his wife loved Spinningfields as they could imagine they were not in Manchester.

Allied London began buying land in the 23-acre Spinningfields site as an alternative for the banks, insurance and firms based in the semi-medieval street pattern around King Street. This had been home to Manchester's 'suits' for generations, with its charming little cafés and specialist shops in the surrounding warren of narrow streets. Lawyers and accountants shopped in the high-class boutiques on the cobbled lower King Street, and in hostelries like Sam's Chop House the property boys networked and feasted on roast beef and draught ale.

The 'big bang' in the City of London had created Canary Wharf but had impacted very little on the way Manchester's offices worked. Ingall and Bernstein looked at the small-town nature of the finance community's neighbourhood and thought that Manchester was ripe for a financial district fit for the new age. 'Most people thought I was from a different planet,' said Ingall in *The Times*, speaking of the 'taboo' of competing with King Street. He was convinced he could shift the 'square half-mile' community by offering ultra-modern offices for the 'suited and booted' young professionals who followed the tieless Tony Blair–George Bush 'yo summits' and ditched the neckwear.

In 2004 Ingall hired my PR firm to gain profile in the media for his plans, which he liked to describe as the largest single city-centre development site in Europe. We came up with the idea for a New York-style skating rink and started to get Spinningfields known in the business media. His property agents blitzed the finance and professional sector with deals. Spinningfields offered three million square feet of commercial space, and by 2007 it was all filled by corporate occupiers.

Ingall badly needed shoppers and diners to go with the new commuters, and in June 2007 he asked me to launch the area as a destination by inviting a thousand people to an outdoor party. The entertainment and logistics were organised by Steve Smith and Jon Drape's Ear to the Ground outfit. The launch marked the evolution of the city's music scene into the corporate era. Smith made his name organising warehouse parties on the old Boddington's brewery site, and Drape was the Haçienda's final manager in its dying days. A solo PA from M People's Heather Small and a set by Haçienda DJ Graeme Park topped off the entertainment.

The crowds filed in to be served canapés and gawp at giant screens showing the development filmed from a helicopter above. Heads craned upwards to see roped-up 'aerialists' throwing themselves around the roof of one of the new office buildings. Haçienda graduates and the city's music stars had been hired to lend credibility and cool to its new home for corporates. Wilson's party sidekick Ross McKenzie was hired to wow the suits for the launch of the Century Buildings apartment scheme at nearby St Mary's Parsonage, dressing the space in the same louche style with which he promoted carnivalesque club nights like The Circus.

People who have worked with Spinningfields' Ingall describe the experience as anything between a nightmare and inspirational. I certainly can recall both. He was dysfunctional in PR terms, as he had a habit of giving reporters premature 'exclusives' about big deals without telling anyone else. The journalists would publish his top-of-the-head thoughts and everyone would be very confused. Ingall considered himself a branding whizz. He had chosen the new area's name from a historic source. Spinning Fields was a narrow westwards-running street on the site, and most agreed the name was authentic and appealing. But he stuck doggedly to his belief that every building, street and square in Spinningfields should include the name 'Hardman', after a local street, despite much advice against. Many years later, this naming system still causes confusion. He hired Manchester 'cool hunters' like Katie Popperwell to travel to world cities looking for the next big thing in urban lifestyle, and he was quite happy to put dozens of consultants first class on the expensive early train to London, where he would inform all present that he had junked the work they agreed at the last meeting, he just hadn't told anyone.

The mercurial Ingall does things his own way and made good on his audacious vision. Over a twenty-year period, he shifted the city's centre of gravity. With Spinningfields, Allied London has built an entire district of flats, offices, shops, bars and restaurants in partnership with a local authority intent on beefing up the city's professional services. In the early 2000s Manchester lacked the large workspaces Spinningfields offered for corporate expansion and new ways of working. Several big firms keen to attract hot young talent took up the large offices, boasting all the must-have facilities for the twenty-first-century executive. Royal Bank of Scotland, Barclays, Deloitte and Halliwells law firm were among the companies to take big lettings.

Ingall had seen the future of offices and it was large floor-plates. But he misread Manchester badly in his early selection of posh shops and eating places. The chains from London like Carluccio's, Giraffe and Café Rouge signed up, but suffered unexpectedly low takings. It became clear that the city's out-and-about-ers favoured the independent sector, staying loyal to the likes of Tim Bacon's Living Ventures bars. Aussie Bacon, a former TV soap actor and flair cocktail barman, had built an empire from drinkeries which caught the city's leisure market just right, and by offering professional training, career paths and respect to bright young things working for him. Ingall needed the Living Ventures' customer base badly and, thanks to sweetheart deals with Bacon and his partner Jeremy Roberts, he brought their bars Alchemist and Australasia into Spinningfields. Sadly, the ambitious and charming Bacon died of cancer in 2016, at fifty-two. Many felt that in his own way he had done as much for Manchester's social life as Tony Wilson.

The retail side of Spinningfields was an even bigger flop. Its retail strip, the Avenue, was hyped to be 'the Knightsbridge of the North' with stores like Armani and Mulberry. But it wasn't long before their managers were complaining to journalists that they had an average of two customers a day. High-end shoppers voted with their feet, sticking to their favoured city-centre boutiques or driving to the Trafford Centre. The Avenue was empty, but of greater concern for those running the city was that, for years, stores selling big-ticket items could not make a go of it in Manchester. John Lewis consistently declined to open despite persistent wooing, and Habitat pulled out of St Ann's Square in 2011, amid widespread feeling that, while there was a lot of money earned in Manchester, high earners spent it out of town.

For all the big talk of aiming to be a modern world city, in these years there was the nagging notion that the city's parochialism was something its people were rather happy with, and that the epithet 'town' which all locals used in describing the city centre was accurate. No one was saying, 'Let's go out tonight to the major world-class city.' It often seems the only way the national media can understand regional stories is to compare them with London, and Spinningfields was being billed as the 'Canary Wharf of the North'. The growing reputation of the booming steel and glass district, however, was sullied by the central role Spinningfields was to play in the collapse of the largest law firm outside London.

Halliwells law firm had a reputation for aggressive entrepreneurialism which saw it swell to 116 partners and 850 staff. It grew rapidly through acquisition and the high-fee-earning work of its deal-making corporate lawyers, and in 2007 it posted earnings of £86 million, a turnover which had ballooned by almost 1,000 per cent since it became a top-100 UK law firm 12 years earlier. Halliwells needed to rationalise seven city offices into one headquarters. The economy was booming, and hubris and greed were in the air. The era's haughty corporate style dictated that head offices needed to be as sleek and well-equipped as possible. Not only would corporate clients be impressed (though their bills were paying for the glistening new offices), the swanky new workplaces would lure in the highest fee-earning lawyers in the war for top talent.

Halliwells had the appetite and Allied London had a tempting solution. Determined to bring the North's biggest legal practice into Spinningfields as an anchor tenant, one that would take most of the 180,000 sq ft curved office 3 Hardman Square and attract other occupiers, a deal was hatched in late 2007. Ingall offered a £20 million 'reverse premium' – an upfront cash handout in place of the standard formula of a three-year rent-free period and a five-year lease extension.

This was a widely used practice, but, instead of being invested into the business, £15 million of the total was paid into the personal pension funds of Halliwells' 45 senior equity partners, who each received between £250,000 and £1 million and, in the most notorious detail of the affair, kept the firm's one hundred other 'fixed share' partners in the dark. Ingall and the senior partners had cooked up the richest of sweeteners, but it would ultimately stick in the throats of all parties.

Swapping rent for capital was part of the mentality which assumes that booms never end. It was designed to be a secret deal and might well have remained secret if it hadn't been for nasty timing. In October 2008, just months after Halliwells' moving in, the Lehman Brothers bank collapse precipitated a global economic meltdown. Halliwells' income was badly impacted at a time when the firm had big bills to pay, chief among them the annual rent of over £4.5 million. In February 2010 the firm's financial pain was acute. The boil was eventually lanced when the main lender, RBS, which was on the hook for £20 million, forced a High Court-ordered administration. The once-mighty firm was parcelled up and sold in a pre-packaged insolvency to four other firms. *Legal Business* magazine called it a story of 'reckless ambition, ineptitude and greed'.

'Trousergate', as it came to be called in Manchester's legal circles, led to open warfare between the partners, and a series of bitter personal claims against the alleged masterminds of the secret deal. Far from burnishing the city's credentials as a professional services centre of excellence, the collapse dented its reputation. Post-crash, with his bold building programme stalled and bank funding dried up, Ingall faced the prospect of a half-completed office district. In March 2010, though, Manchester City Council came to the rescue. The city council bought Spinningfields' final two plots for £15 million and leased them back. Council CEO Bernstein's report to the council executive stated that 16,000 people were employed in Spinningfields and with the two buildings completed this would rise to 25,000. Happily, construction of both the 160,000 sq ft XYZ building and the 340,000 sq ft No. 1 Spinningfields was completed and the loans were repaid.

The shifting of The City's gears towards all things 'culture' started at this point. The City could see how, in the capital, high-finance and its taste for modern art had transformed old East London by building an eco-system of galleries, dealers and artists in formerly undesirable districts: art equalled regeneration. An idea to put a contemporary collection into the clean lines and smooth finishes of Spinningfields was mooted.

In visual art, talents like Chris Ofili had to leave his inner-city Manchester upbringing to find the elephant-dung-meets-blaxploitation muse of his youth. Would he have won the Turner Prize if he hadn't gone to Chelsea School of Art? My experience was that in Manchester those who appreciated contemporary work couldn't afford it, while Northern *nouveau riche* had no interest in the kind of Young British Artists who galvanised London in the late 1990s. However, there was one outlier to the bling-tastic Cheshire set — art collector Frank Cohen, whose journey began as the son of a penniless raincoat machinist in north Manchester.

After selling wallpaper rolls on markets in the early 1960s, Cohen built home improvement retail chain Glyn Webb and sold it for a reported £25 million in 1997. As a youth he had bought and sold cigarette cards and marbles. He got the art-dealing bug, moved into Lowry prints in the 1960s and paintings in the 1970s, and by 2000 he had amassed a UK contemporary art collection second only to Charles Saatchi, stored in a secure warehouse in the West Midlands just off the M6. I introduced him to a client, Comme Ça art gallery, and he exhibited work in their space in Urban Splash's Timber Wharf development in Castlefield, the city's edgy answer to Hoxton. It got London's attention, with BBC Radio 4's Mark Lawson visiting for *Front Row* and Cohen's old north Manchester pal novelist Howard Jacobson returning to pen a mirthfully affectionate piece for *The Guardian* about the market trader's rise to million-pound auction bidder. ('All I ever sold was Vymura, every fucking Jewish house had it.')

'I would love to see more well-off people buying contemporary art, like they buy clothes and diamonds,' said Cohen, who became involved in intense discussions between Spinningfields' overlord Ingall and the city's retained pro-vocateur Peter Saville to site his collection in a large unit close to Deansgate. Despite business planning and mediation by gallerist Stephen Snoddy, these foundered because neither Ingall nor Cohen would agree to equally stump up the set-up costs to gain contributions from the Arts Council and Manchester City Council to assemble a funding package. Cohen's collection remains under lock and key near Wolverhampton, a missed chance for a serious, world-renowned Manchester contemporary art gallery. Perhaps a 2004 Jonathan Jones review in *The Guardian* calling a London show of his '10th rate' and 'dross' may have sowed doubts in Manchester about its true cultural worth. In some way, though, Cohen's aspirations for a Northern market for contemporary art has been realised by the annual Manchester Art Fair run by influencer-entre-preneur Thom Hetherington.

The decade was to present more existential worries, though, for Allied London and the council. The global economic catastrophe slowed progress at Spinningfields, but, despite its missteps over leisure, retail and the aborted gal-lery, Allied London's light remained undimmed in the eyes of The City. Ingall's right-hand man Graham Skinner told *Place North West*, 'We've had the finan-cial support, the backing through recession ... The support we've had from the city has, from day one, been awesome.' In 2010, the year of the Halliwells fiasco, *Property Week* awarded Ingall the title of Developer of the Decade due to his Houdini-like ability to keep forging on through the aftermath of the great crash. His audacious new business district, which looked nothing like the old Manchester, had been launched with the skills and credibility of Haçienda graduates and exploited the music scene's sexy aspirational glamour, and it was grateful to Manchester city council as the lender of last resort. There was no way that The City was prepared to let the small matter of a global economic crisis slow down the growth of corporate Manchester.

13

Manc mafia on the Med

'The same fifty people run Manchester. They always have,' said the doleful voice behind me. North Manchester MP Graham Stringer had entered the busy function room in the Edwardian Baroque splendour of the Midland Hotel, the milk-chocolate masterpiece where Rolls is reputed to have met Royce in 1904 and ever since has been the meeting point for the city's great and good.

It was late 2009 and the event was a farewell reception for Paul Horrocks, the editor of the *Manchester Evening News*. The moustachioed veteran reporter had filed copy on some of the biggest national stories on his patch – the Moors Murders, the Stalker affair and the IRA bomb. Proud of his north Manchester roots, Horrocks was a news man through and through. Reporting was in his blood. His father was the news editor of the *Bury Times* and after 34 years at the *Manchester Evening News* spent on death knocks, crime scenes and police raids, Horrocks had been promoted from news editor to editor. Features subs swapped tales of his ignorance of pop culture, asking if Morrissey was 'Van Morrissey' and referring to 'REM Speedwagon'. But knowing band names was not his scene, and meeting coppers in the pub for a tip-off was.

At the point of retirement as editor, however, he was not quite the ball-breaking reporter of old, thanks to the weight of civic responsibility which went with his accession to the city's top table. In his outside role on the board of inward investment agency MIDAS, he was privy to confidential high-level business news he was trusted not to report on. This was an itchy position to maintain as a hardened news hound, especially when he heard of impending big news in the planning which the authorities were not ready to announce.

Once the bane of the left-wing 1980s council, it was now a time of steadily declining sales for the *Evening News*, then still the nation's largest big-city daily paper. With Horrocks in the chair it was taking a more supportive role in the city's regeneration. This was a tricky balancing act. The reporter's instinct is to publish and be damned. Compelling and controversial stories sell papers. Whether to promote the city or report its seamier stories was a live debate at the time, when 'Gunchester' murder stories made the paper's front page but such reporting was often criticised as too negative an approach, both for the city's morale and as a reader turn-off.

I became aware of the difficult decisions facing the editor when tourism body Marketing Manchester quietly sacked its chief executive in 2001 after five months in the post. Formerly deputy chief at the Northern Ireland tourist board, Mark Alexander had been hired by Manchester after impressing at the interview panel. Within weeks it became clear this was a mistake. He tore through his personal travel and entertaining expenses, raising eyebrows among his new colleagues, and when his girlfriend joined the payroll the alarm was raised. Information came to light that would have been better known before his appointment. A report in *The Irish Times* later described an investigation into his expenses at the Northern Ireland post, after which Alexander had left under a cloud with a £60,000 pay-off. In what was described as a 'monumental scandal' by the Stormont Assembly public accounts committee, it emerged that a recruitment consultant was paid £4,000 to help him find a new job. That, it seems, was the Manchester one. Later reports said the Manchester selection panel had received a positive reference, but in any case Alexander's appointment was trumpeted as a coup. The new boss took centre stage at a press conference when Marketing Manchester declared impressive new visitor numbers to the city.

Perhaps Alexander's enthusiasm for golf endeared him to the hiring panel of old-school business leaders, led by John McGuire, Royal Bank of Scotland's top man in Manchester and Marketing Manchester chairman. It was on McGuire, a bluff and quick-witted leader whose energy belied his near-retirement age, to clear up the mess. Getting rid of Alexander was the easy part. The evidence was overwhelming as he had not been remotely subtle. McGuire's trickier task was to manage the news and prevent any reputational damage about how the organisation, which was still finding its feet, could have hired such a wrong 'un. The Manchester way prevailed. McGuire and Horrocks spoke. A story appeared on a Saturday, when the business community did not read the paper. At the foot of page 2, a single column of four paragraphs headlined 'Tourism supremo quits job' was published. Alexander's departure was put down to 'personal reasons'. Internal candidate Andrew Stokes, an out gay man (and Manchester Pride chairman for six years) who was happier in the urban whirl of the new Manchester than on the golf course, was appointed interim boss.

I lost no opportunity to pitch him my tourism brainwave: as two cast members of top-rated US sitcom *Frasier*, with its twenty million viewers, were born or brought up in Manchester – John Mahoney (cynical ex-cop Martin Crane) and Jane Leeves (playing Mancunian housekeeper Daphne Moon in a distinctly odd accent) – what better way to appeal to educated, well-travelled Americans? Stokes, who has since gone on to become tourism chief of Visit England, did not warm to the idea.

At his leaving bash, Horrocks was wished a fond farewell by MPs, business leaders, city council senior leaders and the chiefs of the expanding Manchester family of public agencies. In many ways it was the end of a golden era for the paper. It could not be laid at his door that its influence was diminishing. The rise of the internet as a source of news drove down demand for print media and the global recession quickened it. The explosion in online news meant the *Evening News* was being home-delivered less, and its decline as a habit purchase badly hit sales.

Regional news websites and bulletins, free to register and made viable by paid-for events, were crowding the space long dominated by the paper. Its business coverage was being undermined by agile challengers *North West Business Insider*, *The Business Desk*, *Prolific North* (formerly *How Do*) and *Place North West*, the latter founded by Paul Unger, son of the former *MEN* editor. Meanwhile, lifestyle websites like the restaurant-focused *Manchester Confidential*, led by the Falstaffian figure of 'Gordo' aka publisher Mark Garner, were eating the *Evening News*'s advertising lunch, and its breakfast and dinner too.

In this tough trading environment, the paper started to give copies away free in the city centre in 2006 and withdrew from the gold standard of the Audit Bureau of Circulations. In 2008–9, it was selling seventy thousand a day and giving away a similar number, a plummet from the mid-1980s when sales were around 250,000, and the heady days of 1975 when its daily sale was 370,000. In 2009, the same year Horrocks retired, Guardian Media Group cut 150 jobs, including 70 journalists, eleven from the *MEN*. As the hub for dozens of weekly papers in and around the conurbation, 22 reporters at local offices around Greater Manchester were relocated to the city centre, which required reporting about Accrington and other satellite districts from the Deansgate head office.

Of the fifty people in the Midland Hotel who in Stringer's view ran the city, a healthy proportion would find a good reason to assemble in Cannes, France, once a year. Here, a month before the glamour of the film festival, was an equally lavish annual convention. This one was for the world's property sector.

MIPIM, for Le Marché International des Professionnels de L'immobilier (the international professionals' property market), had grown to be the dominant European fair at which to promote property schemes to potential investors, partners and occupiers.

It wasn't just for businesses. Countries, regions and cities came to realise that here was the place to meet people, learn about your peers and competitors, and set up deals. And where better to discuss all this than over a four-day week every March, not only in the gigantic Palais de Congrès and the larger pavilions which sprouted every year along the Croisette, but in the bars and restaurants of the elegant seaside town? Manchester was early on the case, testing the water in the early 2000s. Soon the city was leading the nation's cities in being MIPIM-savvy, and bagged a plum location on the balcony of the main building while rivals made do with stands deep in the bowels of the gargantuan Palais.

I attended around ten MIPIMs and was increasingly intrigued and amused at the way it had become the must-attend event for Manchester's decision-makers to network, gossip and plot. Property being the activity that it is, the Manchester reps – and those from elsewhere – swarmed to the Manchester stand like bees round a honeypot. The supply chain in property development is long, from architects to surveyors, from planning consultants to marketers, to the lawyers who draft the contracts and funders who make it happen – and of course, all the construction firms and specialist trades that make a building ... the web of contacts through which a job might be landed over an informal drink or chat is long and convoluted.

Flights to Cannes were filled with businesspeople who worked with the council, all expectant of a private meeting with the regeneration king Sir Howard Bernstein. Rising younger hopefuls were often challenged by their boss to win their spurs by getting a chat with the man whose encouragement, they believed, could make their company's project fly. At the Manchester stand at MIPIM, 'SHB' was in his element, as assistants cued up his presentations and kept the coffees and canapés flowing.

The tailored linen-suited audiences gathered to hear the city's big beasts of the property scene – the likes of Bruntwood, Allied London, Ask and Argent paying £10,000 sponsorships each – talk through their latest plans. Smaller companies were occasionally let in to play with the big boys. Some were permitted to sponsor sessions, and in 2006 a spectacular example of falling foul of the unspoken law of the Manchester mafia was exhibited by the consultant Martin Stockley. A talented, thoughtful engineer from London with a cool Terence Stamp style about him, who had worked with architect Ian Simpson and Rachel Haugh on their Urbis and No. 1 Deansgate buildings, and with city council-sponsored schemes at Spinningfields and New Islington, Stockley had published a book about his work. *The Reluctant Engineer* was launched at the MIPIM stand, a matt-cover, small-format compilation of some of his greatest engineering hits. It was a carefully written account of the germination of some of the projects, such as his giant raking steel columns of No. 1 Deansgate, a dramatic way of separating Marks and Spencer from the £1.5 million apartments above. And here and there, among the stimulating digressions about the purpose of architecture, and the creative, can-do nature of the city's property players, he referred to Bernstein not once but several times.

Presumably to pay the great man due credit — and equally to impress upon his audience how highly he was favoured — Stockley made several references to the chief executive and how he operated. Stockley wrote how Bernstein suggested his name to Edward Ziff, a Leeds property developer whose Town Centre Securities owns the historic Piccadilly Basin site, and in his narrative imagined the thought process taken by 'SHB' over Spinningfields which led to the author being hired. While it was super-innocuous and merely described in basic terms how property projects happen, through recommendations and referrals, these open but naive musings pulled back the curtain. They showed how things worked. Nothing remotely improper had taken place, but it seemed it was a case of 'too much information'. The first rule of The City was that you did not talk about The City. And you certainly didn't write it up in a book.

The text may well not have been cleared with the city council press office and, post-MIPIM, the stink of offending the hierarchy soon wafted from the Mediterranean to the River Medlock. Business for Stockley's consultancy began to tail off. With nothing down for him in Manchester, his next major role was an eye-opener … chief engineer for Moscow-based State Development, in the Russian Federation. People quipped that Stockley had swapped one single-party state for another, but the impression was that he had transgressed the unspoken rules of excessive name-dropping. He had flown too close to the sun king and had seemingly been frozen out of the city. Today back in the UK, he has a senior design role in the HS2 project. Meanwhile, after Stockley's unplanned exit from the business, it was renamed Civic Engineers by his protégé Stephen O'Malley and has prospered mightily.

Most years I attended MIPIM, my agency was representing either Marketing Manchester, MIDAS, local councils with property plans, or property firms. While a large proportion of the cost was met by a battalion of sponsoring businesses, the organisation was by the publicly funded agencies. While the press releases that I drafted explained, for the benefit of council taxpayers, that Manchester was putting itself on the world stage at MIPIM, over time I came to realise this was only fuzzily true. MIPIM was not where Manchester city council met the world's property investors, it was where it went to talk to Manchester's property classes. It was an annual promulgation of the current state of play in the city, and a chance for hundreds of people to have two-minute conversations they never got round to doing at home. As such, there was nothing remotely unethical about the exercise, but the reality was that visitors to the Manchester stand were ignored. I regularly saw parties from Italy or Japan, clearly interested in the exhibition on show, leave without being spoken to. No doubt talking with unbidden foreigners has a low strike rate in getting property deals done. But to tell the Manchester public that the city's civil servants flew to Cannes to have prearranged private meetings with Manchester investors and developers over dinners in fancy restaurants would have pushed all the wrong buttons.

It was often joked that Manchester's entire leadership would be wiped out if the chartered flight from Manchester ever went down carrying the sponsors and delegates. As well as 'SHB', leader Sir Richard Leese, chief executive of the Greater Manchester authority Eamonn Boylan, other city council planning chiefs like Dave Roscoe, and the main property developers and agents, were in some years joined by grandees like the University's leader Dame Nancy Rothwell – indeed these were all on the 2019 flight which was diverted to Italy after extreme turbulence forced three unpleasant aborted landings at Nice. The gallows humour on board as the plane bucked and jolted in the sky speculated who would take command of the city if the worst happened.

MIPIM was a whirlwind of daytime business events and night-time socialising. Stand events began at 8am, the city's support staff worked 16-hour days and the delegates did too, though the evenings were hard-drinking, giving a new physical survival twist on the theme of 'sustainability', a popular seminar topic. Once there, it was easy to be wrapped up in the MIPIM cocoon. In 2008 the Manchester contingent's bubble was burst by shocking news. As the stand filled up with delegates for the morning session, I was reading online that Greater Manchester Police, and indeed the whole city, was in turmoil. GMP's Chief Constable Mike Todd had been found dead on Mount Snowdon, and his chaotic and troubled personal life was starting to emerge. The eventual inquest concluded that his death from exposure occurred with Todd in emotional tumult at the imminent revelation of an affair with Angie Robinson, the formidable chief of the chamber of commerce, and from The City's point of view 'one of us'. Andrew Stokes was running the stand in Cannes and, as a gaggle of PRs and journalists shook their heads disbelievingly, he asked me what the kerfuffle was. I had to inform him of the upsetting news. As the man promoting Manchester's image, he was grim-faced as he took in the potential reputational implications.

That year the property market-induced financial crash was imminent, and the numbers in Cannes spoke of a bloated financial balloon ready to pop. A record number of delegates paying £1,000 each was swelled by non-paying networkers in the cafés, packing the streets outside the halls. Taxi queues at 1am were hundreds of yards long. Drunks of all nationalities brayed and swayed around the town into the wee small hours. MIPIM had eaten itself. It seemed that easy money was everywhere, and the lax credit culture presaged the world banking crash later that year.

Pre-crash, however, Manchester had the reputational mayhem all to itself. With national media all over the story of the city's deceased and disgraced top cop, its leaders focused on their business at Cannes. The Thursday final night was traditionally a time for the Manchester party to let its hair down, a well-earned chance for an evening to relax in balmy temperatures before the bleary-eyed morning flight home to the stubborn British winter. Manchester was used to the danger of knocking copy about its MIPIM activity. Every year, papers such as *The Standard*, *The Times* and *The Mail* would lose no opportunity to reveal which councils paid for a MIPIM stand, claiming irresponsible use of public money. In Cannes all the PRs were wary of the breed of retired UK hacks now living in France, who knew the market for stories about so-called 'rotten boroughs' behaving badly.

Despite this, in 2008, even though Todd's death was national news, the city's contingent looked forward to their end-of-project knees-up at a nightclub, where delegates could boogie on down along with the most important people in the city. It was risky to continue after the scandal emerged; event chief Steve Smith told me he had turned away two uninvited journalists, cannily not disclosing which city had hired the venue. They were just shaking the tree for a story, but, if the journalists had known that Manchester's top brass were relaxing in a Cannes nightspot while their home city was in shock, a bucket full of poisonous PR was surely guaranteed. The photos of a sweaty, intimate niterie hosting Bernstein, Leese, Stokes, MIDAS CEO Colin Sinclair and GM transport chief David Leather – an Ernst & Young consultant being hired out at £250,000 a year – would have been unforgiving.

The West Midlands Police report into Todd concluded that his personal demons might have impacted on the individuals he had relationships with, but that there were no operational failings. It was received in conflicting ways. *The Guardian* talked of a toxic GMP culture, but the findings were reported straight by the *Manchester Evening News*. Clearly there were some interesting insights about leadership. A degree of charisma was an advantage to scaling the peak of public-facing organisations, and perhaps uniformed ones were susceptible to an egocentric personality like macho man Todd, who volunteered to be tasered with 50,000 volts for a publicity stunt in 2005.

Were Todd's indiscretions and tragic death really just a personal matter that did not affect GMP? In the early 2000s I got a clue at a private dinner at Tom and Joanne Bloxham's duplex Castlefield apartment in his own company's scheme Box Works. With its contemporary art collection, extensive roof gardens and firefighters' pole connecting the floors, the 2,000 sq ft apartment offered uber-urbanista views of classic Victorian Manchester gone to seed – wasteland, railway lines and canals. The confidence and clarity of the couple's contemporary living space was in captivating contrast to their grimy urban surroundings. The restored 1920s building stood on the border of Salford and Hulme, and the huge duplex apartment was Northern 'regen' in the new high style, the quintessence of city living for the new millennium.

The Bloxhams had invited four couples to enjoy a privately cooked dinner by the Belgian fine dining chef Francis Carroll. As the drink flowed, people relaxed, and one of the guests regaled us with a tale of how her car had been stolen from the front drive. On an icy morning, she had left the engine running while the windscreen defrosted. She popped inside, only to come out to see the vehicle being raced away. There would have been a problem with the insurance, of course, she said. It wouldn't have paid out. However, good old Mike Todd had come to the rescue. Her husband, the head of a big Manchester organisation, knew the chief constable of Greater Manchester, and he sorted it all out. The idea of the city's top cop fettling some paperwork as a favour should not be surprising given the close-knit nature of the Manchester mafia. But the account highlights the cat's cradle of connections between Manchester's leaders, giving grounds for dissent from the conclusion that Todd's manic personal life had no impact on his force's operations.

The emerging Manc mafia was an equal opportunities cohort. Gender and sexual identity were of no concern to The City. Those who showed their mettle for the pro-Manchester crusade were 'one of us' and got top jobs. Senior councillors included Val Stevens and Kath Robinson, while Vicky Gregory,

Lis Phelan and out gay man Andrew Stokes all took turns at running Marketing Manchester, and MIDAS bosses at various times included Marilyn Steane and Angie Robinson. In the 1980s the top PR officer was Jane Price, followed by Janine Watson, while Margaret Nuttall ran events ... strong characters all, and utterly devoted to the betterment of their city, and to its two knighted frontmen. While the entire crew eschewed the male and stale stereotype of town hall culture, it was undeniably pale. The super-strategic Phelan in particular was drafted in by The City like a special forces operative, parachuted into tough gigs to get bids written and comms straightened out, everything from managing the Commonwealth Games bid to the mid-2000s poisoned chalice of the congestion charge controversy.

The Manc mafia could indulge in some victimless japes. When I launched Pacific restaurant in Chinatown in 2001, I hosted a table for *Manchester Evening News* editor Paul Horrocks, Granada TV regional boss Eamonn O'Neal and BBC Northwest TV news anchor Martin Henfield, and their wives. Martin's wife Maggie was a star in the male-dominated world of the city's media thanks to her track record in national newspapers. As features editor at the *MEN* she had been my former, highly supportive line manager. Drink was taken and the guests tittered at 'glutinous rice' on the menu. Horrocks bet Henfield the newsreader that he couldn't get 'glutinous' on the TV evening news programme. I thought the newspaperman had won the wager, until the very last moment, and Henfield's live end-of-show chit-chat with the weather forecaster: 'The rain was so heavy this weekend,' pronounced the anchor in the dying seconds, 'it was positively glutinous.'

With the glow of the 2002 Commonwealth Games warming the city, Manchester was on a high. The city's venerable Literary and Philosophical Society (established 1781) published the first *Who's Who in Greater Manchester* for many years, with property developers, artists and PRs sharing the reference guide with knights and MPs. For our client Marketing Manchester, my agency's Daniel Kennedy suggested a survey question: 'What is the country's second city after London?' The Ipsos MORI public poll had the city come out on top, beating traditional claimant Birmingham to the title, and the story was covered by BBC and national press. When quizzed about it at conferences, Bernstein quipped that the second-city debate was a matter entirely between London and Birmingham.

In 2006 I was approached to publicise the 'topping out' (the highest point of construction) of 47-storey Beetham Tower, then Manchester's tallest building. The Liverpool outfit behind it was the unconventional Frost family from

Merseyside. Silver-haired father Hugh Frost – posh 'far back' voice, pinstriped suits, the sensible stockbroker type one finds on the Wirral – was flanked by operations son Simon and creative, deal-doing son Stephen Beetham; the latter had changed his surname on escaping, aged sixteen, from the Plymouth Brethren among whom his mother had raised him. Frost senior was in thrall to Stephen's development nous. 'He is a visionary,' he told *The Independent*. 'He sees potential where others can't.'

The family offered a new American concept of half hotel, half luxury apartments, separated by a cocktail bar mid-way up. The Frost track record was strong. They had developed two towers in Liverpool, where they had transformed unloved 1960s concrete blocks into the cool and desirable Beetham Plaza and West Tower, projects housing £1 million footballer pads, blue-chip offices and fine-dining eateries. They called their business the Beetham Organisation, which boasted a ridiculous crest which along with their dark wood Beetham Plaza offices was an absurd clash with their sleek modern towers. They were trying too hard to be seen as reassuring old money, not the brash, meteoric new players they were. I was happy to take their work, but privately I couldn't take them seriously – an assessment shared by 85 banks which all showed the Frosts the door before they managed to convince the Allied Irish Bank, an energetic lender in that era of easy money, to fund their plans.

The location for their Manchester scheme was audacious. There were tall buildings at the north end of Deansgate but nothing dominant at the south end. Their tower was set to vault over the many nearby historic structures, including the G-Mex centre on the north side and the heritage quarter of Castlefield. This meant intense, detailed discussions with English Heritage about its impact on the historic railway arches linking Oxford Road and Deansgate stations, and the sensitively refurbished canal-side cottages and warehouses of Castlefield. Frost told me that Bernstein was advocating the case with the nation's heritage guardian body, and the planning proposal went ahead. Some voices complained that 'bang' had gone Manchester's potential UNESCO world heritage status, which others whispered under their breath was precisely The City's aim. The UN badge was a tick for tourism but, requiring old sites to be left totally untouched, would be the death knell for new development. For the PR, I did some basic research. No one in the development group seemed to realise that, at 554 ft (169 m) tall, this would be the highest living space in the UK. Canary Wharf was higher, but no one lived in its offices; soon it became known who would be living in Beetham Tower, as the scheme's architect Ian Simpson had bagged the penthouse.

The media were hot for the story. We started at 7.30am for a live BBC TV interview on the Rochdale Canal with Sir Richard Leese, followed by national radio. All day long the interest built. In the afternoon, the BBC scrambled the helicopter piloted by Mike Smith, the former DJ who had become the media's go-to chopper pilot. He was hired to send outside broadcast pictures live to BBC *News at Six*. Something technical had to be done on the roof to ensure the BBC got its picture. The lifts had not yet been installed and my PR agency partner Daniel Kennedy had the luckless task of climbing the stairs of the 47 floors for the second time that day.

Since that day, the Beetham Tower has stood for a symbol of the new Manchester, a sign that the city was soaring upwards, unencumbered by its

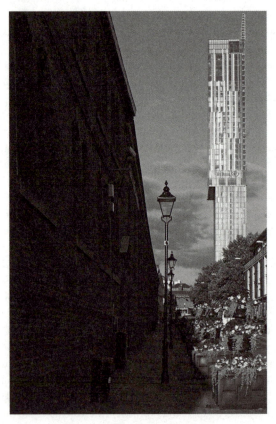

Beetham Tower (photo: Jan Chlebik)

206

weighty past. The *Financial Times* called it 'the UK's first proper skyscraper out of London' and it became a visual signature for TV dramas and documentaries about the city. Manchester's buildings, as grand as they are, had until then never produced the city-association image that Liverpool enjoys with its Royal Liver Building, but the Beetham Tower – one of the slimmest towers in the world, its distinctive profile complete with 20 ft steel lightning rod fin – has become the closest thing to a modern Manchester icon.

While in its final stage of completion, it was the object of much admiration a few months later in 2006 when Manchester hosted the Labour Party conference in the building next door. It was the party's first conference in the city since 1917, and the shift from traditional seaside locations signalled New Labour's perception-change mission. The G-Mex centre was passed fit by the party hierarchy and the state security services who checked out potential sniper views from the new apartment buildings around it. The Westminster bubble floated north for the week to cover what was to be Tony Blair's last conference as prime minister, gifting free media coverage of the changing city centre. On his BBC Sunday morning news programme Andrew Marr remarked on unexpectedly sunny skies against a backdrop of exciting new buildings. Many national reporters referred to the vibrant look and feel of the town, and to the council leadership as the dynamic change-maker.

The Beetham was reported in the media to be a '£150 million development'. When development scheme values are described in this way, they are usually of the development end value – not the cost, but the value after fully occupied completion. As these are an estimate, they are inevitably tickled upwards by the developer and their PRs. The viability of the Beetham Tower project was secured by hotel operator Hilton, which agreed to run the first 22 floors and the 'sky bar', using its staff to service the upper half's apartments. When building work began, Beetham said that 90 per cent of apartments had been sold, the great majority for renting out.

In 2011, exactly five years after the topping out's media blitz, the tower's developer-owner entered administration. The easy credit of the boom years had evaporated in the financial meltdown of the late 'noughties', although the decade might have been better described as the 'naughties' – accounts revealed that the Beetham Organisation had moved around the cash assets in its Liverpool, London and Manchester schemes. While not law-breaking, this was a breach of usual prudent practice to ring-fence each development to prevent financial cross-contamination. Despite the success of the Hilton Hotel, the Beetham development business collapsed under a debt pile as credit dried up. The tower was sold for £47.5 million at a considerable loss to the lending banks, one-third of the end value which our press release had trumpeted in 2006.

Hilton Tower is now in the hands of a London-based company but is still known as Beetham Tower by locals. Its impact on the city centre cannot be overestimated for two reasons: it drove a wedge into heritage defenders' position that that Manchester's cityscape should stay resolutely Victorian, setting a precedent for more towers. And once the market recovered from the 2008 crash, it incentivised landowners to put a tower on their plot, inflating land values. They were encouraged in this by an official position which was never enshrined in a council tall-building policy but became a widely understood approach in property-company boardrooms. There were no public statements which would nail the city down to quotas or guidelines, but the Beetham Tower was a gigantic come-on, a huge beckoning finger for developers in plain sight that Manchester had a growing taste for the high life.

A marker year for the city was 2006, when Manchester entered three public sector competitions, a trio of significant episodes which defined the mid-2000s in the city. The bids highlighted the battle lines between The City and external interests, and ultimately illustrated the limits of the leadership's ability to be master of its own destiny: major competitions for huge funds and development, and Manchester's leaders were, for various reasons, to come out as losers in all three: a major BBC relocation from London, a government contest for a giant casino, and the offer of £3 billion of public transport funding in return for a congestion charge. I was close-quarters eyewitness to and PR participant in all of them.

The first was down to venerable Auntie Beeb. Various leaderships had thought the BBC was unhealthily over-concentrated in London and pushed for a move North for savings and more diverse representation. The BBC had announced in the summer of 2004 that it was to move five departments and 1,800 staff north. The reported move would cost from between £200 million and £500 million, depending over what period the costs were calculated. The corporation had already decided it would move to Greater Manchester and shortlisted two sites each in Manchester and Salford, before narrowing it down to one potential location in each. To most outsiders, the niceties of inter-city politics were academic, and it was all 'Manchester' anyway. The rivalry between the Labour-dominated twin cities, however, with their unequal reputations and resources, led to a feisty neighbour feud over the BBC's contest.

The departments moving North were children's television and radio, sport, new media and R&D, and radio stations Five Live and Five Live Sports Extra – a combined £400 million of direct annual expenditure, with production budgets of £200 million. Then there was the considerable impact on the housing market, as staffers ventured North for their acclimatisation tours with Blue Badge guide Jonathan Schofield and pondered where their hefty relocation packages would be spent. This inward investment prize was a juicy plum, but who would be chosen to pluck it?

Both bids worked hard to maximise the potential of the prize on offer. They sold their sites with a promise of innumerable touch points with the creative types the BBC needed. Their site would be the best physical focus for the BBC and a honeypot attracting supply chain, partner and investment businesses in the growing digital sector, drawing in private studios, education and training centres and research hubs, with a predicted four thousand jobs on top of the BBC staff.

The Northwest regional context was fascinating. The government's Northwest Regional Development Agency, through which much development grant was channelled, was delighted about either side winning, but its civil servants were seen by The City as biased against Manchester when granting state funds. Bureaucrats had to tick boxes about which scheme would bring the most regeneration, and this science was often weighted towards poorer locations like Merseyside. Layered on top of Manchester's suspicion was a personal element – the Salford Quays bid was a consortium of public-sector bodies and the might of main quays landowner Peel Holdings. Its boss John Whittaker was already Manchester's enemy number one for his vast Trafford Centre, whose success was sucking the retail life out of neighbouring towns and threatened the city centre.

Salford Quays, a partnership between Salford City Council and Peel, was a remarkable achievement. The former site of the Manchester Docks had closed in 1982 with the loss of three thousand jobs, but it was a widely acclaimed 'regen' star, in 2001 having welcomed the Lowry Centre – the arts institution named after the household-name Salfordian painter – and in 2002 the extraordinary Daniel Liebeskind-designed Imperial War Museum, across an eye-catching new bridge on the Trafford side. Salford had big sky and sun-glinting expanses of water. It had room on the 200-acre site for the BBC to expand and, crucially, low development costs promised by Peel. In competition, Manchester offered Central Spine. This name, of the kind which master-planning consultants attach before the branding experts are brought in, was the council's internal handle, and it had stuck. My client Ask Developments (major shareholders Simply Red's Hucknall and Dodd) was the preferred developer on this tight 20-acre site bordered by busy main roads, then still a fringe neighbourhood site almost 25 years after the Haçienda opened close by.

Manchester promoted Central Spine on the benefit of clustering. This is where creative and media people played, they stated, along the Oxford Road corridor where the university campus met the nightlife quarter. Manchester had an entitled approach from the start, banking on the fact the BBC had been working for thirty years from its purpose-built New Broadcasting House on Oxford Road, reputedly the busiest bus route in Europe, taking tens of thousands of students and workers daily past two universities, several art galleries, music venues, student unions and the rare green space of Whitworth Park. Didn't media people love being right at the centre of clubland and the arts?

Manchester argued that, when you pile people, resources and ideas on top of each other, creative collaboration is boosted, and everyone wins. Council leader Leese went further, laying it on the line that the BBC should recognise the great strides that Manchester had made, and that backing its site would catalyse the greatest amount of your actual 'regeneration'. A Manchester win would be better for the entire Northwest, ran the script, the implication being that this was because Manchester was the region's capital. Leese said: 'If this city is to continue its growth path … then transformational initiatives like the BBC relocation not only must happen, but should be relocated where the one critical factor is satisfied: and that is where the economic, social and cultural impact of the relocation is maximised.' Salford, however, was winning the PR war. Manchester City Council could see the column inches Salford was getting, despite the bid rule banning overt media relations. Its cheerleader, former BBC presenter Felicity Goodey, was popping up in print and on the air.

The bids were delivered to the BBC in March. A curious round of public lobbying then went on. In May, Ask and the council tasked us to round up the creatives. We had to get a large cohort of luvvies – people in the arts, media and digital – and corral them into Great Hall in the town hall and enthuse them about Manchester's bid. Hundreds assembled to hear speakers tell them how great it would be for them and for the city if the BBC chose Manchester. It was a futile exercise. Public enthusiasm or objection was not a factor, as it is in planning applications, so this pumped-up celebration of all things Manchester to a bemused audience after work on a Friday evening could not affect the outcome.

The BBC selected Salford in June 2006. Weeks later I took another call from Ask's boss Ken Knott. We had to go and meet Sir Howard in his office.

There, the most powerful man in Manchester raged as he urged City Solicitor Susan Orrell to check all options for challenging the decision. Manchester was not used to losing. His anger was intense and sustained and despite its ferocity, I have to say, somewhat comic. The meeting went on for an hour as Bernstein tried to pick holes in the winning bid describing the decision as 'intellectually indefensible'. The solicitor nodded and hummed and haahed, but time and again informed the enraged kingpin that the potential for legal challenge was slim. What was clear from the painful meeting in the city council CEO's office was that the land out in the Salford boondocks was ten times the size of Manchester's five million square feet on offer, and far less expensive. BBC spending is always under scrutiny and the decision-makers had a duty to TV licence payers to get best value. The BBC facilities had expansion room in Salford, and the offer from the Cinderella city was too good to turn down.

Manchester had lost the contest for the BBC, but another race was already starting, and this was equally as big a prize. On the final night of the 2006 Labour Party conference, James Wilson of the *Financial Times* buttonholed Bernstein and found he was already strategising his approach to the government-led contest to award one English location a super-casino. The plan to combat urban decline was to create 16 small and medium casinos, and one giant Las Vegas-style gaming centre with 1,250 slot machines paying out prizes of up to £1 million. 'We have a great chance of winning the casino. You wait,' he told the man from the pink pages. Though it dismayed many in the Labour movement (as well as Conservatives who felt such glitzy vulgarity was un-British) who saw gambling as an immoral way to provide jobs, Labour under Blair was convinced this was a smart way of reviving problem areas.

The casino contest's long list of contenders made it a speculative aspiration. The media thought bids by Blackpool and Greenwich in London were the strongest, but in January 2007 the independent Casino Advisory Panel (CAP) handed the super-casino to Manchester. While its chairman Professor Stephen Crow explained that Manchester had a 'unique formula', ex-Labour deputy leader Roy Hattersley spluttered that the casino plan was 'shameful because it betrays what, long ago, were the best instincts of the Labour Party and exposes thousands of vulnerable people to exploitation'. Those celebrating in Manchester wondered what the Yorkshire Labour politician had ever done for the city, and Bernstein and Leese looked forwards to 2,700 jobs as they were, for once, photographed together (with east Manchester regen chief Tom Russell) popping champagne corks for the cameras on the site next to the new City of Manchester stadium.

Despite reports that Culture Secretary Tessa Jowell was as surprised as anyone when the result was faxed to her, the media were fascinated by the role of Ask Developments and its 17 per cent celebrity shareholder, the frontman of Simply Red, or, as *The Sunday Express* put it, 'crooner Mick, a regular guest at showbiz events at 10 Downing Street'. Conservative MPs queried in the press if there were any links between the unrelated facts of Hucknall's stake in Ask, the company's Manchester victory and his personal £50,000 national Labour Party donation. To complicate matters, Ask had won a 2005 tender from the city council as preferred developer for the casino's huge Eastlands site, and the year before, without thinking of the future optics, boss Ken Knott had approved a £5,000 donation by the firm to the city's central Labour group. Despite a rejection of any wrongdoing by the Standards Board for England, the due process being followed by CAP and government, and the fact the tender would anyway have to be rerun, this was a tasty stew for the tabloids serving middle England.

The media kept the pot bubbling. Soon, however, there was nothing at all to tuck into. Only a year later new Prime Minister Gordon Brown, after all the hullabaloo, quashed the super-casino, the pet project of former leader Tony Blair. The U-turn was announced by culture secretary Andy Burnham, another in the list of misalignments between national Labour and Manchester and one which could hardly have endeared the future city region mayor to The City. The government, now led by the son of an austere Presbyterian minister, dashed hopes for a massive gaming complex on the one-time engine room of the city, providing croupier and bar jobs for the children of those who had worked in coal, steel and chemicals. Bagging the super-casino, it became clear, was not the same as winning the lottery. Only later would it become clear that, when it vanished into thin air, it was only one of a hat-trick of outsized setbacks for a city which had got used to enjoying being on the winning side.

14

PR potholes on the road to hell

In the mid-2000s Mick Hucknall and his partners' property interests in the city centre joined forces with the strategic interests of Manchester City Council in a major conflict about different visions for the future of the city region. It was a disagreement which was to turn ugly, as it was no mere discussion about different approaches to bring growth to Greater Manchester, but one of clashing brute corporate interests, focusing on the land along the Manchester Ship Canal. The clash was complicated by city region geopolitics, spiced with personal leader rivalries, and made toxic by a dollop of culture-war conflict, all of which threatened to rip apart the carefully tended consensus emerging across the ten GM councils.

The cause of the conflict was the plan to exploit the land around the 'Big Ditch', the century old waterway which had demonstrated Manchester's muscle and supercharged its Victorian wealth and power. By digging a 35-mile canal into the heart of rival Liverpool, when it opened in 1894 it enabled merchants to bypass Liverpool taxes on Manchester-bound goods; no mean feat, stealing the sea, a grudge match which continues to this day.

After decades of shipping trade decline, Manchester Ship Canal Company was a moribund business, but it owned those 35 miles of water with land either side of the canal all the way to Liverpool. In 1993 the aggressive property entrepreneur John Whittaker, a secretive tax exile who helicoptered in from the Isle of Man to survey his growing empire, had taken full control of the company and had hoovered up tracts of land along the canal for a planned gargantuan retail mall. His company Peel Holdings' plan for the 300-acre Trafford Centre was greatly feared by Manchester and the smaller nearby towns, having the clear potential to destroy their local high-street shops and associated commerce. Peel faced legal challenges over 12 years from local councils, and the argument went all the way to the House of Lords before being found in Whittaker's favour in 1996.

The battle was rich in symbolism as the ship canal had an existential place in the city of Manchester's history. To get a clear run at developing the site, Whittaker had to buy out two historic Manchester City Council seats on the Ship Canal Company board, dating from the origins of the city's audacious civil engineering project. The council's board seats were now redundant as the other shares were in Peel's control. Council leader Stringer and Whittaker agreed a £10 million deal for the positions, a considerable sum at the time. It meant that both parties could pursue their agendas without conflicts of interest. Stringer said, 'He respected the fact we weren't trying to mess up the business from the inside and he paid a very high price for that at the start. He took a risk but in the end it turned out to be a very low price when the Trafford Centre came to be developed.'

With everything in place for Peel, the waterway was set to become the Manchester shop canal. As construction of the four malls progressed, motorists on the M60 glimpsed a gaudy Rococo-style city taking shape, with replicas of a hundred classical and Art Nouveau statues ringing a grandiose semicircular entrance way, which opened on to a horizon of Italian marble on the shopping mall floor. To future-proof the centre from redesign headaches which bedevilled modern malls, Whittaker's one-off design was what he called a 'people's palace' with 'the Dallas effect'. The aesthetic rankled with Manchester's urban-design aficionados and wannabe loft-livers, who called it rank bad taste. Trafford Council's planning chief called it 'disappointing', but he had to defer to the Trafford Park Development Corporation. With fifteen thousand free car park spaces, the Trafford Centre was also running against the tide of progressive thinking about public transport for environmental gain in high-density cities.

When the new Selfridges store at the Trafford Centre asked if Mick Hucknall would like to perform at its launch, his management saw the chance to take up the cudgels on behalf of Manchester city centre and all those right-thinking people who sniffed at the Las Vegas of the north. It was my task to issue a press release in June 1998 in which the crooner of romantic soul-inflected ballads became the unlikely critic of out-of-town shopping centres. 'A city centre is about the buzz of people and great buildings,' he blasted. 'The Trafford Centre is about the supremacy of Mammon and bad taste.' The media coverage won brownie points in the centre of power in the city, the Manchester City-memorabilia-adorned walls of Sir Howard Bernstein's office. However, under a headline 'Another Helping of Mammon, Mick?' the *Manchester Evening News*'s Paul Taylor lambasted the poor boy made good for seeking to deny

Mr and Mrs Average the pleasures of consumerism. How dare Hucknall deny his paper's readers, the very descendants of the navvies who built the ship canal, their communion in the new cathedral of Manchester materialism?

The newspaper knew the people of Manchester better than Hucknall. The Trafford Centre opened in September 1996 and was a wild success, drawing visitors from all over the North, adding retailers and attractions over the coming years. In 2011 the Peel Group sold the centre for £1.6 billion. The paranoia in Manchester over how its success might hit the city centre proved unjustified, however. 'Town' continued to evolve and, pre-internet, retail held up strongly. However, the battle lines drawn between the City and Peel prefigured an even more bruising conflict to come, over a huge prize on offer to the councils – £2.8 billion of government funding for transport improvements, on condition of bringing in a road traffic congestion charge.

GMPTE, the transport body for Greater Manchester, was responsible for the management and integration of the bus, Metrolink and rail systems. It had in the works a bid for a government scheme to reduce road traffic and massively boost public transport spending. The government's Transport Innovation Fund (TIF) was available to all cities outside London but, typically, Manchester was in for it like a shot. Buses are totemic for former municipal socialists like then council leader Sir Richard Leese, and a big appeal of the TIF was the opportunity to revive bus services. Cuts after the Transport Act of 1985 had deregulated buses, and the privatisation of formerly joined-up routes and timetables meant the experience of using one seemed to worsen every year. In 2007 the *Manchester Evening News* launched a campaign 'to sort out the bus chaos crippling the heart of Manchester'. The over-supplied south Manchester routes had become a 'wild west' in which up to thirty buses an hour arrived at the same stops, with reports of dangerous driving and unsafe vehicles. Yet the real malaise was that many other less popular routes were totally unreliable or axed.

Leese and Bernstein, Manchester's dynamic duo of civic entrepreneurialism, liked what they saw on offer from Transport Secretary and Bolton MP Ruth Kelly – a £1.5 billion grant for not only more, better and greener buses but also a smartcard like London's Oyster card, plus 35 km of new Metrolink lines and longer trains. The £1.3 billion loan to pay for it all would be repaid through road charging. It was clear the city's leaders believed that the politics could be finessed and finagled, with common ground found and the public persuaded. But the train had left the station without a PR plan, and the genie was out of the bottle after the *Manchester Evening News*'s front page splashed: '"Congestion charging: it's coming our way."'

215

The expression of interest to government was duly made. What followed was two years of fierce division which convulsed the Greater Manchester body politic and set off a nasty culture war of competing interests over the place of the motor car in the life of the city. The first signs of the storm to come were the queries piling into the PR office of the city's transport body. In April 2007 GMPTE called in my agency SKV. (We had replaced Spin Media with Spinoza Kennedy Vesey, the names of our three partners.)

Their communications team needed urgent back-up. In early 2007 there were still numerous active local newspapers, and reporters wanted to know what it would mean for readers on their patch. Where would the charging zone start on roads into the centre? Would taxis be charged? What about disabled drivers? What times of the day would it be in force? How would the 'tag and beacon' technology work? How much would the residents on each reporter's patch be out of pocket? Very little of this had yet been worked out, so all we could do was inform them what was known. A rising sense of public anger and frustration was emerging, which the media felt obliged to reflect, and by June a fierce 'hearts and minds' battle was under way in the local papers, on the city's radio and TV news, and in the *Manchester Evening News*, which smelled an easy rabble-rousing win in a time of plummeting sales.

The way language was used was a source of conflict from the off. Instead of '£3bn for public transport', every headline was about the 'congestion charge' or 'C-charge'. Responses gradually emerged to the media's questions from GMPTE's battalion of transport consultants, but these were daunting to under-stand and to explain in plain English. Simply, the plan was for two rings around Manchester, the outer one on the junctions of the M60 orbital motorway and one on the inner ring road. The charge would be between £1 and £5 a day depending on when and how many cordons were passed, and in which direc-tion. While it was complex, it was smart, because the scheme targeted conges-tion when and where it happened, so it would have given lots of opportunity for people to drive when the charge wasn't active. But there was a mountain of technical detail, which we attempted and often failed to clearly communi-cate. One of our given key messages was that behaviour change to challenge Manchester's car-dependency would mean 'facilitating modal shift'.

Saying 'no' to paying more was the easiest message of all to understand. When in July 2007 the Association of Greater Manchester Authorities (AGMA) agreed to submit a bid to government, the headlines and sentiment were hugely negative, and the public mood poisonous. The conflict was enacted along traditionally hostile lines, with the city council's familiar enemy Peel Holdings leading the campaign against. After all, the Trafford Centre was a car-enabled destination (it received a Metrolink stop only in 2020), but the centre and its owners' campaign became something much bigger – a symbolic, libertarian 'cry freedom' against what it portrayed as the over-controlling central Manchester power base seeking to squeeze the little guy. It was astonishing how the media conflated the average Mancunian's concerns with those of the motorist lobby. Whether the consumers of papers, radio and TV were anti-congestion-charge drivers, or whether the media found it simpler to assume that was the case, the result was that the original intention by Bernstein and Leese, for a sensible political consensus to emerge and support the bid, had utterly failed. Some leaders and councillors across the city region saw the plan as a sure-fire vote loser. Some businesses saw it as another unwarranted cost. Some groups, though, welcomed the 'big bang' expansion of public transport, a plan for a greener Greater Manchester with breathable air and lifestyle changes geared to walking and cycling.

Battle was joined. Our client the Yes campaign was funded by the transport body. Agencies were taken on for different roles and one partner outfit, Creative Concern, drew up case studies of typical Mancunians who would benefit from the Manchester bid. While photographs of real people, they were actually 'personas' in marketing speak – photos of alleged (and suspiciously healthy-looking) Mancunians, used alongside their supposed names with details of how they would benefit. In July 2007 the leaflets were delivered to every household in Greater Manchester. I was at a meeting at Manchester Town Hall beforehand when they were discussed, and no one foresaw a problem. However, as PR veterans tell their clients and each other about the comms role, 'We're paid to be paranoid.' Collectively our entire team were not nearly paranoid enough about what should have been described as fictional examples, not passed off as real people.

Firstly, an American blogger realised that 'Kiki', portrayed as a solicitor from Ashton-under-Lyne, and 'Terry', said to be a self-employed van driver from Rochdale, were American models whose photos were sourced from a picture library. The aggressive No lobby couldn't believe its luck with our PR own goal, and the 'case studies' were called out as fakes. This was a serious credibility moment for the whole communications mission to persuade people that the charge was worth it, in return for £3 billion of public-transport gains. And our agency was at the centre of the firestorm. The No lobby tore into the enemy. Articles in BBC online, *The Mail* and the *Manchester Evening News* as well as numerous local papers all carried the story. We firstly stated our belief that case studies were real but the photos were not. Later we had to admit that all the content was confected. Once the dust had cleared, the response we issued on behalf of the transport body described them as 'fictional case studies based on accurate travel plans under current proposals', adding that 'the studies were worked out based on real journeys taken by real people'.

While we had not been the agency responsible, as the media's first point of contact, we were widely presumed to be behind the fiasco. We did not point the finger at our partner and took the flak for a group effort. There was an explosion of media indignation about what was seen as propaganda on the rates, with the *Manchester Evening News* editorial calling it 'cack-handed PR'. Our agency had been the lightning rod and, reputationally, we were burned along with our clients. Our trade title *PR Week* printed that we had been 'named and shamed' for the misdemeanour, a report we hired a libel lawyer to have taken down from its website. It was imperative that I should clarify our role: I spoke to the boss of Creative Concern, Steve Connor, and he agreed to put his hand up. His media statement confessed it was their work. Both agencies had become the story and taken a massive hit for the team. At the height of the controversy, when I was privately moaning about having to eat excrement in public, a senior insider told me something I had not been aware of: 'You took the heat, but all the senior leaders of the TIF bid saw those leaflets, and they all signed them off.'

That summer the confrontation stepped up several gears. Well-organised Manchester Against Road Tolls wrote inflammatory letters to the papers, upping the loaded language stakes by calling the charge a 'tax'. Backed by the Association of British Motorists, MART took out street posters and confronted Yes supporters on online forums. I view this conflict as a presage of Brexit's struggle for hearts and minds, as complex details were reduced to facile and dishonest emotional appeals. In one MART poster, a businessman chomps on a cigar with the slogan, '£5 a day won't even buy me a cigar. Keep the roads free for the rich.' It was not a one-way street. Environmental groups wanted more cars off the road and Clean Air Now and Friends of the Earth campaigned strongly for Yes, but their politely reasoned arguments had less impact.

People and organisations were polarised. Rising pressure on the politicians to let the people decide could not be denied, and in July 2008 AGMA announced a referendum for all Greater Manchester residents to be held in December. The already-charged atmosphere went up a few notches, especially after an IPSOS Mori poll in August found that, in contradiction to the media tone, 53 per cent of residents were in favour of the plans. Big business set up 'for' and 'against' groups. The Greater Manchester Momentum Group was led by Peel Holdings and included Kellogg's, Unilever and breweries. On the Yes side, United City featured many property businesses with interests in the growing city centre. Our agency had been dropped from the TIF bid campaign in favour of another agency, but we were now advising private sector Yes group United City.

Rival developers sat around a table to brainstorm ideas. Celebrities were thought to be prized advocates, and seasoned property man David Russell of Property Alliance Group said he could get Gary Neville and Ryan Giggs to come out in favour. I counselled that he might want to consider that the intervention of millionaire footballers, strangers to the 9 to 5 commute, risked pushing voters the other way. In the end, a letter appeared in the press from the stars' manager. Sir Alex Ferguson, who as a Cheshire resident did not even have a vote, wrote: 'Vote yes for safe, fast and convenient match-day travel and make sure all Greater Manchester people get the public transport they need and deserve.' John Wilkinson, owner of Salford Reds Rugby Club, had his finger more on the public pulse when he said: 'I can't see Sir Alex coming to the games by the tram from Altrincham.'

If some outside the voting boundary wanted their say, an even stranger bedfellow popped up on the other side. Former Manchester leader and now MP Graham Stringer, one-time ally of Leese and Bernstein, was one of the prime movers in the Stop the Charge coalition. It was a group of seven Labour, Tory and Liberal Democrat MPs in the city region and the three councils publicly against the bid. Stringer said he was defending the interests of his north Manchester constituents ill-served by public transport, and that the plan was 'as unfair as the poll tax'.

When it came to the public vote, language once again became the cause of conflict. Even the wording used on the ballot question had its own moment of controversy. During prime minister's questions, Stringer raised the neutrality of the referendum question wording in the Commons, as it did not mention the words 'congestion charge' and simply asked whether voters agreed with the proposals. 'What we're getting is a partial and biased question which doesn't even mention the congestion charge,' he argued. 'Wouldn't it be better,' he asked the prime minister, 'given the current economic circumstances, if this unnecessary congestion charge is cancelled, and the divisive referendum is cancelled, and we brought forward the investment in the tram system in Greater Manchester to an early date?' PM Gordon Brown simply responded that the question was legally approved. Drawn up by independent election expert Sir Neil McIntosh, it did include a preamble mentioning twice both the charge and the potential £3 billion of investment.

Complex issues, simple slogans, questions open to interpretation and disagreement: in the interplay between these, the opportunity for the city region to transform its public transport was lost. It was no surprise, given the attention span of many voters and the focus on simplistic, inflammatory headlines, that the ballot papers counted after the 11 December deadline showed a 4 to 1 victory for the No campaign – 812,815 versus 218,860. While approximately 20 per cent of the voters chose Yes, in fact just 10 per cent of the 2 million voter pool had given the plans the thumbs-up. Given that there are few who neither drive nor use public transport, commentators were surprised that turnout was just 53.2 per cent.

As ever, what Manchester experiences today can be a learning for the nation. Many of the same challenges bedevilling the TIF vote were to be seen writ large in referenda on Scottish independence and Brexit. How to reduce complicated information which crucially affects our lives into leaflets, posters, adverts and slogans? Even the government-funded TV advertising campaign, intended by GMPTE to be in a neutral format to encourage voting, was found to be gaming the information process – broadcast watchdog OFCOM ruled the ad was biased in favour of 'Yes' and in breach of impartiality guidelines. To understand such issues in depth often requires time, patience and knowledge. Experience of absorbing technical detail is preferable. If every voter spent an hour in a closed room with the transport technocrats we worked with, the vote might have been different. But the vast majority simply saw the headlines about costs and bureaucratic control of the freedom to drive.

With the resounding 'No', the application for government TIF cash was stopped in its tracks. Bernstein is on record as saying its downfall was 'a political failure', but it was also a communications failure. The 'go' button was pressed before detailed messaging was worked out, firing the starting gun for over two years of conflict. There was no referendum envisaged in the initial plan, and it emerged only because of the feverish controversy. Yet if all the scenarios had been war-gamed, the public scepticism and the political pushback could have been anticipated and planned for. Launched with the same seat-of-the-pants opportunism which had levered the 2002 Commonwealth Games stadium money from the government, TIF's benefits might have been obvious to the leadership, but they failed to take the public with them. (The 2022 postponement of the Clean Air Zone, forced after white-van owners mobilised in outrage, showed that the passing years had not moved the dial on the public–political discourse around motoring.)

The TIF plan's downfall occurred within an added context. The worldwide economic crash had occurred in autumn 2008. GM leaders presented the TIF plan as an answer to gridlocked roads, but, by the time it came to vote, roads were quiet. The former bumper-to-bumper commute was now as relaxed as summer holiday time as job losses and short-time working took hold. 'I'm sure the economic downturn, which is hitting everyone hard, has had a part to play,' said Leese sheepishly after the result.

However, even while the toxic transport row was in overdrive, 'The City' was thinking big again. Not in development terms for once, but in gathering an evidence base. 'Telling the city region story' using economists and academics would support new strategies, and be a credible prospectus for Greater Manchester 'asks' to government. This was the Manchester Independent Economic Review (MIER), the first high-level in-depth study into a city region. Chaired by Sir Tom McKillop, the chairman of the Royal Bank of Scotland, it was launched in June 2008 by Alistair Darling, chancellor of the exchequer. However, events decreed that the pair were soon to be working together on a more significant project – saving the national banking system and preventing the world economy from catastrophic collapse.

While the five wise persons on the MIER panel – 'prominent economists and business leaders' – and their researchers beavered away, searching for the Greater Manchester economy's strategic strengths and opportunities, Darling and McKillop experienced a nervous summer. The banking system was coming under increasing strain due to a mountain of debt, much of it related to cheap American sub-prime mortgages. On 14 September the US government allowed the most exposed private institution of all, the Lehman Brothers financial colossus, to collapse. In the UK, it fell to Darling and PM Gordon Brown to bootstrap the UK banking system with a bailout package. Darling recalls that on the morning of 7 October 2008 'I remember being summoned out of a meeting to talk to Tom McKillop and he said things were just terrible, that money was pouring out of the door.' The UK bank bailout had not been finalised and Darling recalls how rapidly the situation was deteriorating. McKillop told him that RBS – the biggest bank in the world, about the same size as the entire UK economy – would collapse in a few hours if action was not taken. Darling said: 'If people thought the biggest bank in the world had failed, there would not be a bank in the western world that would be safe … People forget just how close we came to a complete collapse' … 'it wouldn't just have been the banks in ruins, it would have been complete economic and therefore social collapse … It was very scary. That moment will stick with me for the rest of my days.'

221

In the summer of 2008 Manchester was flattered it had secured such an eminent business leader to head up its independent review. But by the time the report was published in April 2009, RBS chairman McKillop had required £20 billion of emergency public money to shore up his bank, 70 per cent of which was now owned by the government. McKillop, who had no banking experience before joining the board in 2005, was held responsible for the downfall of RBS, along with former chief executive Sir Fred Goodwin. The previous credibility McKillop enjoyed, and which Manchester had proudly trumpeted, had been shredded by his failure to rein in Goodwin's high-risk takeover and expansion strategy. Bad timing had struck Manchester's plans. The MIER's vanilla conclusions – greater agglomeration, better skills and conditions for innovation, more robust governance – were quietly buried in articles in the *Financial Times* and *Manchester Evening News*. If there was a distinct lack of enthusiasm to push the report, it was entirely understandable. McKillop was branded by parliament, media and the court of public opinion as having brought a once-mighty institution to its knees and was now hardly the best frontman for Manchester's next economic growth plan.

The crash's effects coincided with the humiliation of the Co-operative Bank, an exemplar of decent, idealistic Manchester with its 1844 roots in Rochdale grocery stores. In 2013 its chairman Paul Flowers displayed his banking ignorance at an MPs' committee, then set out to 'get wasted in Manchester' on cocaine, ketamine and methamphetamine, which a tabloid sting revealed he bought to party with rent boys. Methodist minister Flowers could not resist the lure of party central, which Shaun Ryder once likened to Pinocchio's 'pleasure island' and, as in the fable, made a donkey of the chairman and an ass of the bank. Before its fatal slide, the bank crested on an eco-friendly wave of gooey public sentiment with a TV ad using Bob Dylan's 'Blowin' in the Wind'. First, a disastrous merger with the Britannia Building Society, then the 'Crystal Methodist' affair, were body blows before CEO Euan Sutherland announced a £1.5 billion black hole in its accounts. Moody's downgraded its credit rating to junk. Today the bank is owned by US private equity.

The downturn was felt across the city's property sector. In 2008 a city-centre estate agent was approached to market a package of 20 vacant flats in town from a portfolio owned by TV presenter Anthea Turner's husband Grant Bovey. He ran the biggest buy-to-let outfit in the country, and in the heady days of easy money had snapped up the flats in the Haçienda Apartments, but even the strong sales pitch – come live in the grooviest place in town in the nation's most happening city – could not prevent his company's collapse.

15

Football, fashion and food

Another form of church, football was all that stood between earth and God.

Morrissey, *Autobiography*

When working with Alex Ferguson on his testimonial season, I had loved going to the Cliff training ground in Salford for our early-morning meetings before the footballers turned up. The place had a magical familiarity from bygone TV footage of Sir Matt Busby putting Best, Law and Charlton through their paces as he rebuilt the team after the 1958 Munich air crash. The ghosts were palpable, of Munich as well as Manchester, and the elevated setting, giving evocative views west towards the Irwell Valley and beyond, gave the experience an epic yesteryear charm.

It was a special place, but when the current team arrived for training as I was leaving my meetings with Fergie, you could see it was not fit for the modern era. Set among the red-brick suburban streets of Broughton, the wide old cobblestoned entrance was the haunt of autograph hunters and truanting schoolkids at all times of day. People would wander in, badger the players and take photos of their cars. It couldn't last. Already a global religion, football's journey from communities to commercialism was speeding up, leaving the big new superclubs in danger of losing the ties which bound them to their tribal local fans. In TV presenter Terry Christian's autobiography *My Word*, he relates a remarkable tale in which he and his childhood mates spot rival United and City managers Sir Matt Busby and Joe Mercer chatting in Longford Park, Stretford, in the early 1970s. Young Terry runs the long way home and back to fetch a pen, and there the two football legends are, still minding the kids' football, before signing autographs. Such a scene could never be envisaged in 2000. The gates were literally closing on the world of the players' training ground. The United first team moved to the 100-acre Trafford Training Ground, at Carrington's

223

£22 million 14-pitch complex with security gates, high fences and dense, tall evergreens blocking views for both fans and paparazzi.

The team's success in those years was being enjoyed hugely by the hot young star striker of the property world, Tom Bloxham. As a student from the South, many felt he was the typical United supporter, but no one could accuse him of not putting down United roots, with property interests like his Castlefield penthouse and a house in Worsley, the poshest part of Salford where even the water in the Bridgewater Canal was coloured a tomato-soup red from iron-ore deposits.

Bloxham was a corporate supporter at Old Trafford as soon as Urban Splash took off, and the roots of many a business deal took shape on the canal barges he laid on for match-day socialising, setting off from the White Lion in Castlefield for slow, alcoholic journeys along the Rochdale Canal to the ground. His hospitality is and remains legendary. Bloxham was a new type of party animal, operating at the intersection of the city's social life – regeneration, music and football – and did not go unnoticed by the superstar players of United. Soon Giggs, Cantona and Co. were buddies with Mr Urban Splash, who kept a limo and driver on a retainer, always on hand to lift his friends around the nightspots or to get them home.

His company's success had started with apartment schemes such as the Smithfield Building, which opened on Oldham Street in 1996, a location given momentum by the 1989 opening of Dry bar, owned by Factory and New Order, across the road. The music culture was giving confidence to others to plough their money into the city centre. Even so, Bloxham and Liverpool-based partner Jonathan Falkingham were taking a chance buying Ducie House, close to Piccadilly rail station. It may have been 200 yards away, but it was on a road less travelled in a dead zone. However, Bloxham says he had noticed the business occupiers who had been scattered when 42–44 Sackville Street became Carol Ainscow's loft apartments, and reckoned he could repeat the offer for small creative ventures.

Bloxham's success with his firm's leisure, workspace and increasingly bold residential schemes made Urban Splash a celebrated Manchester export. American urbanist Jane Jacobs was an acknowledged influence, with her emphasis on the importance of street life in city centres, working with the urban grain rather than bringing in the wrecking ball. There was talk of an 'Urban Splash effect' when the company entered other towns, and it all added to the impression of Manchester leading the challenge to tackle the nation's crumbling city centres.

Bloxham's instinct was right; not only were the Ducie House offices in demand from tenants like the experimental dance group 808 State but the party-loving property prince so enjoyed being the host that he opened his own nightclub in the basement. And it was here, at Home (not to be confused with the later arts centre), its bare floor and hard furniture not your typical footballer bling-spot, that his Red Devil pals gathered for their celebration party after winning the league title in May 1997. It was to the United players' credit that they enjoyed the buzz of the city centre rather than hide out in the long grass in Cheshire, the conventional, dull heartland of the Northern celebrity. Indeed, it was an everyday part of the pre-mobile phone camera era that anyone out on the town could see or chat to famous people, such as rugby league stars like Ellery Hanley and Shaun Edwards, footballers from Northwest teams, TV soap stars and visiting actors on shoots, and musicians like New Order, M People and Mick Hucknall, all out in the wild with friends and without minders.

This was the era when United's 'class of 1992', a tight-knit six-strong group who graduated from the club's youth team, went on to win the highest honours in the game – a talent development success story which will never happen in today's big-money transfer culture. The class that played on the pitch also played out together. My Diary desk phone buzzed with who had been seen at the various Saturday night discos. Nicky Butt, one of the United apprentices who graduated to the first team, said: 'Growing up in Manchester in the 90s was just massive … We would be going to the Haçienda, the Boardwalk, to concerts like Spike Island. It was a special time. I remember one time the whole Man United team went to the Haçienda. It wouldn't happen nowadays.'

When United won the 1997 Premier League title, half of the first team descended on Bloxham's nightclub after a riotous day out at Chester races, where the red tops later reported they had brawled with other racegoers who first took the fight to them. They got to Home around 9pm with ripped shirts and ruddy faces to be greeted by Mick Hucknall. The scene was set for a raucous celebration. After arranging some posed photos of them for snapper Eamonn Clarke for the next day's *MEN*, I was on the steps of the exit when someone fell on top of me, then hit the ground hard. It was former United and England captain, the legendary – and, in United circles, legendary drinker – Bryan Robson. The day's wassailing had been too much even for him. His ex-team-mate Dion Dublin helped him up, then carried him bodily into a taxi and threw some £20 notes to the cabbie, shouting, 'Just get him home!' I couldn't resist publishing the incident in the story, with my punchline that 'even foot-ball gods can sometimes have feet of clay'. One of United's youngsters coming through was a young David Beckham, and I lay claim, perhaps a mite patheti-cally, to writing the first gossip piece about him. My Diary story was about him dating *Hollyoaks* actress Julie Killelea, who went on to marry United team-mate Phil Neville.

Far more than the anything-goes approach of today, clothes mattered. In 1985 I had interviewed Vidal Sassoon and he matched a subtly tailored slimline suit with white training shoes, and the effect in grey Northern England was striking. Ten years later, it was a look that Wilson wore for everyday business, but out in the city's nightspots it was Beckham, Lee Sharpe and Ryan Giggs who led the fashion line. The crucial player in the man-about-town league, however, was not a sportsman but a brave retailer, style influencer and lethal salesman. Richard Creme was a great man, a fact unrelated to his 7 ft 3 in height, with hands the size of soup bowls and a nose like a Neolithic axehead. His giantism, a rare medical condition, made him a talked-about celebrity among the gawpers who would snatch glances through the window of his city-centre fashion emporium. If they did spy 'Rich Creme' serving a customer, the effect of his height was exaggerated by the tiny, pale-faced, black-clad woman at his side – his wife Shelley, who I always reckoned wore the trousers, even if they were by Comme des Garçons.

Creme was the first person I heard call a shirt a 'piece'. His wares were not the *schmatte* which my rag-trade uncles dismissively called the products of the fashion business. Creme respected the quality of the cloth, the skill of the tailor, the creativity of the designer, as much he respected the tastes and knowledge of his customers. He stole the street theatre of the buzz-and-enter door from LA's Rodeo Drive for his first store at St Ann's Square, later moving to Barton Arcade and finally Bridge Street. The peripatetic L'homme was a Creme-hosted caravan of fashion, celebrities, art, fun, media and money, and, best of all, Manchester. I observed his client base with curiosity: from the urgent-looking street kid with more cash in his pockets than seemed right for a lad of his age, to the self-made men and the racier lawyers and accountants. If you popped in to see him at his store, he would introduce you to someone interest-ing trying on something interesting.

Creme believed that his mission to bring quality and style to Mancunians was raising his city's horizons, helping to end its cloth-cap image. 'When I first went to the collections the designers laughed,' he told me. 'They'd never heard of Manchester.' He gave world-famous artists a new reason to talk about his city, and he gave me tall tales for the paper. About Morrissey hiding for hours in the changing room because he could not face meeting another customer who stayed and chatted. About dressing Beckham, Bowie and Springsteen, and the day he greeted a cavalcade of limos at 6am from which emerged the 5 ft 3 in Prince – 'It was like shaking hands with a small child,' he told me.

One Creme customer was Eric Cantona, the wilful and wayward football genius who floated around town apparently ignorant of club rules about night-time fraternisation with the locals. He often palled up with Hucknall's pulling partner 'Saltz' Anderson, and the pair rocked up at a Friday night premiere in London for a film screening in January 1996. Player curfews are based on a belief that being out and about affects performance, but Cantona was not the average player. The next Monday, the Frenchman scored the winner away to West Ham and he finished the season the club's top scorer. 'Le God' was not quite so imperious in his car, though; lost and frazzled on Manchester's motor-ways, he would often call Cliff Rullow, L'homme's smooth young assistant from Moss Side, and plead for directions to the United training ground. I revealed in my column that, perhaps to soothe the savage beast inside, the infamously temperamental Cantona was taking lessons in trumpet playing.

From his door, Creme scanned Bridge Street like a human watchtower for celebs walking up from Granada TV. He had a droll sense of humour and there were times we had tears in our eyes as his expressive voice rose and fell, unfolding incredulous anecdotes about the rich and famous: his visits to catwalk shows, an abrasive encounter with Madonna, and who Tony Wilson had pissed off this week. Bitchy US fashionistas, he told me, referred to Rochdale singer Lisa Stansfield, then basking in the success of her 1989 smash 'All Around the World', 'as The Hat, The Coat'.

In the summer of 1989 Creme commissioned the royal photographer Norman Parkinson to shoot a new L'homme brochure, working with the intense young Lancashire graphic designer David Kirkwood. The modelling shoots took place at Agecroft power station, Southern Cemetery and the Esso refinery at Carrington. At 6 ft 5 in, elegant beanpole 'Parks' was almost a height match for Creme, and they turned heads as they strode the streets. Parkinson told me: 'I was fascinated by that fellow called Creme. I so liked his attitude that I said I would do this one.' Creme observed drily: 'The Parkinson breed is a very rare one, and it's not often one finds it up this way … Parkinson has never been let loose before. For four days he did what he liked. We un-caged him.' It was clear the pleasure both were getting from the creative chemistry unleashed in grimy old Manchester. Some of L'homme's selected designers were Yohji Yamamoto, Dirk Bikkembergs and Ann Demeulemeester. The tall guy patiently explained to me what their style was, and how the clothes were created. The designers

'Saltz' Anderson and Eric Cantona in 'The Diary'

meant nothing to me at first. Eventually, very selectively, and at great expense, I was wearing them.

The events which befell Creme were tragic. Following a devastating stroke in 2007, Creme was forced to close his business. Unable to speak and suffering

Richard Creme artwork

from mobility problems, the big man took to drawing with his weaker but still active left hand, creating detailed and accomplished artworks. One was a paint and ink copy of David Beckham's L'homme bill from 24 March 2005. Becks spent a total of £6,480 on items like 'Belt £265', 'Sweat £185' and 'Blk Leather

£1250'. At an auction of Creme's work in 2012 held to raise funds for his ongoing care, I paid £200 for the painting.

In 2018 he passed away, leaving a million Manchester memories and some classic 'pieces' doubtless still hanging today in the wardrobes of penthouses around the globe. Until Beckham left Manchester for Madrid in 2003, Creme would deliver his purchases to Beckham's home in Alderley Edge, the affluent Cheshire town where Beckham had moved with Victoria 'Posh Spice' Adams. Their every move was media news. Even the stylish young buck's taste for clear glass spectacles was a story – the fact he did not need lenses was another world-beating exclusive I revealed for the *MEN* after chatting with him at a film premiere.

Post-Ferguson, the famous old football club and global brand which had benefited Manchester for a generation suffered an appalling slow-motion decline, eclipsed in May 2012 when Manchester City's astonishing victory in the dying seconds of the 2011–12 season pipped United for the Premiership. Weeks later, Bruce Springsteen told 45,000 fans at City's Etihad Stadium, 'OK, now I know

Andy Spinoza interviewing David Beckham (photo: Eamonn Clarke)

there are TWO teams in Manchester.' Even in the US, where people's knowledge of 'soccer' was scanty, there was awareness of the blue moon rising, and in many ways this seismic shift in football would mean that Manchester as a city, too, was undergoing a profound change. The last decade has demonstrated the global attraction of Manchester as an investible location, particularly the 2008 takeover of Manchester City FC by the Abu Dhabi sovereign wealth fund and the 13 per cent investment of £265 million by China's government in 2015 (sold off in late 2022) – valuing the City Football Group at £3 billion and taking the club's relationship with the ordinary fan a long way from the terraces on the Kippax Street stand at the now-demolished Maine Road stadium.

These heady heights were hard to reconcile with very recent memories. In the 1980s and 1990s the blue-supporting fraternity of the Manchester music mafia would gather in Moss Side pubs before a match to moan about their ever-failing team, in the same way most supporters across the country do. In the old-school Gardener's Arms in Rusholme, football fans of the blue persuasion would dimly recall the late 1960s, when their club was as strong as United. To their bitter dismay the Reds had become the one Manchester brand people recognised abroad. There was a big crossover between Manchester's music scene and City supporters; the friendship between the sixteen-year-old Mike Pickering and the older Rob Gretton began when the future Haçienda DJ and rock manager met as away fans under a privet hedge of a Nottingham front garden, where they were hiding from skinhead home fans: 'We lay flat on our stomachs staring eye level at a dozen pairs of well-polished Doc Marten boots, and he extended a hand and said, "Rob Gretton, Wythenshawe, pleased to meet you."' With their hooligan street-running days behind them, Rob Gretton, Mike Pickering and their cronies would sink a few in 'the Gardeners' before heading to the match, climbing the steep steps up to the Kippax's vertiginous standing terrace, to the vantage points they had held for years. And always, despite false dawns and the odd cup run, the glum disappointment expressed by Gretton to me over a pint: talking about the then current book *Manchester United Ruined My Life* by City fan Colin Shindler, Gretton moped, 'Manchester United didn't ruin my life – Manchester City did.'

On a cold, windy evening rush hour in March 2018, Pep Guardiola enjoyed an evening with friends and family at his new restaurant in elegant, pedestrianised King Street. At this private get-together before the official launch, the celebrated football mastermind sought the closest seat to the window for a clear view of the classic Victorian Manchester thoroughfare, completely unnoticed by passers-by. There was no Barcelona-style *passeig*, no multi-generational

Tast opening: Pep Guardiola, Ferran Soriano, Paco Pérez and Txiki Begiristain
(photo: Eric Howard)

groups promenading, pausing and chatting. It was dark and time for the commute home as winter-weary Mancs hurried by without looking. The calm and
relaxed manner with which Guardiola snacked on the fine Catalan cuisine
presented a picture of a man happy with life in Manchester. He was perhaps
still coming to terms with the concrete skies but, only minutes away from
his family's luxury apartment, here he was in the restaurant he co-owned,
surrounded by Spanish and Catalan friends and, importantly for his sanity,
unpestered by passionate fans and nosy reporters as he would be in his home
city of Barcelona.

In 2021 the government's 'cultural industry' champions must have been
purring when Guardiola said, 'Always when I was in Munich, Barcelona, I had
the feeling, the dream, to come here – Shakespeare country, Beatles country,
Oasis country. It's not football. This country is special for many, many reasons.'
The UK's soft power expressed through pop culture had worked its magic,
though the riches of his club's new owners, and the resources they brought the

232

city's Cinderella club, were surely factors in the charismatic Catalan's decision to turn up in the unlikely location of east Manchester.

After a year's sabbatical in New York, he was now close to the home of The Beatles and Oasis (now long departed from the cities which made them). A new friend Manchester had brought Guardiola was the chef Paco Pérez. Strangely given their shared Catalan background, they met for the first time at Tast when I lined them up for an official opening photo, side by side in front of the open kitchen with their partners in the venture, City's football director Txiki Begiristain and CEO Ferran Soriano.

It had been a seismic moment for world football in July 2016 when Guardiola, one of the titans of football management, was reunited in Manchester with his two colleagues, who had left the heat of Spain for the Rainy City three years earlier, lured by 'the Project' on offer by Manchester City's Abu Dhabi owners. As a trio they had delivered spectacular success for FC Barcelona but now, alongside the revolution they were leading on the pitch, Tast was making a statement that life in Manchester was very much to their liking.

This was a watershed moment for the city's gastronomic profile. We had come a long way from the punch-up at Bill Wyman's Sticky Fingers. No burgers and celebrity fisticuffs here. Tast's restrained Scandi design and Pérez's fine-tuned gastronomy had earned him no fewer than five Michelin stars for his restaurants in Barcelona and Berlin. With my business partner, VIP guestlist clipboard queen Geraldine Vesey, I had launched more restaurants in Manchester than City had had managers since 1979 (25 gaffers, including caretakers). The high point had been the 1998 launch of Reform in the baroque splendour of the listed 1870 Liberal Party headquarters in the North. Its grand high ceilings and ornate wooden décor reeked of history. It was a local fable that Liberal politicians Lloyd George and Winston Churchill, when the future wartime leader was MP for Oldham and Manchester North West, addressed King Street crowds from the balcony, even if they actually hadn't.

Designer Bernard Carroll conjured up a psychedelic gentleman's club in its jaw-dropping main room, fitting huge ruby-red drapes, high-backed leopard-print seats and pinpoint-spotlit tables. Tracy McLeod in *The Independent* called the lobby, with its swirling oak staircase and palatial Gothic fireplaces, 'the equal of anything in London or Paris'. Reform was a roaring success from the opening, when two thousand guests crowded into an over-invited launch party. In a scene straight from *Goodfellas*, I had to escort Sir Alex Ferguson and his friend Everton FC manager Walter Smith through a side door, along narrow corridors and eventually through the kitchens into the VIP room. From the off,

Reform was a sensation, the start of a city centre now able to draw the moneyed Cheshire set out for night-time pleasure and play.

There had been many top-calibre chefs who had helmed first-class kitchens in the years before and after the millennium, and the football-star-as-owner trend included Rio Ferdinand's interest in Rosso and United's Juan Mata-backed Tapeo. With Tast, however, I reflected that we had come to a definitive new staging post in the city's leisure offer − a world-famous sport legend tie-up with a multi-Michelin-starred chef, to open a three-storey culinary adventure in one of the city's most historic streets.

Tast (full name Tast Cuina Catalana ('Taste from the Catalan Kitchen') was a project cooked up by Soriano with the operators of the Fazenda South American restaurant group, and I had been hired to help get the venture off to a flying start. I had worked for both sides of the partnership, having launched Fazenda in Spinningfields for Tomas Maunier, an Argentinian-Brazilian whose international background was becoming less unusual among entrepreneurs setting up in the city. I was also well known to Manchester City, having delivered several recent projects supporting its PR office, working to the quite brilliant communications boss Vicky Kloss, one of the very few club employees who was there in the days of 'bad old City' when it was a byword for plucky failure. How Kloss handled the 24/7 pressure of football club PR, dealing with sensitive and urgent media enquiries across world time zones, was beyond me, although her previous job as a Metropolitan Police detective gives a clue to her resilience. She stepped down in July 2022 after 21 years at the club.

Times had changed beyond recognition. Soriano was masterminding the club's fortunes, overseeing City's high-money transfers, managing relationships with sovereign wealth investors Abu Dhabi and China, and fending off Financial Fair Play allegations. The man whom Barcelona media nicknamed 'the Computer' for his relentless business focus had still found time to open a restaurant with his partners. All media information, he told me, was to make crystal-clear that the new business was nothing to do with the football club. The nationalist movement in his native region was very much in the news; when I sent Soriano my draft press release for Tast's launch he sent back one amendment, replacing 'the Catalan region' with 'the Catalan nation'.

Soriano had moved his family, as had Guardiola and a good few of the City players, into the city centre. Those who knew town well realised how different this experience would be from the equivalent lifestyle in Barcelona, and how hard too it would be to make Tast's high-end offer viable in Manchester. Hucknall's Barca had done well for years before it fell out of fashion. Rio Ferdinand's

Rosso was a staple favourite of the city's hen parties and the flashy weekend market, but hardly appealed to diners who knew their food, with a hyper-deluxe drinks list and an Italian menu delivered by a Mongolian chef. Neither pushed the boundaries of world-class cuisine or appealed to the discerning and high-spending dining-out market.

Even so, the city's eating-out landscape had come a long way. In 1996 I had reported for the *Manchester Evening News* that the 120 restaurants in the city centre served mainly foreign cuisine like Italian, Chinese or Indian. The feature was about town being all abuzz over two major new arrivals, the Michelin-star Lancashire chef Paul Heathcote's Simply Heathcote's in the former Register Office on Jackson's Row, and the £1.75 million Mash and Air from Irishman Oliver Peyton, who had taken London nightlife by storm with his pleasure palace The Atlantic Bar and Grill. Yet city-centre living in any numbers was still way off. I got around town of an evening so I knew how unlovely it could be. I wrote, 'Whether Peyton or Heathcote has braved the city centre on a wet Wednesday night in February, with more pigeons sheltering in the bus stops than people on the streets, is doubtful.' Despite their ambition and gut instinct that Manchester's going-out classes would find these two higher-priced, high-quality offerings to their tastes, both were not to last to the final course. Heathcote's had a good run, and closed in 2008, probably because it was a formal affair where you were invited to take the food seriously, not a sustainable approach for a city where socialising around the table is more important than the food itself.

Mash and Air was not formal. It was a riot. The four-storey former mill building took up a whole block, with the entrance on Chorlton Street half-way up Canal Street in the Gay Village, though its official literature described it as Chinatown. It comprised ground-floor bar, second-floor restaurant with a then-rare 'forno' pizza oven and top-floor, up-priced restaurant, with four mammoth beer tuns rising through the height of the building. Floors and walls were gloss painted lime green and orange, and contemporary art photos and paintings hung on the walls. When diners asked for the bill, they were handed a tiny envelope called 'The Damage'.

Sadly, the city's 'suits' shunned this fine contemporary new space for lunch as, even though it was only a few minutes' walk from their King Street offices, their pinstriped neural pathways were habituated to not crossing Portland Street. In any case, Mash (the beer) and Air (the posh restaurant) was a night-time experience. It crackled into life every evening with an exotic array of clien-tele, from bored housewives and office workers to gangsters fresh from plaguing the played-out Haçienda.

Manchester was ready for Mash and Air but the talk of the town was that the restaurant staff had added Colombian marching powder to the range of essential kitchen ingredients. The high-octane foodie haven became 'the scene' in the city for a couple of years, but once the drug dealers who ruined the Haçienda got backstage the end was written. Reputedly, after gunfire in the bar, one manager rang Oliver Peyton to say: 'I've left in a taxi and I'm never going back.' A Sam Taylor-Wood photo was ripped from the wall on one night, but, as Phil Griffin detailed in his collection of stories *Manchester*, Salford gangsters were not up on contemporary art, and they missed a Peter Doig oil painting on a staircase wall, 'big and mysterious, a landscape of mountains and trees', similar to the same artist's painting which sold at auction in New York a few years later for $11.3 million.

Peyton admitted defeat and shut the doors in 2000. In the days of Peyton's and Heathcote's brave gambles, it would have been unthinkable for the city centre to contain five hundred restaurants, the number operating when the pandemic hit in 2020. The remarkable growth was based on rising numbers of visitors and a new army of Millennial flat-dwellers. In April 2020 there was a pipeline of more than twenty new hotels bringing another four thousand new bedrooms by 2023, and the pandemic did not make a dent in it. The cityscape was changing and so were the people, twentysomethings with their lap dogs, rolled-up skinny jeans and wireless ear pods, mooching around what used to be village Manchester and which was now looking something like the 24-hour world city that embryonic *urbanistas* were calling for back in the 1990s.

After years of failing to attract restaurant critics to Manchester for clients, I could relax with Tast; the national media were on it like a flash. Guardiola and Pérez had the pull to get reviewers out of the capital. To be fair to this tiny cabal, they had been increasingly happy to jump into a first-class carriage at Euston for some time, often thanks to key behind-the-scenes operator Thom Hetherington, the tireless promoter of the city's leisure sector. The never knowingly under-tweeted Hetherington has close connections with the big beasts of the London food media, and if Jay Rayner reviews a little-known Korean in Manchester's student district, it will be because Hetherington has a hand, or a tweet, in it.

Critics like Giles Coren and Marina O'Loughlin wield their knives with real power and can stink a new place out overnight. Not long after launch, Tast had enjoyed reviews in four of the national 'quality' papers, easily the best performance for any Manchester restaurant in living memory. The *Guardian* reviewer Grace Dent concluded: 'We eat in the window, where tourists pose for pictures beside Pep's "new signing". I leave feeling that Tast is important, uncompromising, at times lost in translation and possibly not all that much fun. And perhaps, like many wonderful, authentic foods from other cultures, we probably don't quite deserve it.'

Entrepreneur Nick Johnson is a man riddled with certainty. The former right hand to Tom Bloxham at Urban Splash was once so close to The City that he was a two-term chairman of Marketing Manchester (the agency he had torn to shreds in the 1997 branding fiasco). In 2013 he declared he was sick of the dominance of branding and its impact on Manchester. Beneath Johnson's thick-rimmed designer glasses his eyes shone with a new righteousness. His passion now was for a regeneration with a genuine connection to place and people. In *The Curator*, a 2021 online video about his career and philosophy, he said of his relationship to The City, 'We had been absorbed into the establishment.' The 2008 crash and Urban Splash's struggle to recover had led him to re-set his values with a realisation that 'Design didn't matter. It was people that made places.'

After his 2012 exit from Urban Splash, the one-time city influencer behind Atlas and the Independents group reinvented his preferred method of regeneration by, he says, 'curating people'. The once-thriving market town of Altrincham had been eviscerated by the nearby Trafford Centre, but Johnson's mix of artisan food hall and modern craft traders in 2014 hit the spot for locals and visitors, and soon had government policy-makers applauding its reviving magic. Sir John Timpson's 2019 High Street Task Force gave Altrincham the nationwide gold star, making it the pin-up for food-and-drink-led town-centre fightbacks across the nation. Already an affluent enclave, property prices were boosted further after the *Sunday Times* named Altrincham the country's best place to live. Johnson and partner Jenny Thompson's approach (owing much to London's Borough Market) led him to open food halls in Macclesfield and Manchester, and there are copycats in Stockport and elsewhere. Not for the first time, bringing together like-minded people to break sourdough together and down improbable quantities of liquor had shown that the way to Manchester's heart was via its stomach.

The tourist authorities had been desperate for the city to gain a Michelin star to attract the type of high-spending traveller who eats their way around these garlanded establishments. There had not been a star awarded in the centre since 1977. Ambitious chefs set themselves the challenge time and again and then flunked it, a humbling experience for rivals Aiden Byrne and Simon Rogan, as TV viewers witnessed on BBC2 series *Restaurant Wars*. A coveted

Michelin star finally descended on the city in 2019 at Simon Martin's Mana in Ancoats. There are many in the hospitality world who believe Manchester's lack of respect towards the formality of the Michelin machine held back its recognition. It may well be that, for the fine-dining world, there lingers the perception expressed by the late A.A. Gill of the *Sunday Times* in his lacerating description of Manchester: 'A city that drinks first and eats after, with its mouth open.'

16

University challenge

When film critic and broadcaster Mark Kermode addressed an audience of graduates in the imposing Whitworth Hall at the University of Manchester in December 2009, he gave an inspiring speech about how his time in the city had helped him shape and realise his future. Behind the scenes, he was pondering over a new and intriguing opportunity, for which I met Kermode in London at a Soho private screening venue for new releases. There we discussed the prospect of him becoming chancellor of the University of Manchester. The figurehead role is ceremonial, handing out degrees and honours, and making welcome speeches for visiting great minds and award recipients. The honorary position is important not only for the individual holding it but for the academic institution.

A chancellor can add huge reputational value at home and worldwide and, if the holder suffers controversy or criticism, they can be a significant embarrassment. The university (from 1904 the Victoria University of Manchester) had merged in 2004 with the city's science university UMIST, which traced its origins back to 1824. In the new millennium it was fast growing into a billion-pound-a-year institution. As the largest single-site university in the country, as well as the consistently most applied to, it is rarely out of the news, whether it is for its academics winning Nobel Prizes or fronting TV programmes, or the student radicals whose tradition of protest stubbornly runs through its history like a trace of DNA.

I had been approached by the newly merged institution's President and Vice Chancellor Alan Gilbert to chair the alumni association in 2005. Under him, the university was getting closer to The City, understanding that (something wholly underplayed previously) the fortunes of Manchester and its higher-education campus were more tightly bound together than ever before, not least by its huge property estate in the heart of the city. The university wanted to keep tabs on alumni, with an eye on future donations, something American universities have perfected. My role would be ambassadorial and unpaid, chairing meetings and involving myself in the university's social life.

I was happy to be useful to the place where I had earned my Combined Studies degree. I had followed this with a one-year Eng Lit MA which I failed to complete, using my last grant cheque to support myself while setting up *City Life*. In this act of diverting public money from its intended use, which wasted my year of study, I had asked advice from my characterful tutor, the poet and writer Grevel Lindop, author of *The Opium Eater*, a 1981 biography of the city's Thomas de Quincey, the nineteenth-century laudanum-addicted antecedent of John Cooper Clarke and Shaun Ryder.

For his speech receiving his Outstanding Alumnus Award, Kermode drew on his experience of student life thirty years before, and his first published reviews in *City Life*. Donning the required puffed-up tricorn hat over his 1950s-style quiff, he addressed an audience of graduates from Ghana, Nigeria and India who had completed expensive courses in subjects like economics and international business. Accompanied by their parents on this memorable milestone in their young lives, the audience's knowledge of or interest in Manchester in the 1980s would be low. The diverse gathering, dressed for the day in their hired gowns and mortarboards, heard out the movie maven's address with great politeness, clearly waiting for the opportunity when they could collect their certificates onstage to exuberant cheering and whooping.

Cities, as Jonathan Raban articulated in his influential 1974 book *Soft City*, offer us a plasticity that enables us to remould ourselves, trying on and discarding clothes, personas and values as we build new identities. Universities are especially fertile places for people to add new experiences to their behavioural hard drive, before deleting some and saving others. Kermode had more reason than most to see Manchester as a place to reinvent himself; when I knew the graduate who went on to become a national favourite via the BBC and *The Observer*, his surname was Fairey. He completed the first doctoral thesis that Manchester University's English department had allowed on a horror film (his personal obsession, *The Exorcist*), after which he changed his name by deed poll following his parents' divorce. At *City Life*, he drove the van delivering magazines (and wrote it off once on the M56), sold advertising for some low pay, and his unpaid film reviews and interviews carried the byline 'Mark Fairey'. When he moved to London and found work at *Time Out* magazine, he went by his new surname. His career burgeoned and his winning explicatory style and huge enthusiasm for cinema has brought him deserved respect and success.

At the time of his university award in 2009, many in the media world thought him a shoo-in for the vacant presenter role on the BBC's flagship film review programme. Surely the chair made famous by Barry Norman beckoned after Jonathan Ross ended his decade-long stint in it? Kermode was overlooked, it seemed, for the double act of Claudia Winkelman and journalist Danny Leigh (whose own quiff may have caused some to mistake him for Kermode). The show died a protracted death in 2018 when, after chopping and changing the format, the BBC dropped it after a 47-year run. For many dismayed fans, Kermode was the BBC film programme's natural heir, believing his deep knowledge and distinctive personal style could have extended the programme's legacy.

Now, in 2010, the *City Life* van driver turned movie critic had been approached by students who wanted him to be the next chancellor, after the joint post holders of the merged universities had served their terms: former student union president and TV newsreader Anna Ford and UMIST old boy Sir Terry Leahy, the business supremo who grew Tesco into a retail goliath. Kermode agreed that the figurehead role would be a significant honour, but there were two complications. The first was his remote home bases of New Forest and Cornwall, the second the university's constitution, which decreed that the chancellor is decided by a vote of staff and alumni, requiring Kermode to stand for an election of interested candidates. 'I've never got any job for which there was another candidate,' he told me.

The chancellor election gives a chance for staff and alumni to say who should sit on the top of the university's tree. Even though students cannot vote, it is a tradition that they plot to upset the leadership's preferred candidate. Such an alliance had snubbed the university's own nominee back in 1984. With the Duke of Devonshire standing down from the post, the vote had been livened up by staff who proposed Professor John Griffiths, a nonconformist public law scholar. No one expected him to beat the official candidate, the anonymous Marchioness of Anglesey, but the hierarchy's planned *fait accompli* was stymied to everyone's surprise when Griffiths won, and the self-described 'grey-haired old loon' went on to shake up the then cloistered university culture by nominating CND leader Bruce Kent and child poverty campaigner Ruth Lister for honorary degrees.

That cussed spirit was very much alive in 2010 but university leaders could not wait for the awkward squad to put someone up. They searched for an 'official' candidate to reflect the humanitarian spirit and global ambitions of the newly invigorated institution. The alumna Irene Khan, the general secretary of Amnesty International, was approached. As well as studying at Manchester, Bangladeshi-born Ms Khan had worked for the United Nations, and then had run Amnesty for a decade, winning peace awards for the principled work of the global human rights charity. An irreproachable choice, one would have thought, for staff and students to support. Yet the rebel streak runs strong at Manchester. Kermode was still being urged to rekindle ties to the city which shaped him. But he considered the (for him) 'inevitable' scenario – 'Kermode beaten in university poll' – and my cinephile friend politely declined the students' call for him to run.

The disenfranchised students still wanted a robust democratic contest, and approached university alumnus Tom Bloxham, the Urban Splash boss. As well as a Manchester ace face, the king of regeneration had a national profile, but the university had a right to be nervous. Bloxham's crown had slipped after the world banking collapse. In April 2010, Urban Splash announced it had lost nearly £50 million over 2009 and 2010 and started a redundancy programme among its 280 staff. Even if he did continue to sit on the board of the Arts Council, there was the distinct prospect of a crashed property tycoon as the institution's chief ambassador.

When Bloxham won the election against Khan for the inaugural chancellor of the newly merged university, the leadership could have been forgiven for fearing the worst. Yet only a year later, it became clear that a bullet had been dodged, when BBC's *Panorama* revealed that Ms Khan had received a £533,000 golden goodbye from Amnesty in 2009. The news was red meat to right-wing critics in the media, who quipped that she was making her personal poverty history. Peter Pack, chair of the organisation's international executive committee, wrote to Amnesty members apologising 'for the considerable upset'. The reputational damage deeply wounded Amnesty, and her chancellorship would have been embarrassing to the university, too.

The victorious unofficial candidate, meanwhile, was using all his subtle skills to bring Urban Splash back to health. In 2014 Bloxham was able to announce a 'watershed moment' for the property brand he had built out of the poster business he started in the student union hall market. He noted how many other Northern property firms had not survived the crash. Since 2008 Urban Splash had been held back by its debt burden, but now it had refinanced £135 million debt from four different banks, and formed a joint venture with the Pears Group, a long-established London family business with a £6 billion portfolio. Bloxham proved an able chancellor, taking to the cap-and-gown flummery of the Whitworth Hall ceremonies with ease, conferring honorary degrees on luminaries such as his friend Sir Alex Ferguson and proving adept at making dinner toasts to the university's star physicists, the professors Andre Geim and Kostya Novoselov, who had won the Nobel Prize for isolating Graphene, for which they received knighthoods.

When Bloxham's term ended in 2016, the scene was set for more intrigue. Lord Peter Mandelson entered the new election, throwing university mission control at the charming ivy-clad Old Quad on Oxford Road into a tizz. The Labour peer was putting himself about and had gained the requisite number of backers. The news that he was on the ticket perplexed many observers, especially as Manchester had hardly been a frequent destination for him when a minister in the Blair and Brown governments. The university's new chief, Dame Nancy Rothwell, who had become president and vice chancellor in 2010 after Gilbert's death, told me that she had no idea what was driving 'Mandy'. She had never met him. Some canvassed that he could help business links with China and elsewhere. I gave her my view that, if he won, close association with a high-profile political figure was undesirable, as Mandelson's views could be confused with those of the university. As with any figurehead from the political sphere, the ambassadorial nature of the chancellor role would throw up unhelpful perceptions about the institution, which had to negotiate sensitive relations with the government of the day with as little friction as possible.

Reputation has a different context for politicians. Being disliked and voted against is part of the deal. Mandelson stepped up his charm offensive at receptions and events. He was introduced to me at a lecture, schmoozing me with 'Hello, I hear that you are king of the alumni.' Alas for Mandelson, I was in no position to influence the alumni vote and, in any case, my support was with another candidate who had emerged from nowhere. The dissenters had approached Lemn Sissay, and the performance poet from Wigan was up for the challenge. The rival campaigns galvanised the campus. Dave Haslam tweeted, 'Lemn is an inspirer. M is a conspirer.'

No one who has met Sissay can fail to warm to him, and anyone who knows his life story can fail to be moved by what he has had to overcome. It's a heartbreaking story of bureaucratic heartlessness and racism, which he tells movingly in his autobiography *My Name Is Why*. Having carved out a distinctive place in the world of words, both written and spoken, and living in London, he could have been forgiven for wanting rid of Greater Manchester. The borough of Wigan, after all, was the council he had to sue to discover his foster care records, a case finally settled in 2018 with an apology and a six-figure sum.

Sissay, however, sought a deeper relationship with a university set on greater dialogue with developing nations through the burgeoning numbers of international students. With his Ethiopian roots, he knew that, before and during the Second World War, international students in Manchester formed the Pan-African federation, the force behind the decolonialisation movement. The Fifth Pan-African Congress had been held in 1945 just off Oxford Road, where Ethiopia's flag was among those flying from Chorlton-on-Medlock Town Hall and delegates included African nations' future leaders Kenyatta, Nkrumah and Banda.

I had knocked about with Lemn in the 1980s when he was performing poetry alongside some of the live circuit's stand-ups. I had written a piece about him in *i-D* magazine and in the 1990s, when I was promoting live bands, I had put on his acid jazz ensemble Secret Society at P.J. Bells on Oldham Street. We'd lost touch, but now he had picked up the gauntlet in the chancellorship campaign, I was happy to help. As ever, the leadership needed an official candidate, and the conductor of the Hallé Orchestra, Mark Elder, gallantly obliged. Many believed that Mandelson's name recognition would smooth his victory and Sissay would split the vote. However, in the end it was the forty-eight-year-old poet who beat Elder, with Mandelson back in third place.

His confirmation ceremony was the most uplifting of all the grand university occasions I had attended. This care-home boy discovered his real name only when he was seventeen, and he was so desperate to get to Manchester from Wigan that he walked in his bare feet. Now, he live-streamed Dame Nancy Rothwell on his mobile device as she conferred his title. With what has been described as his 'radical vulnerability', the new chancellor spoke eloquently from the podium, and in the days after, about using the role to improve the chances of care leavers like him to pursue education.

Sissay is an artist who made his way, like me, through the more bohemian quarters of the city in the 1980s, the decade when the university's reputation was cemented as a volatile hotbed of student unrest. Running *City Life* magazine in that decade, as recent graduates we had been close to, and reported on, some extraordinary ministerial visits to the student union between 1983 and 1985. The Conservative regime was taking on student unions by clipping their financial wings. From 1983 new restrictions meant that student-union funding was now impossible for a repeat of the Manchester student army descending on London's Grosvenor Square for the huge 1968 anti-Vietnam demo. Money was limited to activities supporting the interests of students, not the causes that students were interested in. Support for striking miners in 1984 was deemed 'improper funding'.

In response to the squeeze, hard-line students soon made Manchester notorious for militant disruption of events. The numbers involved were in the low hundreds, swelled by former and non-students, but the protests made national news. Defence secretary Michael Heseltine was squirted with red paint, then Home Office minister David Waddington was shouted down by, he declared from the stage, 'left-wing fascists'. Most notorious was the 1985 visit of Home Secretary Leon Brittan, which led to shocking violence on the steps of the union building. The minister was prevented by a crowd from entering the main door, and in the police action to get him inside there were 40 injuries and 33 charges for public order offences. The independent police complaints enquiry into the 'Battle of Brittan' took three years, before it found mild police incompetence, and not the excessive use of force by paramilitary police squad the Tactical Aid Group, highlighted by the media, from *City Life* to BBC's *Brass Tacks*.

The militant image of the student union was set hard. The producers of the BBC's 2002 drama *The Project* about the rise of New Labour set its opening scenes on the union building steps on Oxford Road, recreating a violent demo against a government speaker. Its three lead characters meet as students and go on to roles at the heart of the party, embedding the perception of the university union where the essential skills of the political hack – debating, organising, campaigning and 'carving up' – could be learned alongside an honours degree. With a large body politic of around a thousand highly politically active students and the chance to build 'real world' links with pressure groups and unions, Manchester was the ideal compost to grow future Labour MPs. Journalist Decca Aitkenhead, who graduated in the early 1990s, says that on her first visit she was 'bowled over by this amazing exotic display of political energy'. From the 1980s, MPs John Mann, Phil Woolas, Liam Byrne, Nick Brown and Jeff Smith followed Anna Ford and Left luminaries like commentator and one-time NUS president David Aaronovitch into political life.

This energy bled into the entertainment culture, too. Alternative TV comedy of the 1980s was born in a shared house in Didsbury, where drama students Ben Elton, Rik Mayall and Ade Edmondson (and Lise Mayer, daughter of drama professor David) came up with absurdist, aggressively political 'anti-sitcom' *The Young Ones*. Thirty years later a shared Manchester student house was also the setting for co-writer Jesse Armstrong's ensemble TV sitcom *Fresh Meat*, a sound apprenticeship for his creator-showrunner role of the savage HBO business family drama *Succession*.

The universities were critical to the music scene. The union buildings at Salford, the Poly and UMIST offered live performance venues and a ready-made audience. Arcane rules about signing-in non-members were still in place when I arrived in 1979, but soon died out, so gigs were open to all comers. The university union, one of the wealthiest due to historical reserves, was able to finance a new-build live venue, the Academy. Next to the main union building, it opened in 1990 with a show from just-reformed Manchester post-punk heroes Buzzcocks and slotted in a new rung on the ladder of live venues for acts playing to thousand-strong crowds. It made no claim to beautify the campus, being simply a large rectangle with modern stage facilities and ample bars. A lightbox stairwell on one corner softens its ugliness, and an integrated ATM attracts lines of students, signalling its function as an income-generator for the union's finances.

Despite its giant cash-machine look and lack of atmosphere, the Academy became a favourite of the live music industry. Buzzcocks' founder Howard Devoto staged the reunion of his own band Magazine in 2009. Among major cultural events I witnessed in the big shed was the December 1991 show by just-breaking Nirvana, when writer John Robb expanded my musical appreciation by pointing out that The Beatles were the key influence on the grunge pioneers. And one of my most treasured memories is seeing David Bowie on his 1997 Earthling tour, so close to the front I could see his wife Iman just yards away in a baseball cap and bopping away at the side of the stage.

Shortly after the BBC's 2006 decision to move to Salford Quays, broadcaster Mark Radcliffe attended an event to promote the future of Oxford Road. He chatted about his love for the vibrant thoroughfare which binds the university campus tightly to the city centre, and gives the city's universities an urban, urgent character. Radcliffe had, like me, spent the best years of his life bowling along from student union to gig to curry house and, in his case, into work at the BBC's featureless rectangular studios from where he broadcast radio shows. When he and Marc 'Lard' Riley took over Radio 1's Breakfast Show in 1997, their photo-call was at their fave boozer, the Lass O' Gowrie just off Oxford Road, where the real ale was as well kept as the Victorian interiors.

Student days in Manchester make indelible memories. I wonder if the CEOs of multi-nationals, top politicians and world-leading scientists among the alumni also feel the same way about the special ambience of Oxford Road? Do presidents and prime ministers, including leaders of Iraq, St Lucia, Ireland, Mozambique, Palestine and Somaliland, remember the two-mile stretch of daytime study and libidinous after-dark diversions with as much affection as Radcliffe and I do?

No exuberant display of democracy was needed, for once, when Sissay's time was up. The 2022 nominations process for the next chancellor turned out to be uncontested. The unanimous choice of students, staff and the university is Nazir Afzal, former Chief Crown Prosecutor for Northwest England. For the first time in living memory there was no need for plotting and campaigning over who should be the university's figurehead.

As it approaches its two-hundredth anniversary in 2024, from its origins founded by industrialists needing qualified overseers, the university finds itself landowner of the most valuable single-site, city-centre development outside of London, in its words a 'cornerstone of the city region'. The £1.5 billion ID Manchester site is the decanted UMIST campus close to Piccadilly, where I had spent 1979 pioneering urban living in a bijou student bedroom next to the train line to Liverpool. 'This site is about us saying, "what do we want for us, what do we want for the city", because if the city's thriving, we'll thrive,' the University's leader Rothwell told the *Financial Times*' Northern correspondent Andy Bounds. 'We're not master planners, we're not developers. We just feel we need a partner who is really expert at that.'

Despite his urban revival record and honorary professorship there, Sir Howard Bernstein was not asked to sit on the university's ID Manchester working group. A senior city council officer close to him knew I was on the university's board of governors after I was voted in by alumni for an unpaid nine-year stint ending in 2021. He asked me why the UK's regeneration king had not been asked on to the ID Manchester group. 'How can that be right?' he exclaimed. 'With your position there, can you see what you can do about that?' It did seem odd. I asked informally why Bernstein was not on the team. The university had clearly given some thought to perceptions of development contests in the city. 'It's to protect him from accusations of conflict of interest' was the reply, a tactic which may have bruised the Bernstein ego but ensured that everyone witnessed a rigorous bidding contest.

17

The Haçienda must be built

And you, forgotten, your memories ravaged by all the consternations of two hemispheres, stranded in the Red Cellars of Pali-Kao, without music and without geography, no longer setting out for the Haçienda where the roots think of the child and where the wine is finished off with fables from an old almanac. Now that's finished. You'll never see the Haçienda. It doesn't exist.

The Haçienda must be built.

Ivan Chtcheglov, 'Formula for a New Urbanism', 1953

'I wanted a place to go where I could ogle girls,' Rob Gretton was reputedly fond of saying, in his gruffly provocative way, when the New Order manager was asked why he wanted to create the Haçienda. Tony Wilson declared a loftier purpose: 'It is necessary for any period to build its cathedrals,' he said on Channel 4 in 1984. 'It is necessary for youth culture to have a sense of place. Manchester has not had one for two years and we found ourselves the only people in a financial position to do anything about it. It is necessary for a city like Manchester, which is an important city and has been important to music, to have the facilities that New York or Paris have.'

Two strains of Mancunian-ism in the same partnership, one a two-fingered challenge to decorum, one far more suited to feed the media's appetite for pop culture conceptualism. If anyone knew about youth culture and the music which drove its cycles and currents, its twist and turns, it was Tony Wilson. The media loved his fizzy soundbites, while Gretton was unknown outside the music industry, and focused on fomenting his band's mystique by limiting photos and interviews, letting Peter Saville's graphics and music-press writers work their mind games on fans and journalists. Both shared the same civic pride which Bernard Sumner recalls 'bound them together' – that 'you should strive to make the city a better place to live'. As the pair's relationship grew, Gretton was happy to let Wilson do the grandstanding, a natural division of roles that emerged after they agreed to work together to release Joy Division's music.

Led by the shamanic lyricist and singer Ian Curtis until his suicide in 1980, the psychic desolation of the music and its enigmatic sleeve art hit a nerve worldwide and went on to enjoy earth-spinning success. Gretton encouraged a reverse psychology in which record covers did not feature photos of the group and used titles that, as well as having nothing to do with the song lyrics, often did not appear on the sleeve, all assuring mystery and intrigue. After Curtis's death the members regrouped as New Order, which pulled off the feat of simultaneously appealing to the traditionally divided audiences in 'rock', club culture and the commercial pop charts. The group's biographical and musical journey became a deeply compelling story, one into which the Haçienda's own tale became woven.

Flirting with incendiary word association produced stormy media coverage from the start. The names Joy Division and New Order had Nazi connotations and, as the highest-profile name behind Factory and the Haçienda, Wilson took the flak. Being monstered in the tabloid press ('TV man owns Nazi nightclub', yelled one headline) made for uncomfortable conversations, Wilson confessed, with his Jewish friends. We may pause to reflect what such playfulness with extreme political ideologies might provoke today, when ironic or provocative references are sure to call down the wrath of a witch-hunting puritanism.

The Haçienda had its origins in the label and its Factory night, which hired out the Russell Club, a social club for bus drivers in Hulme. The Factory name may have appeared to share its experimental purpose with the culture bunker of Andy Warhol's New York's Factory, but it had been thought up by Wilson's partner, repertory actor Alan Erasmus, who saw a 'Factory Closing' sign and thought 'Let's have a Factory opening instead'. Nevertheless, Manchester's Factory was to have at least as significant a contribution to culture — high and low, popular and intellectual, local and global — as the 1960s New York scene around Warhol.

Under the influence of the oppositional politics and values of their formative years, the prime movers behind both the venue and the record company – Wilson, Erasmus, Gretton, Saville and studio producer Martin Hannett – had embarked upon a radical disruption of the music business. It was a path inspired by Richard Boon and Buzzcocks' 'Spiral Scratch' 1976 EP. The acerbic Boon and his New Hormones label provided ironic, intellectual critique and practical support to the post-punk scene – 'no sex or threat' was his sniff test for new bands – and he first put The Fall into a studio. Factory's business model went further. The conventional way was for major labels to acquire ownership of the artist's work in the standard deal, which began with a large financial advance to the artist to record. This, along with all promotional, distribution and other costs, was later recouped by the company. It was a stranglehold at a time years before superstars George Michael and Prince challenged exploitation in artist contracts.

While the artists on its label received no advance, with Factory they owned the rights to their own music, in a pledge reputedly signed by Wilson in his own blood on a paper napkin and kept in the office safe. Royalties were a fifty-fifty split between artist and company. This idealism, however, had an unforeseen and unwanted effect. Factory released music by new bands which brought the artist sales, fans and profile, and who were then free, as Wilson would opine with customary indelicacy, 'to go fuck with a major label as soon as the manager gets a hard on'. He bemoaned the way Factory's idealism made it a talent-finding operation for major labels. Yet the label was pragmatism as well as idealism at work when it came to Joy Division and New Order. Unlike other disloyal groups, the band were bonded to Factory through the double role of Gretton as label director and band manager.

Both Hook's and Sumner's memoirs recall the lack of agency the band had in their royalties being used to fund the Haçienda. A figure of £70,000 was first mentioned as the total investment, and a Wilson-managed vote among the band and the label directors, with London-based Saville canvassed down the phone, sealed the decision. Consensus among the Factory directors was scarce. Hannett was adamant that Factory should invest record sales from the two Joy Division albums into a recording studio. The label's unstable creative genius saw a studio as a massive musical instrument, locking the band out so he could mix their music alone, a maverick experimentalist who recorded a lift shaft and breaking glass for sound effects on *Unknown Pleasures*. But Gretton had greater clout and, enraged by the Haçienda project, Hannett quit in 1983 and sued, eventually settling for £25,000. In 1991 he became the first of the Factory founders to die, and Wilson would wistfully concede that he had a point, citing the way 1970s Manchester group 10cc opened Strawberry Studios in Stockport, reinvesting in their home city's music infrastructure.

The Haçienda opened in May 1982, and from the start matched its sibling record label in unconventional responses to accepted ways of doing youth culture. 'Punk had levelled the ground,' explained Saville later. 'There was a strong feeling that it was a post-revolutionary moment and that you then had to build the future. The Haçienda must be built was a great statement for that moment in time.' The name was derived, and overtly promoted, as a reference to then-obscure political-philosophical theorists the Situationist International, and it threw open its doors, in Wilson's words, as 'a lab experiment in popular culture'. Original manager Howard Jones said the motivation was: 'Let's not set up a circus, but let's set up a big top and let them [the people] be the circus.' On opening, the club boasted two giant screens above the dancefloor, and video jockeys Tim Chambers and Claude Bessey provided cut-up film content – a diet of horror movies, Nazi rallies and other disconcerting, jarring footage. 'Youth culture thrives on the shocking,' proclaimed an unapologetic Chambers, but half the weirdness was that the visuals were a bizarre complement to often trad Saturday night records, such as Lulu's 'Shout' and jive jazz from the likes of Louis Jordan.

The club's membership application forms read: 'Intention: To restore a sense of place. "The Haçienda must be built."' Wilson proclaimed the Haçienda as 'a gift to Manchester', and in the early days it formulated some extraordinary high-risk escapades in live performance and music culture, by turns audacious, experimental and chaotic. What most remember is how outsize the space seemed, and how cold it was. The beer was alehouse-cheap and there was a smell of chips from the café next to the cloakroom. All part of the mix were film and video workshops, fashion shows, rappers and street break-dancers, and benefits for striking miners. Erasmus made sure reggae nights and artists were programmed, with interesting dub effects in the booming sound. (For one of these, Factory group A Certain Ratio's Donald Johnson brought Leroy Richardson, who was to become a key manager in the club's story.) Jazz-funk DJ Hewan Clarke witnessed with some amazement Mohicans dancing to his New York grooves. As well as literary readings, there was conceptual art, with a commission of a David Mach installation made from thousands of unsold New Order 12-inch singles. On one night, action painter Phil Diggle dripped and sploshed paint while his Buzzcock brother Steve played mad solo guitar. There was even Swing, a salon in the basement run by hair stylist and DJ Andrew Berry.

These were days of adventure. Inspired by the ethos, artists saw it as a chance to push boundaries. In February 1984, electronic German group Einstürzende Neubauten (Collapsing New Buildings) took a pneumatic drill to one of the hazard-striped pillars during its act. The owners appreciated experimentation, but they valued their décor more, and the art-vandals were not asked back; the Haçienda was already so special it was becoming a sacred place. There were envelope-pushing arts centres elsewhere, such as the venerable London

Institute of Contemporary Arts, but was there anywhere else with this kind of daring programming, and operating without public subsidy?

The Haçienda began to command worldwide attention for its radical, witty design aesthetic dubbed 'post-industrial fantasy'. Originally discussed as a Saville project, he handed the design to architect Ben Kelly after they bonded over a mutual fascination with perforated surfaces – Kelly's for a steel London office door, Saville's for a record sleeve. Kelly's design, the Saville graphics and the programming were an integrated vision, providing the perfect setting for a combination of political and cultural philosophies, some curious and obscure, all radical, beloved by Wilson and colleagues.

The pop culture lab was open six days a week, and it lost a fortune in its first year. 'It was a duty, a service,' Wilson told me in 1987 in explaining the financial pain. 'We opened a club with high production values. The people we built it for are the people who are unemployed or doing a couple of odd jobs a week. They can't afford high prices. That's the lesson we learned.' It was a harsh lesson that the counterculture in the city did not exist in the numbers to fill the place, and that political radicals could have different music tastes.

Kelly's design reflected the changes outside the Haçienda's doors. The building for the new venue had gone up in the late nineteenth century, a hulking structure constructed in super-tough Accrington brick, built to stock large quantities of steel on the Rochdale Canal. By 1982, Manchester was post-industrial. The city's steel industry was finished, and the club owners seemed determined to make clear the links between the Thatcher-era hard times and those of days gone by. A crudely photocopied Haçienda leaflet sent to early members explained the history of the location, including a Jon Savage-penned text about Engels's description of the hellish conditions in Little Ireland, the squalid overcrowded neighbourhood close to the Haçienda's location.

This was hardly the usual kind of material mailed out by a nightclub. No leaflets about happy-hour offers here. Instead, the Factory milieu attracted those who wanted some serious thinking with their intoxicants; even self-styled intellectuals needed to get their kicks. The Haçienda in its early period, and Factory as a label, attracted the 'long mac brigade', wearing dead men's clothes from charity shops, and trying not to smile. This look – with both young men and women offering brooding expressions semi-obscured under generous 'one-eyed' fringes – befitted the city's grim ambience, and the bookish mystique of a Gothic musical mood that the rock press dubbed 'Manchester miserabilism'.

The long raincoat worn indoors was first seen on parade in the no-frills ambience of the pre-Haçienda Factory, the Russell Club in Hulme hired out for the label's gig nights. By 1982, though, the Haçienda's opening coincided with a new flowering of youth fashion. The days of men's style in many shades of grey was changing, and it wasn't long before New Romantic style meant that the trusty mac was checked in at the cloakroom. Once inside, there was plenty of eyeliner, gelled spiked hair and zoot suits, a nationwide look televised live every Friday on Channel 4's influential youth show *The Tube*. Fronted by Jools Holland and Paula Yates, one production came live from the Haçienda in 1984. The show featured Madonna in her first UK appearance, performing as a solo act among the dancefloor's zebra bollards and cat's eyes. Post-show, she was forced to spend the night in a Chorlton front porch after a mix-up over door keys with club DJ Mike Pickering.

In the early 1980s, the Haçienda saw itself mainly as a live performance venue, ahead of its other function as a New York-style disco. Wilson had insisted on a theatre-style layout, but the influence of the New York clubs he and Gretton loved produced a muddle in which live performance fared badly compared to the dancefloor sound. Kelly recalls that he fought his corner to ensure that the stage was 'side on' rather than at the end of the space, allowing for varied, flexible uses, even if it caused sound and logistics headaches. Only later, when Madchester exploded, did the owners come to regard the cathedral-like space, now perfect for mass dancing, as a happy accident.

At various points, the unique space was to witness Morrissey flinging gladioli to adoring disciples of the Smiths, just before they broke big, and Oasis and The Stone Roses playing triumphant hometown shows on the crest of waves which would carry them around the world. It was a media social hub, too. Wilson would swan in with colleagues from Granada TV shows after filming, and they would head for the basement Gay Traitor cocktail bar, rather than the main dancefloor bar, The Kim Philby. The reference to members of the notorious Cambridge University Russian spy ring was intended to provoke strong reactions. In the first few years of the Haçienda, the idealistic and financially calamitous over-servicing of what Wilson called 'the interesting community' sprang from the influence of liberal and radical politics in the decade the Haçienda founders came of age, the 1960s. That traction of left-wing beliefs on youth culture, whether a matter of fashion or not, meant there was a greater awareness and interest in politically revolutionary ideas among larger numbers of the young than may be found today.

Situationist, anarchist or generic 'left' sympathies were not the only radical concepts which cast a spell over Wilson and his contemporaries. There was also his devotion to Praxis, the foundation of a variety of philosophical and political concepts. He explained in 1984 that Praxis was, to him, 'Doing something because you have the urge to do it, inventing the reasons later.' This reductionist description shortcut the origins of Praxis in Aristotle, but, as an articulation of an instinctive move to action, it was a good fit with the DIY ethos and dynamics of punk: don't just sit there bored or moaning, go out there and do it – and in the very doing, went Wilson's interpretation, you will discover your reason for doing it.

With his insatiable curiosity about new cultural ideas and possibilities, and with the royalties from Joy Division's first two albums sloshing around in the Factory coffers (*Closer* had sold 250,000 by 1982, ten times as many as *Unknown Pleasures*), in the spirit of Praxis, Wilson and his partners were to rise to the challenge thrown down by an obscure philosophical text.

The Situationist International was an organisation of revolutionary artists and intellectuals which challenged capitalism's domination and perversion of human relations, but in a vividly theatrical way which itself attacked the totalitarianism of creativity-crushing Communist empires. Classic Marxism was about the oppression of the workers, but the SI's intellectual leader Guy Debord described in his 1967 work *The Society of the Spectacle* a world that churned out images, information and ideas. The mass media, from the TV news to cinema to advertising, sold consumption as a way of life, obscuring our authentic desires and masking the 'rigged game' of capitalism. Our very dreams were business schemes to make companies money. What people should do was make revolutions for fun, said Debord, and create alternative spectacles to punch a hole in our controlled, compliant reality.

'Situ' ideas turned complex politics into cool street graffiti. They replaced clunky Marxist-Leninist dogma with guerrilla art and zingy one-liners. True to its roots in Dada and Surrealism, in the UK the philosophy became more of a cultural than a political force, but its utopian activism was there on the walls of Paris in the 1968 uprisings, when students and 10 million workers threatened to bring down the French state. 'Under the paving stones, the beach!' proclaimed one of its most famous slogans, as it called on the disenfranchised to tear up the streets for stones to hurl at riot police. The would-be revolution fizzled out in a back-to-work capitulation after President de Gaulle's televised ultimatum, which acknowledged: 'This explosion was provoked by groups in revolt against modern consumer and technical society, whether it be the communism of the East or the capitalism of the West.'

The much-quoted slogan 'The Haçienda Must Be Built' was found in Christopher Gray's influential *Leaving the 20th Century: A Brief Introduction to the*

Situationist International. Gray's book was published in 1974 and became a cult read, the first introduction to 'Situ' ideas in English. It quoted from the 1953 essay 'Formulary for a New Urbanism' by Ivan Chtcheglov, and, while it may seem preposterous to think that a place of entertainment was intending to reimagine a new city, this playful digression on the ideal city makes it clear that the Haçienda founders intended to draw their own radical sketch on the blank slate of ruined Manchester. It was there, of course, in the club's original membership application forms: 'Intention: To restore a sense of place. "The Haçienda must be built."'

'The Haçienda must be built.' The line has since become a kind of holy text. It has been on a marathon of meanings from the original, in Gray's translation and in Haçienda communiqués and music-press mentions from the venue's 1982 opening until the club's closure in 1997. After the building's 2001 demolition, it became a rallying cry from clubbers, journalists and commentators for a resurrection of the same wild creative spirit the original project embodied.

The line ripped from its source sounded suitably mysterious back in 1982, and I was not the only FAC 51 member who, having never seen the Gray book, was intrigued but baffled by it. It is not hard to see how Chtcheglov's polemic, in among the mumbo-jumbo, struck a chord with punk rockers in drab late 1970s Britain with its opening line: 'We are bored in the town, there is no longer any Temple of the Sun.' In the full version, now online, among the gobble-degook there is a series of provocations calling for love, fun and the power of dreams in the urban experience: 'We need experimental, fluid cities to liberate us from our increasingly banal lives. Modern technology, orderly town planning and efficient city management have taken the mystery and laughter out of city life,' it asserts. 'Everyone will live in their own cathedral. There will be rooms awakening more vivid fantasies than any drug.'

In the slogan's journey, some interpretative punctuation has been employed. It originally sits as an italicised line floating between paragraphs; the emphasis clearly caught the eye of Wilson and Co. Over the years, its initial lower-case letters became capitals, and an exclamation mark was added, as in the title of the book commissioned by the club for its tenth anniversary. Today, 'The Haçienda Must be Built!' has become an ageing nightclubber's catchphrase, recited whenever old ravers gather on Facebook to piece good times and brain cells back together by sharing old tracks and videos.

As Paul Morley identifies, the essay is the missing link between the Situationist art terrorism of The Sex Pistols' shattering arrival in June 1976 and the opening of the Haçienda in May 1982. Chtcheglov's Haçienda is a metaphor for the author's vision of the ideal city, the desire for beauty trumping that of rationalist city planning. For the 19-year-old author, a Parisian son of Russian émigrés, to experience a city imaginatively was a political act, influencing the Situationist practice of psychogeography – the bringing of personal emotion and memory to a place, and particularly in locations layered with the patina of history. 'All towns are geological,' he writes. 'Wherever we go, we meet a figure from the past, armed with all the prestige of its legend.' The psychogeographer's technique is the *dérive* – the drift – a tool for psychoanalysing a city, wandering the streets like a therapist listening to a flow of words.

Thinking about cities in this way can be a subversive act. 'We have no intention of contributing to this mechanical civilisation, to its bleak architecture, to its inevitably catatonic leisure,' continues Chtcheglov, seeing liberation in creating anti-authoritarian spaces and journeys. His postwar notions resonate in the face of today's urban piazzas which have tastefully landscaped over the layers of the past, seen today in a growing privatisation of the public realm, such as the heavily managed set-piece developments of Manchester's Spinningfields and First Street.

The latter's Tony Wilson Place, a square across the road from the Haçienda site, flaunts a 1970 concrete sculpture of Karl Marx's patron, the mill owner's son Friedrich Engels, rehabilitated from a village in Ukraine. Part ideological gesture, part art joke, it is Manchester playing the same game of having your counter-cultural cake and eating it as Wilson's hedonistic commemoration of the traitorous Blunt. Even though Engels died decades before the Russian Revolution, his associations are with the Soviet era. His concrete, lichen-encrusted likeness stands on the very site where he described Little Ireland, the epicentre of rampant nineteenth-century capitalism's human distress.

'Formula for a New City' is not all a stern lecture. The writer's sideways humour envisages a Bizarre Quarter, a Noble and Tragic Quarter ('reserved for good children') and a Death Quarter, 'not for dying but so as to have somewhere to *live in peace*'. He concedes some practicality will be required, so there should be A Useful Quarter. Chtcheglov's fascinating biography has lately become better known in the internet age. It seems he was arrested in 1959 and jailed for five years for plotting to blow up the Eiffel Tower, complaining that its lights shone through his window at night, ruining his sleep. After spells in psychiatric hospitals, he died in 1988.

His essay in the Gray translation was highly influential in spreading Situ ideas. Yet in the punk era it was hard to find a copy outside of specialist bookshops, and no one I knew had seen one. Wilson and his Factory colleagues, it seems clear, owned or had read it, and were turned on by the movement's ideas, which flowed through Factory. (The sandpaper sleeve by Peter Saville for the Factory-released album *Return of the Durutti Column*, for example, is a classic Situ art joke, its abrasive cover meant to wear down adjacent record sleeves on the shelf.)

Wilson was born in 1950. Situ ideas were giddily inspirational for a generation of 1960s school leavers who benefited from an expansion of higher education and public grants for university fees. Less distraction than today meant that the generation that came of age in the late 1960s had to make their own entertainment, and, arguably, worked harder than today's youth at creating political responses to their lives. With only two channels on TV, and minimal radio content for young people, there was plentiful time and opportunity to read and discuss, to be excited by ideas, to dream and scheme, to plan and plot.

In a 1996 seminar at the Haçienda on the Situationist International attended by European academics, Wilson's pop-culture take annoyed serious students of the movement. Said event organiser, the academic Andrew Hussey, 'The intellectuals don't like the way Situationism has been taken up. They are an argumentative bunch.' Mark E. Smith heckled Wilson and challenged him to define what the S-word meant. 'I don't know,' shrugged Wilson. 'I just like the slogans. I think Situationism is funny.' The event's funding by a French government grant was difficult, the London embassy apparently describing the Haçienda, to Wilson's delight, as 'un lieu maudit' – 'an accursed place'.

The politics of Wilson and his cultural co-conspirators in conventional terms was never entirely clear. Personal liberation was, for him, a subversive act. He told *The Sunday Times* in 1990 that his philosophy, developed as a Cambridge undergraduate, was 'Situationism and acid'. He turned to me once and said, unprompted, 'I don't know about you, but I'm into mind-expansion.' Hallucinogenic drugs of all kinds were in common use among the teens and twenties of 1960s and 1970s Manchester. Wilson's first wife Lindsay Reade wrote in *Mr Manchester and the Factory Girl* that 'Tony and I both came from a background of psychedelic music and drugs, smoking pot the way most people drink tea … and using LSD on special occasions'.

Taking drugs was for many young people an everyday part of the counterculture that their favourite music expressed. The city in which Wilson and his friends and associates grew up was one in which grammar-school kids like him and 1953-born Gretton could mix with 'townies' and undergraduates in the city's student bars, music venues and other counter-culture hangouts such as bookstores, record shops, cafés, film screenings and political meetings and debates.

It was in this fashionably radical milieu that the Factory and Haçienda founders were marinaded as teenagers and young adults. The language, if not the practice, of revolution was their default setting, and it was in this febrile anti-establishment atmosphere that Wilson graduated from Cambridge, Gretton tried kibbutz living in Israel, Factory's talent spotter Mike Pickering lived in bohemian Amsterdam and Hannett took to heroin. Gretton's early notebooks, presented in the book *1 Top Class Manager*, reflects the same radical political thinking he applied to the music business. In early 1979, his diary views the emerging DIY music labels as 'a new underground going outside of the system', and his note to himself is telling: 'I would rather adopt a different role with regards to everything – try to approach everything from a different viewpoint – not having everything dictated by *money*.'

The scene around the Factory founders was profoundly anti-authority. The late 1960s had seen seismic shifts in the youth and culture rebellions against the bourgeois pillars of family, monarchy and state, and a generational dissatisfaction with postwar promises of consumer goods and labour-saving devices, all of which Situationists believed were sugary pills served up to sweeten the banality of everyday life.

International radical ideas were given wide public distribution by media coverage of France 1968 and simultaneous protests against the Vietnam War. Radical cultural and political thinking showed up in Manchester as people explored viable ways to run businesses differently, from record labels, music venues and vegetarian restaurants to bicycle-repair shops, art galleries and magazines. Worker co-operatives like Grass Roots Books and On the Eighth Day café at All Saints were destined to be 'alt' lifestyle fixtures for many years. The city was a breeding ground for so-called alternative publications, DIY efforts which predated punk and football fanzines and gave voice to political agitators. Primitively designed print content was sold in the city's student quarter, influenced by the notorious London 'hippy' publications *Oz* and *International Times*, which had published controversial sexual and political material which outraged the national media. In such an atmosphere it is more plausible that Factory Records and the Haçienda's sustained act of financial self-harm, in the declared interest of supporting the interesting community, was rooted less in 1970s punk culture and more in an earlier generation's anti-capitalism. Punk might have provided the spark, but the Haçienda came out of hippy idealism.

The Manchester musician C.P. Lee recalls in his autobiography *When We Were Thin* that in 1969: 'I'd "dropped out", was living in a commune in Salford and had so completely embraced the alternative underground lifestyle that

I'd become the people our parents warned us about.' Lee was in bands like 1960s jazz group Greasy Bear and later the parody-rock Alberto Y Lost Trios Paranoias, which toured extensively and made TV appearances. Lee's later academic research conclusively proved that the famed Bob Dylan bootleg 'Live at the Albert Hall', where his folkie fans cried 'Judas!' at his new electric direction, was recorded in 1966 at the Manchester Free Trade Hall, not in London.

Lee's comrades in music revolution at the city's Music Force Collective were future Factory founder Hannett (aka Martin Zero) and colourful local luminaries Tosh Ryan (later behind the pre-Factory indie Rabid Records), Victor Brox and Bruce Mitchell, all of whom went on to earn distinguished long-service medals in the music industry. Music Force was a chaotic co-operative, booking acts (favoured venues Band on the Wall and Rafters), arranging PA hire and operating a lucrative fly-posting business. The gang based themselves from a building on Oxford Road known as The Squat. Once a music college, it had been reprieved from the wrecking ball and handed over by the university student union for gigs, jumble sales and 'happenings'. Lee says Music Force 'was formed in response to a clarion call from a Trotskyite tendency group', but is better described here by Hannett, quoted in Lee's memoir: 'Supplied with a suitable idealistic contribution, about 80–90 members, a little money from an initial £1 contribution, and a crude sketch of the route to the top, we set about the brain-numbing task of promoting a surly, incoherent mass of local talent … these operations were conducted with a kind of guerrilla consciousness, and a peculiar nihilism reminiscent of a Japanese suicide squad.'

Hannett's wry take should not be taken simply as amusingly quixotic. The deadly seriousness with which he describes the commitment of Music Force's members is reflected in the March 1968 anti-Vietnam War demonstration at the American Embassy in Grosvenor Square, London. Granada TV's *World in Action* accompanied a coachload of Manchester University students. New shoulder-mounted cameras captured a nasty street battle between a thousand police and protestors in the ten-thousand crowd in shocking close-up. 'They claim to be part of worldwide rebellion of youth,' says the narrator. *The Demonstration* documentary hurled iconic images into British living rooms of a violent UK protest to match that spring's uprising in Paris, and in cities around the world from Mexico to Chicago.

This 1960s spirit of 'sticking it to the Man' had not been snuffed out a decade later among politically energised youth, particularly in the big university towns. An alternative press in Manchester emerged to service the city's political militants, cultural subversives, potheads and dropouts. *Mole Express* and *Grass Eye* both started publishing in 1970, as described by Bob Dickinson in *Imprinting the Sticks*, his detailed research into the alternative press outside London from the 1960s to the 1990s. These Manchester underground papers and magazines were not, like the capital's *Time Out*, concerned with selling advertising. Inspired more by London's *Oz*, they were explicitly anti-establishment and employed 'détournement' – the Situ technique of subverting familiar images with shocking messages. Cartoon strips from kids' comics like *The Beano* were reproduced in Manchester paper *Mole Express*, one cartoon character's speech bubbles saying: 'Fuck your TVs, package holidays, cars and unions! We're not fighting to be slaves to your toys and gadgets!'

The publication's first issue, then called *Moul Express*, was in May 1970. It announced (in capitals, not used here): '*Moul Express* is written by and for: acid freaks, agitators, anarchists, angels, apprentices, artists, atheists, Black Panthers, communards, criminals, deviants, dossers, drugtakers, dropouts, flat-earthers, hippies, homosexuals, junkies, mad bombers, magicians, Marxists, motherfuckers, mystics, pacificists, paranoids, provos, pushers, revolutionaries, scum, situationists, skinheads, ten-cents, vegetarians, we're not pushing a line, we can't organise you – organise yourselves. We will have news, music, poetry, survival and the price of pot. We don't want a separation between us and you. We are the fish in the sea of the people. We are the people your parents warned you about. We are the forces of chaos and anarchy.'

Mole Express founder Mike Don explained to Dickinson that in 1971 some new contributors got involved, and directed the content towards British political issues. They included Chris Bott and Hilary Creek, who lived in a run-down terraced house in Moss Side. Don described them as 'very nice people, produced a really good issue'. The pair turned out to be not paper tigers publishing anarchist fantasies but bomb-making revolutionaries. In August 1970, the Angry Brigade began an extended campaign of small bombs, designed to cause maximum media exposure and the lightest possible casualties. For a year, the loosely organised collective managed to target banks, consulates and embassies, homes of Conservative MPs and ministers and a BBC van covering the 1970 Miss World event. In October that year, the group failed to detonate explosives at Italian consulates in Manchester and Birmingham but caused an explosion at the Italian consulate in Mayfair, London, in which no one was injured.

Arrests of eight people were made in London in summer 1971, and, after one of the longest trials in criminal history, four of the accused were sentenced to ten years; at least two of them, Chris Bott and Hilary Creek, were the contributors who steered Manchester's *Mole Express* in its pro-Angry Brigade direction.

Police attributed 25 bombings to the group, which caused mostly property damage; one person was slightly injured during the entire campaign. Others sentenced included Jim Greenfield from Widnes, and Anna Mendelson, former head girl at Stockport High School for Girls, a participant in *les événements* in May 1968 Paris.

The Manchester links are tantalising, but no one would suggest that the next generation of the city's young people supported bombing their way to social change. Don told Dave Haslam in *All You Need Is Dynamite*: 'They had much the same sort of politics as me … libertarian, socialist, anarchist … but they never gave any impression of being involved in planting bombs.'

All the same, to use one of Wilson's memorable phrases, the radical political culture had 'seeped into the water table', and the language of class politics in the mid-1980s, with the so-called 'Hard Times' trope in the style press, was a preoccupation of a generation finding work hard to find as recession hit home. For the Haçienda's third birthday in 1985, Wilson was asked by Haslam in a *City Life* feature if his venue could have done more to support the miners during their doomed strike that year. The reply captured his disdain for placards and marches, and everything about Wilson's mind-expanded view formed in the paradigm-busting 1960s which writer Ian Macdonald called 'the revolution in the head'. He fired back: 'I know by the way you asked that question that you and I have a different understanding of the word "political." All you have to accept is that "Please Please Me" by The Beatles I regard as one of the most political acts of our time. That puts me a million miles away from people who think politics is just meetings and rallies.'

Wilson also had a way-out view of mass unemployment at that time. He believed that joblessness could be a blessing, that with the breakdown of structured work patterns the 'interesting community' could do cash-in-hand jobs, freeing them from the daily grind and letting their creativity blossom. It was a view I tried in 1985 on Alan Bleasdale, the TV dramatist behind the era-defining TV drama *Boys from the Blackstuff*. The writer who so poignantly expressed the personal and communal trauma of Liverpool's mass job destruction shook his head and looked at me like I was mad.

In late middle age, a decade after Factory's crash, Wilson was spending more time visiting churches than any self-respecting anarcho-situationist would be expected to. In his fifties he often sought out Father Denis Clinch at Roman Catholic St Mary's, an 1848 Rhenish Romanesque church on Mulberry Street then obscured by newer buildings, known as the Hidden Gem. It was widely known around town that his personal finances were in turmoil.

261

He hired me in 2002 to publicise the sale of his Little Peter Street loft, the price tag a headline-grabbing £1.9 million. Despite the publicity splurge, no one came forward to buy, and, despite our contract, he wouldn't pay my fee. With amicable pragmatism, we agreed I would hire him out as an event compère until I had been repaid from his fees. The twenty-year-old me had sat at his feet; now I was his agent, hiring him out. Eventually he paid back what he owed me.

It was all very Wilson. As his life moved into its final act, possibly his early Catholic education had, in the Jesuitical manner, begun to claw its way back into Wilson's thoughts. His funeral in summer 2007 at the Hidden Gem was a shock to long-time friends, like Happy Mondays' manager Nathan McGough: 'So the funeral was like a high Catholic mass … It really surprised me, because I thought I knew Tony well and was close to him. But I didn't know that he was deeply religious.' McGough said: 'I know when people are dying … they look to faith as some kind of salvation.'

Could such a cliché really be applied to Wilson? Perhaps he was searching less for conventional salvation then for the new revolutionary spirit within Catholicism. In various interviews before his death in 2007, he referenced Cardinal Arns, the late archbishop of São Paulo. As a TV novice in 1977, Wilson had interviewed the man he later described as 'Mr Liberation Theology, who put the shits up the Vatican for thirty years'. He recounted the exchange in *Q* magazine: '"But Cardinal, are you saying that … to be rich … of itself is a sin?" And he leaned back and said with a grin, "Yes my boy," as if to say, "It's only taken me 45 minutes but you've finally got it."' The discussion was, he said, 'the most profound moment of my life'. It led inevitably to his conclusion that, 'If you believe that' (the cardinal's view of wealth as sin), 'it's very hard to make money'.

If he suffered from classic Catholic guilt, then, it was shot through with the generically left-wing politics of his youth, the same politics with which he argued with his bosses at Granada about alternative ways to describe IRA terrorists. Yet nothing was that simple with Wilson. During a 1980s interview, while digressing on his taste for £30 boxer shorts, he uttered: 'I'll be the first up against the wall come the revolution.' He could never resist adding that he blamed Cardinal Arns for his own 'bad business sense' − a throwaway post-rationalisation justifying him never having to say sorry for running Factory into the ground. On this reading, crashing the label was simply the outcome of his Jesus-meets-Marx belief system, and nothing less than a personal revolution leading straight to the kingdom of heaven.

The merchandising of memory

Manchester, is after all, Spin City, a post-industrial text that produces signs and symbols at the same, barmy rate as it once produced the goods that guaranteed its Victorian prosperity.

Stuart Jeffries, *The Guardian*, 2 October 1999

It may not have been one of the great art heists of the twentieth century, but the grab-and-run robbery of the inspiration for Peter Saville's original Factory club poster from the wall of a Manchester gallery showed that, by 1992, memorabilia associated with Factory and the Haçienda had a coveted quality which drove a certain type of fan to extremes.

Today a substantial marketplace exists, riddled with all manner of over-sold claims, dubious provenance and daft asking prices. In September 1992, just a few weeks before Factory's collapse, Saville's work was exhibited along with that of the city's other influential graphic designers at *Sublime, Manchester Music and Design 1976–1982*. The exhibition, at Cornerhouse gallery, attracted twenty thousand people over six weeks to see the evolution of record-sleeve art of the city's music scene. No other city's music could claim such a sense of community and atmosphere, and it was reflected in the sleeves and posters, now framed and captioned as gallery artwork. I proposed and co-curated the exhibition, though it was an update of *Leave the Capitol*, a show staged by Tim Chambers at the Polytechnic in 1985.

Sublime took over the entire three-floor building and it seemed fitting that the visitor's journey should begin with Saville's iconic FAC 1, the poster for Factory Records' nights at the Russell Club in Hulme. This was the starting gun for both the company's design ethos and its eccentric catalogue system. The poster's main image was Saville's hand-traced version of a health and safety sign which he peeled off a door in Manchester Polytechnic's 3D art department. This image of a man wearing ear defenders and the warning

'Use Hearing Protection' was the debut of Saville's imaginative reinvention of industrialism's found iconography, and set the course for the entire Factory aesthetic. FAC 1 was a design godhead, and it took the Cornerhouse show's pride of place, by the first-floor entrance, accompanied by the actual health and safety sign which Saville had taken to hand draw a copy. Soon after opening, I was given the news that someone had grabbed the A4 laminated holy relic from the wall and had made off down bustling Oxford Road before staff could stop him. It fell to my co-curator Bev Bytheway to break the news to Saville. The sign (which had long gone out of production) was irreplaceable, though Saville was able to produce a copy of sorts for the rest of the show.

Putting aside the irony that Saville's original was a victimless crime (he recalls that the Poly quickly affixed a replacement notice), the brazen theft was an early sign that an obsessive cult was emerging around Factory mass-produced artwork. A poster purported to be from the original print run is, in mid-2022, for sale for £5,142.55 on the Rock Posters Treasure website, described as 'The Factory Russell Club 1979 Joy Division Original Mega Rare Scarce Vintage Music Poster'. On social media, photographer Kevin Cummins names and shames with extreme prejudice thieves who abuse the copyright of his work.

Original inspiration for Peter Saville's FAC 1 poster design

Peter Hook takes a less confrontational tone with bootleggers, writing in his Haçienda book, 'It's a compliment, but …' (he admits he is pals with some of the people who rip him off).

Many of those who grew up with Factory's music are now in late middle age, scattered across the globe, with some having considerable financial means to indulge their obsession and fund their collecting habit. In March 2019, Hook partnered with an auction house to offer four hundred items from his musical past including, for acolytes of the Joy Division myth, mouth-watering artefacts associated with Ian Curtis. The sale took place many miles from any glamorous rock and roll haunt, on an estate of low-rise commercial units outside Warrington, home of the North's premier music memorabilia seller Omega. After online and in-person previews, and producing brochures personally signed by Hook, on auction day Omega welcomed around a hundred people in person, as well as four hundred more bidding by phone and internet. There were collectors from Belgium, Luxembourg and Italy as well as the UK, and the type of fan boy-man (usually solo, though some accompanied by female partners) whose hobby has become a hardcore addiction.

It was fascinating to witness how scraps of paper with once merely functional purposes were fought over for large sums. A framed, typed sheet of lyrics for the Joy Division song 'Failures' by 'I. Curtis. November 1977' was sold for £4,000 and the chimes used on 'Atmosphere' sold to a telephone bidder for £5,800. An original Joy Division flight case sold for £21,000, and 'Hooky's first ever bass guitar' reached £10,000. Auctioneer Paul Fairweather described the sale results as 'unprecedented, with prices often far exceeding our expectations' and noted that Joy Division's pre-Factory 7-inch single 'Ideal for Living' in a picture cover signed by the four band members, which sold for £11,500, 'attained a price in excess of what we would expect for a full set of Beatles signatures, suggesting a fascinating shift in the spending habits of some of the biggest collectors'. I too had a copy, unsigned, of 'Ideal for Living', which I sold after the auction for £1,700 cash to a Belgian dealer who had made his way to Warrington.

Also under the hammer in the 'everything must go' sale was the original Factory Records' snaking hanging table for £9,000. Famously, it was the showpiece of the boardroom in Factory's new HQ building, and the movie *24 Hour Party People* featured a copy, in a scene in which the Factory directors come to blows in a row about money at the height of Factory's financial woes. In the film, Wilson lies to Gretton that he paid £30,000 for it. In real life, the table was not to last long as a functioning piece of furniture – Shaun Ryder

Factory Records offices, Princess Street (photo: Kevin Cummins)

and the Happy Mondays sat on it, snapping the razor-thin steel yachting wires which attached it to the ceiling, another real incident recreated in the film.

In 1990 Factory had just moved into its landmark HQ on Princess Street behind the BBC studios. It enjoyed a property bargain for once, paying just £100,000 for the knackered shell of a former ink factory. Factory announced its arrival by covering it in posters for current releases by New Order and Happy Mondays, Shaun Ryder off-his-face greeting motorists on the busy commuter road in and out of town. The building was a steal but, this being Factory, the interiors budget for Ben Kelly ran to £650,000. Next it had to be furnished, and Alan Erasmus, mindful of rising costs on artist recordings, laid down the law about overspending to the partners.

At this time, I took a call from Wilson enquiring about my friend designer Andy Woodcock, whom I had wangled on to Wilson's late-night Granada arts show *The Other Side of Midnight*: 'Can your designer mate make us a table?' he asked me. 'We've only got £2,000 to spend,' Wilson said. 'I went to IKEA to buy three at £700 each and was going to push them together, but they'd sold out.' Typically, Wilson turned the problem into a dialectic on the business zeitgeist. Woodcock recalled: 'Tony thought the whole meeting culture idea was just painful, so he wanted a table which would be a nightmare to sit at, so that any meetings wouldn't endlessly drag on and on. We also had a bit of a giggle about spilt coffees and expensive suits.'

The Manchester Polytechnic architecture grad was Wilson's kind of designer, injecting a captivating conceptualism into this most basic of projects: 'I came up with the idea of making it seem to float, tense, chaotic and asymmetrical as the thing should be like Factory, somewhat unstable and structureless,' said Woodcock. 'A bonus was that the cables could be tuned, like you would a guitar, and therefore the table could be played and used as an instrument (sort of).'

The 30 ft long MDF-finished piece was designed and made in two weeks for the given budget. Shaped like a long, melting Dali-esque surfboard, it was supposed to be an interim solution, so Wilson named it the Temporary Contemporary and gave it the FAC catalogue number 331. A rough copy of it was produced for the scenes in *24 Hour Party People*, in which London Records executives struggle to eat their meals as the table sways around. Woodcock helped the film-makers by providing his original drawings, and later he discovered the film replica was charged to the producers for 25 times the original cost – '£50K for a shit copy of an original design that only cost £2K!'

One interiors magazine called the table 'unwise', a design put-down, but so it proved after the Mondays thought it funny to test its engineering to breaking point. The original, however, did live to see another day, and it turned out to be an excellent payday for Hook. When the news of Factory's collapse reached him, the bassist-cum-entrepreneur raced to the HQ to retrieve what he could from the wreckage and pulled the table and other artefacts from a skip outside. FAC catalogue number 331 became Lot No. 253 in Hook's auction. The number which ultimately counted was the £9,000 it went for under the hammer. I told its designer 'Woody', now an architect in the Netherlands, the purchase price, and he simply had to laugh at the absurdity of it all.

With the Hook family looking down from the auction house gallery at the giant screen racking up the bids, the total take for the 'Peter Hook: The Joy

Division Signature Collection' by my estimate easily cleared £200,000. The celebrity seller declared that a proportion of sales of certain items was going to three charities, but many in the city's music scene harrumphed about the uncoolness of it all. Others said that Hook had simply held on to a more appealing garage of old gubbins than most, and that if he couldn't exploit the demand for his past, who could? Certainly, he has been an enthusiastic monetiser of the allure around the Haçienda and Factory – a brand, which, as Saville explained to city officials for his Original Modern project in 2004, can have assets, a heritage and an aura. Hook has shown remarkable business savvy in exploiting it, from giving his name to a limited run of six bass guitars with necks made from Haçienda dancefloor maple floorboards, to opening the club and music venue FAC 251 with partner Aaron Mellor in the former Factory HQ in 2010.

He openly acknowledges he is driven by a bitterness that New Order, in his view, has been 'taken' from him. The poisonous language in which he has couched his legal battle with the rest of the group over disputed royalties shocked many casual observers, particularly in a BBC TV interview with Mark Radcliffe. In a manner akin to an Albanian blood-oath, he described how he had told his children to fight on after his death for his share of what he believes he was owed. The other New Order members have for the main part kept their counsel, though Sumner's book *Chapter and Verse* tried to contextualise some of the divisions. It was reported in 2017 that the parties had come to a full and final settlement over royalties, although Hook told *Rolling Stone* in July 2020 that 'we always end up arguing because there's no communication at all. It's a real waste of time, money and effort. Especially when you get to this age. We seem unable to sort out it.' The rift has also left its mark on the city's music fraternity, often forced to side with one camp or the other.

Hook's beefs with his bandmates are personality clashes, but also about money. It appears from the outside that Hook is hellbent on avenging the way Wilson and Gretton pressganged New Order – Hook, Sumner, drummer Stephen Morris and keyboardist Gillian Gilbert – into propping up the Haçienda and investing in Dry bar. Factory's avowed purpose was to put artists first, but the group's naivety and love of a good time meant that accounts were never scrutinised or serious questions asked until the financial hangover kicked in.

The ironies and contradictions of how revolutionary art and value systems have become exploitable marketplaces is a repeated refrain in the Factory universe. The £4,000 inheritance Wilson set up Factory with has led, in a preposterous journey, to the £210 million Factory art centre; FAC 1 was the subject of a reckless and brazen art theft; the company's catalogue system has become a marketplace for dealers, brokers and buyers in a commodification of a generation's deeply personal memories.

While newly found items continue to appear online, often with uncertain authenticity, the genuine provenance of a second Omega auction by Hook in autumn 2021, putting this time his New Order collection under the hammer, only swelled more interest. Yet the marketplace for and fetishisation of Factory objects and paraphernalia has a deep irony. Factory was a satire on corporatism – it was constituted at Companies House as Factory Communications Limited, a future-sighted realisation that its business was cultural content, not just recordings. Its genesis owed much to the success of fellow Mancunians Buzzcocks, whose own New Hormones label under manager Richard Boon released the 'Spiral Scratch' 7-inch EP in 1977. The lo-design cover of a Polaroid snap of the group undercut record business blandness, and 'Spiral Scratch' made the Top 40, selling 16,000 copies.

Buzzcocks' DIY achievement inspired a wave of small labels. Factory was just one of many playful post-punk independent music outfits proliferating in the late 1970s and early 1980s, with Fast Product in Edinburgh, Kitchenware in Newcastle and Mute in London among the ventures slyly mocking music business packaging and promotional methods. Sheffield's Heaven 17 and their 1981 *Penthouse and Pavement* album cover mimicked the visual language of big business with straight-faced humour, all ponytails, suits and skinny ties against a glass tower resembling, prophetically, the Manchester city centre of 2022. More subtly subversive was 1983's ZTT record label formed by Paul Morley and record production team Trevor Horn and Jill Sinclair, its initials resembling bland big business tags but actually lifted from Futurist poet Marinetti's description of the sound of a firing machine gun, 'zang tumb tumb'.

The Factory catalogue system has become the stalking ground of a well-heeled class of international obsessives, despite it being meant as a parody. Even the cat at Factory's Didsbury office had a FAC number. Yet Factory and the Haçienda were real businesses, not just playful Situationist jokes. It was indeed grimly funny that FAC 51 (the Haçienda) led to FAC 61, the catalogue number assigned to the lawsuit by original Factory director Martin Hannett, aka Zero, in April 1982. But his attempt to wind up the company was a real and bitter business disagreement between the founders. A year after the loss-making music venue opened, Hannett ran out of money, accepted £25,000 to walk away and stepped down as Factory director. Yet, as Hook and the others have paid testament, it was Hannett's production of Joy Division that provided them with their legacy. He gave, says Hook, 'the gift of longevity ... We wanted to sound like The Clash, like The Sex Pistols. He saw something in it and gave us a wonderful gift.' The man who did not want to see the Haçienda built was, through his genius with sonic techniques (if not his people skills), crucial in the success of the records which provided the money for it.

The Factory label would not last more than another decade. Its demise in late 1992 was caused, as Karl Whitney details in *Hit Factories*, by offering newly signed acts like Northside, Cath Carroll and The Adventure Babies the standard music-business advances it had once demonised, and these could not be recouped when the records flopped. Factory's liquidators found the company an asset-free entity, as its no-contract arrangement with biggest act New Order left the band free to sign to London Records, the name pointing up an irony not lost on all concerned, given its founders' loathing of the capital and all it stood for.

As the end of the century approached, with the company's collapse and club culture in the doldrums, the next story in the Haçienda legend was to see it taken apart piece by piece. Residential developer Crosby Homes had bought the building from the builder G.R. Morris, which had paid £1.2 million to Rob Gretton for it in August 1998 (coincidentally the same price the Factory and Joy Division joint venture had paid to own it in 1992 after ten years of leasing). As the interior was unsuitable for a residential layout, the whole structure on Whitworth Street West side was slated to go, though the new building profile would retain the scale of the original including the curved elevation on Albion Street. The developer already had its hooks into Manchester, with a block on Princess Street and the postmodern jungle of sprawling, dense towers of its absurdly named Green Quarter near Victoria station.

Given its city connections, Crosby was aware of the legacy of the building it had acquired. To neutralise any opposition, it announced that the Haçienda was now being unbuilt, with loving care. In late 2000, demolition specialists Connell Brothers were brought in with the unusual instruction to tear the place apart ... carefully. The resultant bits and pieces of the Haçienda, it declared, would be available to buy at a charity auction. Crosby's 'corporate social responsibility' would see the proceeds distributed to local youth charities.

The demolition of the Haçienda went ahead under the gaze of a transfixed media and a traumatised fan community. The precision dismemberment was filmed by BBC regional TV. Everything sellable, from the hazard-striped steel girders to the exterior's glazed ceramic bricks, was retrieved and offered for sale in November 2000. The final-stage 'strip out' meant removing the roof, so that the eight main supporting columns could be transported to the auction site.

Everything with a possible value was retrieved. Abseilers were even hired to remove the building's external light fittings. The media gave voice to fans who saw themselves as keepers of the flame. *City Life* editor Luke Bainbridge told *The Guardian*, 'Everyone is furious. The old Haçienda crew and the Manchester clubbing fraternity are up in arms ... The marketing of the new apartments is sick.' ('Sick' was not yet affirmative street slang.) Kelly's distinctive yellow and black hazard stripes were appropriated for the Crosby brochure and the text ran, in classic estate-agent parlance: 'the spirit of the Haçienda lives on as it becomes the epicenter [sic] of stylish, luxury living in a vibrant urban environment'.

The sound of retching could be heard across the city. There was one man everyone looked to for a reaction. Rob Gretton had died the year before and, in November, Tony (now preferring 'Anthony H.') Wilson went on BBC's *North West Tonight* for a live ding-dong with city busybody Carolyn Blain. Hosted by studio anchor Gordon Burns, the recording features the Manchester Civic Society spokeswoman pleading with Wilson to support her call to retain the building exterior. She says: 'I think a lot of young people across the world who want to come to Manchester because of the music scene care.'

'Who cares? It doesn't matter,' Wilson replies. 'The most important clubs in Manchester history, the Twisted Wheel, the Haçienda, and in the middle the Electric Circus in Collyhurst, the home of punk which set this off – they pulled down the Electric Circus in '81 – doesn't change the fact that it was important.'

Burns asks, 'Is the Haçienda as key to Manchester as The Beatles was to Liverpool?'

Wilson says: 'Mancunians stay and reinvest in their city. The Beatles left in 1964 and never looked back and almost betrayed their city.' His payoff line looks forward: 'Carolyn, nostalgia is a disease ...' Ben Kelly, whose creation had been pulled to bits, agreed: 'Wherever I go in the world I meet people who have had the night of their life in the Haçienda. So what if someone puts a new building on top of it?'

I had been approached by Crosby Homes' Manchester office about PR, and soon I was being introduced to the sales director Geoffrey Dickens, whose property CV included a stint as a professional auctioneer. All exhibits deconstructed from Kelly's post-industrial fantasy would be going under the gavel as one-off pieces, bought and sold as at a conventional sale of art and coveted artefacts. The bollards ringing the dancefloor and the massive roof-bearing columns painted in hazard stripes were to be auctioned individually. Planks from the club floor were priced at a fiver, square sections of the dancefloor £20 each.

Tony Wilson and a Haçienda column (photo: Eamonn Clarke)

Even toilet doors, balcony balustrades and the cash register became auction lots. The motorway cat's eyes, recessed into the edge of the dancefloor, were stripped of their plastic light fittings, leaving a rough, rusted, heavy iron object – perfect, enthused Wilson, as an ashtray.

It became clear that he and Hook had decided to go with the flow. The auction would have happened whatever their feelings, but it could not have gone as successfully as it did without their blessing. When pressed again and again, Wilson doubled down on his forwards-looking philosophy: 'It's rock

Peter Hook and Tony Wilson at the Haçienda demolition (photo: Eamonn Clarke)

and roll ephemera – just tear it down,' he told BBC News. Wilson could not, though, be accused of cosying up to the developer. He compared its crass marketing to the botched promotion of Manchester which sparked the formation of the McEnroe Group. The sales strapline, 'Now the party's over ... you can come home', he called 'a crap line ... it misunderstands the mood of the place in almost precisely the same way "We're Up and Going" from McCann Erickson got Manchester wrong before.' It was an odd moment when Crosby allowed Wilson to have a private preview and take home some stuff for free.

He emerged with an armful of the cat's eyes, now ashtrays, for Christmas presents for friends. Then, after hearing that it was all for youth charities, Hook even agreed to play the role of co-auctioneer alongside Dickens.

November 25th was a cold and bright Saturday morning, and the contents of the Haçienda were assembled and laid out in a single-storey industrial warehouse lock-up, the Richard Conrad building, only a few hundred yards from the nightclub itself. Around 150 people present were joined by telephone bidders. As the unlikely auctioneer team of Dickens and Hook churned through the sale of the lots, there was a growing realisation this auction might raise tens but not hundreds of thousands. Not everyone had room for a steel girder and, even if they did, they couldn't move the thing without serious transportation; afterwards, there were tales of people buying one for £30, but spending hundreds to get it to a new resting place.

There was a tangible tension rising as the final lot approached – the Haçienda DJ booth. Most people who had been in it described it as having the dimensions and charm of a garden shed. (It also had a kind of cat flap into which Haçienda owners and managers retreated when pursued by irate creditors who turned up to collect debts). From the pre-event chatter, Dickens knew this rickety black-painted MDF box was talked about in clubland like a holy object and was the most prized of the contents. There were even rumours that Liverpool nightclub Cream wanted to take it to Merseyside, in some kind of inter-city poke in the eye.

When the long-awaited moment arrived, Dickens revealed a talent for showmanship worthy of Steven Spielberg. The wide shutters of the unit rolled up slowly, flooding the place with late morning light. A low-loader reversed in to present the booth to the room in all its knackered glory. There were gasps of awe, as if the chosen people had been reunited with the Ark of the Covenant. The booth was bought for £8,000 by DJ Bobby Langley, a purchase which became legendary not for the acquisition itself but because amateur auctioneer Hook canvassed the crowd for bids, pushing the price ever-higher, and eventually said, 'It's yours Bobby, congratulations. You've been bidding against yourself!' What happened to the hallowed relic is shrouded in mystery and gossiped about in Facebook groups, but reliable sources indicate it was kept outside, and fell to pieces over a couple of Manchester winters.

With the demolition under way, Crosby asked me in confidence in autumn 2000 if I could help them with a problem. They could not market the scheme as 'the Haçienda apartments'. The name was a trademark owned by another company. Dickens looked at me intently, and asked with great seriousness,

'We really do need to find something out. It's important, but it's turning out to be very difficult.' I nodded for him to continue. He said with the straightest of faces, 'Do you know who the three little pigs are?' I stifled a laugh at the kind of question straight out of a spy novel. I replied that I didn't. But it sounded to me like the kind of playful Situationist joke name for a company in the field of subversive pop culture. Dickens went on: the rights to the Haçienda name were owned by a company called Three Little Pigs Limited. And try as they might, none of their approaches to said company had resulted in anything but silence. Dickens and a colleague fixed me with their gravest expressions. Crosby were deadly serious. They wanted to buy the Haçienda name, and they wanted me to find out who was behind Three Little Pigs.

I asked about, and all roads led back to Peter Hook. I asked him, did he want to discuss the matter of Crosby using the Haçienda name? He did, and I set up their meeting and left it at that. It is well known that money changed hands for the use of the name. I did not request a broker's fee from either side, something common in the property world. I was an early member, and the Haçienda had been a guiding star throughout my professional career and my personal life. While I felt no problem at facilitating the deal which saw Crosby snaffle the Haçienda naming rights, I did not want to profit personally. I left the bass-playing entrepreneur and the southern house builders to do a deal between them, and, when it opened, the scheme of 130 apartments priced up to £430,000 each was, and remains, the Haçienda Apartments.

Even as it disappeared, the Haçienda was taking on mythic qualities. It was a site for new pop-culture stories to flourish into legend, and soon, in response for this swelling hunger, the Haçienda was to be rebuilt once again, not just in memory, but literally. This time it was to be recreated in painstakingly accurate detail, for a film which would multiply its meanings to ever greater notoriety, carrying its legend to new generations. This reconstituted Haçienda was to exist for filming key scenes – after which it was destined to be dismantled all over again.

Just weeks after the demolition auction, Ben Kelly was approached by the producers of a film about the Factory story. *24 Hour Party People* tells the record label's story across a fifteen-year period, from 1976 to 1992. The sprawling, rumbustious ensemble tale is threaded through by the lead role of Wilson, played by Steve Coogan. The film did not earn great box office initially but has gained cult status thanks to Frank Cottrell-Boyce's tragicomic, farce-meets-philosophy script, and Michael Winterbottom's immaculate feel for youth cultures from punk to rave.

Ticket for filming of *24 Hour Party People*

The filmmakers discussed with Kelly the idea of rebuilding the club using his original designs, but, when he asked for a fee, the talk dried up. Kelly owned the copyright, but that didn't stop the producers building it without him, using pirated internet versions of his designs. So having only just been demolished, the Haçienda was rebuilt for filming with impeccable micro-accuracy in March 2001. They were in the right city for 3D doppelgängers. From 1988 to 1999, millions of day trippers had visited parts of a recreated *Coronation Street* film set as part of the Granada Studios Tour, which the TV company took to promoting as 'Hollywood-on-the-Irwell'. Soap fans could visit replica homes and shops familiar from TV, based on creator Tony Warren's original inspiration, the long-demolished Archie Street in Ordsall, Salford. On the tour, people could even sup a pint of beer on the real Rovers Return set and stroll the cobbled street on non-filming days. All the sets and the tour replicas were demolished when Granada relocated filming to MediaCity UK in Salford Quays, requiring yet another 'Corrie' set to be built at the new studios in 2013.

Once a classic Fordist producer of goods and machines, in the new millennium Manchester had become a manufacturer of iconic imagery. The Granada tour also included a replica House of Commons used by TV dramas to film parliamentary debate scenes. They could also use Manchester Town Hall to shoot scenes among Alfred Waterhouse's corridors and staircases, a perfect match for the Palace of Westminster. The city centre is also firmly established as the default setting for the contemporary Northern urban backdrop in TV drama, like crime series *Cracker*, *Prime Suspect*, *Band of Gold* and *Life on Mars*, and *Cold Feet* portrays softer stories in shiny new city locations.

The city of making things was now the metropolis of make-believe. Another link in the daisy-chain of Manchester's iconic environments, Winterbottom's movie made the Haçienda reborn, recreated down to its last detail on land in Ancoats owned by Carol Ainscow's Artisan Holdings. Over three nights, the replica interior was used to film scenes for three specific decades of youth music and style, one night each dedicated to the 1970s, 1980s and 1990s. I count myself lucky to have been there for the third and final night, the Acid House night, recreating the crowd scene near the end of the movie which climaxes with Coogan-as-Wilson declaring, 'Let a thousand Mancunians bloom!'

Earlier that day, Wilson had called and offered me two tickets and, while doing so, criticised the producers and Dave Haslam for giving him only a handful. It was his own life story, so I could see why he was upset. From the film-makers' point of view, though, he was plain wrong. Haslam was doing the right thing. His task was to get a thousand extras who looked like the clubbers a decade before having the wildest nights of their lives. He had to source the right crowd, not Wilson's friends and associates, who were now too old, sporting less hair and the wrong clothes, and too self-conscious to throw themselves about with the manic abandon required.

Hook described the passes to the filming as like 'Willy Wonka's golden tickets'. You could tell how many tickets Wilson had managed to procure, because a gaggle of middle-aged people gathered by the main ground-floor bar. The cameras focused on the extras, all going wild to the classic rave-era House tracks, raising their arms high towards the DJ booth to salute the classic pairing of DJs Park and Pickering, whom the producers reunited for the occasion. But around a dozen people – including myself, managers Paul Mason, Leroy Richardson and Ange Matthews, plus musicians Peter Hook, Bernard Sumner, Bruce Mitchell, Rowetta Satchell and Graham Massey – patrolled the area between the bar and the dance floor, both excited and stupefied.

'Has someone spiked my drink?' said Hook. 'I must be hallucinating. This place has been demolished!' It did not help to process the madness when actors playing Manchester figures appeared, such as Paddy Considine looking eerily similar to the deceased Rob Gretton. The whole experience was so realistic that I instinctively opened the door to what I remembered as the men's toilets, only to find a solid breeze-block wall. Everything about the Haçienda interior was perfectly remade, from the bar pumps to the cat's eyes and hazard-striped columns, to details like the exact height of the step down from the dancefloor to the main floor. Kelly later said: 'Watching the film, I sat there absolutely gobsmacked. I went legal on them. It dragged on and on, and eventually it was settled out of court with the distributors of the film. But yeah, they did a great job. The bastards.' Haslam said: 'I didn't want to do a night that was looking back. I feel like us and the audience gave the film-makers the perfect Haçienda night.'

While we were all having a classic Haçienda night in an environment we knew had ceased to exist, other parties were keen to play roles in this real-world simulacrum. Some tickets had gone to 'the Salford' who had found their old territory in the 'E corner' under the balcony, and there was mayhem outside as gangs which used to terrorise the club door tried storming the gates. The producers had to call the police to restore order. It was just like old times.

An independent documentary by film-maker Chris Hughes was screened at Glastonbury in 2015 called *Do You Own the Dancefloor?* It tells the story of the demolition auction and tracked down buyers to discover where the coveted collectables had ended up. In Australia, Miami, Montreal, London and Vancouver, the film shows how the Haçienda lives on in artefacts in homes, offices and gardens of former clubbers, either as decoration or emotion-laden shrines to their personal histories, an era when Manchester had not yet been identified as an asset growth opportunity by fund managers and investment advisers on distant continents.

The remarkable reverence which many had for Haçienda and Factory memorabilia can be seen in the thriving international online market for official
records, posters, T-shirts and household items. Tribute dance-music nights are
common, the most striking being the emptying of the car park underneath the
Haçienda Apartments, paid for by Peter Hook for high-production strobe-lit
raves, charity fundraisers to mark the thirtieth and fortieth anniversaries. The
fetishisation of Factory objects and paraphernalia carries on in yet more surreal
ways. For sale online are Haçienda-striped gin bottles, T-shirts and trainers,
and even oven gloves sporting the pulsar signal readout that Saville used for Joy
Division's *Unknown Pleasures* sleeve – an appropriated image today so instantly
recognisable as to make the word 'iconic' redundant. 'There's just the two
albums,' Saville said in 2008. 'All the rest is the merchandising of memory.'

Pop and politics, Wilson and Burnham

This is Manchester, I believe we do things differently here.

Tony Wilson, *24 Hour Party People* book of the film

Doing Buses Differently.

Consultation on Proposed Franchising Scheme, Greater Manchester
Combined Authority, October 2020

How did Manchester make the metaphysical leap over forty years of time and space, endowing a phrase used by Tony Wilson to persuade Granada TV to televise the Sex Pistols with magic powers of civic populism? 'Doing things differently' is today a twenty-first-century Mancunian dog whistle exploited by politicians and bureaucrats, a mantra deployed both as a badge of civic pride and as a woolly people-pleasing slogan.

Would its coiner spit if he could witness its appropriation on everything from the foyers of new-build apartments and hotel receptions to the websites and press releases of council jobsworths? Or would he be proud of its seemingly omnipresent use by the Greater Manchester Combined Authority, its elected mayor and its many partners, as a tool to power the Manchester brand?

Did its first ever use indeed take place in 1976, as he reported in his movie tie-in book *24 Hour Party People*? Wilson recalls how he summoned up the courage to ask Granada's owner Lord Bernstein to put the Sex Pistols on TV. Came the socialist peer's reply, 'My father was an anarchist, nothing wrong with a bit of anarchy' (though we should take note of Wilson's advice in the same book, 'When forced to pick between truth and legend, print the legend').

In life he showed an intuitive skill for advancing the cause of Mancunian exceptionalism through a kind of psychic vertical integration, achieving single-handedly what no city promotion campaign or PR blitz could. Today's relentless application of the infernal 'DTD' phrase by so many in public life shows us a genius who keeps on giving in death, too.

The dawn of the new millennium seemed to galvanise Manchester's alternative lord mayor into a hitherto unseen interest in traditional politics. He was attending political meetings, if not the Didsbury ward of the city's Labour group, then the conferences and seminars around emerging Labour government plans to give more power to the regions. Wilson's participation in the discourse about new forms of representation was welcomed by those who observed that his rock-and-roll profile could bring along those turned off by conventional politics.

The government could see a growing need to respond to a democratic deficit in which Northern regions continued to decline, matched by a decaying engagement by their citizens with the electoral process. In 2002 its White Paper on the problem was followed by an act of Parliament enabling new limited regional powers. Led by Deputy Prime Minister John Prescott, the experiment in regional devolution had to be legitimised by public votes. The regions were to be asked to approve a new level of autonomy, to be governed by elected regional assemblies. A £5 million information campaign was launched to explain the process and the potential benefits to each region, starting with the Northeast.

Wilson was already an influential voice within Manchester's informal think tanks, and a creative consultant to Lancashire's regeneration body. Now he leapt at the chance for Northerners to prise London's hands off some of the levers of power. This was not quite the republic of Mancunia that many like Wilson had long dreamed of. Prescott and MP Graham Stringer publicly rowed with feeling at one debate, over the former council leader's iron-clad insistence that, as the Northwest's engine, it was the Manchester city region that needed control over its own destiny, and that the North West template did not do the job. At another debate, Faisal Islam (then at *The Observer*, now with the BBC) called for the city to be better able to raise and spend taxes, saying that, without local tax-raising powers, the proposed changes brought little benefit. The Greater Manchester city region model was yet to emerge, and it would take a further decade and more of swirling political discourse, plus a window of breakneck opportunism, to achieve the 'Devo Manc' deal in place today.

First, though, the regional model had to fail. In 2004, the assemblies were aligned to Labour's template in which regional agencies doled out funds from the state. The prospect of an elected assembly having to work with and through the government's Northwest Development Agency based at Warrington appalled Wilson, who was apt to label the body's location, a regional fudge half-way between Manchester and Liverpool, as 'the perineum of the Northwest' (often while onstage at events the NWDA hosted). However, now that a degree of self-government was on offer, the intellectual possibilities excited him. Was not this the mythical landscape of Granadaland, after all, his former employer's warm and fuzzy tagline for its territory as it beamed TV programmes into Northwest living rooms from the Winter Hill transmitter high up on the West Pennine Moors?

Enthused, and rather than allying with any formal political organisation, Wilson set up the pro-assembly Necessary Group. Always mindful of the power of the visual, he commissioned Peter Saville to design a flag for the Northwest region. Saville's design took the cross of St George and highlighted and enlarged the upper left section, the distortion matching up with the Northwest's location on the map of England. This non-aligned push was in the face of a cool response from the city's political leaders. The City saw any kind of Northwest template for precious power, funds and influence as a threat, particularly as civil servants were apt to tilt prestige projects and public cash westwards towards needier Merseyside. If Manchester's leaders kept their heads down about Wilson's group and its flag, the push caused consternation elsewhere. Professional media curmudgeon Martin Regan blasted Wilson and his 'self-important group of regional "movers and shakers"' which included disparate figures Sir Alex Ferguson, singer-songwriter Damon Gough aka Badly Drawn Boy and magazine editor Michael Taylor. Business commentator Regan wrote that they should be pelted with rotten fruit for Wilson's T-shirt slogan 'Necessary Northwesterner'.

Northwest magazine *Entrepreneur* conceded that the Necessary lobby group should at least be congratulated for creating 'more interest in the subject than a thousand dull debates might have achieved'. Furthermore, there was a feeling in the air that, perhaps, decades before Brexit and the Northern red wall turning blue, the political class was genuinely trying to make politics relevant to Northern lives. Kevin Gopal in *North West Business Insider* reported local government minister Nick Raynsford's rose-tinted belief that the 'assemblies entailed a new kind of politics as well as a new type of politician'. I believe Wilson would have seen a natural role for himself, as a political independent naturally, in a Northwest assembly. Dozens of names from Wilson's contacts book (including me) signed a call for 'Northwesterners' to vote 'yes' to an elected assembly in advance of the poll.

The referendum was scheduled for autumn 2004 but Saville's Northwest emblem was destined never to be run up any flagpoles, and the region did not even get the opportunity to vote. Prescott considered the Northeast's cohesive identity and Labour power bases to be the most likely to support devolution, but fewer than half of voters took part in October 2004's poll, and the defeat by 700,000 to 200,000 caused the abrupt abandonment of plans for limited devolution in the Northwest and elsewhere.

The failure of the Labour experiment in regional self-government exposed the deep problems in the Manchester–Labour government relationship. They may have been in the same party, and that party was in power, but there was an undeniable feeling that Manchester's Labour leadership from the early 1980s had got a better shake from the Tories than from their spiritual comrades. While Conservative ministers consistently respected the city's entrepreneurial nous, in 2007 the sight of the city's leader Sir Richard Leese fuming alongside national Labour MPs at his party's G-Mex conference panel was instructive, a cold anger plain to see in a discussion about relations between the regions and the centre under Blair and, now, Gordon Brown. Leese, a master of impulse control, seemed close to self-combustion as other MPs talked about the primacy of the party machine – bearding him in his city, in the building which was the symbolic heart of the Manchester transformation. It was striking to see at first hand the undisguised bitterness between Leese and his own party's machine. Firmly set to central control, Labour was not programmed to reward Manchester for its verve and creativity, can-do attitude and private–public partnerships created as responses to the IRA bomb, the Olympic bids and 2002 Commonwealth Games. The animosity continued into the era of leader Jeremy Corbyn, who in 2015 approved a Northern Future paper calling Conservative-driven devolution a 'cruel deception'.

From inner-city tsar Heseltine's enthusiasm for the city's funding bids to Chancellor Osborne's largesse, Manchester has had a better return under the Tories than under its traditional Labour allies. The City sniffed out opportunities and beat rival cities to further the Manchester pro-business strategy for growth and jobs, often acting with a 'go for it' praxis so beloved of Wilson. One outstanding exhibit was the funding for the XVII Commonwealth Games. The original budget was £68 million but, rather than Blair's Labour government underwriting the events, the onus was on Manchester to deliver them, without a safety net. Memories of debt-burdened sports festivals in Edinburgh and Sheffield loomed large, especially as the true cost of delivering the Games ballooned to £276 million.

The scene was set for a hair-raising ride, as Cabinet Office Secretary Ian McCartney initially told the Commons that there would be no more money, which seemed a Glasgow kiss from Blair via the strong-accented Scot (and local MP) for the city's hopes for a funding rescue. Finally, however, the penny dropped that the nation could ill afford to present a half-cocked event to the world. The City's brinkmanship paid off. The government delivered two big public-cash injections. Overall final costs of the Games were estimated at around £300 million, including funds for the facilities such as the new stadium, with council sources (including Manchester Airport) having to find £45 million of it.

Ray King muses in *Detonation*: 'Did the games have to be "bailed out" or was Manchester's high wire act a deliberate device to procure extra funding for an event of which the nation can be proud?' The episode showed Bernstein's ability to psych out Blair and his cool-on-Manchester stance, which seemed to have no enthusiasm for a spectacular Commonwealth Games. The delivery committee led by Charles Allen of Granada TV, lawyer Robert Hough and accountant Frances Done flew by the seat of its pants, but the nail-biting approach ultimately led to the cash for a superb spectacle with high-production values. After opening by the Queen, the festival of sport was staged with verve and efficiency, the public experience helped by ten thousand volunteers lending a warm Mancunian touch. Following the feelgood glow that the Games lit, first Bernstein and then Leese were knighted. Yet neither was the type to be flattered by such establishment honours. The real prize was the regeneration of the post-industrial east Manchester wastelands. As much as they helped to change perceptions and show off the city worldwide, the ten days of elite sport were only a helpful catalyst in the eyes of Manchester's leaders. The regeneration led directly to Manchester City FC's new modern stadium, for which the council and the football club split the £42 million conversion costs for the 48,000-seater Etihad Stadium, expanded in 2015 to 55,000.

United fans may have derided the stadium as 'the council house', but the Commonwealth Games was a key stepping-stone. Over the next two decades, The City continued to impress governments of all colours and their civil servants that Manchester enjoyed stable, mature leadership. And so to DevoManc, a deal that was no woolly Granadaland footprint offering mild northwest autonomy in the Prescott model. Instead this was the two cities and eight boroughs, home to 2.7 million people making up Greater Manchester. In March 2016, the government agreed to hand the city region control and budgets of its transport, health and social care to add to the existing responsibilities of police and fire services.

The powers were granted by David Cameron's government on condition that the new authority was led by an elected mayor. In 2017 Labour's Andy Burnham was elected as the executive mayor in the first democratic vote for a leader of a devolved UK metropolitan area. He won the next election too, in 2021. Since taking the reins, Liverpool-born, Merseyside-raised Burnham – whose advisers were initially nervous of doorstep perceptions of him as a 'Scouser' – has played a flawless hand in harnessing the city's music heritage to his own agenda. On his way to the first of two walkover elections, as well as wooing the stalwart Labour institutions of unions, public sector and local Labour groups, Burnham was sure to register his music credentials with the voting public. Not long after his win, he informed Twitter followers of his top Manchester bands – Stone Roses in top spot, followed by The Smiths ('life-changing'), The Courteeners, The Verve and New Order, a selection skewed towards melodic guitar bands, rather than the city's more experimental music heard in early Factory and The Fall.

Declaring that Manchester does things differently has, in one of Wilson's favourite metaphors, seeped into the water table. Certainly, it is one of the go-to phrases which Burnham and his speechwriters reach for. In 2002 I had brought together the tyro Greater Manchester MP and Wilson, the ex-record-company boss dabbling in regional public affairs and urban regeneration, whose legacy is frequently quoted by the smart politician who jumped ship from Labour's Westminster woes on to the fast-moving HMS DevoManc.

In March of that year, I was asked to liven things up at a little *soirée* for the new editor of *The Times*. Robert Thomson had got his troops in a tizz, as he had decided to visit Manchester with little warning. I took a call from the paper's Northern correspondent Russell Jenkins, the Thunderer's man in the north. Covering from Liverpool to Hull, top-class reporter Jenkins spent hours writing up stories from courtrooms and press conferences, few making it into print. He sounded genuinely worried: 'I only know boring people, some MPs and some top policemen. You know lots of interesting people. Can you invite some of them to meet the new editor?' He sounded amazed that his boss had taken an interest in Manchester. 'People in the London office can't believe he's coming up in his first days in the job.'

Intrigued by all the talk of the new Manchester, some of which was bubbling up in his own paper's lifestyle pages, Thomson stayed at the Midland Hotel. He had just been promoted from foreign editor by owner Rupert Murdoch, and the predominant adjective for him in the press was 'ascetic'. He had a monkish look, for sure – precise and polite, with a gentle humour. I told him that his

columnist Mick Hume, who went on to launch *Spiked Online*, was a student con-
temporary of mine, and once a leading light in the Revolutionary Communist
Party. I found it amusing to see him writing for the establishment gazette, I said.
'Oh, we have plenty of columnists like that,' Thomson smiled.

This was the season for the ruling class to take an interest in Manchester.
I found myself in a meeting in my office with entrepreneur Ben Elliot, whose
Quintessentially start-up was making waves as a 'luxury concierge' service for
the wealthy. I was intrigued to meet the nephew of Camilla Parker Bowles, lat-
terly the Queen Consort, and he quizzed me about which rich people I knew
in Manchester – a brief conversation, with every word scribbled down by his
unsmiling female amanuensis. I never heard of the company's presence in
Manchester, though it is today an international operation. Elliot is now widely
known as the former fundraising co-chairman of the Conservative Party.

Thomson, meanwhile, wanted to see the changing city, and I put him on
a Metrolink tram outside his hotel to Salford Quays. This ride showed off the
arrestingly mashed-up historic and current Manchesters. The original modern
city's crumbling and ripped backsides were being integrated with classy modern
buildings. The views from St Peter's Square through Castlefield to the Lowry
Centre were, and still are, a brilliant twenty minutes' advertisement for the
resurgent urban centre.

I had invited Tony Wilson, along with consultant Emma Jones, now of
Enterprise Nation business group, and some other interesting types as requested,
to the reception. The gathering was in a reception room at the Midland Hotel
and, if we are to categorise the guest list along Jenkins's lines, then MP Andy
Burnham was one of the host's 'boring' guests. Wilson met Thomson with
'I read *The Times* every day, for me it's the paper of record', and, after a few
minutes of chatting, the new editor moved on to other guests. The canapés
and drinks were served up by waiters circulating with trays. I was in a gaggle
with Wilson, Jones and several others. There was a fresh-faced wine waiter
standing attentively close to our group. He stood fast to one spot and was smil-
ing, as staff at these events do. When it became clear he wasn't holding a tray
of drinks, I realised he was in fact the youthful, recently elected Member of
Parliament for Leigh, the most distant outpost of the Manchester city region. It
appeared Wilson had no idea who he was, but Burnham was gradually drawn
into our group, an informal circle all trying to make contributions to the general
chit-chat but dominated by Wilson's close-quarters style, described by Durutti
Column drummer Bruce Mitchell as 'like a rhino emerging from a thicket'.
Still in his first year as an MP, this was the first time Burnham found himself in

the physical orbit of the man he would come to praise in his successful election campaign, and to quote many times after. None of us, Burnham especially, could have foreseen how the swirls and eddies of national politics, public life and personal ambition could have confabulated a destiny in which he was elected Manchester mayor, with a city machine that reveres Wilson as a spirit guide, publicly appreciated more in death than in his controversial life.

With his skew-whiff England flag and dragnet of B-list names, Wilson's 'Necessary' attempt to make a dent in the world of politics had been derided by some and ignored by most. Widespread apathy for regional autonomy quashed his bid to succeed in politics. Nevertheless, I agree with Paul Morley's suggestion that, had he been alive in 2015, Wilson would have decided to run for the Manchester mayoralty. No doubt Wilson would have had to stand as an independent – no traditional party would have had the nerve to take on the difficult elements of his back story, and his ideals would have prevented his conscience from yoking itself to any manifesto other than his own singular constellation of beliefs.

How would he have managed the presentational challenge? It was hard to see how his universe of cash, chaos and creativity, of drug references and epic effing and jeffing, could be reconciled with a sphere in which politicians need to be 'on-message' for fear of toxic headlines. His proselytising of personal liberation, of the 'revolution in the head', means his beliefs would probably have been labelled 'anarchic libertarianism', at odds with the socialist politics which had shaped his city.

Yet Wilson had nothing to lose reputationally, having been monstered by the press over *So It Goes*, punk controversies, the Haçienda crime scene and the collapse of Factory. He would not have needed media training, as arguing the toss was what he did for breakfast, lunch and tea. Though rhetorical overstatement is rarely a vote winner, he could handle himself in any verbal scrap. He was already, as Morley wrote, "the metaphysical mayor of the other Manchester he helped invent in his imagination …" Wilson would have been sixty-five in 2016, and with a solid claim for much credit for the booming Manchester.

Another factor which would have driven Wilson towards standing will sound unpalatable to many. With his New York contacts going back decades, and his awareness of how stateside media trends pave the way elsewhere, I believe he would have been emboldened, even inspired, by Donald Trump's aspirations in US politics, which between 2001 and 2009 were affiliated to the Democrats. The all-important name recognition to cut through the lack of public interest in policy and politics; a TV personality known to more voters than career politicians; and a personal driving force, in his case, of Mancunian exceptionalism: all these would have driven him to stand. If he had, the tempting counterfactual is: would Wilson have run against Burnham?

Wilson's death in summer 2007 from cancer inspired a wave of genuine grief, and a range of remembrances from public and media figures, the majority loving and appreciative, with the odd sour outlier. It unlocked a mawkish cult of sainthood powered by works like Mike Garry's ode 'St. Anthony' with its refrain 'talk to me'. As sincere as this response was, social media became a yawning sluice-gate for unfiltered public emotion, serving to remind us of the multiple Wilsons, but slapping on a hagiographic gloss which did not do justice to his complexity.

The outpouring led us to overlook the less appealing but fascinating sides of his personality, traits played for laughs with cartoonish hilarity by Steve Coogan. But it would have been wicked fun to hear him debate with official party candidates Burnham, Conservative Sean Anstee and others at the formal hustings for the devolved mayor before the May 2017 vote. Sadly, there would be no chance to hear about how his car-friendly policies would contribute to a cleaner, carbon-reduced city centre, or to listen to moral and philosophical contortions explaining his historic justification of hard drugs, or even his oft-quoted Sid Vicious's verdict of 'the man in the street'. The week after the June 1989 Tiananmen Square massacre of demonstrators by the Chinese state, on his early hours TV magazine *The Other Side of Midnight* Wilson opined that, as regrettable as the events were, it was important not to forget that China had raised hundreds of millions out of poverty. Lack of controversy was ensured by the fact barely anyone was watching.

Given Burnham's Liverpudlian origins, would Wilson have employed an observation he would crack open when dealing with natives of Merseyside, 'Scousers, they've got a mental problem haven't they?' In his TV pomp he used the Northwest airwaves to bait his Liverpool viewers on *Granada Reports*. Perhaps his advisers (and whose political counsel would he have sought?) might even have seen that as a populist vote winner in the football-mad Manc inner-city. Perhaps helping to smooth that strategy would be his friend, ambitious Liverpudlian politician Frank McKenna, who fell foul of Labour Party infighting in Lancashire then reinvented himself with his 'sexy networking' Downtown in Business group.

At the real hustings, we heard from Burnham time and again ticking off the Labour movement's twentieth-century big hits, from trade unions to the Suffragettes, and missing out, it seemed to me, the potential of the post-Haçienda city he was bidding to take control of. He repeated the traditional Labour shopping list of wholemeal staples, but of the spice of life there was little. In addressing businesspeople, he failed to acknowledge the incentive of the profit motive, the adrenalised excitement of the new city centre, or even a nod to the potential of the university's advances in 2D materials like Graphene.

At his campaign launch in May 2016 at the Lowry Centre, along with pledges on transport and youth opportunities, Burnham sought to widen his appeal in a speech which summoned up Wilson's legacy and asked how it could evolve. Post-election, the mayor launched an independent review into the city's music business, revealing his personal connection to the music scene and how, he said, Manchester music and culture had shaped him. Music was worth £169 million to the Greater Manchester economy, he said in the *Creative Tourist* website. Burnham wrote how his younger self landed his first job after graduation on Portland Street at the very heart of blissed-out Madchester. It was summer 1989 and the future politician, before his English degree at Cambridge, had a summer office job with British Telecom, just round the corner from Affleck's Palace. He was in the coach parties thronging Blackpool for The Stone Roses' incandescent show at the Empress Ballroom. 'At the time I didn't realise how lucky I was,' he wrote. 'Looking back, the very definition of being in the right place at the right time.' No visual evidence, sadly, was provided of the future politician – who may yet emerge to lead the Labour Party and potentially the country – as a twenty-one-year-old in a beanie hat and baggy T-shirt. But he skilfully evoked the image of the teenage Burnham, like so many other Northwesterners, receiving his cathode-ray communion in the family living room: 'Gone are the days of watching *Granada Reports* on a Friday evening and hearing Tony Wilson, having finished reading the headlines, say: "And, to play us out, here's Northside …"'

At election hustings held by *Place North West* in February 2017, before an audience of the property industry, Burnham called for a new relationship between Manchester and business, 'to work together to make it the industrial capital it once was, and at the same time to show you can do that by looking after people … where we do want to get on in life, but a place where we leave nobody behind'. This mild appeal to business's conscience led to an ironic paradox at the time: having stood and lost to leader Jeremy Corbyn in the party's leadership contest, among the nation's *Guardian*-istas he was often disdained as a Blairite, yet in Manchester the new mayor's rhetoric was perceived by the city's entrepreneurs as more that of a leftist with no empathy for business.

Following Burnham's win, city council leader Sir Richard Leese continued to hold the city region's economy portfolio, including leading the annual MIPIM showpiece, which calmed the nerves of the Hale wine-bar property crowd. This move gave developers confidence in a firm, long-standing relationship at the highest level, while removing Burnham from the fray over increasingly fractious planning rows about the lack of affordable homes in the city centre's high towers.

The city region's devolution of 2017 was hailed as a first in the history of the North-South divide, but it had a long gestation. The 2014 agreement with the city region by Chancellor George Osborne followed a 2009 pilot, but its culmination was a miracle of timing, when political opportunism and mutual respect between leaders in London and Manchester coincided with tectonic plate-shifting forces. The groundwork laid over two decades had overcome the poisonous emotions stirred up by the congestion charge bid. Aside from drawn knives at election time, councillors from the three main parties bound themselves together in an informal compact. Councils in Bury, Bolton, Rochdale, Stockport and Trafford changed hands over the decades, but even as the party kaleidoscope turned the political colours, a consistent pattern was emerging.

Osborne, effectively a Manchester MP, as many of his Cheshire constituents had work ties to the city, was in earshot of the mood music, and the sound volume was rising. There was an increasing recognition that the centre would hold as a strong political and economic base, and it was in the interests of all ten councils to ally with the economic force of the bullseye on the GM dartboard, Manchester city centre. Pulling together began as early as 1986 after the abolition of Greater Manchester County Council. The ten councils formed the Association of Greater Manchester Authorities (AGMA), a voluntary grouping, and its base in Wigan was symbolic because it is the most westward of the city region's boroughs, one of only two not to share a border with the city of Manchester, and in fact only part of GM since 1974.

If a town centre ten miles from Manchester Town Hall and well on the way towards Liverpool could sign up to collective working, they all could. It would have been easy for Wigan to ask, 'What's in it for us?' No doubt the question was asked time and again there, as Manchester grew in leaps and bounds. But the man answering the question to Wiganers was one of their own. Lord Peter Smith (strictly speaking a Leyther from the town of Leigh which felt hard done by when friendly local rival Wigan was given the borough's name). The highly esteemed politician had been on the council since 1978, when he won his ward by a single vote. Ever since, and increasingly after taking over as chair of AGMA in 2000, he had fostered the devolution dream.

The year 2005 saw a new Greater Manchester Economic Development Plan. The report's owner, Manchester Enterprises, wanted people to know that this dry-sounding document was a blueprint for the local authorities to work together, for the good of all 2.7 million residents. It fell to my PR firm to promote it. Just the words 'economic development strategy' were certain to have them yawning by the final syllable. The challenge was overcome by my bright spark colleague Richard Bond, who devised a jigsaw 12 ft across with ten removable pieces in the shape of each council area. The jigsaw was toured around the town halls and each local authority-shaped piece was signed by a council leader and countersigned by Manchester Enterprises' urbane chief Daniel Dobson-Mouwad.

No fireworks were set off by a celebrating populace. There were limited circles of interest for this kind of thing. But the local papers covered the photo of their piece of the jigsaw. It was important to send the message to the politically active in the social clubs, the local party meetings in church halls, not to mention the civil servants in the ten town halls, that the days of fighting like cats in a sack were fading. Differences there would always be. But showing London that 'GM' could deliver its responsibilities as a coherent, well-run conurbation demanded respect from Whitehall, which was used to viewing local turf-war politics from London. Believing such perceptions are unimportant can be unwise; recall PM David Cameron's off-mic remark in 2015 ahead of a speech in Leeds: 'We just thought people in Yorkshire hated everyone else,' he said. 'We didn't realise they hated each other so much.'

If DevoManc was hashed out in Manchester and London, its tender shoots were nurtured in Wigan. The borough was not only the back-door bolt that held Greater Manchester together, it appeared to be a local back channel for the ambitious Burnham, whose Leigh constituency was in Smith's fiefdom (indeed his title was Baron Smith of Leigh, ennobled in 1999 for his services to local government). Splitting his week between Wigan and the House of Lords, the council leader took regular midweek meetings with Burnham. Smith and Burnham's relationship is contested. Locals such as long-time Wigan councillor Chris Read talk of a supportive mentor dynamic, with Smith aiding Burnham's MP constituency selection and prepping him for a DevoManc mayoral poll – despite the nasty hiccup when his 2015 Labour leadership forced vote-seeking Burnham into declaring his fears for a 'Swiss cheese NHS' in a devolved health service. It went down badly in The City, and personal and policy tensions still exist between high-level players. 'They couldn't stand each other,' says one. 'Peter thought Burnham wasn't serious and that he was the playboy of the

Greater Manchester jigsaw (above) Lord Peter Smith and Daniel Dobson-Mouwad bottom
far left and in media coverage (below) bottom right

western world.' Burnham spins the discs at DJ sets in Northern Quarter bars;
austere, high-minded Smith might be spinning in his grave. One local MP says,
'Peter helped Andy at the start but things cooled when he thought Andy as an
MP didn't deliver for Wigan.' When Smith retired in 2019, Burnham described
Smith as 'a great friend and mentor' and Leese called him 'the glue that held
Greater Manchester together'. Smith accompanied Leese and the impressively
young Trafford Tory leader Sean Anstee to hear George Osborne spell the
DevoManc deal out. Reportedly, with an eye on governance propriety, Smith
asked for the elected post to be called 'leader' not 'mayor', but Osborne was
having none of that politically correct language. Mayors are intended to excite
the interest of people who have lost faith in politics, and the title carries with it

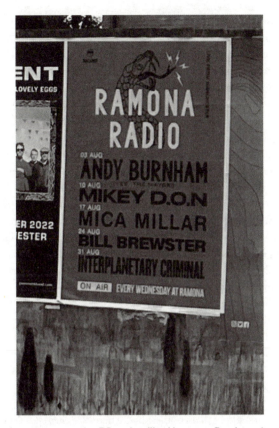

Ramona bar poster promoting DJ sets headlined by mayor Burnham, August 2022

the tabloid ring of the big-city boss, even if Burnham is a mayor whose wings are clipped in comparison to his London equivalent, as the big decisions must be agreed by him and all ten council leaders.

Lord Smith stood down as leader in 2018 and died in 2021. That low-income Wigan should be the custodian of the resurgent Northern soul of self-governing politics is no surprise to those who understand its tradition. Wigan's story includes George Orwell, whose 'pier' was a hoary old music-hall joke at the time of his 1930s account of the Northern mining town, as the original was just a coal-loading jetty on the Leeds and Liverpool Canal.

Even now, Wigan is a byword for Northern nowheresville. Yet Wigan's famous children show that provincial stereotypes do injustice to its more sophisticated nature. Quite apart from its legend as the lodestar of Northern Soul, it has produced Georgie Fame, Buzzcock Pete Shelley, radio presenter Shaun Keaveny, photographer and film director Elaine Constantine, and Richard Ashcroft and The Verve. Seeking an even higher brow? I give you playwright Colin (*Kes*) Welland (an Oscar winner for *Chariots of Fire*), political thinker Paul Mason, writer-broadcaster Stuart Maconie, not to mention the life-affirming story of poet Lemn Sissay, though it is one which taints its institutions. 'If Prince came from Wigan he'd have been slaughtered by now,' Morrissey told me in a 1985 interview, 'in England they're always ready to pull your trousers down and slap your bum.' Prince did not of course hail from the town, but in the evolving push towards self-determination for nations, regions and cities, generations to come may be thankful that a different Smith from Morrissey did. For that, respect is due to the stalwart devolutionary Lord Smith. 'He was not a people person,' says Read. 'But he could sell the room with the big idea, that if Wigan weren't in the game, we didn't have a voice.' Many describe him as shy but direct and articulate when required; GM council leaders undertook psychometric tests, which found that Smith was the only one with strong convening skills.

We can safely say: no Wigan, no DevoManc. Lord Smith was to consistently argue that, if Wigan paid towards the Manchester city region's tourism, promotion and inward investment, its star would rise along with the Manchester mothership. Granted, relatively few tourists would arrive at the 'cultural destination' of Wigan's Orwell-related locations. They could not pay homage any longer to the enduring legend of the demolished Casino, the 1970s flowering of a transatlantic blue-collar brotherhood where working-class Northern kids danced all night to music from American smokestack cities forsaken in its homeland.

There was a far greater prize at stake. Growing international visitor numbers across the entire city region helped fill the ten council coffers, a process boosted by a second airport runway in 2001. Manchester Airports Group (MAG) is the zenith of British municipal entrepreneurialism, being part-owned by the ten councils, Manchester holding the largest stake. Today the city owns 35.5 per cent and the other nine authorities own just over 3.2 per cent each. MAG was formed in 2000 and became a cash machine for twenty years, swelled by acquiring East Midlands and Stansted airports. Over the two decades of growth, Manchester council received dividends of £473.08 million and the other nine councils almost £41 million each. Nine years of successive revenue growth was stopped in its tracks by Covid-19 in 2020, but the impressive MAG profits helped fund the so-called 'Manchester family' of agencies and other projects across the city region. The income sweetened the pill for any borough councillors dumb enough to think about rocking the Manchester family boat, helping to end traditional petty bickering and showing the way towards devolution. It could also be said that the arrangement lent The City what academics call 'meta-governance' – in this case, a measure of influence, if not control, over the other councils beyond the city of Manchester's borders.

Since 1999, the ten councils had signed up to working together to harness the airport's growing benefits through agencies Marketing Manchester for tourism and MIDAS for investment. This was in effect a takeover, a process of co-opting the whole of Greater Manchester to identify as 'Manchester'. Mere fluff, you might think, if you're a stranger. But mark these sentiments from a senior Rochdale public executive around the turn of the millennium: 'I am not a Mancunian, I am a Rochdalian … If you said to a Rochdalian that the city centre of Manchester dominated their lives they'd slit your throat. So you must be careful.' This was a person tasked with bringing 'the locals' into the city region fold, as part of an exercise asking all 2.7 million of the wider conurbation to consider themselves citizens of 'Manchester'. An unmissable (pre-Peter Saville) manifestation of this were giant advertising totems, metal 'M's 40 feet high installed at both ends of the city's elevated Mancunian Way urban motorway, which left visitors in no doubt that the empire they were entering was ruled by the mighty 'M'.

The challenge for local politicians outside Manchester was for the process not to tip over into coercion. Across the ten councils, when it came to facing the world, discipline was maintained, oiled by airport dividends. As a senior civil servant told *The Guardian* anonymously in 2015: 'It's like a sausage factory up there: you don't want to know what goes on inside.' Governments over the decades recognised that Greater Manchester had leaders who could sit down and look national politicians and officials in the eye, credibly presenting themselves as the architects of an ever-strengthening machine with a track record of economic achievement.

The voluntary association of the ten councils, AGMA, was superseded by the Greater Manchester Combined Authority (GMCA) in April 2011, the first of its kind in the UK. The evolving co-operation laid the ground for devolution by showing government that Greater Manchester had proved it could deliver. Now it wanted more power over its own destiny.

The City was knocking on government's door, and it was already ajar. A plan for city mayors had been brought forward towards the end of the Blair

Manchester 'M' (photos: Aidan O'Rourke)

government, and the 2010 Conservative–Lib Dem coalition also backed the idea, granting elections for city mayors in 11 large cities in 2011. The view from a nervous Manchester leadership was that we were doing well enough, thank you, and did not need this unwanted innovation; the Manchester referendum result of 47 per cent for and 53 per cent against (on a 25 per cent turnout) was tighter than expected. An equivalent poll in Salford the next year voted for a mayor by a slim margin. The direction of travel was set, and it morphed into the city region mayor model, imposed by the Conservative government with no referendum.

Chancellor George Osborne, MP for the affluent Cheshire constituency of Tatton (home to many of Manchester's wealthier commuters), was the unlikely provider of the agreement to go much further than governments of any colour before, not just by imposing the mayoral model on the city region, but by granting historic new powers to the original modern city. In August 2016, six months before he retired from politics, I chanced upon him at a late summer fête in the rural fringes of his patch, at Crag Hall near Wildboarclough, in the estate of the Earl of Derby. He strolled about chatting with close friend the Earl, a four-strong close-protection detail in their weapons-concealing Barbour jackets a discreet distance away. Osborne is often described as pale. Even at the end of the summer, his near-transparent pallor was disturbing. In the nearby Labour heartlands, he was the much-despised architect of economic austerity; now, contrary to that reputation, and indeed to his undead demeanour, he was busy pumping new lifeblood into a Northern city that many in his ideological tribe saw, quite mistakenly, as a citadel of red-hot socialism.

20

Devolution and dissent

We want our city back.

Sir Howard Bernstein, *The Guardian*,
12 February 2015

When Chancellor Osborne's offer of Manchester's devolution was made public in 2014, the Labour Party called Sir Richard Leese to ask him to publicly reject it. The city's leader replied with a curt two-word response. This was revealed in Simon Jenkins's long read in *The Guardian* in February 2015 about the DevoManc deal, which drew back the veil in mouth-watering detail on how deep the Manchester–Conservative relationship went. Making positive noises off were Lord Heseltine and native son Jim later Lord O'Neill, the Goldman Sachs economist and Treasury minister. With PM Cameron's consent, Osborne sidelined the rest of his party and all in Whitehall, bar some handpicked civil servants, to get the mission over the line.

Jenkins likened Osborne and Bernstein to mafia bosses carving up territories. Stephen Hall, president of Greater Manchester TUC, said that the process had made 'a complete mockery of democracy'. What was jaw-dropping for the in-the-know witnesses to the willing surrender of state power was the degree of raw Treasury muscle exercised on Manchester's behalf. Papers were restricted in circulation and, when released for others to sign off, stamped 'with the chancellor's approval'. Manchester's sherpa was Mike Emmerich, then head of the Greater Manchester think tank New Economy, a former Downing Street and Treasury official. (Proving once more that civic renaissance is about culture as well as business, this lover of serious classical music is an evangelist for the city's self-made classes to support its beaux arts, and in 2019 revived Manchester Baroque by funding performances of seventeenth-century music at St Ann's Church.)

In 2017 Sir Howard Bernstein, now a portfolio man with Deloitte and the University of Manchester, was free of the diplomacy expected of the city's top official. He told *The Guardian* of Labour's reaction to the city's self-reliant entrepreneurialism: 'Because of our pragmatism in working with a Conservative government, particularly during the late 80s and early 90s … "Well, you sold out to the Tories" … John Prescott spent most of his life telling me that on a daily basis … "Manchester should be punished for working with the Conservatives."'

The Labour council and the Conservative government made strange bedfellows, but this was after all a long-running affair. Not for the first time was a different game played out behind a Punch and Judy show of political conflict. The City's dealings with Labour and its London biases had always felt like pushing water uphill, yet fraternisation from the redesign of Hulme through to the IRA bomb reconstruction had seen Tory ministers consistently plough money into Manchester. Bernstein told Jenkins that Osborne knew the existing model was not working: 'By 2014 he could read the tea leaves: Scottish devolution, the NHS and social care, skills, criminal justice, he looks at it all and sees it is bust.' Osborne believed 'SHB' had shown mature leadership and always looked to create opportunity rather than whinge and plead. The respect in Downing Street for Manchester's leadership was off the chart. Osborne described Bernstein as 'the star of British local government and frankly I can't think of anyone who comes close to him'.

When the devolution deal was signed in November 2014, it was a blizzard of Christmasses coming early. The city region was being given control of transport, planning, housing and economic growth, plus the £500 million budget for further education and skills training. It would, too, be the first place in the nation where local health and social care budgets and services would be fully integrated – a £6 billion budget, a £2 billion cut from the former model. So complex was the challenge of creating a new joined-up system of health and social care that Bernstein joked privately that Manchester had thought about handing that one back. With the coronavirus pandemic's merciless effect of exposing the weakness in England's care homes and hospitals, the importance of the 'Manchester model' has become greater than ever and is being monitored as a pathfinder by government, and viewed with interest by Harvard University.

Osborne doubled down on the goodies from the state money tree. The chancellor greenlighted Bernstein's audacious HS3 bid, approved a Metrolink tram extension to the airport, funded the huge £250 million Rutherford materials science centre, and, with a final flourish, gifted £78 million for an arts centre which was first jokingly referred to as The Factory between him and Bernstein in private conversation. The name soon became nailed on. In December 2014, when Osborne made his parliamentary address confirming DevoManc, the *Manchester Evening News* front page proclaimed, 'We Are All Winners Now'.

There was no dancing in the streets. Even today, most citizens would be hard pressed to describe any ways in which devolution has changed their lives. The government has put HS3 on ice. The Factory emerges slowly, resembling a gigantic beetle, with occasional bulletins about its rising costs. The legal tangle around reregulating buses means that basic need is only finally coming into view after a court ruling paved the way for the combined authority to control routes, fares and operators. Yet DevoManc posed questions which embraced both serious politics and popular culture. Had Bernstein and Leese managed to fire up Wilson's dream of getting London off Manchester's back? Could the link between local tax powers and self-governance – rejected out of hand by Labour's Tony Blair and John Prescott – take a great leap forward under Tory rule? Some in government concede that the devolutionary genie cannot be put back in the bottle. Leese went on record to boldly proclaim, 'Our ultimate ambition is for full devolution of all public spending in Greater Manchester', eyeing the city region's entire £22 billion of state spending. Another question was raised: whatever would the colourful cast of flaky misfits and revolutionaries behind the Factory and Haçienda make of the nation's rulers hosing public money at their city in a bid, so it seemed, to create more of the special sauce they had cooked up in their counter-culture lab?

Manchester city council announced the retirement of its chief executive in autumn 2016. Bernstein, the city's top civil servant who had joined as tea boy and gofer 45 years earlier, departed as a knighted regeneration star. A charity dinner in his honour was attended by city grandees in the town hall, the Gothic palace's exterior lit blue for his football team Manchester City. It had been an extraordinary rise which marked the impact of one man's ability and drive writ large across his home city in real physical change – in bricks and mortar, steel and glass, jobs and investment, as well national and worldwide profile and respect.

The overlaying of the powerful city authority by new Greater Manchester mayor Burnham was not without friction. Though invisible to the public, political cultures clashed behind the scenes. Bernstein's people let it be known that, as one told me, 'Andy doesn't seem to appreciate the Manchester partnership way of doing things.' While at the launch of new hotel Mamucium in 2019, council leader Leese told me, a full two years into the mayoral system, 'Andy is finally understanding that you don't just put out a press release saying you're going to do something, but you discuss it with people first.'

Many frustrations focussed on Burnham's Westminster special adviser Kevin Lee, a former public affairs consultant and ardent Manchester United fan who continued to commute to Westminster throughout his parliamentary career, returning to his home in Prestwich at weekends. Lee led Burnham's election campaign and afterwards emerged as his stern gatekeeper, stymying the property world figures wanting the ear of the new city region boss. Urban Splash's Tom Bloxham had Bernstein and Leese on speed dial, but with Burnham, he told me, the city's business community moaned about 'the Kevin problem'. Westminster-style command and control was the only way these returning Northerners knew, and it was clear that there was no open door to some established property business leaders in the new regime.

Commentators began sniffing for clues to who was taking over the reins of power now that the city council was outmuscled in executive reach by Burnham's Greater Manchester authority. There was the air of a wrangle over which was the dominant power now, the city council or the wider ten-council city region. As when any strongman leaves the scene, the fear factor which once limited open discussion began to break down.

In September 2016 a column in *Manchester Confidential* tiptoed into sensitive territory. The online news and lifestyle website has been a consistent platform for the staunchly independent views of city observer Jonathan Schofield. He wrote: 'Some in the city will also see Sir Howard's retirement as an opportunity to create a situation in which the Town Hall not only listens to intelligent criticism but responds to it. There has been a feeling amongst some in the city that there's an autocratic element to the way power, certainly over development, seems bilaterally shared between the Leader and the Chief Executive offices, with secondary input from the private sector but not necessarily from the general public, no matter how wise their comments are. Manchester's public consultations have become a byword for being empty of meaning.'

He continued: 'As a writer and commentator on the city I've had conversations with architects, entrepreneurs and others about how nothing goes ahead without a Town Hall nod. There are rumours of commercial favourites, of cosy relationships. Nobody will go on record to say anything, of course … Perhaps, after such a long time, such rumours are inevitable. Perhaps the point is that the Bernstein/Leese axis approach works. It delivers.'

The column reflected a changing weather system. Developers were used to local difficulties around their plans being ironed out in a mix of private meetings and public consultations, arrangements which had brought Manchester so much physical change since the IRA bomb twenty years before. Now things were changing. One controversial scheme became the pivot for shifting sentiment. In March 2017 I received a voicemail from footballer-turned-entrepreneur Gary Neville. His plans to build a luxury hotel, offices and residential development in the heart of the city had run into trouble, and he wanted PR to help him turn the tide of public sentiment. Funded by Singapore stockbroker and investor Peter Lim, the St Michael's scheme was designed to transform the 1.5 acre site on Jackson's Row, just off historic Albert Square and Manchester Town Hall. Neville promised to bring 'a world-class, mixed use development … a 200-bed, 5 star brand international hotel, 153 high quality apartments, a brand new Grade A office building and ground floor and rooftop retail and leisure units'.

His plan was for two towers of 31 and 21 storeys linked by a split-level public plaza, two 'sky bars' and a shopping centre, all aimed at tourists and wealthy residents. The plan pushed all the wrong buttons for many, attracting strong and widespread opposition, not only to the towers so close to the Victorian heart of the city, but because it would wipe away the now-vacant Bootle Street police station and the Sir Ralph Abercromby pub – an unremarkable hostelry but reputed to be where wounded protesters in the 1819 Peterloo Massacre had been carried.

After an honours-laden career, the ex-Manchester United and England full-back had risen to prominence as a Sky Sports TV pundit whose straight-talking style impressed even Manchester City fans. But when he announced his plans in July 2016 without anticipating much push back, Neville was widely viewed as a tasteless ex-footballer teaming up with a Far East billionaire to trample over hallowed Manchester heritage. After taking a beating in local and national media and on social media channels, Neville paused the plans. Government body Historic England's view was that it would cause substantial harm to the city's heritage, and in those circumstances the plans would never get passed by Manchester City Council.

Of course, all planning applications had to jump through the requisite hoops of public consultation and pass suitability tests before getting the green light. Councils assess all information provided, including the kind of economic impact studies provided by the likes of Deloitte consultants which, for Neville's scheme, estimated an £80 million added-value contribution to the local economy, £147m million in government tax revenues over ten years, and nearly fifteen hundred new jobs in the development. These reports are part and parcel of any new plans going before councils, although I have never met a single person who fully believes such projections.

A local authority whose leaders prioritised jobs and investment could make all the difference to where a billionaire's footloose cash might be invested. Certainly, 'SHB' was celebrated in the property community for his willingness to chat over a cup of tea in the Midland Hotel as early as 7am with potential investors. This approach was unusual among the highest rank of local government official. Developers working in Liverpool, a city with similar regeneration aspirations, could not expect any such high-level liaison. In 2002, Warren Smith, who for LPC Living had transformed two run-down tower blocks in Liverpool into key-worker flats, compared his experiences. 'I can see Howard for breakfast in the Midland any time I need to, but when I write a polite letter to Liverpool council's chief executive, I don't even get a reply,' fumed Smith, a man who as Greater Manchester's Lord Lieutenant, was not unused to dining with the Queen and Prince Philip on their visits North.

Would the Neville plans, paused just as Bernstein was departing, be a tower too far? This was a key moment for the property sector. How would the scheme fare in the absence of an apparently omnipotent city boss who had overseen remarkable transformation during his tenure? Neville's plan was, for some, a sign that developers had too much of the upper hand, with a growing body of opinion furious at the lack of affordable or social housing in the city centre. Those mistaking Neville for a flash and uncaring ball-kicker had got him wrong, I discovered. His plan was an unashamed bid to bring international money and visitors to the city, and he was sincere in his belief that Manchester people would also want to enjoy the restaurants, bars and shops.

In business affairs Neville is a one-man northern powerhouse. He was on the consortium behind the 2014 takeover of non-league Salford City FC. He owns a hospitality company with former team-mate Ryan Giggs, which opened restaurants in Manchester and Leeds, building the £24 million, 133-bed Hotel Football next to the Old Trafford ground, in the face of opposition from his former employer. With the same dogged industriousness that he displayed on the pitch, Neville is on a mission to help young people into work, and launched UA92 vocational university in Trafford. While still with United, he was a partner in a property services firm and educated himself in sustainable building techniques. He tried to create a futuristic, underground eco-home outside Bolton for his family, powered by wind turbines. Mocked by the media as a Teletubbies house, it became mired in planning wrangles and he put the land up for sale.

Neville lives by the adage 'Attack the Day', drilled into him by his father Neville Neville, who ran Bury FC as a lifetime labour of love. The macho family motto appears in foot-high letters on the wall as you enter Neville's Knott Mill offices and not for nothing is his property firm named Relentless. He partnered with Lim, who has taken stakes in many of his ventures, one being the 2015 purchase of the city's Stock Exchange for a boutique hotel, with a restaurant by TV chef Tom Kerridge in the domed marble interior of the 1904 Grade 2 listed building. During its fit-out in the winter of 2015–16, a group of homeless people squatted in the grandiose Edwardian Baroque building. Neville was moved to explore their plight in detail, making intelligent media contributions to the issue which had become a major humanitarian and image problem for the city. In March 2020, Neville and Giggs closed their two Manchester hotels in the pandemic and offered the rooms to NHS staff for free.

Somehow during 2016, with all his business projects on, he had spent four volatile months as the manager of Valencia FC in Spain. He was parachuted in by the owner Lim, and then left by mutual consent after an awful run of results, the home crowd chanting 'Gary Vete Ya!' – Gary Go Now! Being around his restless energy was draining. He sucked the oxygen out of the room with his non-stop unfiltered monologues and he exhausted relationships too, changing architects half-way through 2017, from London's MAKE to Manchester's Hodder Associates. A third architect took over in 2018, though Hodder was still attached.

Being around hyperactive Neville is a full-on, caffeinated experience. In 2017, he would turn up in the morning with new configurations for apartments he had drawn overnight on his i-pad and then get his architect to flesh them out. The 8am meeting would be followed by back-to-back sessions, all carried out at breakneck speed. Even a coffee at Piccolino was a rushed conversation before he paid the bill and dashed off to the next thing. Neville seemed to leave very little time for careful consideration of what was discussed at the previous meeting, or enough time to reflect and hear others' views about the ramifications of his decisions.

Anyone visiting Bootle Street and Jackson's Row could see how a property developer could view the narrow old streets and the police station site as a wasted asset, ripe for transformation. Only yards from some of the busiest streets of the city, its use was mainly for parking meters. Neville saw it as disused and unwelcoming, yet a Situationist practising a psycho-geographic *dérive* might see these as some of the more interesting areas in the city centre. There are glimpses of the layers of urban evolution, from the ghost signage of the

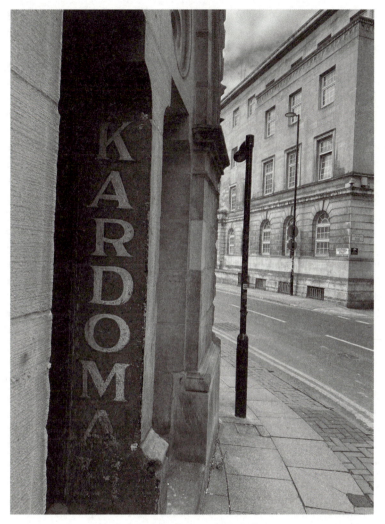

Former Kardomah café, Southmill Street junction with Jackson's Row
(photo: Andy Spinoza)

long-lost Kardomah café in the side doorway of the Fountain House pub, to
the synagogue at the Deansgate end of Jackson's Row. The muscular bulk of
the city centre's former cop shop yields on to a forbidding courtyard and yawning doorways, and we can add the Peterloo legend of the pub (supposedly also

inspiration for the 1970s boozer in TV series *Life on Mars*). As far as the public mood was concerned, this was a characterful pocket of town and, to use a football analogy, Neville had gone in recklessly with his studs up.

This was one game though, as property owner and developer, in which he could not be sent off the field of play. And when he returned to the action, the statement he hired me to place in the media stressed he was now keeping the legendary pub 'in recognition of its emotional importance to the community', and retaining the former police-station frontage. Perhaps most importantly for planning approval, he now offered a single tower, rather than the original two. Stirling Prize-winner Hodder's new design, for a narrow-waisted lozenge-shaped tower in the International style, was two metres lower than the previous plan's highest point.

Historic England was mollified, but a new public consultation flushed out some unlikely opposition. Alongside the local history and conservation groups and affordable-housing champions were some of the highest-altitude residents in the city. Both objectors were seasoned property veterans, and both lived in nearby high towers. Lesley Chalmers was the former chief of public-private developer English Cities Fund and lived in the 25-storey, slope-roofed Great Northern Tower less than a hundred yards from Neville's site. Ian Simpson was the Beetham Tower architect who bagged the 47th and 48th floor duplex in his own creation on nearby Deansgate. Simpson was featured in glossy magazines about his penthouse, filled with Scandinavian and Italian furniture and glassware and thirty olive trees. He was for a time living in the highest apartment not only in the city but in the country. 'I'm an architect by training but I am contributing to the regeneration of a place,' he said in 2016, 'I just see myself of the equivalent of an artist or musician.' This was not thought to be a reference to the high-pitched whistle made when strong winds hit the thin steel blade atop the south face of the tower, causing recording hassles on the nearby Coronation Street set in 2007, and forcing remedial work on what had become a giant tuning fork.

Chalmers's petition against the scheme gained 3,750 signatures, and Simpson caused a stir at one of Neville's public consultations in 2017. City-centre residents gathered round as he held forth on how he would have done things differently. The issue for both complainants was that the tower, despite now being lower, was simply too close to the revered town hall. However, for me, there was an unmistakably comic smell of NIMBYism, or perhaps in this case 'not in my back sky'. People in glass skyscrapers …

My relationship with Neville ended brusquely, after a disagreement about PR tactics. He rejected my view on how he planned to present results of a public consultation. 'I have never seen such an unprofessional email in my life. If you have an opinion you consult me first … Please stand down.' As one property consultant said to me: 'Gary very much values the views of his consultants – as long as they agree with his own.'

The government did not block St Michael's and the development is under construction. There was a feeling that the controversy around it meant schemes were more vulnerable to challenge since Bernstein's departure, and as his replacement Joanne Roney was expected to focus on child social care and education, areas that remained stubbornly unimproved during her predecessor's time, a weakness finally showing signs of turnaround with a 2022 Ofsted rating of 'good' for its children's services, eight years after they were found to be 'inadequate'.

St Michael's was not the only scheme to face greater resistance than before. A loose coalition of shrill anti-development views could be heard getting challenges in. One strident voice was that of Manchester Shield, a campaign led by psychotherapist Adam Prince, a city-centre resident and self-appointed guardian of urban design. This self-described 'little piranha in a big pool' could be relied upon to object hyperbolically to any scheme which did not meet his own views, which was almost all of them. Reporter Jonathan Schofield noted he was 'not everybody's cup of tea, rather their mug of arsenic'.

Prince's poisonous social-media rants scared enough developers to invite him inside their tents. The Kampus scheme asked him into detailed discussion, and he was encouraged to input his community-minded thoughts for London Road Fire Station, an Edwardian Baroque gem fallen into a lamentable state under Britannia Hotels before its rescue by Allied London. The Mayfield scheme in the derelict expanse next to Piccadilly rail station also allowed Prince and friends an 'Imaginarium' to sketch out visions for the site.

In 2016, concerned at Peel Holdings' plans for waterfront flats at Pomona Docks, Prince contrasted its official vision to 'create sustainable environments' with a photo of swans swimming through surface dreck: 'Sadness at Pomona. Not only have all trees been destroyed by Peel Holdings … seeing Swans nest in trash, is doubly heartbreaking and shows how the Manchester "green rhetoric" is only that. Empty rheotic [sic].' Though many of his three thousand Twitter followers were nervous property people, Prince's small band thrilled to his outrageous claims, such as: 'In Manchester under one autocratic, technocratic, disingenuous, #fauxsultation culture, not only are people not valued, transparency refused.' Prince left Manchester in 2019 to an almost audible sigh of relief from the city council.

Yet Prince's hyperbole did catch a wider public mood. In March 2018, a *Place North West* property forum for three hundred delegates was the scene of an extraordinary exchange. Senior planning officer Dave Roscoe, a familiar figure at MIPIM alongside Bernstein, was widely surmised to wield great influence in city planning matters, and, if that was true, much of the look of the new Manchester would stem from his officers' support for new developments. A delegate asked Roscoe whether Manchester would still be using 'favoured architects' to deliver city-centre projects following Bernstein's exit. The unsaid that was frequently discussed in private had finally been aired in public. A tense silence followed. Perfect strangers made eye contact among the rows of seating, raising eyebrows. Others simply sat with mouths gaping open. Roscoe firstly sat upright in umbrage, and, as *Place North West* reported, 'dismissed the idea that the council had favoured practices', stating that it had 'no control whatsoever over who people choose to use as architects or planning consultants'. Then, calmer, he expressed the view that it was the council's responsibility to ensure that the buildings were of the highest design quality. The culture of silence in the Bernstein era was melting away.

In March 2017 as Bernstein was packing his boxes to leave the town hall, *Place North West* editor Paul Unger made his way to Room 212, 'the physical centre of a web of power which stretches across the north-west' as described by *North West Business Insider* magazine, which regularly ranked 'SHB' number one in its annual Northwest Power 100. Undaunted, Unger put to Bernstein his property-sector reader sentiment: 'We hear a lot from readers and privately among property professionals about you working with a set group of people on major city centre projects such as Ian Simpson on architecture and Deloitte on planning. What would you say in response to those comments?'

Bernstein: 'I don't think Ian's designed every building in the city, or at least I'm not aware he has. Ian's designed a number because he's one of the country's and indeed Europe's leading design practices. There's a whole range of different architects and indeed some of the letters I've received over the past few weeks from a whole array of architects wishing me well and thanking me for the support I've given them. London practices, international practices. OMA designing The Factory is the latest example. So I wouldn't believe all you read or what the impressions are.'

Unger: 'So there's never any pressure on developers to use a certain architect or planning practice?'

Bernstein: 'Why would I say to a developer "I think you should use X or Y architect?" Most of the time developers come in with their chosen architect.'

Unger, whose research found that 80 per cent of major city-centre planning applications listed Deloitte as adviser, pressed again: 'And in terms of using Deloitte as the favoured town planner?' Bernstein: 'Well we have a framework ... It's horses for courses.'

Surely if the same few companies repeatedly won work on big property schemes, went the official line, that was a simple matter of developer choice? Property professionals, however, had anecdotes to the contrary. In 2018, a developer who had emerged from a meeting with senior council planners to discuss his plans for a new Manchester hotel told me, 'I can't believe what I've just heard. I've just been told that I have to drop my architect and use one of three named firms.'

When meeting Bernstein, journalist Michael Taylor described him as the country's most pre-eminent example of 'a new class of civic politician and city official prepared to think differently to get what they need. They use European initiatives, lottery funding, cultural funding and regeneration budgets, they cosy up to the buccaneers of the private property sector to fund capital projects that improve their cities in their own image.' Taylor noted that 'He has an aura and an intensity to him that makes his arguments, his vision and his purpose all the more compelling ... But if he was a politician, would you vote for him?' Taylor was let known that this observation was not well received. It was well made, however, because Bernstein was not a politician, and as a civil servant he enjoyed the public mandate not from the electorate but from his own 'boss', council leader Leese.

Their partnership as 'The City' made Manchester a fine-tuned machine focused on gobbling up opportunities. Some of the most spectacular wins can be seen in east Manchester. After the 2002 Games, its stadium (later Manchester City FC's home) created a wave of development. From 2001 a new urban regeneration company, New East Manchester, stimulated activity. Apartments and a large ASDA went up alongside the ground, along with a stunning 53 m high, 1,000-tonne sculpture by Manchester Polytechnic alumnus Thomas Heatherwick. The 180 steel spikes expressed the explosive force of an athletics starting pistol. 'The B of the Bang', the UK's tallest sculpture, made an exciting statement in 2005 about the area's momentum. But in 2009, the much-loved landmark was taken down after sections of spikes fell off or came loose, risking making passing City fans into human kebabs. After a court wrangle about liability, the core was melted down for £17,000 scrap and the spikes remain in storage. Heatherwick's palpable sorrow over The City's lack of resolve to fix a solvable problem is expressed by his iPhone wallpaper – a photo of the sculpture.

Another prize exhibit is a business park in nearby Newton Heath, which boasts the most dramatic and eye-catching tram stop in the country. Resembling a giant science-fiction insect, a great copper-turned-verdigris roof is held up by slender steel ribs. This is the Central Park 'transport interchange' on a 450-acre council-owned estate to which Greater Manchester Police relocated in 2010. Over two-thirds of the £36.5 million landmark structure was funded by government and European funds, while Greater Manchester contributed £11 million. Completed in 2005, it would be seven years before Metrolink rails ran through it, and today it stands as a striking but underused bus and tram hub much driven past by police officers on the way to their HQ car park.

Another testament to the city's powers of strategic form-filling and political persuasion exists as part of today's Etihad Campus of sports facilities, run by partnerships of the council, sports bodies and Manchester City. The £10 million Connell College for sixteen-to-nineteen–year-olds opened there in 2013 with the aim of raising educational standards in an area of low attainment. It is today run by the Co-op Academies Trust, the set-up cash having come through the Free School funding stream pet project of then education minister Michael Gove. It was unsurprisingly not something publicised locally that the Tory alternative to state schools was flowering in the Labour heartland. This pragmatism brought to mind something Tony Wilson recounted after visiting China in the late 1980s. 'The Chinese have a phrase,' he told everyone who would listen. 'It's not important whether the cat is black or white, it only needs to catch the mouse.' Manchester was being led by mouse-catchers *extraordinaire*.

In April 2017, the week after his last day at the city council, Deloitte announced that Bernstein was joining its strategic advisory team, a part-time role to support the consultancy's global growth plans, and it was stressed that his role would not take in local real estate. *Place North West* commented that 'the appointment will raise eyebrows across the property sector …'. Not for nothing was 'SHB' known for being, ran the joke at MIPIM, 'a property developer disguised as a town clerk – and not very well disguised, either'.

Architecture critic Owen Hatherley describes many of Manchester's new buildings as 'pseudomodern', damning them as handmaiden to rapacious forces which do little to improve the lives or life chances of the majority, 'neoliberalism with a human face'. By contrast, the Civil Justice Centre in Spinningfields has won admirers, not least Hatherley himself. Sir Richard Leese described it as his favourite new building in Manchester upon opening it in 2017, and says it still is. Designed by Melbourne's Denton Corker Marshall, Leese's snub to home-grown architects is pointed because, for once, the city council was nowhere near its creation, the client being Her Majesty's Courts Service, meaning that the process was entirely unbothered by the usual ways of Manchester procurement.

I had invited the design guru Stephen Bayley to a pre-opening visit of this ingenious building, nicknamed 'the filing cabinet' for its irregular, cantilevered floors in a Mondrian-redolent colour scheme. Unfortunately for an architecture writer, Bayley suffers from severe vertigo, but he bravely managed the views from the tenth floor and *The Observer* headlined his review: 'What a perfect place to get divorced.' The former creative boss of the Design Museum applies a simple test 'that if a building enhances your mood or excites curiosity, then it has real quality that transcends style'. He agreed with Leese. The nation's first major court complex for more than a century was a radical and exhilarating piece of work, 'certainly Manchester's best'.

In 2018 the Bernstein and Leese era came under the cold-eyed scrutiny of Professor Karel Williams and colleagues at the Alliance Manchester Business School, who identified a 'golden circle' of ten property companies developing most residential schemes in the city centre, and questioned developer-led regeneration designed to attract the young professional 'urban monoculture of private rented blocks'. In the unsparing analysis-cum-polemic, the AMBS academics accused Manchester of running a neo-liberal economic regime in plain sight, calling time on 'the 30-year experiment in regeneration for competitive success', commenting acidly that 'Developer regeneration has produced an expanding new town in the centre whose shiny external appearance impresses London journalists on a day return rail ticket. But it offers very little to most Greater Manchester citizens beyond more choice of city-region shopping destination, a Saturday night in the centre or a holiday flight from the airport.' It was not a lone blast. The Manchester academic Paul Kennedy gave vivid expression to this critique in his 2019 book *Vampire Capitalism*. The proffering of the city's welcome mat to unfettered private capital, he believed, sucked the wealth from cities like Manchester and reinvested little, as profits went abroad or were untaxed offshore. For solutions, Williams proposed a return to 1945 NHS-style principles of universalism, with improved accountability to the public using new, experimental governance structures. Without such a change, he concluded, Greater Manchester's future 'could be decided by local elite conversations between confident private developers and amenable town halls in Manchester and Salford'.

If that seemed an overstatement, on Bernstein's retirement, Allied London chief Mike Ingall, the developer whose firm received a (subsequently repaid) city

council bail-out after the 2008 crash to save his paralysed Spinningfields development, paid tribute: 'In partnership Sir Richard Leese and Sir Howard Bernstein
have created a city that has not just opened its doors, but actively gone out and
encouraged a private sector, with a similar vision, to walk through them.' In his
no-filter style, Ingall continued, 'People involved in those partnerships will know
the marked difference Sir Howard makes to key projects. There is never a time
in the day or night Sir Howard has not been available when I have called.'

Ingall planned luxury towers at St John's on the old Granada site but his idea
did not get off the ground. Other luxury skyscrapers were sprouting, however,
overlooking areas of deprivation. It wasn't the dizzy height of the 36-storey
Angel Gardens that provoked nausea in 2019. On the city-centre fringe, next
to the Co-op's HQ, Apache Capital, a UK and Middle East investment firm,
targeted high-end renters with the promise of a five-a-side rooftop football
pitch, a state-of-the-art gym and mini-cinema. Other perks include Uber credit,
cookery classes, free use of co-working space and private party dining area. 'In
what sense are they going to be Mancunians?' asked Piccadilly councillor Sam
Wheeler, concerned that the tower block would be 'hermetically sealed off'
from the city around it. As the 466 apartments started at £900 per month for a
studio, the question arose: how many locals could afford to live there?

Wheeler was the left-wing spearhead for councillor unhappiness at 'the
Manchester's miracle', calling it in the *Morning Star* 'a Faustian pact', listing the
conditions which the revival hardly touched – 'the second worst life expectancy
in England after Blackpool, the second worst rate of child poverty in England
after Tower Hamlets, wages that have fallen since 2002 and 15,000 families on
its housing waiting list'. He added, 'Some might call those revolutionary conditions.' Wheeler acknowledged that, for all Manchester's political radicalism, the
forces of business always seemed to win out: 'The history of Manchester shows
that, just as the city creates revolutionaries, it is equally adept at breaking them.'

The remarkable changes in the city overseen by Bernstein and Leese could
never have been achieved without a politics stabilised by ironclad leadership.
In a 2015 dissection of DevoManc in the *Financial Times*, John McDermott
observed that 'there is something almost Chinese about the way Manchester is
run'. David Thame's online column in April 2021 said: 'A super-sized group of
91 Labour councillors – the largest Labour council group in the country – are
largely spectators, rather than participants, in the big decisions.'

In neighbouring Salford, Paul Dennett won the vote for the city's mayor in
2016. An out gay man from a low-income upbringing in Warrington, he came
to know his adopted city well, where poverty means politics has a hard edge;

in its 2012 mayoral election, one candidate was Paul Massey, a pre-eminent gangland figure and one of the mobsters who had caused mayhem at the Haçienda. 'Mr Big', as the local press called him, took almost two thousand votes, 4.45 per cent of the poll, and came seventh out of ten candidates. Massey did not get the chance to stand against Dennett in 2016, as the year before he was gunned down outside his Clifton, Salford home by an assassin paid £10,000 by underworld rivals.

Dennett's role effectively makes him the leader of Salford council. His pro-active intervention in the affordable housing controversy has contrasted with Manchester. He deployed astute slogans designed not to scare the property sector – Greengate, Middlewood Locks and MediaCity UK being Salford developer hot spots – but also to satisfy his own political beliefs. 'No ghetto rich or poor' was his smart response to the swelling concern about locals being priced out. Dennett agrees with the charge that, in planning, local authorities have come to be, in his words, a 'Thatcherite model of hollowed-out councils as procurement hubs for private contracts'. Yet he admits that the private-sector-led property boom has benefited the city's regeneration. Between 2017 and 2019, Dennett calculated, £1 billion of new development raised the council tax base, injecting £40 million into the council's coffers. Always adept with a savvy PR line, he calls his council's direction 'Putting growth to use'.

In 2021 Dennett created a council-owned arm's-length social housing organi-sation to deliver the largest council-house-building programme in the city for fifty years. Five hundred homes will be built, he says, in 'our determination to put people before profit'. The new body is named Dérive – a council-house-building company named after the Situationist reverie of wander-and-wonder which so entranced Tony Wilson and his fellow dreamers. Dennett gives every impression of providing a Salfordian counterweight to developer-led growth in Manchester, which followed with its own social housing arm This City.

The pandemic hardly dented the pace of the Manchester property-development boom. November 2020 produced a typical blast of crisis oppor-tunism, a plan called *Powering Recovery*, in which the city council set out its post-pandemic ambition to cement Manchester's position as 'the UK's premier growth city'. Deloitte's annual crane survey in 2022 revealed that more than 5,500 new homes were completed in 2021 in the city centres of Manchester and Salford, the largest number since the survey began in 1999, adding to the almost five thousand built the year before.

All European cities have faced the convulsions of Brexit, Covid and 2022's ongoing war-influenced economic challenge. Manchester also had to cope with the 2017 Manchester Arena bomb outrage and to come to terms with subsequent appalling revelations of official incompetence which might have prevented it. Poet Tony Walsh channelled the outpouring of love and grief in his response 'This is the Place', declaiming it in mocking May sunshine as the world watched leaders Burnham (fresh in his new role) and Leese struggling to comprehend the obscenity visited upon youngsters in the entertainment capital of the north. They had come from as far as Scotland, many for their first-ever concert, to be transported by the positivity of Ariana Grande. Twenty-two were killed and eight hundred were injured, 116 seriously, and the trauma remains for many there that night, and their families.

Grande returned on 4 June with a stellar bill of global pop's new royalty for a tribute concert to the victims at Old Trafford cricket ground, leading the line with astonishing grace and courage for one carrying so much pain. She took the stage at the finale with organisers including a rare sighting of the reclusive Simon Moran, the force behind major league promoter SJM, who started out putting bands on in the Madchester era. Ratings showed that 22.5 million watched live on UK television, with worldwide audiences on fifty foreign TV networks and online. Scooter Braun, the most powerful artist manager in commercial pop, told *Billboard* that 'the City of Manchester was the Hero'. Only a week after the atrocity, Happy Mondays' singer Rowetta Satchell summoned up all that was best about rave-era Haçienda to sing the club classic 'You've Got the Love' on BBC1's Andrew Marr *Sunday* – a raw, deeply affecting performance powered by a Manchester Camerata string quartet and the senseless waste of it all. A one-year anniversary event at a packed Albert Square saw massed school choirs singing Elbow's 'One Day Like This' and poet 'Longfella' Walsh telling the crowds, 'This is what love sounds like.'

21

'Who wants to live in a city without culture?'

This rhetorical question was put by Sir Richard Leese to his audience in 2015 at the launch of the publicly funded HOME arts centre, which sits across Whitworth Street West and the railway line west to Liverpool, a stone's throw from the Haçienda Apartments.

Yet it is only comparatively recently that what we think of as culture has been turned upside down. Back in the 1980s, at *City Life* we featured indie musicians with agit-prop, anarcho-punk or 'rad-fem' ideas, sounds and hairstyles, none of which anyone called 'culture'. We mocked 'the yarts' even as we listed classical music concerts. 'Culture' was posh and privileged, lacquered brittle with history. Government policy for music and the arts came under the Department for National Heritage. It was renamed the Department for Culture, Media and Sport in 1997, and Digital was added in 2012.

In the 1980s not much had changed since the attitude sent up in 1968 film *Charlie Bubbles*. Albert Finney's famous Northern writer returns home and a waiter in the sparkling new modernist Piccadilly Hotel asks: 'Do you just do the writing now sir? Or are you still working?' Salford prodigy Shelagh Delaney wrote the script, and it was surely a line that the bus driver's daughter was familiar with, after the notoriety of her 1958 play *A Taste of Honey* and her screenplay for the 1961 film version which exploded British attitudes to class and sex.

Creative work wasn't real work, then, and creative endeavour wasn't part of the real economy. After the millennium turned, digital technology collapsed the boundaries. Today popular culture is the mulch of modern life, the always-on, real-time, omnipresent 'content' on our multi-screened lives in posts, memes, gifs, videos and podcasts. Unlike the cultural waves of punk and rave, today's youth music and fashion, even when it is authentic, is everything, everywhere, all the time.

New music now can go from a cult to a cliché in an instant, but Factory Records emerged in the shadows. It felt like a guerrilla foothills opposition taking on the fortresses of high culture, fighting to get heard and seen. Only a handful of media shared its strange, powerful art in an era when carrying an album sleeve on the street was your way of starting a conversation about music. After the label collapsed, Factory's legend flourished, and today it has an undeniable claim as that rare thing, popular art which also commands the cultural high ground.

Factory, Joy Division, New Order is an exceptional, self-contained universe: rock and dance music lauded for innovation and originality, record sleeves exhibited in galleries, fine artists commissioned for band videos, the Haçienda globally recognised as a rules-busting redefinition of what a music venue can be. Factory refused to play by the rules, making unexpected moves like releasing classical music. In 2019 the Royal Albert Hall in London hosted the Manchester Camerata chamber orchestra playing arrangements of *Unknown Pleasures*. An April 2022 editorial in *The Times* hailed Joy Division's national cultural impact as at least the equal of Benjamin Britten or Gustav Holst, and presumably not because football fans have reworked 'Love Will Tear Us Apart' into a match-day chant.

That such an influential art movement had arisen in their city was an irresistible opportunity for Manchester's leaders as they wrestled with the giant question mark over its future. The city's leaders realised that culture in all its manifestations was the ace up its sleeve, but also knew that the magic could not be faked or manufactured. The council had seen positive changes flow from its game-changing 'Let's work together' letter in summer 1987 to the Conservative government. Now the powers-that-be understood they should help create the conditions for artists to produce their work. While the Factory art project was being wound down in 1992 by liquidators scratching their heads at the zero cash value left, The City understood that the music culture gave Manchester an 'aura', in brand-speak, that could help in the audacious 1993 bid for the 2000 Olympics.

Tony Wilson later told *Building* magazine that, even as his club was hosting a carnival of crime, council leader Graham Stringer had declared that the Haçienda was to Manchester what Michelangelo's David was to Florence. This was classic Wilsonian chutzpah. Stringer does not recall saying it, but he does remember being in Chicago and hearing how highly its citizens regarded his city's pop culture. Stringer received foreign business delegations at the town hall who, after politely touring the old building, asked to be taken to the Haçienda. Bernstein had been to New York and enjoyed two hours with 'Hizzoner' Michael Bloomberg, and had spent time with Barcelona's Mayor Pasqual Maragall, finding out from both about the cultural excitement that had made their cities places where people wanted to be after years of decline. The visits took place as Manchester music was sweeping the world. Rather than banging on about Victorian railways and Bobby Charlton, the *Newsweek* Madchester cover feature gave the city currency.

Even so, the city centre in the 1990s was still largely hollowed out. Its economic decline made the penny drop — Manchester's potent past as a globaliser was over. Its status was now as another second-tier European city fighting for visitors, publicity and investment. The task for all regional cities was clear: media spectacles, from the Haçienda to the Commonwealth Games, from empire-building sports teams to city-set TV dramas like *Queer as Folk*, from the biennial Manchester International Festival to the £210 million Factory arts centre — all could put the city on the must-visit lists of globe-trotting thought leaders, and lure curious, talented people who had the whole globe to choose from.

Yet Manchester struggled with a cultural cringe: it was known for partying and pop, *Coronation Street* and football. To rise above its fur-coat-and-no-knickers image, in the council-creatives conclaves of the early 2000s, Wilson and others lobbied The City to improve its image and communications. As part of his Original Modern recommendations, the homegrown designer-savant Saville returned, to explain that Manchester's growth strategy should be based on new culture, sending out a global signal that something interesting was happening here. His prescription was it should take the form of new work — either premieres, collaborations or new ways of tackling classics.

And so the Factory founders fathered the Manchester International Festival. Exemplifying this clear, direct lineage, it was an article of faith that, as music from the Hallé to the Haçienda was the city's strong suit, the festival must feature music of all kinds at its core. Since the first biennial in 2007, the festival has built up an outstanding international reputation. In 2017 *The New York Times* called MIF 'possibly the most progressive arts festival in the world', though it is less loved in its own backyard, where fragile arts organisations fill in their grant applications with dread.

The MIF will be based at The Factory International, opening in 2023 after years of cost rises, design issues and construction delay. The origins of the twin-auditorium, seven-thousand-capacity performance space was as a hobbyhorse of Royal Opera House chairman and former BBC director-general Tony Hall.

Lord Hall of Birkenhead, a proud Northerner, sought a regional outpost of Covent Garden, and the Victorian venues revived by the impresario Sir Bob Scott, the Palace Theatre and the Opera House, were mooted. National budget cuts kept the project on ice, but the idea of a top people's palace to raise the very brow of Manchester grew as its devolution ambitions swelled.

In December 2014 the £78 million pump-priming of the project as part of the DevoManc deal seemed an astronomical sum when announced by George Osborne in Parliament. The chancellor spiced up his financial statement with details of the Northern Powerhouse, the 'supercity' concept he first floated in a speech at MOSI in June of that year. 'The cultural life of the North will get a boost too, including a major new theatre space in Manchester,' he told MPs. 'Manchester City Council propose to call it The Factory Manchester. Anyone who's a child of the '80s will think that's a great idea.'

BBC arts reporter Ian Youngs took one look at the sums involved in Factory and asked 'Austerity? What austerity?' Hadn't the city council only just found £19 million from its budgets for the £25 million new arts centre, HOME? This building by Dutch architect Mecanoo in 2015 relocated two atmospheric but antiquated venues, the Library Theatre and the Cornerhouse cinemas and galleries, both institutions held in mighty local affection. Steered by community arts stalwart Dave Moutrey, there is a palpable sense of public ownership in HOME, and its name had been arrived at after long-winded consultations with a partisan arts crowd initially disturbed by the move.

Despite Manchester's social problems, its unskilled young people, its lack of secure jobs and lamentable health and education outcomes, there seemed an almost improper eagerness to find money for palaces of entertainment. Clearly still sensitive to this charge nearly a decade later, on launching MIF 2023, city council chief Joanne Roney stressed the venue's provision of creative, culture and digital skills, and how key this will be to the new economy. 'There is a reason George Osborne backed it,' she said. 'That's because we are using culture to contribute to economic growth and create jobs. Its significance to the North can't be overplayed.' (The 2022 announcement of a new DCMS hub for four hundred staff in the city, to create its biggest base outside London, reflects this government and council alignment.)

The genesis of The Factory was known only to a tight-knit cabal. In the loop were Manchester's cultural commissars Alex Poots and Maria Balshaw. With the city's king of soft power, MIF chairman Tom Bloxham, smoothing their paths, the pair had gained the confidence of The City with decisive, well-resourced missions in taste-making and media profile. In a remarkable concentration of curatorial authority, Balshaw had jointly run the City Gallery as well as the university's Whitworth Art Gallery, where she bossed its highly praised £19 million extension. Poots was simultaneously recommended by Saville and shortlisted by the council. He took up the post of MIF boss, leaving the English National Opera after a year for what he described to the council as 'the Original Modern job'.

From the off, the MIF programme was militantly avant-garde. Contemporary artists worldwide responded to the city's call to capture the zeitgeist in Manchester, though initially due more to Factory Records' reputation rather than to the city itself. At the first festival in 2007 it rained for what seemed three weeks solid, but even this could not dampen the enthusiasm for such an audacious assault on the UK establishment festivals. Edinburgh's main festival was still very much about 'the yarts' and various London and outdoor festivals had well-defended slices of the cultural diary. But MIF was inescapably urban and contemporary, and intentionally risky. An early curtain-raiser, a live show by Damon Albarn's Gorillaz at which Bernstein looked on bemusedly, was followed by some truly challenging events, not just for audiences but for the authorities. One of its first headline shows was *Il Tempo del Postino*, an ensemble of performance art happenings which included a woman peeing onstage and a live bull being encouraged to mate with a motor car. David Ward in *The Guardian* said it was 'stuffed with self-indulgent excess. But the show had to happen to make Edinburgh tremble and prove that the Manchester International Festival was all about today, or even tomorrow and the day after that.'

Poots secured leading artists seldom spotted up North for his audacious cross-hatchings: new performance art by Marina Abramović, a Björk premiere complete with Icelandic choir, a Damon Albarn opera in Chinese, an immersive haunted house experience by Punchdrunk. Jeremy Deller led a Northern surrealism parade down Deansgate, choreography star Wayne McGregor returned to his home city to premiere *Tree of Codes* with the Paris Opera Ballet, Olafur Eliasson's set and light design and a score by Jamie XX.

The starchitect Zaha Hadid made a swoosh of a pavilion for Bach's solo work inside the City Gallery, and Kraftwerk pressed buttons on their computers to play their hits, as Olympic Gold medal track cyclists sped around the Velodrome for an audience wearing 3D glasses.

It was all a colossal shift from the city's late twentieth century festivals, when music promoter Phil 'Napoleon' Jones scratched around for a programme of bands out on tour. Jones had staged Spike Island for The Stone Roses. There was no need now for his streetwise skills, nor for the hippy hangover duo of Jeremy Shine and Ann Tucker, whose Streets Ahead theatre group had been the mainstay of Manchester's memorable street carnivals for two decades. They were old stagers out of step with the times. Manchester now aimed to commission cultural product it could export, raising profile, kudos and intellectual-property income.

As the biennales came and went, we got the idea that the Manchester International Festival was very much about the International. Poots told arts professionals he wasn't here to do community arts. The festival, then, was never going to be for Ancoats Annie and Beswick Bob, even if the lamp posts in their neighbourhoods were festooned with MIF banners and some cut-price tickets were on sale for the jobless. The MIF got good press. The city had friends in high media places in 'that there London': Paul Morley, Waldemar Januszczak, Miranda Sawyer, John Harris and Mark Kermode were some of the metropolitan taste makers who had fled hairy-arsed Manchester to build their careers in the capital.

A 2017 *Manchester Confidential* interview asked Sir Howard Bernstein and associate Mike Emmerich if The Factory would be worth all the money. 'There is no doubt at all that this will be a transformative project for Manchester in the long term,' said Bernstein. Emmerich spoke more freely: 'As big a fan as I am of MIF ... I sometimes wonder if the balance of art is completely accessible to

the mainstay

output

people, and whether *avant-garde* for the sake of it is going to be right.' The elite art/mass appeal is a stark dichotomy in Manchester. At the Arena's twentieth anniversary Bernstein told VIPs: 'Not everyone wants to go to the Opera House, not everyone wants to go to the Bridgewater Hall.' The Arena, he said, was 'a place where families can actually come and enjoy themselves.' In contrast to Leese, who takes in new homegrown music like LoneLady and WH Lung at the small indie venues Yes and Gorilla, it's well known that 'SHB's' personal taste does not embrace MIF esoterica, even if he does sit on its board. Property-world pals josh with the dealmaker who changed the face of Manchester. 'What's MIF all about?' he says. 'Don't ask me!'

Bernstein once returned from a weekend in Rome to declare to colleagues that its piazzas were just as good as Albert Square. They looked for the irony. None was visible. A man of the people in his own middle-of-the-road pastimes, he is very much in his comfort zone around the deal in which the city is tightening its grip on the mantle of entertainment capital of the North. Post-council, one of Bernstein's hats includes Manchester City's strategic development adviser on the Etihad Campus, where a 23,500-capacity indoor music and sports venue is taking shape next to the football stadium. Co-op Live says it will create a thousand jobs on opening in late 2023. When the twenty-thousand-seater Manchester AO Arena (so renamed under new sponsorship since 2020) complained that the new venue would undermine it and threaten the city's night-time economy, I was reminded of the unrealised fears that the Trafford Centre would turn the city centre into a ghost town. US company Oak View Group's plan was approved, a £365 million investment bringing the biggest music and sports events. One backer is pop heart-throb Harry Styles from nearby Cheshire, injecting a 'significant figure that makes Harry a minority equity shareholder'.

Meanwhile, from its 2017 start on site, The Factory International, designed by Ellen Van Loon of Rem Koolhaas's OMA, has been hit by design muddles, cost overruns and Covid, racking up headline-hogging build costs which the latest disclosure declared to be £211 million. Commercial mass culture in Co-op Live, subsidised elite culture in The Factory, would appear to be the way big-ticket events will play out post-2023. Totting up the investment, including the £50 million upgrade at the AO Arena, the doors will be thrown open in 2023 to, astoundingly, more than £630 million of new entertainment infrastructure in the city.

Manchester has pivoted its new economy around culture and entertainment. In doing so, it could do well to remember the significance of The Factory's location. Its painful birth is on the site of the former Granada Television studios, where Manchester and Salford meet among the coal-and-cotton cradle of capitalism, that elemental criss-cross of canals, river and the world's first inter-city passenger railway. Here is where the ley lines converge, not only where the conjoined twin cities meet at their original modern hearts, but where the roots of today's visual and music culture, and its contribution to the political self-confidence of Manchester-Salford, were dug deep into the Northern psyche.

Brothers Cecil and Sidney Bernstein, owners of the successful southern England cinema chain Granada, began broadcasting to the Northwest during the advent of commercial television in the 1950s. The company's purpose-built studios were opened in 1955, predating BBC Television Centre by four years. Granada became the nation's vanguard for postwar popular culture outside London – many programmes which defined the late twentieth century came from Quay Street, from the seminal, moving dissection of class in the 7 Up! documentary series to investigative weekly reports from *World in Action* which challenged politicians and big business. It televised the first British by-election in Rochdale in 1958 and broadcast the news of President Kennedy's assassination in 1963 half an hour before the cautious BBC was telling the rest of the nation.

The station's talent-spotter Johnnie Hamp broadcast the first TV turns by The Beatles, often as fillers in teatime news programmes, over a decade before its cameras rolled for The Sex Pistols and Joy Division. It nurtured Tony Warren's Northern kitchen sink drama *Coronation Street*, and made long-running quiz show *University Challenge*, the irreverent *What the Papers Say* and lavish productions for international audiences such as *Brideshead Revisited*.

For over fifty years, Granada's backlit red logo was a defiant beacon, visible for miles around on its eight-storey granite and glass HQ on Quay Street. Perhaps it served the whole Northwest patchily, but it gave Manchester a sense of itself as a modern, glamorous place where big ideas, grand challenges and high emotions were the city's as of right.

Granada was not defined by being 'not London'. Its identity was born of Manchester's history as a city hewn from its land and weather by the skill and industry of its people, a self-created metropolis without the ancient wealth and privilege of the feather-bedded capital. Its programmes oozed the condescension that Anthony Burgess said Mancunians had towards Londoners when they travelled south. The tone of company culture was set by Sidney Bernstein, who noted the North's 'home-grown culture' while London was 'full of displaced persons'. He observed: 'I think that what Manchester sees today, London will see eventually.'

Bernstein adorned the studio's corridors with his modern art collection, and was the ultimate insider-outsider, a Jewish socialist with a seat from 1969 in the House of Lords, and the man who, in Wilson's half-remembered version of events, indicated that his TV station could televise a music group whose fans (almost certainly without the knowledge of the staunch anti-fascist owner) wore swastikas to shock Britain out of its mid-1970s lethargy.

The box in the living rooms of the terraced streets of Granadaland shaped dreams and engendered pride. There was no highbrow or lowbrow about Granada. Bernstein believed it was 'impolite to talk to people in terms they do not understand'. While adventurous and risk-taking, it made classy but classless programmes with intelligence and panache.

After *The Guardian* dropped 'Manchester' from its masthead in 1959, Granada took up the baton as the city's home of intellectual discourse. As Granada's regional output dwindled and it was absorbed into ITV's focus on mainstream entertainment, it is the MIF now that is the city's institution with the financial and reputational heft to bring the big beasts of art and ideas together, to play out the challenges of today's world.

Despite their roles making The Factory International happen, taste makers Poots and Balshaw departed for the glittering prizes in New York and London. Under director John McGrath, MIF has continued to stage intriguing performances in established venues and art happenings in unknown places and promenade spaces. A new Phillip Glass work and a Yoko Ono livestream took headlines in 2019, but my favourite was A Drunk Pandemic – a Japanese art collective Chim↑Pom set up a micro-brewery in a cobbled undercroft beneath Victoria Station, after the 1830s practice of drinking beer instead of cholera-infected water. I still have their takeaway beer mat with 'A Drop of Pandemic' printed on it.

I was and remain a supporter of MIF. I have been a modest sponsor, following the example of high-minded arts lovers like lawyers Geoffrey Shindler and Stephen Sorrell, who have given massive support to arts venues, and believe that people who have done well out of the city should contribute to make the life of the city interesting. In the same spirit, hedge fund rich lister Andrew Law, from Cheadle, stumped up £7.8 million in 2022 to save Lowry's painting *Going to the Match* for the Lowry Centre.

Manchester putting on a show has a long tradition. The upstart city wanted to show it was cultured as well as booming when it staged the Grand Exhibition in 1857. While the Duke of Devonshire was not persuaded ('Why can't you stick to your cotton spinning?'), the city's industrialists pledged £74,000 for a vast temporary glass-and-iron pavilion at White City. The event hosted 1.3 million visitors in 142 days, displayed sixteen thousand works, set the template for the way art was presented for the next 150 years and created the Hallé Orchestra from the musicians it assembled.

If its update is the MIF, its early incarnations felt like a satellite, associated with but not quite owned by The City, with a licence to roam 'found' places hosting quasi-guerrilla art happenings, its social spaces moving from Albert Square to Cathedral Gardens. Its mobility made it appear intriguing and stealthy. Now the festival's base is inside The Factory International, it risks the perception as the giant spoiled baby of the city council, a £210 million solution to a problem that no one knew existed.

As the city expanded and its property classes thrived, the MIF has mushroomed in significance, running costs and personnel. The MIF–Factory combine employs about 165 arts professionals. Its prodigious sponsorship boss, Lancastrian force of nature Christine Cort, launched *Time Out* in New York, so knows how to work a room, and a city. The festival's early cash calls started with teeth-pulling frustration but Cort (who left her managing director role in 2021) reputedly forced a pen and sign-off form into the hands of Spinningfields' Mike Ingall. His autograph was the signal to the property world's big dogs to follow suit. Since then, the big-ticket sponsors behind the MIF are the companies developing the biggest property schemes in the city – corporates like Aviva, Allied London and Bruntwood. Gary Neville joined the MIF board in 2022 and told a crowd of sponsors: 'You can't come into this city, walk in and take the money and walk away, there is an expected return. There is a Mancunian tax.'

The legacy of the mysterious and unpredictable Factory feels, oddly, to be Official Culture, paid for by property developers and their lawyers. Are those who pay the pipers calling the tune? I can't see it. Poots recalled in 2015 that the council agreed to make MIF free of funders' influence and independent of council policy: 'When it comes to the arts they've been utterly hands off.' Poots did, however, lay down the law to Turner Prize-winning artist Douglas Gordon after he took an axe to the wall of HOME in 2015, echoing the German metal group's drill attack on a Haçienda pillar in 1985. Festivals are meant to make sparks fly, but the message to artists is unchanged: 'Say what you like, but don't mess with our buildings.'

Undeniably it is wonderful, if not vital, that big companies fund the MIF in the time-honoured manner, of 'business giving back'. Perhaps the grandest civic munificence of all, though, is the saga of how Tony Wilson's £4,000

Tom Bloxham and Christine Cort

inheritance seeded an improbable property boom and laid down the cosmic crazy paving leading all the way to the Factory International. Deliciously, of course, the Haçienda gang were inept property players, always overpaying or forced to sell cheap. When it came to the Haçienda, Dry bar and the Factory HQ, the directors had not the guile, greed or luck to make money out of real estate, all of which has sustained the narrative as a project of edgy art activism.

'Factory mistook financial incompetence as the hallmark of Situationist rebellion,' says Eric Longley, the ex-Ernst & Young entertainment-division accountant who was Factory's managing director for a brief period from 1990. He describes his and financial director Chris Smith's doomed task to balance the books as 'King Canute versus the profligate tide'. Longley says, 'There is something in the romance of death that Curtis' demise gave to Factory. Manchester became the hip cool university town to go to, and in its own self-confident identity as a city leading popular music, to think about new ways of being pop, of bringing art into pop.' Of the idea that Manchester's renaissance is founded squarely on its music culture, he says, 'It has an attractive appeal to it. I don't think it is supportable by the facts, although it meets Tony Wilson's own dictum: forget the facts, the legend is more important.'

In 2015 then council leader Sir Richard Leese said anyone linking Factory's late 1970s high water mark with the poverty of those days would be talking 'absolute bollocks'. He told John Harris in *The Guardian*: 'Stuff about needing poverty to get creativity – it's clearly bollocks. There is more creativity now in the city than there ever was 35 years ago.' He did not dwell on the impact of property values on artists. A clear sign that The City was sensitive to any notion that Manchester could lose the creative juices making it a tasty proposition to investors was exhibited in 2017, when 97 studio artists were evicted from the nineteenth century Crusader Mill. Rogue, the largest artist-led studio collective in the North, had enjoyed cheap space in Crusader Mill in the scrappy Back Piccadilly red-light area since 2000, and now had to make way for apartments.

The artists kicked up a fuss. Rogue's David Gledhill told *Artist's Newsletter*: 'I think it's time artists understood that their strength lies in their economic clout with the Council … We can claim some of the value that we create.' In 2014, 150 contemporary artists signed an open letter to the city's curators, asking them to 'have more confidence and pride in Manchester artists.' Apparently stung by attacks like these, Maria Balshaw replied to reassure the city's artist community she valued their work, and one of her last acts before taking up the role of Tate director in 2017 was, along with Leese, to shepherd most of Rogue's artists into a vacant school building in Openshaw, a few miles out of the centre. Perhaps she spoke for The City when she told Rogue's practitioners that working artists – around 50 in the 1980s, today over 500 – would have to get used to not being based in the city centre, where property values now made it unrealistic for artists to find a garret to work in.

Crusader Mill featured in BBC TV's *Manctopia*, following its new owners Tim Heatley and Adam Higgins of Capital and Centric. In one scene, Heatley discovers structural problems that will cost him an extra £1 million, a reminder that developers suffer big risks and sleepless nights. In their uniform of trainers and anoraks, the pair present as conscientious operators, 'creating communities', selling off-plan apartments to owner-occupiers only and subsidising artists. Across the city, developers employ 'meanwhile uses', gifting artists space in edgy locations. After the creation of buzz, footfall and value, artists are often shown the door once the area has 'come up'.

Three miles out of the pulsating centre, could a Factory-style cultural force emerge from an unremarkable three-storey redbrick building, at 1394 Ashton Old Road, in Bradford, one of the city's lower-income neighbourhoods? Here black entrepreneur Michael Adex ('it's just Adex') has based NQ, his '360 talent

Michael Adex with Andy Burnham

and entertainment company'. With its motto 'Northern roots, Global influence,' NQ has next to no profile in the Manchester media, but is hot news in the international music business.

Adex, twenty-six, was born in Germany of Nigerian-Liberian parents and moved to England at ten. He began representing artists after befriending grime and rap musicians online, then in person, and set up in business at twenty-one. 'By reading up, by discovering for myself, the history, Factory Records, Tony Wilson,' he says, 'I understood that there was something special about Manchester. I could have gone to London … it's surreal to see what I was envisioning being a reality now. I stayed to grow with the city.'

In 2021 an early visitor to Adex's new base was Mayor Andy Burnham. He told youngsters there, 'I feel in life sometimes – and certainly when you have a working-class background, we do ourselves down too much.' Not really requiring the pep talk was Adex's biggest act, NQ's in-house rapper Aitch, a cocky, cursing charmer whose collaborations with Ed Sheeran, Stormzy and others get millions of streams. He has a Spotify following of 5.8 million with over 29 million streams, and his online videos are devoured by a global fan base that places Aitch and his multicultural mates in the north Manchester back streets where Bernard Manning was once the local cultural export.

The NQ building bears no signs of Factory-style statement interiors, just a smart and simple boardroom, studios and open-space offices. But there is an echo of Wilson's artist-centred ethos: 'Despite all the data that goes into music now, there's still a big thing to be said about stardust that you can't recreate,' says Adex. 'An unexplainable energy.'

If they want to stay and be prophets in their hometown, who knows what futures await Adex and Aitch in the new Manchester? A classic career path of the new city, from the musical margins to the top table, can be observed in the super-achieving example of school exam failure Sacha Lord. His first promotion in July 1994 flopped when he hired the Haçienda for a student night but timed for when his audience had left for the summer. He just got away without losing his shirt and learned his trade hosting 3,500-strong dance nights at the Bastille-like Victoria Warehouse and the former Boddington's brewery site at Strangeways. His commercial success and social media platform led to him being appointed by Burnham as Greater Manchester's first night-time economy adviser in 2018. The pandemic thrust 'Sacha' on to the national stage in his unpaid role in spring 2021 when he launched a private high court case against health minister Matt Hancock's hospitality lockdown. From nightlife huckster to the mayor's right-hand man – yet again, the influence of that cavernous danceteria on Whitworth Street West is clear.

Adex is a modern example of how immigrant communities have contributed to the Manchester music scene, notably the Irish backgrounds of The Smiths and the Gallaghers. Manchester, indeed, was not a creation of 'Mancunians'. The nineteenth-century manufacturing big bang threw up townships drawn from poor rural Lancashire to live around new mills and chimneys. The city of immigrants soon embraced Irish, Germans, Greeks, Italians, Lithuanians, Armenians and Poles, joining an earlier community of Jews. The twentieth century saw communities from the West Indies, India and south Asia, and later Poles, Iraqis, Afghans, Somalis, Cantonese Chinese, Portuguese and Latin American nationalities. In the wake of the 2017 Manchester Arena bombing, the city learned that it contained numerous Libyan exiles. As I write, the Ukrainian community established after the Second World War has organised to help refugees fleeing what we are warned could be the start of the next one. Many new arrivals, of course, stay for a few years' studying. During the Covid pandemic, Manchester and other universities chartered private planes to bring high fee-paying students from China so they could start their course in the city, not on Zoom.

In October 2021, at Marks and Spencer, Piccadilly, I watched two young Chinese women loading up twin packs of rump steaks into their baskets.

Struggling to pay at self-service machines, and speaking no English, the new students, a bit giggly and nervous in a strange land, opened their purses to show me their problem − £50 notes, in wads thicker than that even of the Happy Mondays' promoter in 1990, when he finally paid me up for stealing my words on his band.

22

Intention: To restore a sense of place

London's gone. It's drifted off as an independent city state … London is exclusive and impenetrable to the young. Manchester has an extraordinary opportunity. Manchester is the capital of the rest of the UK.

Peter Saville, interview, July 2022

The Romans who built a fort on a sandstone bluff above the River Medlock in AD 79 named the place Mamucium. The soldiers garrisoned to hold off the Brigante tribe would have believed it had a *genius loci*, its own guardian spirit. Romans dedicated their altars to specific forces that protected their fields, towns, neighbourhoods and even buildings, which they named and pictured on doors, on walls and on homeware. It's lost in time, but perhaps their spirit of place for proto-Manchester was a river goddess, inspired by the Medlock and 'the breast-shaped hill' which gave Mamucium its name.

Two thousand years later, the creator spirits of the new Manchester seem to hover in the air, big personalities who own and run the corporations bringing whole new districts to life. Today's new neighbourhoods bear the stamp of these firms and their bosses. Office business quarter Spinningfields and its St John's extension, home to the long-awaited Factory International, is Allied London territory. Its boss is the mercurial Mike Ingall, who has beaten a stubborn stammer and rollercoaster property markets with future-gazing creativity and council support. His vision stuttered in its early days, but Spinningfields now claims 24,000 workers and the city's swankiest eateries. Perhaps we could call his now well-established business district 'Ingall-stadt'.

Make your way to the Oxford Road corridor, and a benign spirit presides along the student strip from the old BBC North site, now Circle Square, and its adjacent Hatch shipping container-aesthetic leisure scheme, along to the life-science workspaces and clean labs on the university hospital estate. All around here, the family business Bruntwood dominates, its old-school philanthropy the legacy of founder Michael Oglesby, a Lincolnshire man who started out by buying a derelict Bolton factory in the 1970s. A country gent in the city, he died in 2019 aged eighty, leaving a £1 billion portfolio including 20 per cent of Manchester city centre's commercial space, and the lead developer role of ID Manchester, in the hands of son Chris. Bruntwood are hard-nosed operators, but not hard-hearted. Their family charitable trust, run by Mike's wife Jean and daughter Kate Vokes, is one of the North's major giving organisations, having donated over £16 million to three hundred charities in arts, education, medical research and social inequality.

Both Greengate and the area where the city centre meets Hulme display stunning evidence of the market in full spate, with clusters of tall towers produced at high speed by ruthlessly efficient constructor-developer Renaker. It builds so fast that it can seem as if the central Manchester hot zone is a Sims-style computer game. When a new Renaker obelisk was approved close to Salford Cathedral, Salford councillor Bob Clarke fumed: 'That cathedral out there, that is architecture. This is just Jenga.'

The firm has delivered the 1,500-unit Deansgate Square tower quartet (fast rivalling the Beetham as the latest city icon). And more of its towers are under way – two 51-storey Great Jackson Street towers branded Blade and Cylinder – with 988 flats, and the gargantuan Trinity Islands, 1,950 apartments in four towers of 39, 48, 55 and 60 storeys. Both schemes were approved without a single unit of affordable housing on site, though the developer is paying £196,000 for affordable homes elsewhere and agreed to contribute £1.5 million towards a new school. The quoted value of Trinity Islands is £494 million, reported market observer David Thame of *Place North West*. No wild-eyed leftie, he headlined his story 'No End of Shame'. Renaker's boss is matter-of-fact Yorkshireman Daren Whitaker. Despite his seismic impact on the twin cities' skyline, Whitaker remains invisible to the public.

A name better known to the average Mancunian is Middle East royal Sheikh Mansour. He owns Manchester City FC through his Abu Dhabi United Group (ADUG) investment fund. It is the partner with the city council in Manchester Life, the buy-to-let landlord owning nearly 1,500 homes in the historic Ancoats area. Sheffield University research in summer 2022 thrust the billionaire Emirati into a different spotlight, accusing the council of a hidden sweetheart land deal with ADUG and asking scathing questions about the relationships between the partners.

Legendary Tom Bloxham, aka Mr Urban Splash, is never seen without a trilby, and the indoor hat-wearer could lay claim to two areas as Bloxham barrios – the audacious extension to 'Castlefield' that his schemes created in what was the Hulme–Salford border west of the A57, and in New Islington, with Will Alsop's Chips, a free school, marina and nicely done groups of new builds on small infill sites.

North of the city centre the Irk trickles through the city's own Jurassic Park, a hidden river valley with intriguing views of greenery snatched from passing trains and trams. Here, the substantial figure of David Chiu and the deep pockets of his Hong Kong-listed Far East Consortium is delivering Victoria North for the council, shooting for a target of 15,000 homes across 400 acres over twenty years. FEC's first buildings are emerging around the attractively undulating Angel Meadow, under which lies a Victorian burial site where tens of thousands of paupers were interred in mass graves. As a result of the FEC owner's feng shui beliefs about ghosts, his marketeers are instructed to omit any upsetting mentions of the historic dead.

Among all these outsiders welcomed into the city (unlike in Liverpool, where development seems a closed and clannish game) is local boy Gary Neville. He is also ambitious to leave his mark on the cityscape with his grandiose St Michael's project. The development is finally, as the property crowd say, coming out of the ground, with a 2024 completion target date. Talk at the highest echelons is of Neville's political ambitions, speculation fuelled in early 2022 by a Labour Party fund-raiser with Keir Starmer at an Asian restaurant in east Manchester, and a BBC radio interview with Nick Robinson. A Labour-backed Neville run for the post-Burnham mayoralty in 2024, or even a parliamentary constituency, is openly discussed. Yet no one asks how seemly it is for any aspiring Manchester politician to be developing a 40-storey hotel-and-offices complex just 100 yards from the city's town hall.

These signatures writ large on the cityscape make clear The City's commitment to progress at scale. Development at critical mass supports master planning and design cohesion and cuts the energy-sapping torpor in which residents grow old waiting for areas to improve. The big operators can be trusted to deliver, not flip sites for easy gains or fold in a cold economic snap. They have responded to The City's call, creating numbers of homes and workspaces only dreamed of back in the naive 1990s, when renovating a few old arches was seen as the lofty aim.

Yet more others could lay claim for their spirits to be anointed as creator-gods. We could add Dave Roscoe, the senior planning officer honoured by *North West Business Insider* in June 2022 with the Game Changer Award, who 'worked incessantly for decades to improve the fabric of Manchester for its residents and investors'. And let us not neglect the tower designer supreme, the city's 'starchitect', the cloud-dwelling, softly spoken Ian Simpson, or his long-time, lesser-known practice partner Rachel Haugh, who have ten of the city's towers to their name to date. The urbane Simon Bedford, the Deloitte partner and key council adviser, responded to a 2016 call for London-style tall buildings policy to protect city views; the fine amateur cricketer responded with a straight bat. The council, he said, 'has given some thought to clusters of towers, which has to be right, and Manchester can cope with more – but it is debatable whether it needs lots more, especially very tall towers where demand is unproven.'

For this Manchester group which works closely together, constructing a new city centre has been their life's work. Not among their number is the celebrated Mancunian Sir Norman Foster, lauded as the nation's greatest living architect, who grew up in tough circumstances in Levenshulme. The pioneer of 'high-tech' building design across the world's big cities, he returned in 2015 to give a lecture in the town hall, where he began his career as a 16-year-old office clerk. Asked by *Place North West* why his practice's only work in the city centre is a medium-sized office scheme, Hardman Square in Spinningfields, he said: 'I'm looking at projects all over the world; in California, New York ... You go where you're invited as an architect. But that means the people who invite you have a wider view, a wider perspective. They're looking for talent, they're looking for enthusiasm, they're looking for commitment. But you have to want that, and if you don't want it ...' Reporter Jessica Middleton-Pugh noted Foster's shrug, before he added, 'It's always easier to take the easy way out and choose someone you know.'

Perhaps Bernstein and Leese in partnership are the true *genius loci* of the new city centre: a symbiotic, all-seeing, all-knowing consciousness hovering at the highest altitude, whose policies and practices have been the drumbeat behind the mission to build, build, build. The two knights of civic reinvention – one the political leader of the apparently permanent one-party state, the other unelected yet wielding huge power – cannily refused to be pinned down by heritage protection status, London-style tall building policies or affordable housing quotas, and, with tight political management sweetened by Manchester Airport dividends, they achieved a powerful overarching control, ensuring the city centre was a magnet for developers.

The SHB–SRL partnership lasted almost three decades and seemed almost telepathic. They were rarely photographed together, even (or especially) at MIPIM, although exuberance got the better of them with the super-casino site

Tom Russell, Richard Leese and Howard Bernstein at super-casino site

win. Neither publicly undermined the other, an external unity presenting a collective iron discipline. Councillor rebellions were damped down by cabinet decision-making, or tea and sympathy one-to-ones from councillor Pat Karney, whose city centre remit made him a key aide going back to the Stringer era.

This constellation of star players has also achieved a new Manchester of the mind, changing the way the city is perceived, from the dirty old town to a skyscraper city. At his council retirement event, Bernstein described his achievements as stemming from 'spotting opportunity and threat, dogged determination, irrational optimism', adding that 'Manchester is a place that reaches for the stars'. Music indeed to the property players seated in the Great Hall – including his old adversary, the Peel Holdings' billionaire John Whittaker – benefiting from what some critics fiercely describe as the grand illusion of a Labour council 'protecting jobs and improving services' while ushering in a shining new city to attract young professionals to live in the sky.

It is remarkable to observe the dislike with which Sir Richard Leese is held in some quarters, whether due to disquiet at the way the city centre has changed, or for his combative personal style. In November 2021, aged seventy, he stood down after 25 years as leader and 39 years on the council. Manchester Central banqueting hall resounded to speeches and applause. The dinner and drinks bill for a thousand guests was not paid by the austerity-hit council – one which has taken out a £330 million loan for the top-to-bottom future-proofing refurb of Manchester Town Hall – but was paid for by Deloitte.

Gordon Brown and Sir Keir Starmer paid tribute on video. Bruntwood boss Chris Oglesby praised the council's 'conscious capitalism' (echoing Salford mayor Dennett's 'sensible socialism,' perhaps, the phrases rubbing shoulders on the spectrum of policy in which social justice aspirations must accommodate the forces of business). Leese's response welcomed 'comrades, colleagues and partners', nods to his council, Labour and business constituencies. Rather than the aspirational hot buttons Bernstein pushed at his leaving bash, Leese flicked through slides of achievements for everyday Mancs – arts centres, schools, nurseries, health centres – in humdrum corners of the city. His emphatic tone seemed to underline a subtext: 'trickle-down works'.

Perhaps the animosity against Leese is because, set against the high-cresting waves of towers, the public benefits can seem just that, a trickle. Deep-seated issues counter the Leese narrative. In early 2022 *Manchester Evening News*'s Jen Williams (now at *Financial Times*) interrogated official figures on Manchester's spiralling homelessness crisis, due to the lack of rented homes genuinely afford-able to the less well off. As a result of people unable to afford rising rents being evicted from private tenancies, Manchester had the highest rate of people in emergency accommodation outside the capital, except Luton. But there is almost nowhere to house them. In the decade of the city centre's rapid growth, the numbers of children living in emergency housing had shot up from the low hundreds to almost four thousand, many forced away to outer boroughs away from their schools. 'Those on lower incomes here face a perfect storm,' she wrote. 'The city around them has become the poster-child for northern eco-nomic renaissance, pushing rents beyond their reach.'

A Centre for Cities report revealed that, despite their makeovers, cities like Manchester lack high-productivity exporting businesses in 'tradable' sectors. While it is doing well on low-productivity 'non-tradable' activities – hospitality, the arts, entertainment and leisure – in *Cities Outlook 2022*, Paul Swinney commented that, along with other regional cities, 'Manchester's pro-ductivity looks much more like Cumbria's than Bristol's, and trails far behind Munich's'. It blames not the council but the government grip on Greater Manchester's finances, the same rigged game that the chamber of commerce appealed to Margaret Thatcher to change back in 1986. DevoManc was, in truth, devo-lite, and the mayor Andy Burnham continues to push for a full-fat devolution, under which GM has the same fiscal powers as Scotland or Wales. March 2023 saw this move closer with the government's Trailblazer deal.

Meanwhile, in 2023 the effects of a property investment-led economy are all around. The post-pandemic city revealed new handsome privately owned public spaces (POPS), areas with tastefully landscaped urban realm around the gleaming towers or hipsterly refurbished mills. These squares, piazzas or spaces between buildings may appear to be council-run and publicly owned. But if you want to kick a football, ride a bike or busk for small change, you may find that you are in a privately managed environment, often patrolled by security operatives. Some believe they have a civilising effect, although for academic Dr Morag Rose, these lovely looking spaces could also have 'an unwelcoming atmosphere, the sense you have to look a certain way or need to spend money'. Back in 2007 the first of these new hybrid areas, Spinningfields, produced a brochure promising it as 'a place to Eat, Shop and Explore'. We were free to spend in the shops, bars and restaurants, but in truth there was little else to explore, no flower stalls or newspaper kiosks, the humanising outposts which soften vanilla corporate environments. Later additions brought outdoor seating, flower beds and that Mancunian answer to most regeneration problems, an outsized licensed premises, the Oast House.

National calamities visited upon the city centre, the crises of cladding and homelessness, have had severe impacts. The former will take years for official justice to make good, if it ever will, while the mayor deserves credit for driving his 'bed every night' programme to solve, at least partly, the seemingly intractable epidemic of rough sleepers in the city centre. Combined with a pandemic, these might have been enough to cut off growth at the knees, as happened after 2008's 'Great Recession'. Well-informed voices, however, believe that a new economic epoch is close to hand, of Manchester as a globally significant centre of digital technology. An independent 2020 report put Greater Manchester as the nation's digital capital, and the GMCA estimate of 86,000 tech workers at the last count is fast rising to 100,000.

My work in the city's digital economy goes back to 2001 when MIDAS asked me to convene a meeting of tech businesses, among them Tony Wilson and his music download start-up Music33. The strong view was that the city's emerging sector lacked representation, and so Manchester Digital trade association was born. As founding chairman, an unpaid role, I worked with Shaun Fensom, whose pioneering work at pre-internet electronic network Poptel provided Tony Blair with one of the UK's first email addresses and who, with Manchester City Council's digital chief Dave Carter, created the nation's first municipal network, linking up city services and enabling its 'electronic village halls' to connect with peers worldwide. Manchester was making groundbreaking forays into the digi-verse, but was the capital taking note? The answer came during the banking crash days of 2007 when the new economy looked like it could collapse along with the old one. I secured the Blair government's digital e-envoy Andrew Pinder to speak at the city's annual Big Chip Awards. Only the day before the prestige event at Imperial War Museum North, when I tried to confirm arrangements, an embarrassed civil servant confessed that Pinder and his people had completely forgotten and that he could not attend. I drew the conclusion that the path-finding tech community in this city of innovation firsts was clearly of little interest to national government.

How the sector's fortunes had changed little more than a decade later. At a 2018 property seminar, city regeneration chief Eddie Smith held a bullish Q and A session. Big tech occupiers, he reported, would soon be bringing thousands of new jobs. Signs of sky-high confidence in the city from Booking.com (a new global HQ), Amazon, Google and even government spy base GCHQ (in a very public location opposite the town hall) were all telling him that their opening job numbers were only the start. We were set for a new army of millennials and Gen Z-ers, coming to live their best life right here in surging Manchester–Salford, not in the San Francisco sunshine or at London's government-hyped Silicon Roundabout.

After the pause of Covid, the indicators are turning green again. The high numbers of young new Manchester and Salford residents indicate both centres' success in drawing the young to live in towers, attracted down to the streets for a full menu of leisure and culture from their swimming pools and cinema rooms. In summer 2023 the centre has no empty blocks in which overseas owners stash dubious money for capital growth (as many believe is the case from reading about the practice in London). Manchester city centre does not provide that growth, but it does provide better rental income than London. The patient capital of big institutions owns 40 per cent of the residential stock, while 15 per cent is occupied by owners, and the rest held by private landlords of varying sizes from all four corners of the earth.

Manchester is full. Foaming demand for rented flats and a post-pandemic slowing of the supply of apartments means that properties are rented the same day they are advertised. Rents are at a 16-year-high, not only in the centre but throughout the entire city. Such gravity-defying conditions often presage a popping of a market balloon, but agents report no let up. A predicted recession is sure to stress test its viability, but in summer 2023 the city-living community appears to be a real mix, of building types, rent levels and facilities, and also of occupiers – influencers, Only Fans exhibitionists, baristas, key workers, lawyers and grey-haired city councillors, though the residents taking the lift to the top floors are likely to be the footballers. All disdain the Airbnb brigade who love to come to town to party riotously.

The four-tower Deansgate Square complex is the icon of the new Manchester. A 2022 *Manchester Evening News* report listed lifestyle facilities for occupants of fifteen hundred apartments: swimming pool, gym, spa, rooftop gardens and concierge. A typical monthly rent is £1,500. It's not just the tech bros digging the views from the 67-storey West Tower. Services entrepreneurs are there, a sign of a maturing economy in which a big city feeds off itself – a skin clinic owner, a personal chef and a hair stylist talk rapturously about the 'elite hotel vibe'. Says one: 'It's got a sense of magic about it.' Purrs another: 'Living in the towers you feel like a king.'

It is common now for fifty storeys of 'luxury living' to eclipse the tiny old pubs. Another 28-storey apartment scheme close to the emerging 65-storey South Tower, set to be the highest building outside London, has been greenlighted by the Planning Inspectorate, overturning a rare council refusal. A gold-coloured 15-storey apartment block has been approved near Piccadilly rail station, its youthful developer speaking of its Dubai-inspired 'architectural magnificence'.

Who can ignore the towers? They demand a response. Many believe they look 'cool', the most common word for expressing that the future has arrived. Others think that the skyline is a triumph of engineering over design, or that the blank glass edifices are evil, devoid of humanity. If we ask ourselves, 'what mood do these techno-modern buildings put me in?' it may also lead to the question of whether the towers are an expression not so much of architecture, but of corporate profit and loss accounts.

No coherent or transparent aesthetic case has been made for such an extraordinary facelift. While council planners consider levels of harm to existing views and amenity in developer proposals, there has been no meaningful public debate beyond a TV doc here, a newspaper noting 'Manc-hattan' there. As he pounds the pavements, self-appointed critic Jonathan Schofield is a lone voice debating in his online columns about the good and bad of the building spree. Perhaps the Manchester International Festival should provide a forum for this debate?

In July 2022 I meet former council leader Sir Richard Leese at the Briton's Protection. The atmospheric pub dating from 1806 is waiting to hear if plans for a 26-storey tower on a ludicrously tiny footprint next door will progress to planning stage. The crushing over-scaling will put the beer garden we are sat in in the shade. 'There is regulation,' he insists. 'This is not the Wild West. I don't see how they are ever going to bloody build it and I hope they don't.'

He is no longer the city's top politician, however. The new leadership duo of leader Bev Craig and chief executive Joanne Roney have made no pronouncements that they wish to halt, or slow, the wave of development, or building heights. Despite their stepping down from council service, there is a tangible sense that Manchester's civic planning machine assembled by the former city bosses runs smoothly due to its deep-grooved imprint on the way things are done, not to mention the still highly active, many-hatted former chief executive. In September 2022, an *Estates Gazette* profile ran: 'Some may argue Sir Howard Bernstein never really went away. Since retiring as chief executive of Manchester City Council in April 2017, he has taken up roles at Manchester City Football Club, Deloitte and Vita Group.' A wry phrase does the rounds among the property community: 'Development in Manchester has been outsourced to The Office of Sir Howard Bernstein Limited,' referring to the company he formed in 2017.

His long-time colleague Leese describes himself as someone whose career has been spent solving problems. He not only led the council but was also a board director of Manchester Airport, with the public oversight of the money tree which smoothed the political path to devolution. Today he leads on the knotty problem that is the devolved city region's integration of health and social care. Leese displays the remorseless logic he is well known for when reminding critics that city centre development 'prevents everywhere else in Greater Manchester from having to churn up green fields ... we are building on brownfield sites.' Of the tower clusters, he says that 'the future of the planet, not just the city' depends on doing dense urban living well: 'We recognised if you want to have all the amenities and parks and everything else, we had to have a public commitment to high-density.'

Leese describes a walk up the 600 ft Billinge Beacon, outside Wigan, where clear-day uninterrupted views of both Liverpool and Manchester revealed the comparison between a 'big urban sprawl' and, he says with pride, 'Manchester, you see a city!'

Leese's childhood was spent in a Nottinghamshire pit village, and he lives in a semi in the ungentrified inner suburb of Crumpsall. He derides suburbanites who moan about the brash new centre but who love the big city's culture offer, which he says is made viable by the packed-out centre. He is on record (by Joshi Herrmann in *The Mill*) saying of his critics in long-running dissent over so-called affordable housing: 'They are middle-class tosspots and I hate them.'

The discourse about 'affordable' in Manchester is toxic, made worse by slippery official language. As campaigning online bulletin *The Meteor* points out, 'The government normally regards homes to rent or buy which are 20% or more below local market rates to be "affordable."' As the price of homes has rocketed, there is no way that average income earners can afford the averagely priced home.

The government's 'affordable' definition is a misnomer, for some cynically encouraging the idea that low-income groups can buy in. What people often think it means is housing for the poorest in the city. Says Leese of affordable housing in the sense of families on benefits, 'We can only provide that with serious public subsidy. In a crude sum, we can build more affordable housing in Beswick than we can in the city centre. If we're serious about affordable housing, that's what we have to do.'

Leese was unflinching in 1987 when selling his 'jobs, jobs, jobs' policy to the city's left-wing councillors and unions. As leader he was happy to confront received wisdom by blogging that many street people being loaded up with pizzas and change were beggars with addresses. He maintains: 'The bottom line is, this was a dying industrial city. By pre-Covid, this was the fastest-growing city, economically, in Europe. And getting younger. All that says to me: this is working. When I moved here in 1979 it was a shithole. Working-class Mancs now feel very proud of their city in a way they didn't previously.'

For a 1987 *City Life* interview marking the Haçienda's fifth anniversary, Tony Wilson told me: 'I always use the image of the Aeolian harp – the winds of the culture blowing through it and the individual just being a part of that.' I wasn't entirely sure what he was on about, but I included the quote about the harp in Greek culture that plays itself when the wind blows through it, often used as a metaphor for the poetic imagination. Wilson had dashingly reworked his classical learning into a way of describing the impact of the Haçienda on his city's live music scene.

It sounded almost as preposterous when, years before the metastasising of the city's towers, Wilson said in Grant Gee's 2007 documentary *Joy Division*: 'I don't see this as the story of a rock group. I see it as the story of a city … The revolution that Joy Division started has resulted in this modern city.' Yet as the years roll on, we can look back and see the links, effects and influences. A slow-motion epiphany reveals itself – the Haçienda founders' intention 'to restore a sense of place' is substantially a mission accomplished.

The Joy Division legend is surely a kind of spiritual song-line across Mancunian time and space. Long after the titanium-clad penthouses have fallen, great songs will never die. Even so, as the city centre has risen higher, and Tony Wilson Place emerged at First Street in 2015 (his collaborators were consulted and felt a statue was inappropriate), I understand that tentative suggestions for a statue of Ian Curtis in Albert Square to join the city's founding fathers were met with ignorance of his name.

If the silk town shaman Curtis was not known at the highest levels of official-dom, gig-goer Leese is, of course, aware of the legacy. I ask him to consider the thought experiment 'no Factory-Haçienda, no new Manchester'.

'Oooh,' he exclaims, the technocrat brain whirring, computing the notion. 'It would have happened without Factory. Yeah it would, basically.' Its contribution? 'A bit overstated.' He acknowledges, though, 'Manchester had to become a place where people wanted to be. Music was a very big part of that.'

Peter Saville is the only one of the five Factory founders alive and happy to talk. (Factory's will o' the wisp Alan Erasmus travelled to Ukraine in 2022 to raise money for displaced children but is otherwise elusive.) Irrefutably for the eloquent design guru, the 'investment' of Ian Curtis's life, and the eye-watering funds poured in by his bandmates and their associates, contained the seeds for the city's revival.

'Modern Manchester stands in part on the sacrifice made by Ian Curtis,' he says. 'His untimely death was the capital investment in Factory Records and inevitably that which has followed on as a consequence of Factory – the Haçienda, the regeneration it inspired, Original Modern, the Festival, and now the Factory arts space. Much of the aura of Manchester today is founded on the charisma of Factory, and Factory's charisma was founded on Ian.'

Saville regrets that the Original Modern project, for him both a route map and a way of organising Manchester's response to today's world, petered out under Leese's watch. Saville thought that the 'brand positioning' could change the way the city did things: 'It is not the most beautiful or has the best climate, but it has addressed the challenge of the world in the modern era and that is the essence of Manchester.

'I thought in 2005 there was a strong enough direction there for the city council to initiate it as policy, that there would be an office of Original Modern, asking whether what we are doing in architecture, manufacture, health-care, transport, sport – is it pursuing Original and Modern thinking?' Saville laments that it became a soundbite, handy for headlines and book titles. Leese jokes that it is now 'Original Post-Modern', meaning that it is over, not refer-ring to any aesthetic style.

As the snappy go-to it wasn't supposed to be, Original Modern served the city well. It gave intellectual rigour to leaders not content for Manchester to simply be magnificent in defeat. In their own way, rather like the Sex Pistols, the city's leaders exhibited a frightening seriousness. Along with its high-altitude brand position, Manchester's post-industrial pragmatism put out the welcome mat to private money, holding its nose about ethical and moral questions, and snaffled whatever it could of public funds.

Former senior civil servant Mike Emmerich, the Mancunian who returned home and became the city's DevoManc go-between with government, now speaks openly about 'Whitehall's contempt for Place'. The City's response was not the 1980s Liverpool way, to get mad, but to get even – or as much as was possible, given the headlock that London has regional cities in.

As it fought the death spiral of deindustrialisation, Manchester hustled and pitched, first up and best dressed, craving cleaner lines and more business-like buildings. The leadership brought inside their tent the misfits, dreamers and artists for media spectacles and groovy times. They gave the creatives house room, but privately there was a belief that Manchester's unique music culture was just juvenilia or mere ephemera next to the grown-up stuff: grade A office space, rental yields and transport improvements. Saville the designer-savant says: 'I never sensed from Howard and Richard any particular aware-ness of the significance of Factory.'

Forget about those poetic Situationist visions of urban mystery and delight that so engrossed Manchester's hippy-turned-punk generation. Land has a monetary value. Through the lens of the real world, a property market has simply gone through the gears as rising land prices have utterly changed the city. As Manchester shapes up as a global locus for property investment, there is the dawning realisation of a corporate takeover (something true of all major cities). Today's Manchester represents a two-square-mile irony the size of the city centre: 'Factory didn't care if you bought their records,' Saville reminds us. 'It wasn't about profit.'

Put that device in your pocket. Look up. The view is changing fast. There's a pride, often sarcastic, about 'Manctopia' and the thrill of a new future emerging. In the inner-city districts, the unskilled left-behinds and have-nots can gawp at the eye candy, the twinkling lights hovering in the dusk across the serpentine Irwell, but they may feel the real benefits for them are elusive.

Yes, this is still Manchester. You can still dream a dream by the old canal, and not even a pandemic could stop the the immortal rhythm of big city life. The stench of skunk will slap you in the face, and there is forever trouble in town. The skull beneath the city's skin is in plain sight: in Piccadilly Gardens, dozens of eastern African delivery bikers gather at twilight, the low-wage service economy made flesh. This is what a successful modern city in a neo-liberal economy looks like: gig-economy workers taking food to the tower

Haçienda Apartments, September 2022

dwellers above, journeying through a city whose history may well have little meaning for them.

The time may be gone when pop culture was a matter of life and death, when it taught us the things we didn't get from our parents, teachers and politicians. My feelings towards today's city centre, I admit, are like a petulant music fan who resents that my indie darlings now pack stadiums, resentful of glory hunters and guilty that my evangelising was partly responsible.

Analogue Manchester had the heroic atmosphere of a lost empire, caught between crumbling Gothic streets and an unwritten future. Writing this recent a history risks an easy nostalgia, which Wilson warned against even as his beloved pop culture art-lab was being torn apart, but the Haçienda was the first regeneration project of today's Manchester–Salford revival, when the unloved centre was open to anyone to come and play. Today there is a perhaps inevitable push back about the cultural value of the Factory-Haçienda art project; revisionism presents it as a white male-dominated culture, with merciless read-across charges of racism and misogyny, all context, complexity and nuance disallowed. If we follow the money, however, it is incontestable the Factory directors (and less enthusiastically, New Order) could have taken their royalties and departed to Cheshire mansions, tax havens or, the most appalling destination of all, London, for Wilson the 'dead city'. Stephen Morris has totted up the Haçienda's losses at £18 million. No grants were applied for, no government forms were filled in. The Haçienda was Manchester celebrating itself, and if culture is in any sense political, then it was the expression of a place starved of power and simply making its own fun.

My participation in the city's story from the post-punk era to the pandemic gave me the interesting existence I was searching for. Forty years after I dragged my suitcase full of records through the heart of the crippled city, people often refer to me as an adopted Mancunian. They won't know the pointed meaning of that phrase for someone given away at birth; most people have the story of the people they come from, when for me there is a blank page. But my adoptive parents loved me, and Manchester made me. Countless others, I know, feel the same, that the city has made them who they are. I told stories of the city on my own blank page, and in trying to make sense of Manchester, I am still making sense of myself.

> I bring my past I bring my future
> I bring my rights and I bring my song
> I stand atop the Haçienda and shout
> We belong Here. We belong.

Lemn Sissay, 'Belong', 2013

Postscript to the paperback edition

This paperback edition, published in November 2023, contains some additional text and amendments to the hardback edition of February 2023, which was titled *Manchester unspun: Pop, property and power in the original modern city*. Since the current edition went into production, the name of Factory International has officially changed to Aviva Studios.

Pictures and credits

Maps

Central Manchester, 1980. © Ed Howe.
Central Manchester, 2022. © Ed Howe.

Introduction

Andy Spinoza Haçienda card back and front. Courtesy of Andy Spinoza archive, John Rylands Research Institute and Library.
Factory Records and Haçienda founders founders Peter Saville, Tony Wilson and Alan Erasmus. Photo © Kevin Cummins.
Factory Records and Haçienda founder Rob Gretton. Photo © Kevin Cummins.

Place names: a stranger's guide

Manchester, from Charlesworth, Derbyshire, September 2022. Courtesy of Andy Spinoza.
This is Not a Barth. Courtesy of Eric Jackson, Statement Artworks.
CIS Tower. Photo © Peter J. Walsh (peterjwalsh.com).
Beetham Tower in clouds. Photo © David Blake.

Chapter 1

Cannon Street, October 1979. Photo © Kevin Cummins.

Pictures and credits

Chapter 3

Central Station, 1981. Photo © Ian Capper, CC BY-SA 2.0.

Chapter 4

Andy Spinoza, Ed Glinert, Chris Paul, 1983. Courtesy of David Lubich.

City Life No. 1, December 1983. Courtesy of Andy Spinoza archive, John Rylands Research Institute and Library.

City Life No. 2, January 1984. Courtesy of Andy Spinoza archive, John Rylands Research Institute and Library.

City Life No. 32, May 1985. Courtesy of Andy Spinoza archive, John Rylands Research Institute and Library.

National Union of Journalists card, 1987. Courtesy of Andy Spinoza archive, John Rylands Research Institute and Library.

Chapter 5

Max Clifford, Derek Hatton and Muhammad Ali at Cheerleaders opening. Courtesy of Andy Spinoza archive.

City Life No. 100, April–May 1988. Courtesy of Andy Spinoza archive, John Rylands Research Institute and Library.

Morrissey letter, 6 July 1988. Courtesy of Andy Spinoza archive, John Rylands Research Institute and Library.

Peter Hook and Caroline Aherne, *City Life* No. 256, June 1994. Courtesy of Andy Spinoza archive, John Rylands Research Institute and Library.

'A right hook', *Manchester Evening News* front page, 12 November 1996. Courtesy of *Manchester Evening News*.

Andy Spinoza with Joe Strummer. Courtesy of Andy Spinoza archive, John Rylands Research Institute and Library.

Andy Spinoza with Tara Palmer-Tompkinson and Darcey Bussell. Courtesy of Andy Spinoza archive, John Rylands Research Institute and Library.

Andy Spinoza with Coronation Street cast members, Courtesy of Andy Spinoza archive, John Rylands Research Institute and Library.

Andy Spinoza with Noel Gallagher. Photo © Eamonn Clarke.

Andy Spinoza with Anthony Burgess. Photo © Martin O'Neill.

Andy Spinoza with Alan Clark. Courtesy of Andy Spinoza archive, John Rylands Research Institute and Library.

Chapter 8

Haçienda dancefloor. Photo © Peter J. Walsh (peterjwalsh.com).
Haçienda leaflet for *The Hitman and Her*, 18 January 1989. Courtesy of Andy
Spinoza archive, John Rylands Research Institute and Library.

Chapter 9

Andy Spinoza with Lynne Cunningham, Joy, 1989. Photo © Peter J. Walsh
(peterjwalsh.com).

Chapter 10

City Life advert for Simply Red at Tropicana. Courtesy of Andy Spinoza archive,
John Rylands Research Institute and Library.
Barca launch. Ferguson and Hucknall. Photo © Eamonn Clarke.
Ferguson, Hucknall and United players. Photo © Eamonn Clarke.

Chapter 11

Steve Coogan in Hulme. Photo © Richard Davis.
Travellers in Hulme. Photo © Richard Davis.
Howard Bernstein with model of reconstruction of city centre after the IRA
bomb Photo © Unknown.
McEnroe Group invitation. Courtesy of Andy Spinoza, John Rylands Research
Institute and Library.

Chapter 13

Beetham Tower. Photo © Jan Chlebik.

Chapter 15

'Saltz' Anderson and Eric Cantona in 'The Diary', *Manchester Evening News*.
Courtesy of Andy Spinoza.
Richard Creme artwork. Courtesy of Andy Spinoza. © Richard Creme.
Andy Spinoza with David Beckham. Photo © Eamonn Clarke.

Tast opening: Pep Guardiola, Ferran Soriano, Txiki Begiristain and Paco Pérez. Photo © Eric Howard.

Chapter 18

Original inspiration for Peter Saville's FAC 1 poster design. Courtesy of Peter Saville.

Factory Records offices, Princess Street. Photo © Kevin Cummins.

Tony Wilson and a Haçienda column. Photo © Eamonn Clarke.

Peter Hook and Tony Wilson at the Haçienda demolition. Photo © Eamonn Clarke.

Ticket for filming of *24 Hour Party People*. Courtesy of Andy Spinoza archive, John Rylands Research Institute and Library.

Chapter 19

Greater Manchester jigsaw. Media coverage. Courtesy of Andy Spinoza.

Ramona bar poster promoting DJ sets headlined by mayor Burnham, August 2022.

Manchester 'M'. Photo © Aidan O'Rourke.

Chapter 20

Former Kardomah café, Southmill Street junction with Jackson's Row. Photo © Andy Spinoza.

Chapter 21

The Factory, August 2022. Photo © Len Grant.

Tom Bloxham and Christine Cort. Courtesy of Andy Spinoza.

Michael Adex with Andy Burnham. Courtesy of Michael Adex.

Chapter 22

Tom Russell, Richard Leese and Howard Bernstein at super-casino site. Courtesy of *Manchester Evening News*. Photo © Len Grant.

Haçienda Apartments, September 2002. Photo © Andy Spinoza.

Sources

Chapter 7 relies heavily on Ray King and Andrew Nott's *Detonation: Rebirth of a City* (Clear, 2006) which, along with much detail about the 1996 IRA attack, benefits from the authors' insider contacts and knowledge to produce a thorough and insightful account of the city's politics and regeneration both pre- and post-bomb.

A significant part of Chapter 17 is indebted to Robert Dickinson's *Imprinting the Sticks: The Alternative Press beyond London* (Arena, 1997), in which he sourced and captured interviews about Manchester's 1970s counter-culture publications, which touched my early days in the city but which I could never hope to recall.

I undertook face-to-face interviews with Graham Stringer MP in April 2022 and Sir Richard Leese in July 2022 and had several conversations with Peter Saville in summer 2002. I also interviewed Michael Adex in June 2022.

This book was inspired by two works which, in their own way, enthrallingly reveal the soul of the cities that are their subjects: *Liverpool: Wondrous Place* by Paul Du Noyer (Virgin, 2002) and *City of Quartz: Excavating the Future in Los Angeles* by Mike Davis (Verso, 1990).

Archive sources

Andy Spinoza Archive, John Rylands Research Institute and Library, University of Manchester.
Margaret Thatcher Foundation Archive.

Newspapers and magazines

BBC.com
The Big Issue
Businessdesk.com

Sources

cerysmatic.factoryrecords.org
City Life 1983–2005
ENtrepreneur
Manchester Confidential
Manchester District Music Archive
Manchester Evening News
Manchester Meteor
The Mill
North West Business Insider
Place Northwest

Books and articles

Champion, Sarah, *And God Created Manchester*. Wordsmith, 1990.

Christian, Terry, *My Word*. Orion/Hachette, 2007.

Conn, David, *Richer than God: Manchester City, Modern Football and Growing Up*. Quercus, 2012.

Cooper Clarke, John, *I Wanna Be Yours*. Picador, 2020.

Crick, Michael, *Michael Heseltine: A Biography*. Hamish Hamilton, 1997.

Crick, Michael, *The Boss: The Many Sides of Alex Ferguson*. Simon & Schuster, 2002.

Cummins, Kevin, *Looking for the Light through the Pouring Rain*. Faber & Faber, 2009.

Curtis, Deborah, *Touching from a Distance*. Faber and Faber, 2019.

David Beckham: Made in Manchester, an Unofficial Photographic Record. Dewi Lewis Publishing, 2004.

Davis, Richard, *Hulme 1980s–90s*. Café Royal Books, 2019.

Dickinson, Bob, *Imprinting the Sticks: The Alternative Press beyond London*. Arena/Ashgate, 1997.

Donnelly, Jimmy, *Jimmy the Weed: Inside the Quality Street Gang*. Milo Books, 2012.

Fac229! The Music Week Factorial, 15 July 1989.

Forman, Denis, *Persona Granada*. André Deutsch, 1997.

Froud, Julie, Mike Hodson, Andy McMeekin, Anne Stafford, Pam Stapleton, Hua Wei and Karel Williams, *From Developer Regeneration to Civic Futures, A New Politics for Foundational Service Provision in Greater Manchester*, Manchester Alliance Business School, 2018.

Glinert, Ed, *Manchester Compendium*. Penguin, 2008.

Goulding, Richard, Adam Leaver and Jonathan Silver, *Manchester Offshored*. The University of Sheffield, 2022.

Grant, Len, *Regeneration Manchester: 30 Years of Storytelling*. Manchester University Press, 2020.

Greater Manchester Digital Blueprint. Greater Manchester Combined Authority, 2020.

Gretton, Rob, *1 Top Class Manager*, ed. Abigail Ward. Anti-Archivists, 2008.

Griffin, Phil (words) and Jan Chlebik (photographs), *Manchester*. Mancunian Books, 2014.

Hartnell, Clare, *Manchester*, Pevsner Architectural Guides. Penguin, 2001.

Haslam, Dave, *Manchester, England: The Story of the Pop Cult City*. Fourth Estate, 1999.

Hatherley, Owen, *A Guide to the New Ruins of Great Britain*. Verso, 2010.

Hook, Peter, *The Haçienda: How Not to Run a Club*. Simon & Schuster, 2009.

Hook, Peter, *Substance: Inside New Order*. Simon & Schuster, 2016.

Hook, Peter, *Unknown Pleasures: Inside Joy Division*. Simon & Schuster, 2012.

Hutton, Chris and Richard Kurt, *Don't Look Back in Anger*, Introduction by Bob Dickinson. Simon & Schuster, 1997.

Kennedy, Michael, *Barbirolli*, McGibbon & Kee, 1971.

Kermode, Mark, *It's Only a Movie: Reel Life Adventures of a Film Obsessive*. Random House, 2017.

King, Ray, *Detonation: Rebirth of a City*. Clear Publications, 2007.

Lawson, Alan, *It Happened in Manchester*. Multimedia, 1998.

Leaving the Twentieth Century: The Incomplete Work of the Situationist International, trans. and ed. Christopher Gray. Rebel Press, 1998.

Lee, C.P., *When We Were Thin*. Hotun, 2007.

Manchester Independent Economic Review, reviewer's report, Tom McKillop, Chairman, 2009.

Marr, Andrew, *My Trade: A Short History of British Journalism*. Pan, 2004.

McGibbon, Robin and Rob McGibbon, *Simply Mick: Mick Hucknall of Simply Red*. Weidenfeld & Nicolson, 1993.

Messinger, Gary S., *Manchester in the Victorian Age: The Half-known City*. Manchester University Press, 1985.

Michaelides, Tony, *Moments that Rock*. This Day in Music Books, 2022.

Middles, Mick, *Factory: The Story of the Record Label*. Virgin, 2009.

Middles, Mick, *From Joy Division to New Order*. Virgin, 1996.

Middles, Mick, *Red Mick*. Headline, 1993.

Middles, Mick and Lindsay Reade, *Torn Apart: The Life of Ian Curtis*. Omnibus, 2006.

Morley, Paul, *From Manchester with Love: The Life and Opinions of Tony Wilson*. Faber and Faber, 2021.

Morley, Paul, *The North (And Almost Everything in It)*. Bloomsbury, 2013.

Morris, Stephen, *Fast Forward*. Constable, 2020.

Morrissey, *Autobiography*. Penguin Classics, 2013.

Parkinson-Bailey, John J., *Manchester: An Architectural History*. Manchester University Press, 2000.

Peck, Jamie and Kevin Ward (eds), *City of Revolution: Restructuring Manchester*. Manchester University Press, 2002.

Phipps, Simon, *Brutal North: Post-War Modernist Architecture in the North of England*. September Publishing, 2020.

Price, Jane (ed.), *The Mancunian Way*. Clinamen, 2002.

Pullan, Brian and Michele Abendstern, *A History of the University of Manchester 1973–90*. Manchester University Press, 2003. Available open access at: www.manchesteropenhive.com/view/9781526137197/9781526137197.xml.

Raban, Jonathan, *Soft City*. Collins Harvill, 1988.

Redhead, Brian, *Manchester: A Celebration*. André Deutsch, 1993.

Redhead, Steve, *The-End-of-the-Century Party: Youth and Pop towards 2000*. Manchester University Press, 1990.

Robb, John, *The North Will Rise Again: Manchester Music City 1976–96*. Aurum, 2009.

Rogan, Johnny, *Morrissey & Marr: The Severed Alliance*. Omnibus Press, 1992.

Ryder, Shaun, *Twisting My Melon*. Bantam/Transworld, 2011.

Savage, Jon, *England's Dreaming*. Faber & Faber, 1991.

Savage, Jon, *This Searing Light, the Sun and Everything Else – Joy Division: The Oral History*. Faber & Faber, 2019.

Savage, Jon (ed.), *The Haçienda Must Be Built!*. International Music Publications, 1992.

Schofield, Jonathan, *Illusion and Change Manchester*. MCR Books, 2015.

Schofield, Jonathan, *Lost and Imagined Manchester*. MCR Books, 2015.

Sherriff, Graeme, 'Communication and Governance Challenges in Greater Manchester's Congestion Charge Referendum' in *Road Pricing: Technologies, Economics and Acceptability*. University of Salford, 2018.

Signature Collection, Peter Hook auction catalogue. Omega Auctions, March 2019.

Sources

Southall, Brian with Mick Hucknall, *If You Don't Know Me by Now*. Carlton, 2007.

Stockley, Martin, *The Reluctant Engineer and Other Manchester Stories*. Martin Stockley Associates, 2006.

Sumner, Bernard, *Chapter and Verse: New Order, Joy Division and Me*. Bantam Press, 2014.

Taylor, Kevin with Keith Mumby, *The Poisoned Tree: The Untold Truth about the Police Conspiracy to Discredit John Stalker and Destroy Me*. Pan, 1990.

Taylor, Michael, *Never Mind the Bankers, Here's the Interviews 2002–2012*. Northern Monkeys, 2017.

This Is Ray Lowry, exhibition catalogue, See Gallery, Crawshawbooth, Lancashire, 2008.

Towards an Urban Renaissance, final report of the Urban Task Force, Lord Rogers of Riverside, Chairman. Department of the Environment, Transport and the Regions, 1999.

Urban Splash, *It Will Never Work: 25 Years of Urban Splash*. Urban Splash, 2018.

Urban Splash, *Urban Splash: Transformation*. RIBA Publishing, 2011.

Wainwright, Martin, *True North: In Praise of England's Better Half*. Guardian Books, 2010.

We Are Bored in the City, Chelsea Space exhibition: Use Hearing Protection: FAC 1 – 50 / 40, curated by Jon Savage and Mat Bancroft, 2019.

Whitney, Karl, *Hit Factories: A Journey Through the Industrial Cities of British Pop*. Weidenfeld and Nicolson, 2019.

Who's Who in Greater Manchester. Manchester Literary and Philosophical Society, 2002.

Williams, Joanna M., *Manchester's Radical Mayor*. The History Press, 2017.

Wilson, Tony, *24 Hour Party People*. Channel 4/Pan Macmillan.

Witts, Richard, 'Building up a Band: Music for a Second City' in Benjamin Halligan and Michael Goddard (eds), *Mark E. Smith and The Fall: Art, Music and Politics*. Ashgate, 2010.

Young, James, *Songs They Never Play on the Radio: Nico the Last Bohemian*. Bloomsbury, 1992.

Films and television

24 Hour Party People, 2002, dir. Michael Winterbottom.

Charley Bubbles, 1968, dir. Albert Finney.

Control, 2007, dir. Anton Corbijn.

Joy Division, 2007, dir. Grant Gee.

Madchester The Sound of the North, 1990, dir. Simon Massey.

New Order – Play at Home, 1984 (RPM Productions for Channel 4).

Many of the television programmes referred to can be viewed thanks to public-spirited uploaders on You Tube, including Granada's 1968 World in Action documentary *The Demonstration*, Granada TV broadcasts of the Sex Pistols and Joy Division, the BBC's 1977 *Brass Tacks* about punk rock, some of *The Hitman and Her* at the Haçienda in 1989 and substantial sections of *The Mancunian Way*, a short 1993 Granada regional series about music and the city by presenter Jon Savage and Steven J. Lock, on which I acted as informal researcher.

Acknowledgements

Sometime near the end of the twentieth century, Jon Savage told me, 'You go mad when you write a book.' *Manchester Unspun* is the result of a conversation we had in August 2020. He suggested that I could write this story. That's where his responsibility ends.

That meeting was one of a series resulting in my archive being acquired by the British Pop Archive at the John Rylands Research Institute and Library at the University of Manchester, which launched in 2022. I must thank Jon, now Professor Savage, and Professor Hannah Barker for their interest in my twenty-five boxes of yellowing print, and in particular pay tribute to curator Mat Bancroft, for whom nothing ever seems to be too much trouble.

I'm grateful to Matthew Frost, senior editor at Manchester University Press, without whom …

For support during three years of drafting, editing, correcting and catastrophising, and what I hope is mere temporary insanity, I give sincere thanks production manager David Appleyard and copy editor John Banks

For reading and their feedback either whole or in part: Stephen Bayley, Michael Crick, Phil Griffin, Paul Ogden, Michael Taylor, Paul Unger, Trevor Ward; and to the archetypal man about town Howard Sharrock for reading both early and later drafts.

For help with historical facts, hard-to-find records, hard-to-decipher documents or hard-to-recall memories: Ed Glinert, Paul Morley, Samuel Lowry, Simon Greenwood, Eric Longley, David Thame, Lis Phelan, Ian Ransom, Dave Wilson, Stephen Snoddy, Andy Dodd, Leroy Richardson, Neal Keeling, Jen Williams, Anthony Cross, Kath Robinson, Chris Fletcher, Simon Sperryn, Professor Bob Bennett, Jeff Cunningham, Steve Diggle and Rose Marley.

Acknowledgements

Thanks to my two brothers Marc and Robert and their families, for being themselves, and being cool with me being me.

Thanks, finally, for Lynne and our daughters – Leah, Elinor and Ava – for humouring me, and for knowing there was no point in getting in my way.

Index

Note: page numbers in *italic* refer to illustrations

Index

Index

Index

Index

Index

Index

Index

Index

Index